# Renaissance Mad Voyages

*Renaissance Mad Voyages is one of those exciting scholarly books that make you realize how important and interesting its apparently obscure subject is. Parr provides a rich historical contextualization for the English "mad voyage" which demonstrates that it is caught up in, and also a vivid epitome of, the main currents of shifting religious, economic, and colonialist practices for at least 200 years. Historians and literary critics alike will find it engagingly written, magisterial but never overwhelming in its command of historical detail, and skillful in making a wide range of unfamiliar texts legible and accessible.*

– Jeremy Lopez, University of Toronto, Canada

*Anthony Parr displays a firm grasp of early modern cultural history in this charming but scholarly account of recreational travel and madcap journeys and adventures. His deep research in Elizabethan and early Stuart texts yields vivid vignettes of ingenious stunts, scams and wagers, pioneer tourism, and the feats of English eccentrics. Parr illuminates the worlds of London finance, legal chicanery, and literary reputations, while tracing intrepid travelers across the British Isles and as far afield as Venice, Istanbul, and Jerusalem. This is a lucid and illuminating work that displays a warmth and sympathy toward its subjects, and respect for the work of other scholars.*

– David Cressy, The Ohio State University, USA

A vogue for travel 'stunts' flourished in England between 1590 and the 1620s: playful imitations or burlesques of maritime enterprise and overland travel that collectively appear to be a response to particular innovations and developments in English culture. This study is the first full length scholarly work to focus on the curious phenomenon of 'madde voiages', as the writer William Rowley called them. Anthony Parr shows that the mad voyage (as Rowley and others conceived it) had surprisingly deep and diverse roots in traditional travel practices, in courtly play and mercantile custom, and in literary culture. Looking in detail at several of the best-documented exploits, Parr situates them in the ferment of such ventures during the period in question; but also reaches back to explore their classical and mediaeval antecedents, and considers their role in creating a template for eccentric English adventure in later centuries.

*Renaissance Mad Voyages* brings together literary and historical enquiry in order to address the implications of an interesting and neglected cultural trend. Parr's investigation of the rash of travel exploits in the period leads to extensive research on the origins of the wager on travel and its role in the expansion of English tourism and trading activity.

*Anthony Parr is Professor Emeritus of English at the University of the Western Cape, South Africa.*

# CULTURES OF PLAY, 1300–1700

## Series Editor: Bret Rothstein

Play looms ever larger in academe: a growing body of scholarly literature lies at the nexus of strong current interest in material culture/the study of objects, performance studies, and childhood studies. At the same time, play has also begun to transform aspects of pedagogy – most notably, perhaps, through the rise of games as vectors for instruction. With these transformations comes, across disciplines, a concomitant shift in historical interest, one to which this series is dedicated.

Dedicated to the ludic Renaissance in Europe, this series serves two purposes. First, it recounts the history of early modern wit, humor, and games, from backgammon and tops to bulls and tractates. Second, in addressing its topic broadly, Cultures of Play, 1300–1700 also provides a forum for reconceptualizing the play elements of early modern economic, political, religious, and social life. We welcome proposals from a range of disciplines, including history, religious studies, the history and philosophy of science, literature, theater history, philosophy, and the history of art and visual culture.

# Renaissance Mad Voyages

## Experiments in Early Modern English Travel

*Anthony Parr*

Routledge
Taylor & Francis Group
LONDON AND NEW YORK

First published 2015 by Ashgate Publishing

2 Park Square, Milton Park, Abingdon, Oxfordshire OX14 4RN
52 Vanderbilt Avenue, New York, NY 10017

*Routledge is an imprint of the Taylor & Francis Group, an informa business*

First issued in paperback 2019



**British Library Cataloguing in Publication Data**
A catalogue record for this book is available from the British Library.

**The Library of Congress has cataloged the printed edition as follows:**
Parr, Anthony, 1949–
Renaissance mad voyages : experiments in early modern English travel / by Anthony Parr.
pages cm.—(Cultures of play, 1300-1700)
Includes bibliographical references and index.
ISBN 978-1-4724-5709-7 (hardcover : alk. paper)

1. English literature—Early modern, 1500–1700—History and criticism. 2. Travel in literature. 3. Travelers' writings, English—History and criticism. I. Title.
PR428.T73P37 2015
820.9'3209031—dc23

2014043575

ISBN 978-1-4724-5709-7 (hbk)
ISBN 978-0-367-88103-0 (pbk)

*For Laura*

# Contents

# Illustrations

## Figures



## Colour Plates

4 Terracotta model of Coryat's shoes, in the church of St. Peter and St. Paul, Odcombe, Somerset. (Author's photograph.)

5 Simon Stevin's *zeil-wagen,* or wind car (c.1600), from Joan Blaeu, *Novum ac magnum theatrum urbium Belgicae* (Amsterdam, 1649). (Huntington Library, San Marino, California.)

# Acknowledgements

This book has its origins in a talk I gave many years ago at the Huntington Library in California, and that extraordinary institution has continued to facilitate my research ever since, both with the provision of short-term fellowships and more generally through the stimulus and support it unfailingly offers to visiting scholars. I am particularly indebted to former Director of Research Roy Ritchie, to the staff of Reader Services, and to Mary Robertson, Alan Jutzi and Stephen Tabor for their help with manuscript and early printed materials. Lawrence and Susan Green have been wonderfully supportive friends and colleagues during my California sojourns, while Peter Mancall and Lori Ann Ferrell kindly invited me to explore several of the book's topics in their respective seminar series at the Huntington.

Progress with completing this project was inevitably slowed by my university duties in South Africa over the past decade, but I must record my appreciation to that country's National Research Foundation for a grant at the outset of my research that enabled me to travel to London and California. My institution, the University of the Western Cape, has been generous with research funding, and I am grateful to my colleagues in the English Department for making possible two crucial periods of sabbatical leave.

Over the years of working on this book, I have incurred more personal debts than I could possibly list, but I would like to express particular thanks to Richmond Barbour, Graham Bradshaw, the late Christopher Brooks, David Cressy, Wendy Jacobson, Julia Martin, Carla Mazzio, Karen Press and Laura Stalker for fruitful suggestions, valuable conversation, and insightful comments on my material. Ashgate's anonymous reader provided a generous and constructive review that helped me to reshape parts of the book. I am also grateful to James Loxley and Julie Sanders for allowing me to see their transcript of Ben Jonson's 'Foot Voyage' before publication. The late and much-missed Kevin Sharpe was a constant source of encouragement, and frequently nagged me to complete my labours. Delegates at several conferences where I have aired research for this book have helped me to clarify my ideas, and I am especially grateful to members of the USC-Huntington Early Modern Studies seminar and the British History seminar at the Huntington Library for their questions and responses. All remaining deficiencies are of course my own.

Earlier versions of some material appeared in the journals *Studies in Travel Writing* and the *Southern African Journal of Medieval and Renaissance Studies*, and I thank their editors for leave to develop them here. I have received splendid assistance from staff at the Bodleian Library, the British Library, the National Archives at Kew, and the Folger Library. The photographic departments at the National Portrait Gallery, the National Trust, the Rijksmuseum in Amsterdam, and the Huntington Library have been models of efficiency in supplying illustrations and permission to use them.

I would like to record my sincere thanks to Erika Gaffney at Ashgate for her enthusiastic and collegial approach to publication of this book. Its dedicatee will be thankful that my odd journey is at an end, but her love and support have been crucial to my safe arrival.

Cape Town, August 2014

# Note on Citation Methods

Quotations taken directly from early modern printed books and manuscripts are given in the original spelling, but I have silently normalised i/j, u/v, and the long s. Contractions used in the manuscript records discussed in Chapters 4 and 5 have been expanded in the interests of legibility, and obsolete symbols for currency have been replaced by their modern equivalents.

Major writers are cited from modern collected editions of their work, where available. Quotations from Shakespeare are not ascribed to any particular edition, as the few references made to his plays are easily located.

In documenting books printed before 1700 in the notes and bibliography, the place of publication is given but not individual details of publisher and printer unless they are of particular significance.

## Abbreviations

| | |
|---|---|
| *CSP* | *Calendar of State Papers* |
| EEBO | Early English Books Online |
| HMSO | Her Majesty's Stationery Office |
| *ODNB* | *Oxford Dictionary of National Biography* |
| *OED* | *Oxford English Dictionary* |
| *PMLA* | *Journal of the Modern Language Association of America* |
| UP | University Press |

# 1

# A Very English Journey?

My point of departure is that of an English traveller one afternoon in July 1607, and I quote from the account of his voyage published in the following year:

> The Governour of the Pynace … finding all things sufficient, and stronge for his proceeding … came downe cheerfully, and with a resolute heart to goe forward on his journey, But many of his friendes both learned Preachers, and others went about to disswade him from this adventurous enterprise: Alleaging his attempt too venturous, his purpose dangerous; and his presumption egregious, and to be a great sinne in tempting the mercie of God in so strange and unhearde-of manner of boldenesse. WHO sodainelye made answeare that this [deliverance] being so wonderfull, and beyonde hope, did more encourage and anymate his proceedinges, than any mans perswasions could possiblye prevayle to the contrarie: For now hee felt the helping hand of his mercifull God to bee readye to assist him in all his actions, especially in this his journey[1]

This reported dialogue stages one of the defining myths of the European 'Age of Discovery', recapitulating the historical moment when the admonition *Non Ultra,* which warned against ventures beyond the gates of the Mediterranean, is answered by the assertion *Non sufficit orbis,* and the traditional impediments to exploration are overcome. It echoes the famous episode in Canto 4 of *The Lusiads,* the Portuguese national epic, where on the eve of Vasco da Gama's embarkation for India the old man of Restelo steps forward to condemn the voyage as futile and overweening; and it mimics the epic posture of Camoes' scene in suggesting that the pious warning must yield to destiny and an equally pious sense of mission. The expansionist argument had indeed for all practical purposes prevailed in England by the early 1600s, with the first voyages of the East India Company and a determination, at the end of a long war with Spain, to match and surpass the Iberian achievement in colonialism and trade. Yet the old debate seems to survive as a sort of container for more specific arguments about the purpose and value of overseas ventures. Travel still had its critics, as English tourists grew in number and set their sights on distant destinations, and bitter disputes over foreign policy that came to a head with the Essex revolt in 1601 continued to affect colonial endeavours and naval strategy after the Jacobean accession. Richard Hakluyt's *Principal Navigations,* first published in 1589, decisively endorsed a mercantile vision of empire and did much to promote it, but this did not immediately resolve the conflicting priorities that helped to vitiate so many expeditions, or stifle conservative criticism of overseas ventures. In the 1580s and 1590s, England's most spectacular maritime exploits were attacks on the Spanish mainland and colonial territories, but even the more successful of these – Drake's piratical raids or the taking of Cadiz in 1596 – were a source of considerable controversy at home. Similarly, remarkable courage and faith in God's helping hand were much in evidence in the early attempts to colonise Virginia and discover a northwest passage to Cathay, but these efforts had failed nonetheless and encouraged sceptical voices to ask whether such enterprises were really worth investing in. Francis Bacon, arguing in 1606 for the creation of a council to oversee the settlement of Ireland, notes that there is 'the precedent of the like council of plantation for Virginia', but that, he says, was 'an enterprise in my opinion differing as much from this, as Amadis de Gaul differs from Caesar's Commentaries'.[2] Bacon changed his mind later about Virginia, but, as J.H. Elliott and Jeffrey Knapp have argued, England's early overseas enterprise offered little to satisfy its more ardent propagandists and frequently lent fuel to the arguments that its efforts were rash, timorous or simply misconceived.[3]

However, the occasion of the passage quoted above is not the fresh effort in 1607 to colonise America with the founding of Jamestown, nor the first of Hudson's doomed efforts in the same year to find a way through the Arctic ice to China. The scene is a more homely one, a churchyard in a Berkshire village, where a small ship is suspended 40 feet from the ground on a cable stretched from the top of the church tower to a winch on a platform below. The ship, we are told, 'was orderly rigged with ropes and sailes, and in all poyntes had all manner of tacklings provided for her as fit and necessarie, as belongeth to a ship of her burthen: Shee had twelve peeces of Ordinance in her, that went off by a strange devise in just order one after the other … and no man neere them at their discharging' (B4). (See Figure 1.1.) The cautionary words I started with, in which the shipowner's friends try to dissuade him from his enterprise, are prompted by an accident in which spectators on the tower lean against the cables and winching equipment and are injured when the structure gives way. But William Bush, the self-styled captain and builder of the vessel, being assured that nobody is seriously hurt, is determined to go ahead with his project, which is to travel by air, land and water in his ship from Lamborne to London. To fulfil the first part of this plan, the pinnace is winched up to the top of the tower, and then lowered 20 feet, where

> As shee so hunge in the Ayre, her Ordinance went of[f], and no man neare her by Twentye foote with many fire woorkes, and other strange and worthy devises, to satisfye the peoples expectation.

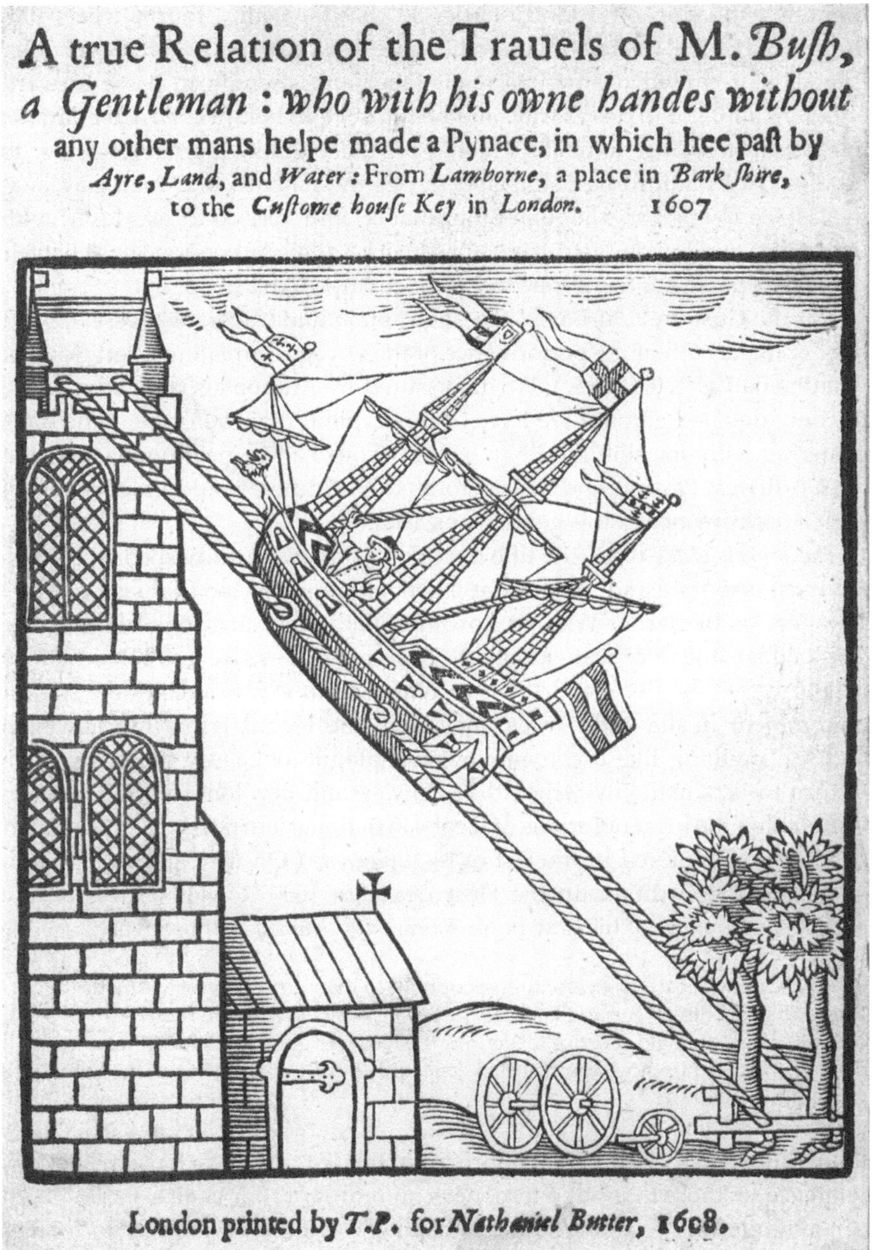
A true Relation of the Trauels of M. Buſh, a Gentleman: who with his owne handes without any other mans helpe made a Pynace, in which hee paſt by Ayre, Land, and Water: From Lamborne, a place in Barkſhire, to the Cuſtome houſe Key in London. 1607

London printed by T.P. for Nathaniel Butter, 1608.

1.1 Titlepage of Anthony Nixon, *A True Relation of the Travels of M. Bush* (London, 1607). (Private Collection, California.)

But the people are not satisfied, and demand that 'one come downe from the toppe of the Tower in the same boate or Pynace' (C2); so the operation is repeated with the captain at the helm. The crowd of country folk, the 'most part' of whom we are told 'never sawe shippe, or pynace before' (Cv), nonetheless seem to know what is needed in a just representation of a voyage. Next day begins the land journey, which covers 26 miles and is effected by mounting the ship on a kind of tricycle chassis, with a fourth wheel that 'turned in her [i.e. operated within the vessel by the driver], with divers other Engyns that caused her by one mans labor and strength to passe forward either up a hill, or in deepe way, and he himselfe in her' (B3–v). After various misadventures, Bush joins the Thames for the 100-mile journey by water to London. At Brainford he paints and re-rigs the pinnace, and then leaves on the last leg to London, shooting off ordnance, and 'passed forwardes ... with Drummes, and lowde Instruments of Musicke' (E4). At London she is hauled out of the water near Somerset House and 'carried into a house in the Strande', and at the Custom House next day the captain and 'divers witnesses ... did offer to make oath of the performance of the voyage, intreating a certificate of what he had effected' (E4v). We are assured by Anthony Nixon, who wrote the only detailed account we have of this exploit, that even those who have conferred with 'the skilfullest Navigators of our Land', including veterans of the Northwest Passage and the sea route to the Indies, 'could never report of such a performance as this gentlemans' (B2).

*The Travels of M. Bush* (the title of Nixon's pamphlet, published in 1608) is the most elaborate and spectacular example known to me of a rash of 'mad voyages', as the writer William Rowley called them, that took place in late Elizabethan and Jacobean England. The craze seems to have reached its height in the first decade of the new century, but it was already the subject of comment in the early 1590s; inevitably the record is patchy, however, and for anything like a contemporary catalogue of these efforts, we have to turn to lists made by writers like Rowley and Ben Jonson – the latter in introducing the most notorious of Jacobean fictional journeys, the 'most liquid deed' commemorated in the last of his *Epigrams* ('On the Famous Voyage') of a rowing expedition up the Fleet Ditch. In 1609 Rowley addressed the prospective buyers of his new book *A Search for Money* as those who

> have beene either eare-or-eye-witnesses or both to many madde voiages made of late yeares, both by sea and land, as the travell to *Rome* with the returne in certaine daies, the wild morrise to *Norrige*, the fellowes going back-ward to *Barwick*, another hopping from *Yorke* to *London*, and the transforming of the top of *Paules* into a stable ... [4]

Rowley includes Continental tourism in his list, as does Jonson with his reference to 'those that put out moneys on return / From Venice, Paris' – both of them alluding to the custom of making wagers on a journey to foreign destinations; but the majority of their examples are rather more idiosyncratic. Predictably, both writers refer to Will Kemp's famous morris dance from London to Norwich, the 'nine days wonder' of 1600, and each includes also the showman Banks and his performing horse Morocco who climbed to the top of the steeple of St. Paul's Cathedral in 1601, a much-discussed event which John Chamberlain in one of his letters lumped together with another exploit where 'one came hopping from Charing Crosse into Powles bounde in a sacke', noted 'divers other such wagers', and commented that '[w]e have dayly here many new experiments made.'[5] Several of the more ambitious stunts were written up as pamphlets that directly invite comparison with the 'real' travel narratives, similarly issued in cheap quarto format, that by the 1590s were coming off the presses in large numbers. (Just before he wrote his description of Bush's exploit, Anthony Nixon had published an account of the Sherley brothers' adventures in Italy and the Middle East.) Other exploits are known to us from a variety of sources, including private memoirs, legal records and anecdotal histories, that help to illuminate some of the contexts in which the staged journey was conceived and the urges that it tried to satisfy.

In his poem Jonson alludes as well to the many adventures by water, humorously claiming that the challenge faced by his rowers is '[a] harder task than either his to Bristo', / Or his to Antwerp' – references that are repeated in a catalogue of maritime exploits drawn up by the pamphleteer Samuel Rowlands in 1612:

*Ferris* gave cause of vulgar wonderment
When unto Bristow in a Boate he went:
Another with his Sculler ventered more,
That Row'd to *Flushing* from our English shoare.
Another did devise a woodden Whale,
Which unto *Callise*, did from Dover saile,
Another, with his Oares and slender Wherry,
From *London* unto *Antwerpe* o're did ferry.
Another, maugre fickle fortunes teeth,
Rowed hence to *Scotland*, and ariv'd at *Leeth*.[6]

The list would have reminded readers that, amidst the ingenious and varied stunts singled out by other writers, there was a core group of ventures that drew playfully but specifically upon English seagoing skills and experience. Like Jonson, however, Rowlands has an ulterior motive for his maritime references, since the lines occur in a commendatory poem prefaced to *The Sculler*, the first published pamphlet by John Taylor the Water Poet, offering a mock-pedigree both for the latter's regular work as a waterman on the Thames and his new career as a writer – skills, he insists, that make these previous ventures (and presumably any written accounts of them) 'but triviall things'. Rowlands' complimentary verses proved prophetic, since Taylor was later to turn the travel exploit into a sustained commercial operation, making numerous excursions within Britain and to the Continent and selling his accounts of them on a subscription basis. Some of the earlier mad voyages anticipate aspects of Taylor's business move, as we shall see. Others who showed signs of making a professional habit of such journeys were the actor Will Kemp, who reportedly followed up his dance to Norwich with another over the Alps, and Thomas Coryat, whose successful walk to Venice in 1608 prompted him to undertake an overland trek to India four years later. Both men hoped to profit by their ventures, and the attempt to turn travel into a commodity was certainly a factor in creating in the minds of contemporaries a category of 'mad voyages' that readily embraced many different kinds of excursion. The economic motive behind these exploits, which I shall explore in more detail in later chapters, needs to be acknowledged now because it has so often been ignored in traditional analysis of pastimes and unusual customs. But it is also evident that the flurry of interest in travel exploits, both for those undertaking them and for the curious onlookers, cannot be explained purely in these terms. Why should such 'happenings' suddenly become marketable? What drew the large crowds that attended the progress of Kemp or Bush through the English countryside? And what moved numerous performers to specific feats of endurance or ingenious contrivance that amounted over several years to a running burlesque of 'serious' travel and adventure? 'Exploits of this description,' suggested Joan Parkes in a 1925 study of English travel, 'were very popular alike with gentry and commonalty, before Puritan ascendancy overwhelmed Merry England',[7] but the dated notion of a carefree pre-revolutionary world ruled by stable customs reveals its limitations particularly sharply in trying to account for a craze like this one.

The mad voyages undoubtedly sprang from tangled roots in mediaeval and Elizabethan culture, but as a phenomenon they were unprecedented: the conditions for such a vogue did not exist before the late sixteenth century. Far from being a marker of what was lost – a fabled Merry England – they are a sign of a new world that is taking shape in this period, one marked by increased mobility, opportunity and enterprise, and in fact the travel stunt has been with us ever since: as a gentlemen's wager it became something of a social institution in the eighteenth century, and it survives today as the charity fundraiser or feat of self-promotion. Some of those linkages will be briefly explored later. But the fact that we have become habituated to such exploits can make us lose sight of what was novel and distinctive about the Renaissance vogue. The mad voyages are part of the ferment of travel activity in Tudor-Stuart England, and they cannot be entirely disentangled from other enterprises that for the English were also new or greatly expanded initiatives, such as continental tourism or various kinds of maritime venture. These exploits do not play out against a background of stable and long-familiar itineraries, but participate in a volatile theatre of travel where most kinds of journey were risky and might easily be regarded as outlandish. Devices like William Bush's ship distinguish themselves from 'serious' travel, apparently, by the spirit of play and burlesque they bring to their exploit, but they are also tapping into the spirit of adventure and taste for derring-do that fuelled so much overseas enterprise. The jostling of all these projects, whether it be the personal travel stunt or weighty ventures like East India trade, Atlantic privateering, voyages in search of El Dorado or land journeys to Constantinople, produced a kind of melting-pot in which game and earnest are often surprisingly bound together, and where the relationship between the two is unstable and suggestive. When William Rowley refers to the 'many madde voiages made of late yeares', a good number of his readers would have applied his words to much more than a current fashion for ludic exploits.

In later chapters, I shall try to tease out the implications of Rowley's phrase for several aspects of English travel and enterprise in the early-modern period. But let us first look at the more elusive meanings it might have had for his contemporaries. In early-modern usage, the word 'voyage' could describe many kinds of travel, including land journeys, and as we might expect, it is a fairly acute register of shifting attitudes and practices during a period of growing mobility. In mediaeval times it frequently carried the implication of official or formal travel, being used *inter alia* to describe a military expedition, a royal venture abroad, or pilgrimage. By the seventeenth century it was being applied to the various parts of the Grand Tour (as in the 'Voyage of Italy') and had come to dignify educational travel; it was also starting to be recognized as a literary category, describing accounts of oceanic travel as well as the journey itself.[8] In these ways the patrician and religious associations of the word in the Middle Ages yielded to the secular and bookish interests of a new class of traveller. But 'voyage' had also long carried the looser sense of a personal enterprise or undertaking, potentially applicable to a wide range of initiatives, and we can watch this meaning come into its own at a time of growing entrepreneurial activity. Banks's feat of taking his horse Morocco to the top of St. Paul's is a voyage in this sense, as is the act of hopping in a sack from Charing Cross: both play with the idea of travel but are not easily compared either with each other or with epic rowing feats or with walking to Rome. These things seem like disparate events, yet contemporaries were ready to link them as 'facts' in the archaic sense of deeds, as acts of assertion or innovation that collectively meant something. John Chamberlain, as we saw, described the stunts taking place in London as 'experiments', which then as now meant a test or proof, and his word presumably acknowledges their challenge to what is thought to be feasible or normally conceivable. Rowley's classification of a whole set of exploits as 'mad' also recognizes this outlandish element, though it leaves open the question of whether they should be seen as decadent follies or as inspired initiatives; we might recall that Jonson, who declares that his Fleet Ditch rowers in 'On the Famous Voyage' make the trip 'in worthy scorn' of the real-life mad voyagers, nonetheless was himself described as being admirably 'mad' (i.e. driven by creative *furor*) in his most vivid fictions – of which this poem is certainly one. But it seems to be true that for many commentators the rash of exploits was a harbinger of something like the 'foolish madd world, wherein all things are overruled by fansye' to which Gabriel Harvey accused Spenser of subscribing, a world of shifting boundaries and new uncertainties.[9] If 'voyage' appears to be an elastic term in this period, we need to remember that our contemporary use of the word has expunged from it any notion of a controversial act.[10] In early-modern times, by contrast, the element of proscription or admonition that often hung over the act of travel seems to have encouraged a more flexible understanding of what it might include, reading it potentially as an act of inversion or travesty – the ship on land, the horse on top of Paul's – that defied the conventions limiting people's freedom to move around or to experiment with the time and space available to them.

This is not to suggest that the mad voyages should be seen simply as acts of 'transgression' (an overused word in cultural analysis that I shall try to avoid), but that they are a complicated reflection of changing social conditions. Historians have traced the sharp increase in human traffic within England during the later decades of the sixteenth century, a development that heightened anxieties about vagrancy and the breakdown of settled customs, but which also revealed the benefits of mobility for internal trade, regional development and gentlemanly recreation. The walking tours that became fashionable amongst students and gentry, following Robert Burton's advice that 'the most pleasant of all outward pastimes, is ... to make a petty progresse, a merry journy now and then with some good companions',[11] were encouraged by humanist emphasis on the benefits of perambulation, and as we shall see, they made a direct contribution to the vogue for travel exploits. The lower orders of society were also more mobile. A majority of the population might still stir very little beyond their immediate neighbourhoods, but they were able to observe the growing circulation of migrant workers, itinerant traders and entertainers, demobilized soldiers and sailors, and an expanding system of posts. 'While Tudor moralists insistently proclaim the virtues of place', argues Andrew McRae, 'by the early seventeenth century texts increasingly consider the importance of mobility, depicting men and women of middling and lower degree on the move',[12] and this shift in attitude helped to create the conditions for several adventurers of humble origins on England's roads and waterways. By the 1630s, when the waterman John Taylor was using the mad voyage to promote the economic benefits of making the country's rivers more navigable,[13] the trend noted by McRae had helped to legitimize numerous forms of internal travel; at that point, similarly, foreign ventures of all kinds (and undertaken by all classes) were becoming increasingly routine. But these later developments had uncertain and contested beginnings, and at the turn of the century, when the vogue for bizarre travel stunts was apparently at its height, the picture is a more muddled one. It shows all the signs of cultural change that has not yet been rationalized and fully comprehended, and the mercurial testing of boundaries that is the hallmark of these exploits is part of a larger response to the novel challenges posed by both social and geographical mobility.

In the late sixteenth century, there was dispute about virtually every aspect of foreign venturing, whether it be Continental tourism, long-distance trade, maritime warfare or American colonialism, or simply the extension of travel opportunities to the middling sort. There was also considerable panic over the problem of vagabonds on English roads. The arguments were intense because increased mobility promised, or threatened, to bring great changes to English society, and the value of travel remained a debating point until the country's newer 'traffiques and discoveries' (in Hakluyt's phrase) were effectively institutionalized in the seventeenth century. Travel was fashionable, of course, because the English were now visiting the Continent in greater numbers, and the book trade made travel writing available to many more. Yet excursions to Italy and Spain by Protestant Englishmen were among the most controversial of journeys in the later Elizabethan period, and the burgeoning literature of travel highlighted the daunting challenges faced by all would-be adventurers. It is not difficult to see how foreign travel could be viewed by many as an irresponsible gamble or a piece of bravado, and equally, why those who decided to mimic or parody its more flamboyant gests often seem to be engaging in what we would call a dare or a prank – two words that seem to acquire their modern senses in the late sixteenth century, suggesting respectively a private challenge and a practical joke or exploit.[14] ('Dare' as a noun is first recorded in 1576.) More than one European trip in the period was consciously conceived in this spirit, and it is worth observing that the literature of jest and prank written by an emerging class of popular writers in the 1580s and 1590s often makes use of the new tourism – Nashe's *Unfortunate Traveller* is the most conspicuous example – and treats it in effect as a series of risky stunts. The wager-journey into Europe and the Middle East was identified by Rowley and Jonson as blurring the boundary between 'real' travel and playfully staged 'voyages', and invites us to explore further the links between the two.

We should also note, however, that while the mad voyages are clearly stimulated by the contemporary interest in travel, they are likely to have drawn some of their inspiration from more traditional sources. The travel stunt is often built upon the notion of a superhuman or virtuosic feat, performing the previously unattempted – an idea that had a popular pedigree in the stories of peripatetic folk heroes with extraordinary powers of transport, as in the 'mad merry pranckes of Tom of Bethlem' or '*Garragantua* that monster of men', a legendary giant (before Rabelais adopted him) who crossed into England on a cloud and fought for King Arthur, or Tom Thumb who is given 'a payre of shooes ... which no sooner on his feete, but he was carried as quicke as thought into another world, where hee sawe wonders'. This was a kind of travel writing that the market in printed romances, chapbooks and ballads kept in the public consciousness and lent a place in the growing literature of picaresque heroes and their escapades. Tom o' Bedlam boasts in a seventeenth-century song that

From the top of high *Caucasus*,
To *Pauls wharf* near the Tower,
In no great haste I easily past
In less than half an hour. ...
In a Boat I went on dry Land
From *Carthage* to St. *Albons*,
I saild to *Spain*, and back again
In a vessel made of Whalebones.[15]

These fantasy-journeys quickened the imaginations of ordinary people long before travel of any kind became an option for them, and supplied a set of metaphors for the impossible dream of mobility that retained their appeal even when travel reports began to bring them more realistic versions of transport. As Mary Campbell says, fiction provides 'the shoes of flight',[16] and as long as travel in general remained a rare activity, or the preserve of particular social classes, and its purpose was strictly defined as pilgrimage, commerce or education, the fantastic voyage of popular legend was a chief repository of thoughts and impulses held in check by the sedentary life. With the erosion of traditional restraints on mobility, such tales must have helped to create a space for parodic acts of transport drawing upon the folklore of extraordinary enterprise – impossible vehicles, heroic feats of agility, the patently absurd challenge.

Were the real-life 'mad voyages' an exclusively English affair? The answer in part depends on how widely we define the phenomenon. The epidemic of travel stunts or 'experiments' noted by observers like John Chamberlain has to my knowledge no parallel in other European countries, and the craze must be explained – if it can be explained at all – in terms of local conditions and responses.[17] But it is closely bound up with activities, like the wager on a journey and related forms of speculation, that certainly occurred and even originated elsewhere. In thinking about how English pilgrimage and tourism became involved in these practices, certain developments in other countries will need to be considered. The same is true with regard to projects like William Bush's, whose remarkable ship invites comparison with the experiments of scientific virtuosi elsewhere in Europe, and specifically with their interest in ingenious machines. More generally, the European context is vital to an understanding of how attitudes to travel developed and were disseminated, and of how humanistic modes of thought brought ideas into play that allowed *literary* mad voyages to flourish across the Continent. Renaissance writers effectively reinvented the ancient genre of the fantastic or extraordinary journey that was particularly associated with Lucian, and used it to create what Elizabeth Chesney calls a series of 'countervoyages': revisionist fictions of travel by Ariosto, Rabelais and Cervantes that parodied much of the epic tradition from Homer to Dante and reflected the restless and sceptical temper of much early-modern enquiry.[18] And while we would not expect the journeys of Orlando or Don Quixote to stimulate direct imitations by actual travellers, there is no doubt that they spring from, and probably make a contribution to, changing conceptions of what travel, be it knightly crusade or picaresque adventure, means to the European imagination in this period. Nonetheless, it is only in England that the fantastic voyage takes root as an *idée fixe* both in popular literature and in social practice and weaves a complicated relationship between the two. In the remainder of the present chapter, I shall examine some of the reasons why the mad voyages should have been a distinctively English phenomenon, and look briefly at some of the intellectual, literary and political developments that generated particular attitudes to adventure in sixteenth-century England.

## Eccentric Acts

The travel stunts that are the germ of this study have been little studied, but they are often lightly invoked as an illustration of English eccentricity, something that is assumed to be a permanent feature of the national character without ever being fully defined. Such a notion informs Arthur Freeman's introduction to a section on 'Improbable Journeys' in his book *Elizabeth's Misfits*:

> When Elizabeth II of England laid Sir Francis Drake's old sword upon the shoulders of Francis Chichester, at Greenwich on 7 July 1967, knighting a mariner for circumnavigating the world alone, she was recognizing and even canonizing ... a tradition of 'dare' journeys, self-imposed tasks and travels, which her earlier namesake might well have similarly admired, if not so formally rewarded.[19]

More a sort of journalistic label or folk myth than a tested category, this notion of perennial eccentricity is supported by evidence of some striking continuities in behaviour, such as the making of bizarre travel wagers in the late eighteenth century that often closely resemble those of two centuries before, and a recurrent addiction to flamboyant stunts that proudly insist on their lack of serious purpose or utility. From such a perspective, the round-the-world balloon attempts of Sir Richard Branson in the 1990s, or his record-setting crossing of the English Channel in an amphibious vehicle in 2004, are the most recent in a long line of English mad voyages, part of a popular tradition that celebrates monomania or deliberate perversity.[20] Unlike Chichester's circumnavigation, they also promote the cult of the amateur in much the same way as did Richard Ferris, the earliest of our documented mad voyagers, who rowed round the coast from London to Bristol in 1590 and insisted that his 'attempte' was 'the more straunge in respect that I was never trayned up on the water',[21] and maverick adventurers who swim in Arctic waters or walk across deserts remain charismatic figures in our own day, although their exploits are increasingly supported by specialized, quasi-professional training.[22] The tradition has also generated books for the general reader like Peter Nichols' *A Voyage for Madmen*, about a round-the-world yacht race in 1968 sponsored by the *Sunday Times*, in which one English participant set out with no previous sailing experience (though he had just crossed the Atlantic in a rowing boat), whilst another, the unfortunate Donald Crowhurst, faked radio reports of his rapid progress whilst meandering in mid-ocean, where he finally committed suicide. A general survey is offered in John Keay's book *Eccentric Travellers*, whose protagonists are nearly all English, including the nineteenth-century tourist James Holman of whom Keay remarks that 'had he not been totally blind, he would never have felt the need to embark on his improbable journeys'.[23] And behind such accounts lie numerous anecdotal histories in which English travel stunts and wagers feature regularly: a representative example is *English Eccentrics and Eccentricities* (1866) by the prolific John Timbs, one of whose stories is about 'Jerusalem' Whalley, the reputed founder of the Hellfire Club, who in 1788 took a £20,000 bet that he could walk to and 'have a game of ball against the walls of Jerusalem' and return within a year.[24] But these chronicles of outlandish activity tend to rely on generalizations that they make no attempt to explain or interrogate. Early-modern English culture yields a set of responses to travel and adventure that does seem to create a pattern for bizarre enterprises in later centuries, but rather than treating those responses as a kind of God-given eccentricity, or one that can be simply accounted for by reference to an eternal stereotype, we should try to see them as part of a formative historical moment in which all the categories are unstable. To put it another way, the mad voyages may allow us to ask where 'English eccentricity' comes from and what it means in the early-modern period.

The late-eighteenth-century exploits just described no doubt reinforced the view of G.F.A. Wendeborn, a German visitor to England who published his impressions of the country in 1791, that a 'spirit of gaming ... exerts itself more powerfully among the English, than among any other nation', and he asked: 'where is there any people so fond of frequent and oftentimes high betting, not seldom about extreme trifles, as the English?'[25] Historians have made similar observations about upper class gambling in Tudor and early Stuart England, and the wager on travel was recognized at the time as part of the extension of aristocratic preserves to other classes, paving the way for the later perception that the nation as a whole was obsessed with idiosyncratic betting. But the English reputation for eccentricity has more complicated roots than this, and we should remember that the country's relationship to the rest of the world was transformed in the two centuries following the establishment of the East India Company and the European Grand Tour. What later appeared to foreigners to be the perverse habits of a world-dominating race were forged in a very different climate of relative isolation and insecurity.

At the end of Samuel Rowley's history play *When you see me, you know me* (1605), Henry VIII greets the Emperor Charles V on the latter's visit to England, which historically took place in 1520:

We dwell heere, but in an outward continent,
Where winters ice-cickles hangs on our beards,
Bordring upon the frozen Orcades,
Our mother-point, compast with the Artike sea,
Where raging *Boreas* styes from winters mouth,
Yet are our bloods as hote, as where the Sun doth rise,
Wee have no golden mines to leade you to,
But hearts of proofe, and what wee speake, weele do.[26]

Looking back 80-odd years, Rowley imagines an England that found in its own insularity and remoteness a source of spiritual strength. This self-image was particularly cultivated by the English after the Reformation had isolated them from much of Continental Europe, and as they struggled to meet the challenge to their dreams of overseas expansion posed by Spanish conquest in the Americas ('Wee have no golden mines'), but it was underwritten by the classical perception of the British Isles as *penitus toto divisos orbe,* wholly divided from all the world (Virgil, *Eclogues*, 1) on the very edge of Europe, facing an uncharted sea.[27] This view was sustained by mediaeval authorities: the fourteenth-century historian Ranulf Higden cited the belief that 'Anglia hath that name as it were an angle and a corner of the worlde', though adding that it contains 'grete plente of all good' and 'is worthy to have the name of another worlde'. In 1614 John Speed repeated this affirmative view: 'This *Iland* is so spacious and ample, that *Cesar* (the first Romane discoverer thereof) supposed that he had found out *another World*.'[28] The British archipelago, further declared Speed, 'hath been taken for those fortunate *Ilands* whereof the Poets have imagined a perpetuall spring time' (156), and like many historians before him, he looked to the Britain of antiquity, before the Roman and Anglo-Saxon invasions, for the sources of national identity and pride. But 'Britain' did not exist as a political entity in mediaeval and Tudor times, and it was in the service of an *English* nationalism that the argument for insular self-sufficiency was made during the sixteenth century, using what Kate Chedgzoy calls the 'misrecognition of England as an island' to appropriate the whole of mainland Britain in England's self-definition as 'a boundaried nation'.[29] This is what makes it possible for John of Gaunt in Shakespeare's *Richard II* to apostrophize England as a 'precious stone set in the silver sea', and a 'fortress built by Nature' whose 'rocky shore beats back the envious siege / Of watery Neptune' (2.1.43–63). But such assertions were also a way, by the late sixteenth century, of rationalizing the country's loss of her French dominions, the erosion of English dominance in northern European waters by the Hanseatic League, and the fact that the Iberian nations had stolen a march on her oceanic ambitions.

However, the refusal by Rowley's Henry VIII to let geography define and set limits to his country's reach ('what wee speake, weele do') confirms another standard view of the English alive in this period. The classical image of 'Britons ... fully separate / From all the worlde ... / Walled with the sea'[30] may have been a hardy perennial, but curiously, it co-existed with a set of folk traditions about the English as compulsive wanderers. This tendency is repeatedly noted by writers in the late Middle Ages and early Renaissance, and as Christian Zacher points out, it is frequently explained astrologically: the English, as befits a maritime people, are ruled by the moon, which Mandeville in the most popular of all travel books described as 'of lightly mevynge' and the 'planete of weye', provoking those under her influence 'to go diverse weyes and to sechen strange thinges and other dyversitees of the world, for the mone envyrouneth the erthe more hastily than ony other planete.'[31] William Caxton writing in 1490 declared, 'For we englysshe men ben borne under the domynacyon of the mone which is never stedfaste but ever waverynge', and John Gower had said the same 100 years earlier, adding that as a consequence 'thei travaile in every lond'.[32] Caxton emphasized internal movement, travel *within* the country, and it may be that a vigorous tradition of domestic pilgrimage partially accounts for this reputation, though the most visible literary outcrop of that tradition, Chaucer's *Canterbury Tales*, also acknowledges the popularity of the major foreign shrines for English pilgrims and has the Wife of Bath claim to have made three visits to Jerusalem on top of pilgrimages to Rome, Compostella and Loreto. Her obvious exaggeration may be intended by Chaucer to show how a national reputation for extravagant travel gets embellished, but it feeds on a substantial record of traffic during the Middle Ages. George Parks suggests that 'the road to Rome has probably never been so well travelled by Englishmen as it was in the years from 1100 to 1500'[33] – by diplomats and officials on church business as well as by pilgrims and a few tourists – and at its height, the Anglo-Norman sphere of influence extended to the Pyrenees and southern Italy and dominated the northern seas from Spain to the Baltic. There were English trading communities in every country, and although the country's commercial might declined in the fifteenth century, particularly after the virtual collapse of its navy during the Wars of the Roses, its merchants, pilgrims, political agents and soldiers of fortune remained a major part of the European network of travel. There is, then, plenty of evidence for Gower's mediaeval claim that the English 'travaile in every lond'. What is intriguing is the concomitant belief that they are somehow intrinsically restless and exorbitant, a quality that might be put to good use in the daunting search for trade routes through the Arctic but which is also seen, especially after England's horizons were clouded by the Reformation and setbacks in foreign policy, as a problematic feature of the national character.

More than a century after Caxton declared that the English were ruled by the moon, William Camden in his *Remaines* was still pondering the 'mutability' of his countrymen and wondered if they were particularly susceptible to foreign fashions because 'we as all Ilanders are *Lunares* or the Moones men'.[34] By then the national reputation for flightiness was being fed by the rapid growth in European tourism and living examples of the *inglese italianato* and Frenchified fop that many observed in London's streets. But the idea that the English were culturally unstable, preferring foreign novelties to their own traditions, long predates the early-modern surge in private travel. It was probably in the main pleasure-seeking pilgrims in Italy that provoked the remark of a fifteenth-century pope (again recalled by Camden) 'that the Englishmen were fit for any thing, and to be preferred before other nations, were it not for their wavering and unsetled lightnesse'[35] – a view that we shall find one of his Counter-Reformation successors having occasion to echo. The same report found its way into the Tudor translation of Higden's *Polychronicon*, which condemned the English for preferring the customs of 'ferre and straunge londes' to 'theyr owne herytage'.[36] There is no evidence that English pilgrims to continental shrines in the late-mediaeval period were any more numerous than or different in behaviour to those from other countries, though John Wyclif believed that his countrymen were especially prone to the vice of curiosity that was believed to infect most pilgrims, already labelled as 'light-minded and inquisitive persons' by Jacques de Vitry in the thirteenth century.[37] Memories of how English mercenaries, highly respected for their fighting skills, terrorized Italian communities in the later 1300s while participating in the peninsula's wars might also have helped to shape views.[38]

But whatever the reason for the papal judgement, what is interesting here is the early-modern readiness to repeat it, as if such statements held a clue to the contemporary state of the nation.

Ralph Waldo Emerson famously called the English 'a nation of humorists', and his belief that they were typified by 'Mr Cockayne', the man who cultivated oddness and singularity, was of a piece with eighteenth-century statements like Joseph Priestley's: '[t]he English, they say, have least of a uniform national character, on account of their liberty and independence, which enables every man to follow his own humour.'[39] When Priestley made this remark in 1788, the term 'eccentricity' was newly coined, and its connotations, as Paul Langford explains, were those of harmless individualism: 'whim, caprice, singularity, folly'. The same was true of the word 'humour', which had lost most of its physiological associations and was being applied more loosely to quirks of personality or idiosyncratic habits. But an earlier period was less tolerant of quixotic deviations from the norm: Langford reminds us that before the later eighteenth century the common term for such eccentricity was 'originality' – an altogether more alarming concept – and the genial acceptance of oddness and obsessive behaviour was much less evident.[40] These tendencies were evidence of a disordered personality, perhaps of heresy, or various kinds of madness, and in the troubled *zeitgeist* of sixteenth-century Europe were unlikely to be understood as mere character traits. Idiosyncracy was virtually synonymous with folly, a capacious category that for practical purposes included all deviations from the Christian ideal and was widely taken to epitomize the human condition. The figure of the fool has been described as the dominant 'non-religious icon'[41] of the late-mediaeval period, and it retained its hold on the public imagination well into early-modern times, complicated and enriched by humanist ideas of 'wise folly'. As late as 1621, in *The Anatomy of Melancholy*, Robert Burton mustered numerous authorities and copious evidence to support the proposition that 'all the World is melancholy or mad, dotes, and every member of it', and demanded, 'who is not a Foole, Melancholy, Mad … who is not brain-sick?'[42] When the norm is already distempered, when everyone is seen to deviate from right living, 'originality' might have difficulty making itself visible, let alone winning acceptance as a legitimate lifestyle.

Yet this sweeping view hides some complicated trends. As scholars have recently reminded us, Burton found his vision of universal folly epitomized in the curious map 'made like a Fooles head', published in about 1590, in which the face beneath the jester's cap was replaced by the latest version of Ortelius's world-map.[43] (See Plate 1.) This image, which Burton describes as 'a crased head, *cavea stultorum*, a Fooles paradise', was brought to theatrical fruition nearly half a century later in Richard Brome's play *The Antipodes* (1638), where the hero Peregrine has a head full of geographical fantasies as a result of his single-minded devouring of travel books and is cured by a lengthy series of charades. Brome was heavily influenced by the *Anatomy* in this play and probably took his central conceit directly from Burton's invocation of the fool's-cap map. Peregrine's derangement is however quite specific, and peculiar to him; it is not a demonstration that 'all the world is mad', and it is worth asking whether the focus on his travel fixations represents a new way of thinking about obsessive behaviour, one that may in fact be anticipated in the relevant passage of *The Anatomy of Melancholy*.

As suggested, Burton treats the fool's-cap map as an emblem of general reality rather than a comment on wayward conduct, and approves the archaic emphasis on worldly *vanitas* that is expressed in the map's numerous quotations from classical and biblical sources. Yet in his repeated invocation of 'hellebore', a herb said to have been used in ancient Greece as a cure for madness, Burton tilts his critique in the direction of satire on particular modern developments. He declares that because 'most men are mad … they had as much need to goe a pilgrimage to the *Anticyrae* [the Greek locations where hellebore grew] as in our daies they run to *Compostella* … or *Lauretta* [Loreto] to seeke for helpe … it is like to be as prosperous a voyage as that of *Guiana*, and … there is much more need of *Hellebor* then of *Tobacco*.'[44] Burton's catalogue of the vanity of travel deftly suggests that the English search for Eldorado or the new fashionable vice of smoking imported from America are cultural addictions that have replaced the rituals of Catholic pilgrimage, but the playful recommendation of an antique, long-abandoned remedy for madness hardly compels us to see a taste for travel experience in itself as a sign of the imbalance of humours, a sickness in need of cure. Burton freely confesses in the *Anatomy* his fascination with geographical subjects, and his own fantastic voyage later in the book, when he imagines himself as 'a long-winged Hawke … still soaring higher and higher', and 'having now come at last into these ample fields of Ayre, wherein I may freely expatiate and exercise my selfe, for my recreation a while rove, wander about the world', ushers in a virtuosic, flamboyant meditation on contemporary exploration and discovery that ends with a ringing endorsement of travel and 'change of ayre' as a salve for melancholy.[45] The 'Digression of Ayre' is an obsessive piece of writing, one that seems exorbitant in its torrent of geographical enquiry, but for all Burton's insistence that he is as mad as anyone else (1.109), his disquisition comes across as a deliberately eccentric performance, one that proclaims the 'originality' of the single-minded scholar.

The stern conception of some kinds of travelling behaviour as 'mad' in an older clinical sense (one shaped by humours theory) is certainly detectable in the fiercer satirical assaults on tourists and venturers in this period, but it is evident that these ideas were under some pressure by the end of the sixteenth century. In Ben Jonson's *Every Man Out of his Humour* (1599), the satirist, Asper, is angry about the current 'abuse of this word humour', which Cordatus agrees is 'racked and tortured' in fashionable society. It is not that it cannot be used figuratively: Asper acknowledges that the doctrine of the humours

may by metaphor apply itself
Unto the general disposition,
As when some one peculiar quality

Doth so possess a man, that it doth draw
All his affects, his spirits, and his powers
In their confluxions all to run one way,
This may be truly said to be a humour.

But what infuriates him is its trivial misappropriation:

But that a rook, in wearing a pied feather,
The cable hat-band or the three-piled ruff,
A yard of shoe-tie or the Switzer's knot
On his French garters, should affect a humour,
Oh, 'tis more than most ridiculous.

Jonson's prize exhibit in the play of such affectation is Puntarvolo, a 'vainglorious knight, over-Englishing his travels and wholly consecrated to singularity', who 'deals upon returns and strange performances'[46] – exploits to which we shall return. If Puntarvolo's 'singularity' were seen as somehow pathological, this would make him 'humourous' in the old sense, a grotesque example of travel's capacity (as Tudor moralists saw it) to unbalance minds and ruin characters. But Asper's reluctance to credit the eccentricities of flamboyant young men with the title of 'humour' reveals a belief that odd behaviour is becoming more voluntary, a matter of lifestyle and social performance rather than a compulsive departure from God-given norms. It is another of the ways in which the early-modern period is one of transition: people are not yet ready to see individualism as harmless whimsy, but a space is opening up in which the notion of a man 'following his humour' (in a later sense of the word) is beginning to exert its own fascination. This is perhaps why some of the enduring forms of English eccentricity take shape in this period. When, for instance, Paul Langford describes the eighteenth-century obsession with long-distance walking, which foreigners 'found it difficult to believe … did not arise from some kind of abnormality',[47] it is apparent that the practice, and probably also its reputation for oddity, has its roots in the pedestrian feats of several early-modern adventurers, including Ben Jonson and Tom Coryat, and the publicity that their exploits engendered. What had been regarded as an involuntary pathology (in this case, the wandering habits of '*Lunares* or the Moones men') was becoming part of a repertoire of behaviour, taken up by individual actors as a chosen vehicle of self-expression.

This diminution of the fear of 'originality' was clearly necessary before independent exploits like the travel stunt could generate positive publicity and make it possible to be 'mad' in a way that did not alienate or alarm one's fellow citizens. A long tradition of hare-brained English adventure is born at this point. But it is not yet the whimsical counterpart to solid national success that it would be in later centuries. The mad voyages are in varying degrees a kind of *reductio ad absurdum* of the act of travel, introducing elements of parody and nonsense to physical recreation, and as such they both defy and strangely chime with the arguments of those who criticized the taste for adventure as frivolous and destabilizing. This ambiguity is at the heart of the vogue and will be explored throughout this book: it reflects a moment in English culture when expectations of the nation's growing mobility were high but were also the source of considerable anxiety and controversy and had not yet yielded the stable institutions of the Grand Tour, settled colonies or East Indian trade. Nor was it simply a question of material development: as I shall argue further in what follows, sixteenth-century Europe wrestled with competing ideas of folly and madness, and of the role of play in educating young men, that had particular imaginative and social outcomes in Elizabethan England and may help to explain what precipitated this curious rash of events.

Travel in this period was a volatile theatre of activity in which ludic stunts and speculative ventures displayed a family resemblance and often relied on similar sources and methods of support, as later discussion will show in detail. The mad voyage phenomenon cannot be viewed in isolation from the 'normal' travel practices of the period, in particular the custom of wagering on a journey that was usually (and perhaps invariably) part of the vogue. This is the point made by William Rowley when he includes in his list of mad voyages 'the travell to *Rome* with the returne in certaine daies' – the 'bargain of return' that brought a sporting element into early-modern tourism. The protocols of the travel wager will be discussed briefly in Chapter 2, in introducing the analysis of domestic exploits, and more extensively in Chapters 4 and 5, which deal with English adventures abroad and examine the role of such bets in facilitating long-distance journeys long before tourism became commonplace. Before turning to the games with travel that were played so energetically and inventively in this period, however, I want to explore a little further the cultural origins of the mad voyage in some of the texts and ideas that comprised the mental furniture of early-modern Europeans, and look at their particular manifestation in Tudor England.

## The Ship of Fools

Past discussion of the mad voyages, as already indicated, has tended to assign them to a special category of eccentric exploits, ignoring their social and economic contexts, and if we are to find anything new and useful to say about these events, it is necessary to situate each of them as fully as possible in the individual circumstances from which it sprang. At the same time, however, the fact that contemporary observers were ready to lump together a variety of elaborate stunts, wager-journeys and betting challenges as an identifiable trend, and to treat the lone endeavour, however bizarre, as a kind of odyssey, does suggest that the vogue for travel exploits tapped into a fund of stories and journeying tropes that had shaped the collective mind for generations. The traveller as author of a significant ordeal is a figure that spans many cultures, and mediaeval Europe inherited some potent examples from the classical world, peregrinating heroes like the Argonauts, Odysseus, Aeneas and Alexander, whose exorbitant journeys left their mark on folk tales, peripatetic romances, picaresque fiction, learned satire, and secular travel writing itself.

This was an oral and literary heritage of great antiquity, and from early times it had contained strong elements of travesty and burlesque. As Neil Rennie points out, in the Hellenistic period 'many elements from the accumulating tradition – of primitivism, mythical islands, and ideal societies – were given the form of imaginary voyages to fabulous lands', stories whose enduring popularity meant that more than 200 years later, in the second century AD, the Greek-Syrian writer Lucian could write parodies which depended upon his readers' familiarity with them.[48] Long before Renaissance satirists attacked Mandeville and lying travellers, Lucian was pouring scorn on classical writers who 'have written about imaginary travels and journeys of theirs, telling of huge beasts, cruel men and strange ways of living', and responding to their fabrications with his own deadpan accounts of far-fetched voyages, noting in the preface to one of them that 'everything in my story is a more or less comical parody of one or another of the poets, historians and philosophers of old, who have written much that smacks of miracles and fables'.[49] This was a learned burlesque, of course, and it was to prove useful to humanists who had their own uses for the fantastic voyage, but mediaeval cultures that knew little of Lucian also relished the tall tales they inherited from antiquity and elaborated them in ways that would be indispensable to Ariosto and Rabelais in their revisionist epics of extraordinary travel.

Much later, a critical industry was to grow up in eighteenth-century Europe around the concepts of the 'fantastic', 'imaginary' and 'extraordinary' voyage, one that reached its most developed form in France, and later still, students of science fiction saw the extraordinary or speculative journey as a kind of theoretical actualization, made possible by technological developments, of the imaginary dream-voyages of an earlier period.[50] These categories tend nonetheless to overlap, and trying to distinguish them precisely is of limited value here. But it is worth noting that the distinction between 'imaginary' and 'speculative' voyages that has been useful to critics writing about Jules Verne can profitably be applied to early-modern fictions that used the journey of discovery as a tool of rational enquiry: thus More's *Utopia* and Bacon's *New Atlantis* take on a scientific appearance and purpose that is absent from the mediaeval or classical *somnium*.[51] These are fantastic voyages that are also 'experiments', to use John Chamberlain's term for the travel stunts he witnessed in London, and they bring the imaginary journey of folk legend or Christian allegory (the flight of the soul to God) into the novel context of early-modern discovery and innovation and examine the cultural questions that flow from them. Similarly, we may conclude that when English adventurers started to experiment with new peripatetic opportunities, they were participating in a process where time-honoured ideas of fantastic travel were being modified by the pressures of the time.

For instance, in writing up the adventures of William Bush and his versatile ship with which I began this enquiry, Anthony Nixon laid considerable stress on their supposed contribution to experimental science, claims that may be hard to take seriously but which raise pertinent questions about the project's purpose or utility. As we shall see in Chapter 3, Nixon affects to present Bush's ship as a speculative venture and not as simply a fantastic *jeu d'esprit*. On the other hand, there were observers who were content to describe the same episode in loosely hyperbolic terms, like the allusion in a pamphlet by Thomas Dekker to 'the rowing over steeples by lande in a wherry',[52] which aligns it with the impossible peripatetic feats of Tom Thumb and other folk heroes. In these contrasted perspectives, Bush's ship-on-land is being made to do two very different kinds of cultural work, modern and progressive in the first case, and safely traditional in the second.[53] But Dekker's apparently stable fantasy is not quite what it seems, and hints at a more sceptical alternative to Nixon's optimistic manifesto.

The imaginary voyage might be purely fanciful, or it might be (as in More and Bacon) a vehicle for new ideas, but it also provided the occasion for one of the most influential moral tropes of the early-modern period, that of the ship of fools. Robert Burton seized on this idea in elaborating his vision of universal folly and error, declaring that 'a company of brainsicke dizards … may goe *ride the asse*, and all saile along to the *Anticyrae*, in the *ship of fooles* for company together',[54] and he gives it a light classical gloss with another of his allusions to the Greek source of a cure for madness, like those that I quoted earlier. But the ship of fools is essentially a late-mediaeval construction that came into its own in the sixteenth century, and by Burton's day it was a well-worn trope, one repeatedly invoked by Tudor writers and, no doubt, a familiar colloquial allusion for decades. The phrase 'ship of fools' entered the language via two English versions, both published in 1509 with that title, of *Das Narrenschiff*, a hugely popular verse satire by the German jurist and scholar Sebastian Brant that was first printed in Basel in 1494. Brant's encyclopaedic survey of worldly folly was enlivened by a series of expressive woodcuts (many of which have been ascribed to Dürer), one to illustrate each type of fool, and images like that in Figure 1.2 provided several generations of European readers with a mental picture of folly epitomized in the contemporary explosion of maritime travel. For many observers they would have been irresistibly recalled by the madcap adventures involving vessels of various kinds in the 1590s and early 1600s.

Brant did not fasten on the conceit of the ship until he was well into the composition of his poem, and only a few of the woodcuts in the first edition feature it, a pattern that would be repeated in the numerous adaptations that followed (at least a dozen by 1512), but as the work spread across Europe it seems nonetheless to have been the ship that caught the imagination of readers, especially in France and England. An early sign of this was the publication (c.1515?) by Wynkyn de Worde of *Cock Lorel's Bote*, a burlesque version of the ship of fools that was to have a long popular life of its own and reproduced four of the woodcuts that adorned Henry Watson's version (also published by de Worde) of *The Shyppe of Fooles* in 1509. They included a fine reworking (Figure 1.3) of one of Brant's woodcuts that probably became for many English readers the definitive image of the ship of fools. The illustrations have only a

1.2 Engraving attributed to Albrecht Dürer, in Sebastian Brant, *Das Narrenschiff* (Basel, 1494). (Special Collections, University of Houston Libraries.)

tenuous relation to the text of *Cock Lorel's Bote*, which describes the assembly of a wide assortment of craftsmen, artisans and rogues by a legendary outlaw, Cock Lorel, and their nationwide excursion, and the woodcut in Figure 1.3 provided a purely generic model for a remarkably adaptable vehicle:

Then Cock weighed anchor and hois[t]ed his sail,
And forth he rowed without fail;
They sailed England thorough and thorough,
Village, town, city and borough;

1.3 Engraving from *Cock Lorel's Bote*, c.1515, published by Wynkyn de Worde. (Huntington Library, San Marino, California.)

They blessed their ship when they had done,
And drank about Saint Julian's turn.
Then every man pulled at his oar,
With that I could see them no more:
But as they rowed up the hill
The boatswain blew his whistle full shrill ... [55]

The lines have a festive air that anticipates the holiday mood generated by the later mad voyages (as described in the pamphlet accounts of several of them), and they cloak the journey in the same figure of *impossibilia* (rowing uphill and so on) that Dekker used to satirise William Bush's ship-on-land. *Cock Lorel* is the liveliest and most irreverent treatment of the ship of fools theme, and its eponymous hero became an English cultural legend still remembered at the turn of the seventeenth century. Samuel Rid, in his *Martin Mark-All* (1610), portrays him as the creator of the vagrant fraternities that populate Elizabethan rogue literature and is tolerant towards his topsy-turvy regime, as is Ben Jonson in a rather similar invocation in his masque *The Gypsies Metamorphosed* (1621). These two treatments reflect something of the Jacobean debate about what constituted lawful recreation at a time of sharp religious disagreements over the value of festivity, and the masque, which shows 'aristocrats encouraging and even participating in incipiently riotous pastimes',[56] prompts us to consider what kind of comment is offered by Cock Lorel's exorbitant travels on the itinerant stunts in which Jonson and many of his courtly friends were actively interested.

As Lawrence Manley suggests, writers of Tudor complaint literature used motifs like the ship or cartload of fools 'to figure the overturning of traditional order' and to delineate 'the bewildering profusion of social roles, classes, species, and distinctions that were linked to socio-economic change', and the best-known English version of the *Narrenschiff*, by Alexander Barclay, in many ways epitomizes the conservative response to social dislocation and mobility in the earlier sixteenth century.[57] Its central image of the overloaded bark of folly is even more sharply drawn in *Cock Lorel's Bote* where, as Manley points out, 'the sheer magnitude of the boat's swollen population adds an aggressive edge to the poem's topsy-turvy'.[58] But the aggression in *Cock Lorel* is inseparable from an infectious spirit of carnival, which seems to express a popular will to defy the restraints on mobility that Barclay's more traditional design is anxious to enforce:

With this man [Cock Lorel] was a lusty company,
For all rascals from them they did try;
They banished prayer, peace and sadness
And took with them mirth, sport and gladness;
They would not have virtue, ne yet devotion,
But riot and revel, with jolly rebellion.
They sung and danced full merrily,
With swearing and staring heaven-high.[59]

The poem is ambiguously poised between censure and celebration, graphically evoking the threat of disorder and vagrancy but at the same time acknowledging the social perspectives of tradesmen and itinerant workers and their vigorous claim to new freedoms of movement and association. Whatever the poem's overall satirical design may have been (only a fragment of 400-odd lines survives), it plays with the fashionable literary trope of the foolish ship in ways that partially subvert its orthodox message and hint at the countercultural purposes to which it might be put. In its flamboyant and confrontational rendering of a journey, *Cock Lorel* is a recognizable precursor of Jonson's epigram (to be discussed in Chapter 6) about a voyage through the Fleet Ditch, a poem which is combatively aware of the vogue for travel 'experiments' that this much earlier piece of writing seems strikingly to anticipate.

Alexander Barclay does not make as inventive use of the voyage motif as the author of *Cock Lorel*, but his poem (with the relevant illustrations) helped to keep it alive and encouraged readers to associate the ship of fools with a number of strategic criticisms of contemporary travel – to some of which he was careful to give a native twist, as in the list of foreign university towns where English students waste their time and 'retournyth home agayne / More ignorant / blynder and gretter folys / Than they were whan they firste went to the scholys' (fol. LXI v), and in a pointed attack on early Tudor tourists and adventurers. The latter comes in Barclay's vigorous reworking of Brant's brief chapter (34) about foreign travel, which had dealt solely with the pitfalls of over-curious pilgrimage (a common late mediaeval theme, and only slightly elaborated by Watson). In contrast, Barclay mounts a sustained critique of those in modern times who wander abroad and 'besyly enquere / Of all marveyles':

And so they labour alway from londe to londe
To se all wonders / but nought they understonde …
Some unto Fraunce and some to Flaunders ren
To so the wayes / and workes of cunnynge men
And to be shorte over all they range
Spendynge theyr goodes about unthryftynes
In countrees knowen / unknowen and strange (fol. LXXIII)

His Horatian admonition (following these lines) that travellers 'chaunge the place' but not 'theyr mynde nor maners' is conventional enough, but it is interesting that at this early date Barclay is already making the kinds of complaints about secular touring that became routine in the second half of the sixteenth century. More remarkable still is the way in which his critique operates reflexively, using a strategy that would be common in later urban satire, to suggest that England's metropolis has become part of the hazardous circuit of contemporary travel, importing foreign vices and losing its former identity:

To passe the se[a] to lerne Venus rybawdry
It is great foly / for thou mayst lerne thy fyll
In shoppis Innes and sellers / ye[a] sometyme openly
At saynt Martyns Westmynster or at the tour hyll
So that I fere all London / in tyme it shall fyll
For it is there kept in lyght and in darke
That the pore Stuys decays for lacke of warke (fol. LXXIII v)

Lawrence Manley notes that in the earlier Tudor period London 'became in the popular imagination a kind of Cockaigne, a fool's paradise that … turned England upside down', and he suggests that this was partly a result of large-scale migration to the city that 'signified an empowering liberation from peasant servitude', with urban life creating opportunities for working people that were unimaginable in England's villages.[60] But for Barclay the topsy-turvy vision of the capital is clearly more worrying. His London is one where he dares not dock the ship of fools:

From London Rocks almyghty god us save
For if we there anker / outher bote or barge
There be so many that they us wyll overcharge ...
We kepe the streme / and touche nat the shore (fol. XI)

The sheer profusion of fools keeps the ship from what looks like its natural destination, the dystopian place where its passengers will find the most company and will be most at home. The paradox is expressive of profound tensions in the conservative vision of change, which recognized but could not accept that London was becoming a different kind of city. Barclay's way of dealing with the siren image of Cockaigne, which is a vital if ambiguous element in the ship of fools trope, is an interesting symptom of English attitudes to this most popular of imaginary voyages, the fabulous journey to the land of ease and pleasure, at a particularly fluid historical moment.

At the start of the climactic chapter that Barclay calls '[t]he unyversall shyp and generall Barke or barge', named individuals and tradesmen ('Jacke / charde / my brother Robyn hyll / With Myllers and bakers that weight and mesure hate') are summoned to join the company before embarkation:

Come to Companyons: ren: tyme it is to rowe
Our Carake fletis: the se is large and wyde
And depe Inough: a pleasaunt wynde doth blowe
Prolonge no tyme / our Carake doth you byde
Our felawes tary for you on every syde
Hast hyther I say ye folys naturall
Howe oft shall I you unto my Navy call (fol. CCLXII)

A roll-call follows of the nations that flock to take part in the voyage, all of whom will

sayle to that londe where folys abounde and flowe
For whether we aryve / at London or Brystowe
Or any other Haven within this our londe
We folys ynowe / shall fynde alway at hande. (fol. CCLXII v)

The sense of anticipation here derives ultimately from Brant's energetic description of a voyage to Schluraffenland (the German Cockaigne), which was variously treated in subsequent adaptations, including the Latin and French versions from which Barclay worked. (Brant's original woodcut, shown in Figure 1.4, is closely copied by Barclay.) Brant left the reader in no doubt about the eventual fate of the voyagers, whose ship is blown off-course and finally swallowed up a whirlpool,[61] but his vivid storytelling evoked the spirit of boon companionship that is indispensable to the folk myth of Cockaigne or poor man's paradise. The legend still flourished in German culture when Brant

1.4 'Ad Narragonia', possibly by Dürer, from Sebastian Brant, *Das Narrenschiff* (1494). (Special Collections, University of Houston Libraries.)

was writing, and it leaves its mark on *Cock Lorel's Bote*, but Barclay is much more ambivalent about this festive version of the mad voyage, as is apparent in the change of mood following his lively opening. Whereas Brant invents a compelling symbolic destination ('Ad Narragonia') for the ship of fools, and maintains narrative momentum with various pseudo-Odyssean adventures, Barclay draws down and declares that 'No speciall place will I chose for our rode', emphasising that the voyage is endless and without clear direction:

About we wander in tempest and in tourment
What place is sure / where Foles may remayne
And fyx theyr dwellynge sure and parmanent
None certaynly: The cause therof is playne
We wander in the se / for pleasour bydynge payne
And though the haven of helth be in our syght
Alas we fle from it with all our myght (fol. CCLXIII)

The perplexity sounded in these lines ('We wander in the se') would find an echo in later commentary on English maritime affairs,[62] and it is deepened by the traces of the Cockaigne legend that remain, adding to the distrust of wandering a sense that the voyage in search of 'pleasure' is one that perversely avoids the 'haven of health'. This intuition continued to inform conservative objections to travel in the century ahead, and was to be especially provoked by the growth of English tourism abroad and by the spectacle of New World adventurers pursuing quick riches and immediate gratification. Some of the ways in which those expeditions were caught up in the indictment of foolish travel in this period will be examined in later chapters. But influential as Barclay's book and Tudor complaint literature in general were in shaping attitudes to worldly adventure, their perspective was challenged not only by the rebellious spirit of Cock Lorel but also by the humanist reinvention, at the same time as *The Ship of Fools* was spreading across Europe, of the ancient trope of the fantastic voyage.

In composing their revisionist travel fictions, writers as different as More and Rabelais were compelled to draw the *mythos* of a land of ease and plenty into the ethical debate about the good life, recognizing that Cockaigne and its cognate forms had their origin in ancient sources (like the classical journey to the Isles of the Blest) and behind the fantasy of self-indulgence harboured important questions about work and leisure and the distribution of wealth.[63] But they were also very aware of the paradoxical potential of such stories. If Cockaigne began life as a Golden Age myth of classlessness and common ownership, it had become by the Middle Ages a kind of cultural sport: E.M. Ackerman traces its role in the development in Germany of the 'lying tale', a popular rhetorical exercise that in the thirteenth century was usually just 'a list of impossibilities', but later picked up on the popularity of travellers' tales to create the 'voyage to a fabulous land of plenty'.[64] According to Louise O. Vasvari, the earliest surviving complete description of Cockaigne is the French *Li pais a non Coqaigne* (c.1250), a burlesque tale of pilgrimage 'in which the poet claims he went to Rome to receive absolution and that the Pope sent him to do his penance in Cockaigne'.[65] It was an obvious vehicle for parody and satire, especially of the anticlerical sort (Luther was fond of saying that 'life in the monastery is the real life of Cockaigne'[66]), and these oral and literary games paved the way for the intricate humanist uses of the fantastic journey in the early-modern period. But it was the example of Lucian, championed by More and Erasmus in the early sixteenth century, that did most to shape the emergent genre of ludic travel narratives. Lucian's frequent use of imaginary journeys in his writings helped to ensure that the fantastic voyage emerged as a prime vehicle of Menippean fiction, with its emphasis on intellectual play and detached observation, in a tradition that was eventually to yield such varied achievements as *Gulliver's Travels, Candide* and *Alice in Wonderland*. His most popular work, the ironically titled 'A True Story' (*Vera Historia* in the Latin version) parodies the tall tales of antiquity with an account of a journey to the moon, and it provided to the Renaissance a kind of prototype for the narrative of travel or exploration that mocks its own claim to truth and in so doing, ensures that the discoveries it charts are seen in teasing relation to the reader's world and normative conceptions of progress.

*Serio jocum* made possible a new kind of satire, one in which fantasy and playful hypothesis played a large role and created a fictional dress for new ways of appraising the social and moral problems facing sixteenth-century Europe. It was not always understood or approved in the period: Lucian's own writings were frequently condemned as frivolous and immoral, while ebullient humanist fictions that had absorbed his example and mounted a cunningly indirect attack on pretension and hypocrisy, like the later books of Rabelais' *Gargantua & Pantagruel* and Erasmus' *Praise of Folly*, were some of the most controversial publications of the age. More's *Utopia*, less flamboyant in manner and (in part 1) overtly critical of the status quo, was misread in other ways: contemporaries often overlooked the fable's ironic framing devices and simply took part 2, as did Philip Sidney or Nashe's Jack Wilton, as 'a perfect plot of a commonwealth or government'.[67] In some cases, of course, they may have been fully appreciative of More's methods but wanted to insist on the seriousness of his conception, recalling perhaps that More had chosen specifically to translate Lucian's satires on the abuse of wealth, and that one of these, the *Menippus*, 'can be seen as an imaginary voyage of sorts (into Hades) in which an egalitarian society is used to show up the inadequacy of conventional materialistic values'.[68] The humanists defended their endorsement of Lucian by stressing the pedagogical value of his elegant Greek and his affinities with respectable Roman satire,[69] but the literary qualities that most excited them were his use of paradox and ludic plotting devices. Humanist *serio jocum* – what Erasmus called *lusus ingenii*, or erudite joking – extends and complicates the Lucianic model, tightening the use of paradox to make of it a more rigorous tool of 'witty' enquiry. The same process also strengthens the ethical intent of such literary play, making it clear that it is not merely a surrender to relativism or scepticism but an attempt to stimulate in the reader a positive exercise of moral judgement. At the heart of Lucian's vision, as Douglas Duncan stresses, is the Cynic concept of *kataskopos* or detached observer, typically offering a narrator who 'belittles human concerns by seeing them from a great height', as in the dialogue *Icaromenippus*, where Menippus on a flight to Zeus's throne has a stopover on the moon and gazes down upon human beings swarming like ants in an anthill.[70] It is a perspective which – allowing for Lucian's flippant tone and his debunking of the (pagan) gods – has something in common with mediaeval *vanitas*, and humanist writing that was influenced by his playfulness tends also to qualify his mordant view of the folly of human existence with a more compassionate irony and an emphasis on the complexity and difficulty of right judgement. The fantastic voyages that convey Erasmus' Dame Folly from the Isles of the Blest or Raphael Hythloday to Utopia are metaphors of initiation, designed to awaken the responses of readers to the multiple challenges of the *vita activa*. The utility of this literary stratagem, as Duncan well expresses it, lies in encouraging the reader 'not so much to distinguish heresy from dogma, the false from the true, as to recognize the complexity of truth, to face the paradoxes and moral dilemmas which arise in the pursuit of truth, and to see that these cannot be simply resolved without loss of wisdom.'[71]

It is evident that the wise fooling of these humanist voyage narratives responds in complicated ways to a more conservative tradition of complaint literature and moral satire that is saturated with images of Christian and worldly journeying. Lucian's vision of universal folly has its correlates in writers as different as Alexander Barclay and Robert Burton, but his sceptical example allowed humanists to see the world not as a primrose path but as a labyrinth, one demanding orientation skills more complex and experimental than the dead reckoning required by traditional Christian teaching. This is the awareness that John Donne struggles with in sermons that have a voyaging theme. The ship of fools looks from one perspective like the quintessential container of human travail, the vessel in which we are all fated to ride, but in early-modern Europe it became possible to see it as a different kind of vehicle, one whose folly and madness were strategic, a means of experiment and enquiry, and an expression of personal will. In a chapter of *The Shyp of folys* entitled 'Of them that wyllynge and knowyngly put them self in jeopardy and peryll', Barclay excoriates the fool who takes unnecessary physical risks and concludes:

To prove a peryll / is foly certaynly
Whether it be done in ernest or in game
They that so doth may theyr owne madnes blame[72]

It was advice that increasing numbers of Englishmen were disposed to ignore.

## Notes

1 Anthony Nixon, *A true Relation of the Travels of M. Bush* (London, 1607), C3v–C4.

2 'Certain considerations touching the plantation in Ireland', in James Spedding, ed., *The Works of Francis Bacon* (Boston: Brown and Taggart, 1860–64), xi.123.

3 Jeffrey Knapp, *An Empire Nowhere* (Berkeley: U. of California Press, 1992); J.H. Elliott, *The Old World and the New, 1492–1650* (Cambridge: Cambridge UP, 1992).

4 William Rowley, *A Search for Money* (London, 1609), A4–v.

5 N.E. McClure, ed.,*The Letters of John Chamberlain* (Philadelphia: American Philosophical Society, 1939), I.118 (3 February 1601).

6 John Taylor, *The Sculler* (London, 1612), A4.

7 Joan Parkes, *Travel in England in the Seventeenth Century* (Oxford: Oxford UP, 1925), 292.

8 Hakluyt uses the word in this sense, but the handsome illustrated volumes about America by the De Bry family, collectively known as the *Grand Voyages*, probably did more to create this definition, which was cemented in the great voyage collections of Churchill and others in the eighteenth century. On the 'Voyage of Italy', see Edward Chaney, *The Grand Tour and the Great Rebellion* (Geneva: Slatkine, 1985).

9 E.L.J. Scott, ed., *Letter-Book of Gabriel Harvey, 1573–1580* (London: Camden Society, 1884), 86; and see Nick Davis, *Stories of Chaos* (Aldershot: Ashgate, 1999), ch. 4.

10 Compare its common application at this time to sexual conquest and exploitation, as in Shakespeare's *Cymbeline* (act 1, scene 5) when the exiled Posthumus, looking very like a Jacobean tourist in Rome despite the play's ancient setting, accepts a wager upon his wife's virtue ('if you make your voyage upon her') that requires Giacomo's duplicitous journey to Britain. The episode is a particularly pointed reference to the contemporary practice of betting on a journey, and it shows a familiar colloquialism being sharpened by its reinsertion into the dangerous world of travel from which it sprang.

11 Robert Burton, *The Anatomy of Melancholy*, ed. T.C. Faulkner, N.K. Kiessling and R.L. Blair (Oxford: Clarendon Press, 1989), 2.72.

12 Andrew McRae, 'The Peripatetic Muse: Internal Travel and the Cultural Production of Space in Pre-Revolutionary England', in G. Maclean, D. Landry and J.P. Ward, eds., *The Country and the City Revisited* (Cambridge: Cambridge UP, 1999), 41–2.

13 An accessible anthology of Taylor's adventures is John Chandler's *Travels through Stuart Britain* (Stroud: Sutton, 1999), and they are usefully analysed by Andrew McRae in his *Literature and Domestic Travel in Early Modern Britain* (Cambridge: Cambridge UP, 2009), ch. 6.

14 These words had long been associated with malicious injury, terror and conjuration (see *OED*'s examples), and are slow to lose some of these connotations – as in the fairy 'pranks' of Puck and Oberon in *A Midsummer Night's Dream* – but they become available at this time to less uncanny purposes.

15 Richard Johnson, *The most pleasant history of Tom a Lincolne* (London, 1631), A2v, B8v; *Le Prince d'Amour … with a Collection of several ingenious poems and songs by the Wits of the Age* (London, 1660), 164–6.

16 Mary B. Campbell, *The Witness and the Other World* (Ithaca: Cornell UP, 1988), 146.

17 There is some evidence of sporadic related Dutch activity in this period: see A.T. van Deursen, *Plain Lives in a Golden Age: Popular Culture, Religion and Society in Seventeenth-Century Holland* (Cambridge: Cambridge UP, 1991), 105. See also Chapter 4, note 3, below.

18 Elizabeth A. Chesney, *The Countervoyage of Rabelais and Ariosto* (Durham, NC: Duke UP, 1982).

19 Arthur Freeman, *Elizabeth's Misfits: Brief Lives of English Eccentrics, Exploiters, Rogues, and Failures, 1580–1660* (New York: Dorset Press, 1978), 167. Freeman's

entertaining survey brings out the miscellaneous sense of 'voyages' as covering rash and bizarre ventures of various kinds.

20 Richard Branson's exploit earned him a cameo appearance in a recent film version of *Around the World in Eighty Days* – leaving us to ponder whether his stunt is dignified by literary precedent or whether art (the movie) is imitating a celebrated contemporary career. The film's 'quotation' from life, giving a contemporary nudge to the story, also places Branson in a line of culture heroes, both actual and fictional, who testify to the English flair for adventure.

21 Richard Ferris, *The most dangerous and memorable adventure* (London, 1590), sig. A2–v.

22 Much of this activity is now supported by the sports industry, but the modern chronicle of such exploits includes figures like Eddie the Eagle, the spectacularly incompetent Olympic skier who some years ago became a national hero through his unerring ability to come last in competition, and who made a fortune by selling his story to a newspaper and recording a pop song.

23 John Keay, *Eccentric Travellers* (London: BBC, 1985), 10.

24 John Timbs, *English Eccentrics and Eccentricities* (London: R. Bentley, 1866), 1.196–7. The feat was recorded in the *Annual Register* for September 1788, together with an identical wager on a walk to Constantinople, and a bet by a baronet that he could go to Lapland and return with two native women and two reindeer. John Ashton, *The History of Gambling in England* (London: Duckworth, 1898), 163.

25 G.F.A. Wendeborn, *A View of England towards the close of the eighteenth century* (London, 1791), 1.412–13.

26 Samuel Rowley, *When you see me, you know me* (London, 1605), ed. F.P.Wilson (Malone Society: Oxford UP, 1952), K4.

27 The implications of this view are ably explored by Jeffrey Knapp in *An Empire Nowhere*, but I dissent from his principal thesis that England and its literature 'trifle' with the idea of empire, and argue for a different kind of playfulness in the country's engagement with the challenges of greater mobility and overseas expansion.

28 Ranulf Higden, *Polychronicon*, trans. J Trevisa (London, 1527), fol.xli v; John Speed, *The History of Great Britaine* (London, 1614), 155.

29 Kate Chedgzoy, 'This Pleasant and Sceptred Isle', in P. Schwyzer and S. Mealor, eds., *Archipelagic Identities*, 25, 41. For a different view that posits a purely British nationalism in the sixteenth century, see Philip Schwyzer, *Literature, Nationalism and Memory* (Cambridge: Cambridge UP, 2004), 5–10. I tend to agree with Claire McEachern that 'to deny a Tudor-Stuart moment of the English nation is to obscure the very moment of its invention' (*The Poetics of English Nationhood*, 7). This appropriation had direct consequences for ideas about the national character: as Paul Langford puts it, 'It is difficult to discover any alleged British characteristic that does not in practice coincide with an alleged English characteristic. Nor is it easy to find any supposed characteristic of one of the so-called Celtic nations that was not specifically contrasted with an English characteristic. English character, so to speak, was the dynamic force, squeezing out Celtic claims to determine what made Britain British' (*Englishness Identified* [Oxford: Oxford UP, 2000], 14).

30 Alexander Barclay, *The present Boke named the Shyp of folys* (London, 1509, with a second edition in 1570), fol. 127.

31 Quoted from Christian Zacher, *Curiosity and Pilgrimage* (Baltimore: Johns Hopkins UP, 1976), 141.

32 W.J.B Crotch, ed., *The Prologues and Epilogues of Wiliam Caxton* (EETS: London 1928), 108; G.C. Macaulay, ed., *The English Works of John Gower* (EETS: London 1900–1901), II.253; both quoted by Zacher, *Curiosity and Pilgrimage*, 142.

33 George Parks, *The English Traveller to Italy* (Roma: Edizione di Storia e Letteratura, 1954), x–xi.

34 William Camden, *Remaines Concerning Britain*, ed. R.D. Dunn (Toronto: U. of Toronto Press, 1984), 198.

35 Camden, *Remaines*, 19. The pope in question was Eugenius IV, who restored the papacy to Rome and reconstituted the English hospice there in 1446.

36 See Higden, *Polychronicon*, fol. lvi. Andrew Galloway observes that 'Higden made a trope about English instability in social identity into a set feature of national ideology', and partly as a result, '[v]ariable identity … is seized on by many late-fourteenth-century vernacular writers as their common bond' ('Latin England', in K. Lavezzo, ed., *Imagining a Medieval English Nation* [Minneapolis: U. of Minnesota Press, 2004]), 60, 86.

37 Jonathan Sumption, *Pilgrimage* (Towota, NJ: Rowman and Littlefield, 1975), 257–9.

38 Parks, *English Traveller*, 393–4.

39 Ralph Waldo Emerson, *English Traits*, ed. Mumford Jones (Cambridge, MA: Harvard UP, 1966), 93. Priestley is quoted in Langford, *Englishness Identified*, 291.

40 Langford, *Englishness Identified*, 301. While we might detect a benign view of eccentricity in the more jovial references to travel escapades, it had to contend with a long-standing association of mobility and various kinds of derangement. Wandering was seen as a prime tendency amongst lunatics and something of which they needed to be cured. No doubt the general fear of vagrants fed (or was fed by) this diagnosis. There was also a long history of the mad being taken to pilgrimage sites in the hope of restoring their wits, and while this practice offered travel as a cure for rather than a cause or example of madness, it did so as a corrective to derangement or frenzy that was typically described as 'a roving, wandring, vagrant, extravagant course; which knowes not which way to flie … a going without a path' (Thomas Adams, *Mystical Bedlam* [London, 1615], 46).

41 Robert S. Kinsman, ed, *The Darker Vision of the Renaissance* (Berkeley: U. of California Press, 1974), 276.

42 Burton, *Anatomy of Melancholy*, 1.109, 25.

43 See Anne S. Chapple, 'Burton's Geography of Melancholy', *Studies in English Literature* 33 (1993), 99–130; Richard Helgerson, 'The Folly of Maps and Modernity', in A. Gordon and B. Klein, eds., *Literature, Mapping, and the Politics of Space in Early Modern Britain* (Cambridge: Cambridge UP, 2001), 241–62.

44 Burton, *Anatomy of Melancholy*, I.25.

45 Burton, *Anatomy of Melancholy*, 2.33. For a different view, see Patricia Vicari, *The View from Minerva's Tower: Learning and Imagination in 'The Anatomy of Melancholy'* (Toronto: U of Toronto Press, 1989), 41. Burton could be dismissive about travel, as in 'See one … Mountaine, one Sea, one River, and see all' (1.364), but this remark is part of a general attack on curiosity and sounds like the offhand comment of the sedentary scholar. Contrast his enthusiastic recommendation of European tourism in 'Exercise Rectified' (2.73).

46 Ben Jonson, *Every Man Out of his Humour*, 'Induction', 101–12, 'Characters', 11–15, in *Works of Ben Jonson* (Cambridge: Cambridge UP, 2012), 1.254, 266.

47 Langford, *Englishness Identified*, 40. Particularly famous was 'Walking' John Stewart, 'whose wandering exploits extended over three continents and whose memorable stride was still fascinating onlookers during his last years in Regency London. It was not always appreciated by those who first encountered this phenomenon that it had very little to do with "getting from A to B". The English had no respect for those walking merely as a means of self-transport' (41).

48 Neil Rennie, *Far-Fetched Facts* (Oxford: Clarendon Press, 1995), 9.

49 Lucian of Samosata, 'A True Story', in *Works*, trans. A. Harmon (London: Heinemann, 1921), I.251 (Loeb).

50 A key element in the emergence of science fiction as a genre was a detailed interest in the mechanics of locomotion, so that the technical means of interplanetary flight or a venture into the earth's core could become central to the story and be plausibly represented. Most specialists in the field date this development to the mid-nineteenth century, but see Adam Roberts, *The History of Science Fiction* (Houndmills: Palgrave, 2007), Ch. 3.

51 Cf. Geoffroy Atkinson's definition of the 'Extraordinary Voyage' as a 'fictitious narrative, purporting to be the veritable account of a real voyage ... to an existent but little known country', as opposed to 'Fantastic' or 'Marvelous' types that make no claim on credulity or philosophic interest (*The Extraordinary Voyage in French Literature from 1700–1720* (Paris, 1922), 7.

52 Thomas Dekker, *The Great Frost* (London, 1608), A4.

53 Compare the folk tale of Sir Gammer Vans, a version of which survives in a seventeenth-century newsbook: 'last Sunday morning, at four o'clock in the afternoon, before Sun-rise, going over Highgate-Hill in a Boat, I met a man I overtook' (K.M. Briggs, *A Dictionary of British Folk-Tales in the English Language* [London: Routledge, 1970], 559).

54 Burton, *Anatomy of Melancholy*, 1.59.

55 K.W. Gransden, ed, *Tudor Verse Satire* (London: Athlone Press, 1970), 35.

56 James Knowles, introduction to *The Gypsies Metamorphosed*, in *Works of Ben Jonson*, 5.473. On the issue of 'lawful recreation', see Leah Marcus, *The Politics of Mirth* (Chicago: U. of Chicago Press, 1986), 106–14.

57 Lawrence Manley, *Literature and Culture in Early Modern London* (Cambridge: Cambridge UP, 1995), 77. Barclay's *Shyp of folys* was published in London in 1509, with a second edition in 1570.

58 Manley, *Literature and Culture*, 82.

59 Gransden, *Tudor Verse Satire*, 34.

60 Manley, *Literature and Culture*, 88.

61 See Sebastian Brant, *The Ship of Fools*, trans. Edwin H. Zeydel (New York: Columbia UP, 1944), ch. 108, and C.H. Herford, *Studies in the literary relations of England and Germany in the sixteenth century* (Cambridge: Cambridge UP, 1886), 332–3.

62 See my essay 'Cales and Guiana' on late sixteenth-century views of English maritime policy as 'idle wanderings upon the sea' and 'Idolatrie to Neptune', in *Southern African Journal of Mediaeval and Renaissance Studies* 19 (2009), 69–73.

63 Rabelais in the *Quart Livre*, ch. 48ff describes the isle of Papimanie 'whose inhabitants worship the pope … and in return receive all the delights of Cockaigne' (E.M. Ackerman, *'Das Schlaraffenland' in German Lit and Folksong* [Chicago, 1944], 44). Christopher Kendrick argues that 'More's text silently presents Utopia as the negation of Carnival, as its impossible logical end' (*Utopia, Carnival, and Commonwealth in Renaissance England* [Toronto: Toronto UP, 2004], 74).

64 Ackerman, *'Das Schlaraffenland'*, 81–2.

65 Louise O. Vasvari, 'The Geography of Escape and Topsy-Turvy Literary Genres', in Scott D. Westrem, ed., *Discovering New Worlds: Essays on Medieval Exploration and Imagination* (New York and London: Garland, 1991), 183.

66 Ackerman, *'Das Schlaraffenland'*, 97.

67 Thomas Nashe, *The Unfortunate Traveller*, in R.B. McKerrow, ed., *The Works of Thomas Nashe* (London: A.H. Bullen, 1904–10), 2.246.

68 C. Robinson, *Lucian and his Influence in Europe* (Chapel Hill: U. of North Carolina Press, 1979), 133.

69 See Douglas Duncan, *Ben Jonson and the Lucianic Tradition* (Cambridge: Cambridge UP, 1979), 26–30.

70 Duncan, *Ben Jonson*, 15; Lucian, *Icaromenippus*, in A.M. Harmon, ed., *Works*, II.301.

71 Duncan, *Ben Jonson*, 40.

72 Barclay, *The Shyp of folys*, fol. LXXXXV.

# 2

# Strange Returns and Performances

Apart from a small clutch of pamphlets that describe individual travel stunts, there is sufficient contemporary testimony to the 'many madde voiages made of late yeeres', as William Rowley put it in 1609, to indicate that the vogue was seen as something new and remarkable. In letters, prefaces, poems, entertainments and prose tracts of various kinds, numerous commentators refer to these exploits, sometimes as single events but more often as a collective phenomenon, with responses that range from mild wonder and amusement to satire and fitful attempts at diagnosis. On several occasions, as I indicated at the start, they are invoked as an analogue to a writer's own fictional project, and this serves to remind us that, despite their novelty as social events, the mad voyages have a substantial literary pedigree in the ancient trope of the fantastic or imaginary journey and influential Renaissance treatments of it such as More's *Utopia* or Ariosto's *Orlando Furioso*. Some of those connections will be explored in later chapters. Here I want to consider what the more miscellaneous evidence can reveal about the mad voyages as a social phenomenon and try to provide a fuller context for analysis of the pamphlets dedicated to particular exploits. It should be said at the outset that because contemporary observers were often baffled or disconcerted by what they saw, and did not usually interrogate it, my attempts to read events through those responses are inevitably speculative. But the scattered evidence, fragmentary though it is, often provides perspectives on the vogue unavailable from the carefully fashioned narratives that are the only detailed accounts we have of any of these ventures. What contemporaries saw as a localized rash of 'experiments' also had roots in an established practice of travelling on a wager, and the present chapter will consider how some significant domestic examples of this were caught up in and affected by the fashion for 'madde voiages'.

One of the most elaborate comments to have survived on the fashion for travel stunts in late Elizabethan England occurs in the revels mounted by the students of Gray's Inn during the Christmas season of 1594–95. Recorded in a contemporary account later published as the *Gesta Grayorum* (1688), these revels are famous for including a performance of Shakespeare's *Comedy of Errors* on 28 December, but the entire proceedings stretched over the 12 days of Christmas (the traditional period of licensed 'misrule') and beyond, and turned Gray's Inn into a make-believe kingdom ruled over by the Prince of Purpoole. This elected figure apparently held office for several weeks, and the charade of his court replicated much of the structure and ceremonial of government, with a Privy Council, gentlemen attendants and an armed guard. Pardons were issued, ambassadors received and masques performed, and a 'royal' progress was made through the city on 4 January. This sustained collective fiction was not simply a spoof of courtly ritual; it is closer to what Steven Mullaney calls a 'rehearsal' of culture, a 'period of free-play during which alternatives can be staged, unfamiliar roles tried out, the range of one's power to convince or persuade explored with some license'.[1] The tradition of appointing a mock-monarch to preside over Christmas festivities probably originated in the universities during the fifteenth century and later spread to noble households and the royal court itself, but in Elizabethan England it became particularly associated with the Inns of Court and reached its most developed form there. The wardens of the Inns apparently sanctioned this type of charade in order that the students 'should in time to come know how to use themselves', and the parodic exercise of courtly and rhetorical skills took place in what Noel Malcolm describes as 'a peculiar hothouse world of court wits, lawyers and poets engaged in mutual ridicule and emulation'.[2] At the end of the sixteenth century, the Inns were the focal point of London's cultural life, since they provided lodging not only for training lawyers but also for the sons of the gentry looking for jobs or connections in the capital and young men down from university hoping to make their way as writers. They were the seedbed of much of London's literary activity, and their formal revels created some of the city's most imaginative charades.

The range of ideas and motifs covered by these games is like a prospectus for the mad voyage craze. For instance, having obtained ratification of 'His Highness's Title to the Land of the Amazons, and to the Cape of *Good Hope*', the Prince receives 'Another Letter from Sea', which reports that 'in the Straits of the Gulf of *Clerkenwell*, there was an hot Skirmish between a Merchant of St. *Giles*'s, called *Amarpso*, and the Admiral of the *Amazons*, called the *Rowse-flower*' – presumably a well-known brothel.[3] This licentious journey into London's underworld is a fantasy stimulated by the notoriously permissive lifestyle of the Inns' residents, and demonstrates their proximity to a metropolitan culture that made considerable use of such voyage tropes to explore the consequences of rapid urban growth and development. On a very different note, the Prince is earlier addressed by the members of his Privy Council, who give him expert advice on a range of topics. One urges him to take sports and pastimes seriously: 'Let other men's lives be as Pilgrimages, because they are tied to divers Necessities and Duties; but Princes Lives are as Progresses, dedicated only to Variety and Solace' (41) – advice that turns the well-worn metaphor of life as a journey into a teasing question about the legitimacy of recreational travel. A previous speaker counsels the Prince to make his court a centre of culture and progressive ideas, with a library, garden, zoo, a 'goodly huge' curiosity cabinet, and 'a Still-house so furnished with Mills, Instruments, Furnaces and Vessels, as may be a Palace fit for a Philosopher's Stone' (35). It was long thought that Francis Bacon, then a Reader at Gray's Inn, was the author of some or all of these speeches, partly because here we have an early sketch for Salomon's House in *New Atlantis*, and the topical issue it raises of scientific experiment and innovation was to be focused by a number of travel exploits.

Close to the end of his reign, and nearly a month after the holiday season had officially ended, the Prince of Purpoole and his retinue boarded 15 barges 'bravely furnished with Standards, Pendants, Flags and Streamers' together with 'Musick and Trumpets' (54). According to the *Gesta Grayorum*, they sailed down the Thames to Greenwich, where the Queen was expecting them, but did not land as requested, and the Prince sent a message ('Dated from Ship-board, at our *Ark of Vanity*, the 1st. of *February*, 1594 [o.s.]' (55)) pleading sickness after his arduous journey. This nautical fantasy taps into the imagery of the ship of fools that was so pervasive in the period, but it subdues it to a courtly language and purpose by play-acting the return of one of Elizabeth's celebrated navigators, a Drake or a Cavendish, and thereby makes the mad voyage serve royal authority even while pretending to rebuff it. It is a witty and graceful manoeuvre that bids to exempt the Prince and his student-followers, as lords of misrule, from their own earlier critique of travel 'performances' that are thought to violate decorum and good sense.

These performances came under the spotlight in a ceremony held on 3 January, in which the Prince of Purpoole invested his followers with the Collar of the Knighthood of the Helmet and commanded the articles of the Order to be read. Two of these articles are particularly relevant:

> *Item*, No Knight of this Order shall put out any Money upon strange Returns or Performances to be made by his own Person, as, to hop up the stairs to the top of St. *Paul's*, without intermission; or any other such like Agilities or Endurances, except it may appear, that the same Performances or Practices do enable him to some Service or Employment; as if he do undertake to go a Journey backward, the same shall be thought to enable him to be an Ambassador into *Turky*. *Item*, No Knight of this Order, that hath had any Licence to travel into Foreign Countries, be it by Map, Card, Sea, or Land, and hath returned from thence, shall presume, upon the Warrant of a Traveller, to report any extraordinary Varieties; as, that he hath ridden through *Venice* on Horse-back Post, or that in *December* he sailed by the Cape of *Norway*, or that he hath travelled over the most part of the countries of *Geneva*; or such like Hyperbolies ... (29)

It is clear from the first of these edicts that what John Chamberlain in 1601 described as 'daily ... new experiments made' had several years earlier become sufficiently common to be identified as a trend, with St. Paul's and its tower something of an urban focus, and the students confirm that the craze is organized around a very elastic concept of 'voyage'. They also imply, however, that the freedom to travel and to turn travel into recreation is at the heart of this vogue, and suggest ironically that these ridiculous enterprises should, like official journeys, constitute 'some Service or Employment' if they are to be justified. The second article (which directly follows the first) gives a provocative sketch of the developments that are said to have created this situation. The growth of tourism and other foreign ventures means that the returned traveller, always notorious for his lies, is now to be found in all companies, offering tall tales that pose as his own 'Agilities or Endurances' and, it is implied, provide a potential cue for more preposterous exploits. It should be said that the law students at the Inns of Court were as likely as anyone to be undertaking travel stunts and dining out on their tourist adventures, but they reveal here a sharp eye for the social and cultural shifts that have brought the craze into existence.

We know from the contemporary lists of 'mad voyages' cited in the opening chapter that certain types of Continental venture featured in people's perceptions of the travel stunt, and this is ultimately because in the latter half of the sixteenth century, if not before, tourism abroad became associated with the wager on a journey. This was the practice called 'putting out', whereby the traveller laid out a stake to be repaid at an agreed rate of multiplication if he returned safely and met a particular set of conditions. William Rowley, we recall, singled out 'the travell to *Rome* with the returne in certaine daies', and Ben Jonson mentions Venice and Paris as favoured destinations for a wager, while the Middle East provided some of the prime sites for this sort of bargain. The traveller Fynes Moryson, who has a good deal to say about the custom, testifies that 'this manner of giving out mony upon these adventures, was first used in Court, and among the very Noble men', and he sets it in the context of their general proclivity for gambling, whether on horse racing or in the custom, 'used time out of mind', says Moryson, 'to put out money to be repaied with advantage upon the birth of their next childe'. For a man to be 'hired … so he may get a boy' is 'a base gaine', he thinks, 'compared with the adventures of long journies' which 'alwaies bettered the mind',[4] but Moryson is glossing the custom with his own priorities as a serious tourist. Aristocrats may not have regarded a bet on European travel as qualitatively different from, say, the swimming race in the Thames to which Sir John Pakington challenged fellow courtiers in the early 1570s,[5] or the many wagers on the Queen's possible marriage. Gambling, which Henrician laws permitted only to the upper orders, no doubt always included a good many bizarre challenges and contests designed to sustain the competitive and exclusive ethos of the governing class; and when, with the advent of the Tudor peace, travel abroad became an option available to a growing number of that class, tourism or 'venturing', whatever its other purposes, was an item to be added to the repertoire of patrician wagers, placing it in the same category as the traditional feats that had helped to shape a courtly culture at home.

In Chapter 4, I shall look in detail at the emergence of the wager on travel and its role in shaping English fortunes abroad in the later sixteenth and seventeenth centuries. But Fynes Moryson's comments also help us to identify the early 1590s as the moment when perceptions of the travel wager began to shift, regarding both its social acceptability and the uses to which it could be put. When Moryson returned from his first continental tour in 1595, a few months after the Gray's Inn students made their satirical proclamations against foolish escapades, he found himself having to confront changing attitudes. On reaching home, he discovered his brother Henry preparing to set out for Jerusalem and Constantinople, having put out £400 on a three-for-one basis, and decided to make a similar arrangement and join him. But he quickly finds himself being dissuaded by his friends, who tell him that 'these kind of adventures were growne very frequent, whereof some were undecent, some ridiculous; and ... in great part undertaken by bankerouts, and men of base condition'.[6] A little further on he adds 'Stage-players' to the list of those who 'have drawne this custome into contempt' (1.428), although it is not clear whether he refers to satire in London's theatres or to actors going on such journeys. The 'common opinion', he says, has changed during his three-year absence from England, but he stoutly defends traditional wagers against the critics:

> Surely they must spare them, who undertake long voyages, ful of great dangers: who doe not put out their money in Tavernes, or at feasts to any man without distinction, but dispose of their money with their friends upon reasonable adventure of gaine.... I say the detracters must spare these, and distinguish them from others who make cursorie journies, without any desire to better their understanding thereby, and more from those, who in these courses rather make triall of their bodies strength, then of their mindes abilitie. (1.429)

Moryson reserves a special contempt for those who undertake 'base and ridiculous adventures ... in undertaking desperate actions for gain.' As a beneficiary himself of the expanding opportunities for tourism in this period, he is anxious to draw a line between his own cultural adventures and what he sees as less salubrious imitations of aristocratic practice. The phenomenon he and his friends recoiled from was evidently real enough, in the sense that the growing number of tourists and adventurers inevitably meant that more people were trying to exploit these financial arrangements, whether it was to speculate on a journey or simply to raise money for the trip. The disapproving mention of 'bankerouts' conjures up another kind of traveller we shall meet in the drama, and the distaste with which Moryson mentions wagers made in taverns precisely anticipates the comment made more than a century later, on the case of a poulterer who in 1731 bet £50 that he could 'walk 202 times round the area of Upper Moorfields in 27 hours', that 'Wagers are now a favourite custom with too many of the Londoners; they very frequently ... originate over the bottle, or the porter pot.'[7] The scanty evidence we have suggests that increased social mobility and an entrepreneurial urban culture in Elizabethan England had already led to the appropriation of traditional gambling methods, and sometimes to the imitation or parody of the travel practices to which the upper classes had applied them. Yet the distinction Moryson draws, between serious journeys and stunts, did not follow class divisions as closely as he wished to believe.

Like Moryson, though in more playful vein, the Gray's Inn students also register a sense that travel exploits have become increasingly bizarre, and rule them off-limits to their knightly order, but their satire is directed as much at the habits of the privileged classes (and at each other) as at the travesties mounted by their social inferiors. By the end of the sixteenth century, upper-class gambling in England had turned, in Lawrence Stone's words, from 'a pastime into an obsession', and the courtly wager was subjected to a proliferation of trivial subjects for betting and a sharp rise in the stakes. Gambling became the expression not of a self-regulating aristocratic ethos but of unfettered opportunism, in an environment where careers and fortunes were increasingly prey to the instabilities of political faction, jeopardizing the delicate balance on which noble concepts of gaming and 'hazard' depended. As Stone points out, 'Lord Burghley had himself painted engaged in a card game for high stakes', and as these tendencies deepened in the Jacobean years, Sir John Holles described the times as 'fruitfull of strange, and extraordinarie accidents' and likely to 'return through this corruption to their first confusion; that the ould game ended the cards may be new shuffled for that which followeth'.[8] The courtiers and gentry who were players in this dangerous game were less tied to their rural fastnesses and generally better travelled than their predecessors, and some of them were more than ready to turn established wagering practices to their advantage. It was not just social upstarts who were attracted to travel exploits that 'rather make triall of their bodies strength, then of their mindes abilitie.' When Moryson came to write his memoirs, he reflected that the changing practice of the travel wager was another example of the way in which courtly rituals lose their exclusivity, and expressed the view that 'when they come to be vulgar ... Courtiers and Gentlemen think them uncomely to be used' (1.428). But while some of the 'better sort' were no doubt discouraged by popular stunts from betting on travel in the old way, many were not, and the surge in 'cursorie journies' and other escapades that struck Moryson and his friends as a sign of social breakdown did not preclude the participation of several well-born young men in the mad voyage craze. His patrician explanation of the fashion for travel stunts will only take us so far, and we need to look at other pressures that were coming to bear on the English appetite for adventure in this period.

An instructive case is the career of the Queen's cousin Sir Robert Carey, who in 1603 undertook an epic ride to Scotland to bring James Stuart the news of Elizabeth I's demise – a coup on which Sir John Harington commented wryly that Carey 'was Prime in his Scottyshe intelligence of the Queenes deathe.... St. Paul hathe saide, that *the race is not alwaie givene to the swyfte.* I dowte Sir Robert will give the Sainte the lie, for he is like to get both *race* and *prize*, and, as fame goethe, creepethe not a little into favoure.'[9] In the event, Carey's opportunism earned him disapproval in official circles and he was excluded from court employment until 1605. Fourteen years before his ride, in 1589, Carey showed that he already had an eye for the main chance when he undertook a timed walk from London to the Scottish border. As he recalled it in his memoirs, 'having given out some money to go on foot in twelve days to Berwick, I performed it that summer, which was worth to me two thousand pounds, which bettered me to live at court a good while after.'[10] (See Plate 2.) One of those who took this wager was Sir Robert Sidney, who in January signed a bond for £100, so presumably Carey was gathering sponsors over several weeks or months in a gaming ritual familiar to his circle. This is 'putting out' of the traditional sort, but it took place in a highly volatile context. In the years prior to his walk the English government used Carey on sensitive political missions, including one in 1586 when, following the execution of Mary, Queen of Scots, 'her Majesty sent me to the King of Scots, to make known her innocence of her sister's death, with letters of credence from herself to assure all that I should affirm' (*Memoirs*, 7). On that occasion Carey did not dare to cross the border but negotiated with James VI from Berwick, the garrison border town where his father was governor. In 1588, however, when Elizabeth sent an embassy to James intended to keep him onside in the conflict with Spain, Carey was passed over in favour of Sir Robert Sidney, the very man who took his wager the following year. The irony might not have been lost on Fynes Moryson, who made his own highly discreet journey to Berwick in 1598, almost certainly acting on behalf of the Essex faction as a line of communication to the future English king.[11] There is some indication that the walk from London to Berwick became a standard challenge amongst the Elizabethan gentry: during his dance to Norwich in 1600, Will Kemp was introduced to a country gentleman who had performed it, and who offered him advice about how to handle the long-distance excursion,[12] so we have the curious situation, in the last decades of the sixteenth century, in which a tortuous diplomatic path was effectively being retraced by a popular stunt and turned into a playful ordeal. It is possible that 'putting out' on this particular journey became fashionable in courtly circles rather earlier: Berwick, as a frontier town, was the site of enormous investment in military defences from the middle of the century, and this may have helped to make wagering on the way thither (for a generation of courtiers starved of foreign military adventure) into a home-grown act of knightly assertion and a sort of secular and nationalistic pilgrimage. But in the tense circumstances of Elizabeth's final years, and in the changed environment of James I's succession to the throne, the walk to the border could take on a more ambiguous appearance.

Robert Carey was one of a group of ambitious young men seeking place and fortune at the Tudor court; another was Philip Gawdy, member of a prominent Norfolk gentry family who, being a younger son, was forced to make his own way, which he attempted to do with a variety of foreign adventures. In 1591 he joined Grenville's last sea campaign against Spain and, following the celebrated destruction of the flagship *Revenge*, was captured and imprisoned in Lisbon. Much later, in 1611, he was to undertake a wager-journey to the Holy Land. But Gawdy never solved his money problems, and in 1602, whilst embroiled in an obscure dispute with various creditors and debtors, he complained that 'Every body is very hasty uppon me, thoughe I fynde very fewe ready to paye me, and I had as lyve adventure my mony to Ostend, as put it out to Barwicke unlesse his honesty wer the greater.'[13] 'Barwicke' turns out to be one Roger Barwyke, who is said to be extorting money from Gawdy, but even if no pun on the name of the border town is consciously intended, Gawdy's phrasing is surely influenced by its topical associations and by the fashion for wagering expeditions across the North Sea (with Gawdy's 'adventure ... to Ostend', compare the rowing ventures to Flushing and Antwerp mentioned by other writers). The likelihood that he is thinking primarily of the long-running Spanish siege of Ostend (1601–1604), to which English forces had been sent in 1601, merely illustrates the way in which military adventure could become a speculative activity in the minds of impecunious courtiers, and comparable to whatever kind of 'putting out' bargain might be involved with 'Barwicke'. It also hints at the complicated conditions in which the patrician wager was operating by the turn of the century. As we have seen, there were insinuations that a noble custom had been hijacked by base imitators – a prime example being William Rowley's reference in 1608 to 'the fellowes going back-ward to *Barwick*', echoed by Ben Jonson a few years later, for whatever is meant by this pedestrian feat, it suggests some kind of travesty of the trip that Carey and others undertook. Rowley's word 'fellowes' does rather imply a plebeian trespass upon aristocratic custom. Yet Gawdy's language indicates the readiness of his own class to participate in the current wagering craze. The performance recalled by Rowley and Jonson is clearly akin to, and may even be identical with, the stunt that the Gray's Inn students are alluding to in their ironic assertion that if a member of the order will 'undertake to go a Journey backward, the same shall be thought to enable him to be an Ambassador into *Turky*'. This well-informed joke[14] neatly suggests that 'strange returns or Performances' are now part of the repertoire of those who were traditionally responsible for diplomatic missions. For men like Moryson the travesty of official travel was one of those 'base and ridiculous adventures' that brought the custom into contempt, but a less class-bound perspective would have found 'desperate actions for gain' equally present in more elevated quarters.

In fact, when we look more closely at the circumstances of Robert Carey's walk, it takes on a parodic dimension of its own. Carey is quite open about what provoked him into setting off: he declares that 'my lord of Essex stole from court to go that journey, and left me behind him, which did so trouble me, that I had no mind to stay in the court' (*Memoirs*, 12). 'That journey' was the naval expedition to Spain and Portugal in April 1589 to avenge the Spanish Armada of the year before, and the Queen had expressly forbidden her favourite, the Earl of Essex, to take part. Essex defied the ban and rode secretly to Plymouth to join the voyage, not even sharing his plans with the close friend who had hoped to be part of the adventure. Bitterly disappointed, Carey took to the road instead. Doing the walk to Berwick was no doubt good for his self-esteem as well as his pocket, but he had probably hoped to do even better financially out of the Portugal voyage. Essex had embarked on the latter declaring 'I will adventure to be rich' – hoping to pay off his debts by ransom and plunder, yet in the event he was rather less successful than his friend in fulfilling this aim. Essex was also short on military success in the venture, despite a highly theatrical performance at the gates of Lisbon when he dared the commanders within to single combat. It is an intriguing thought that at much the same time as Carey was performing his wager, Essex was gambling on his knightly reputation 'with a red scarf on his arm and a great plume of feathers on his casque'.[15] The Queen later condemned the commanders of the Portugal expedition both for 'an haviour of vainglory which will obfuscate the eyes of their judgment' and for putting profit before service,[16] and the two charges were far from incompatible in the curiously mercenary world of aristocratic venturing. In his memoirs Carey boasts of his ability to maintain an extravagant lifestyle, and implies that he managed it by gambling: 'God so blessed me that I was ever able to keep company with the best: in all triumphs I was one; either at tilt, tourney, or barriers; in mask or balls: I kept men and horses far above my rank, and so continued a long time' (*Memoirs*, 7). Since it was common knowledge that the Portugal voyage had been a fiasco, we might think that, by recalling Essex's impetuous move, Carey is giving himself the better half of the bargain. But in presenting his walk as a consequence of Essex's desertion of him, he also acknowledges that the customary wager has come under strain. Within the system of values that bound him to Essex, and which ruled both of their journeys, his own expedition becomes a kind of compensation for failure rather than a marker of aristocratic freedom and authority. This may have mattered little to Carey once he had acquired the means to continue living, as he himself put it, 'far above my rank', though that boast itself reveals how gambling might undermine rather than affirm traditional status-relations and the customs that expressed them. But more important, the courtly game of travel wager in this loaded political context could not fail to come under pressure, just as the 'bargain of return' to Rome could not remain an innocent activity in the fraught doctrinal atmosphere of the 1580s. Carey's walk, however traditional the custom may have been, takes place in a crowded cultural space that restricts the autonomy of aristocratic play, and forces out of it a parodic suggestion that may have made it all the more easy to parody in its turn.

The foot journey to northern Britain was to figure largely in later wagers, as the English predilection for long-distance walking took hold, and it became something of a showcase for the kinds of parody and inventiveness that flourished at the height of the vogue for travel stunts. Before coming to these developments, however, I want to look at an exploit nearly contemporary with Carey's walk that had a similarly complicated relationship to courtly culture and national politics.

## The Adventure of Richard Ferris

In the summer of 1590, a government employee named Richard Ferris undertook a hazardous voyage around the south coast of England that, by virtue of the pamphlet that was quickly issued about his exploit, is the earliest documented example we have of the vogue that was to flourish for the next three decades. Samuel Rowlands' catalogue of maritime travel stunts gives the impression that Ferris inspired a number of seagoing imitators, and he may have been the first to create a venture that was not simply (as the Gray's Inn students put it) a piece of 'agility' like hopping up the stairs of St. Paul's or a 'strange return' to mimic a patrician wager. Instead, the 'most dangerous and memorable adventure of Richard Ferris', to quote the title of the account printed by John Wolfe in 1590, was a story substantial enough both to fill a newsbook (one of Wolfe's specialities at this time) and to be recounted in the style of a long-distance voyage narrative like those found in Richard Hakluyt's just-published *Principall Navigations* (1589). Like many such narratives, Ferris's account is an unsophisticated piece of writing, a straightforward chronicle of the journey that offers enough of the drama of 'dangerous Flawes and rough Seas', not to mention a narrowly averted capture by pirates, to justify its title. Proudly, and with an apparently straight face, Ferris dedicates the tale of his 'late dangerous attempt, rashly by mee undertaken, to row in a small Boat to the Citie of Bristow'[17] to Sir Thomas Heneage, one of the Queen's privy counsellors, and describes at the start how the wherry – a rowing boat with a single sail – was painted green, 'and the Oares & sayle of the same collour, with the red Crosse for England and her Majesties armes'. On the day of departure, he and his two companions embarked at Tower Wharf, and with a flotilla of boats accompanying them 'rowed to the Court at Greenewitch, where before the Court gate we gave a volley of shot' (A3). After landing and being entertained at the palace, they are bid farewell by various dignitaries, including Lord Burleigh and the Lord Admiral, armed with the written 'leave given us from the right Honourable of her Majesties counsell, for our quiet and safe passage' (A4v). Whatever the doubts of the 'sundry persons' who Ferris says were sceptical about the venture, the most powerful people in the land seem to have regarded it as anything but unworthy of England's maritime traditions.

Richard Ferris was a pursuivant, a court messenger and bailiff in the service of the Privy Council, and thus used to travelling throughout England on official business; his job was not without its particular dangers, for it involved having to arrest recusants and others wanted for questioning.[18] Since he admits that he 'was never trayned up on the water' (A2–v), it is not obvious how he came to undertake this new venture, but his professional standing with the government seems to have won high-level recognition and support for his stunt. It was indeed a formidable undertaking, covering about 600 sea miles and requiring skilful navigation of some treacherous stretches of coastline, including the difficult rounding of Land's End.[19] Ferris prudently engaged an experienced mariner to take charge of the wherry (together with a third man to assist with rowing), and the voyage was completed in 40 days, putting in for the night at a succession of harbours and taking care to obtain certificates of arrival and departure in the major ports. The voyagers were apparently well entertained wherever they stopped, and Ferris claims that his position as a royal servant stood him in good stead both in the homes of the gentry and with the naval captains he met in Plymouth. It may also have helped to ensure an official reception at the end of the journey, where 'the Maior of Bristow, with his bretheren the Aldermen, came to the water side, and welcomed us most lovingly, and the people came in great multitudes to see us'. The next day Bristol put on what amounted to a civic pageant, with the wherry as its centrepiece:

> The people of the citie gathered them selves together, & had prepared Trumpets, Drummes, Fyfes, & Ensignes to go before the Boate, which was carried upon mens shoulders round about the Citie, with the Waites of the saide Citie, playing orderly in honour of our rare and daungerous attempt atchived. (Bv)

And this celebration, Ferris informs us at the end of his account, is due to be repeated in London where, after the boat has been transported by land to the capital, 'the watermen & sundry other have promised to grace the saide Boate with great melodie, and sundry volleyes of shot' (B2).

There is no way of confirming the details of Ferris's narrative, but the plain and sober manner in which the story is told creates confidence in its basic veracity, and it would not have been in Ferris's interests to embroider a venture that relied for its success upon independent confirmation of what had been achieved. Those buying his pamphlet might have welcomed a more colourful narrative, but some of them had a financial stake in the project and wanted an exact account of how Ferris managed (as he puts it) 'to performe my promise'. In verses by James Sargent that Ferris appended to his narrative (and which were probably also issued as a broadside ballad), we are told that

> From London Citie this wager sure,
> Was for to bring his Wherry small,
> On surging seas, if life endure ...
> To Bristowe Citie of worthie name,
> Where Ferris now hath spred his fame. (B2v)

And later he confirms that 'three men hath this voyage done, / And thereby wagers great hath wonne' (B3). He does not say who accepted these wagers or exactly what form they took, though it is possible that the mercantile communities of London and Bristol were both involved. But Ferris was a Westminster man, and it is reasonable to assume that a large number of these bets were placed in the court circles where he regularly moved, especially given the elegant scene he paints of his reception at Greenwich. We know that wagers were sometimes made between courtiers on the performance of a third party, and this may have happened here, but Sargent appears to be emphasizing that Ferris and his companions have won money in their own right. This suggests that the courtly travel wager, contracted between men of rank and relying on word of honour, was rapidly mutating in response to new circumstances. The 'severall certificates' that Ferris assures Heneage had been obtained en route were obviously a condition of the wager: they testified to the sailors' unaided passage through key points on the journey and could be used to answer any suspicion of fraud. And the pamphlet account that quickly emerged (something that could not be imagined accompanying Robert Carey's wager, for instance) capitalizes on the verification of the journey to produce a saleable book of 'true news'. Ferris may have been regarded by the court as one of their own, but his stunt brings their exclusive gaming rituals into contact with a more public and commercial sphere.

Yet we should not assume a definitive move into the marketplace, for there is an intriguing possibility that the small quarto volume telling the story was an intrinsic part of the wager process. Its title-page bears the unusual legend 'Published by the sayd Richard Ferris' (above the information that John Wolfe printed the book for Edward White at whose shop it will be sold). This strongly suggests that Ferris put up the money to have it printed, and this would mean that instead of the conventional arrangement whereby a writer was simply paid once for a manuscript in which he had no further economic interest, in this case the author might have had copies to dispose of as he saw fit. The title-page ascription may simply acknowledge that Ferris funded publication, presumably with his winnings from several wagers, but we know from Privy Council records that he had difficulty getting those wagers paid out,[20] and the fact that the pamphlet appeared quickly after the event prompts us to consider other possibilities. A plausible scenario is that Ferris hit upon (or was encouraged to adopt) a type of subscription system as a way of launching the venture and turning a profit. Finding the money to 'put out' in the customary way – lodging a wager of, say, £10 in order to get £30 back – was considerably easier for a gentleman than for a humble pursuivant and his even less wealthy companions, and those interested in his venture might instead have been persuaded to do some of the putting out themselves, giving him a sum in return for a copy of the printed account when the voyage was over.[21] A similar form of sponsorship was later adopted by John Taylor in his travel ventures, and despite its commercial character the arrangement remained, as Alexandra Halasz points out, a wager on the probability of the journey being completed: '[t]he subscription is … not an exchange so much as an elaborate game, for which the minimum cost of entry is something above the price of a pamphlet and greater investments are encouraged.'[22] It is easy to see how courtly circles might have found such a game attractive, modifying traditional practices to include the ventures of the middling sort but keeping the idea of a strict monetary transaction at a distance.

Like Robert Carey's walk to Berwick, Ferris's voyage took place in the shadow of a greater expedition, but in this case the private exploit claimed to draw strength from recent political events. Two years earlier, the coasts of the British Isles had witnessed the destruction of the Spanish Armada, as the enemy's huge galleons were scattered by bad weather and outfought by the smaller but more manoeuvrable English ships. The victory promptly gave rise to a national myth about the triumph of English pluck and versatile seamanship, and this feeds into the unlikely claim that Ferris makes in his dedicatory epistle, that his voyage

> may be a just occasion to pricke forward other of my native cuntrymen to practise an ordinary passage thorough the like dangers in such small wherry Boates, especially when necessary occasion shall serve; the better to daunt the enemies of this nation, who in such flawes and frets at Sea, dare not hazard their Gallies to go foorth, though they be of farre greater force to brooke the Seas. (A2v)

The argument is pushed into a more inflated register by James Sargent's verses, with the suggestion that ''Twill make the Spaniardes harts waxe cold, / If that this newes to them prepare', and a resounding demand:

> Hath seely Wherry done the deede,
> That Gallyes great dare not to trye? (B3)

These extravagant declarations recall the promotional literature (often in similarly excruciating verse) that was generated for the voyages of sailors like Humphrey Gilbert or Frobisher, but here the assertions seem merely playful, with the special pleading of the epistle tipping frankly into burlesque in Sargent's couplet. The Gray's Inn students seem to be alluding to such claims when they affect to ban all travel 'Performances' that do not contribute 'to some Service or Employment' – a joke perhaps aimed at unsophisticated readers who were taken in by the appeal to practical utility. Yet playfulness of this kind may be more complex and purposeful than it seems. All the evidence suggests that this exploit was enthusiastically supported by people in authority who understood its propaganda value at a time of national emergency. No one supposed that three-man rowing boats could take on Spanish galleons, but the mock-heroic assertion – that Ferris has gone where mighty ships fear to follow – appealed to recent memories of Armada vessels wrecked in the Channel and put some juice into a more practical proposition: that English seamen were uniquely equipped to defend the 'narrow seas' around the British Isles. In the midst of a maritime war in which at least half of England's fighting ships were privateers, the spirit of individual enterprise was one that the government was keen to harness to the national effort. And to patronise an effort that dramatized English initiative and daring on the sea evidently seemed worthwhile to the Lord Admiral and his colleagues, perhaps to the point where their patronage extended to material sponsorship.

In short, Ferris's expedition seems to have been regarded by the dignitaries who saw it off at Greenwich in a spirit of *serio jocum* – serious play. It was simultaneously a real voyage, encountering all the normal hazards of coastal sailing, and a piece of sport that served no useful purpose, but its detachment from humdrum utility – the moving of goods or passengers – turned the wherry into a vehicle for maritime aspirations that could be entertained and focused by participating in the game of promoting it. This *lusus* has some points of contact with the revels at Gray's Inn discussed above, not least when each creates a pageant on the Thames in which the heroic navigator salutes his Queen with ordnance and colours. The student fiction works within a framework of humanist and courtly ritual, testing its boundaries with the extended voyaging conceit, whereas Ferris uses the court as a starting point for his personal adventure. But if the above analysis is correct, his appropriation of the patrician gamble on a journey was one that the court found easy to recuperate and turn to its own purposes. In 1590, celebratory sentiment about defeating the Armada was mixed with chagrin at the failure of a retaliatory expedition in the previous year: the Portugal voyage that provoked Carey's walk to Berwick. The political and military gamble of striking back at Spain had spectacularly misfired, and with it (as I explained earlier) the mercenary hopes of some of Carey's fellow courtiers, who may have regarded his wager winnings with the same cold eye that fell on his opportunistic ride to Scotland in 1603. About that we can only speculate, but it is suggestive that at this perplexing moment in national affairs, court officials should have supported a rather novel version of the bet on travel, one that, unlike Carey's consolation prize, reaffirmed the symbolic value of ludic activity in promoting a serious cause. The visibility and popular appeal of Ferris's venture would have been incentives: Samuel Rowlands claimed it was a cause of 'vulgar wonderment', and we may doubt whether everyone got the serio-comic point, but the project's influential patrons apparently believed, or hoped, that they were enabling an effort that could bolster confidence in English naval skills.

## Making History

No documented example of courtly involvement in the mad voyages survives from the last years of Elizabeth's reign, but in the early summer of 1605 a Yorkshire gentleman called John Lepton, 'his Majesties servant, and one of the Groomes of his most honourable Privy Chamber',

> undertooke to ride five severall times betwixt London and Yorke in sixe dayes, to bee taken in one weeke, betwixt monday morning & Saturday following: he began his jorney upon monday being the 20. day of May [1605], betwixt two and three of the clocke in the morning forth of S. Martins, neare Aldersgate within the City of London, and came into Yorke the same day betwixt the howres of 5. and 6. in the afternoone, where he rested that night …

Completing two return trips in four days (which this account tracks in detail), Lepton rode to York for the third time on the Friday, 'so as hee finished his appointed journey, (to the admiration of all men) in five dayes, according to his promise: and upon Monday the 27. of this moneth hee went from Yorke and came to the Court at Greenwich upon tuesday the 28. to his Majesty, in as fresh & chearefull maner as when he first began.' Once again we have a glimpse of a courtly milieu in which the travel exploit was welcomed and supported – and no doubt was the focus of energetic gaming, notwithstanding the polite silence about money in this account. We know about Lepton's ride only because it was recorded by Edmund Howes in the 1611 edition of his *Abridgement of the English Chronicle*, where he declares that Lepton 'performed so memorable a journey, as I may not omitte to record the same to future ages, the rather for that I did heare sundry Gentlemen who were good horsemen, and likewise many good Physicians affirme it was impossible to bee done without daunger of his life'.[23] Howes' enthusiasm for the stunt is striking in view of his censure elsewhere of writers who 'have very vaingloriously recommended unto endless memory, many land leapers ... to be right noble valiant & adventrous', and, he argues, have thereby dishonoured the memory and 'high merit' of the great Elizabethan explorers.[24] His primary target in these comments is not the mad voyagers, but his phrasing leaves little doubt that he disapproved, like Fynes Moryson, of 'base and ridiculous adventures' that garnered publicity at the expense of genuinely heroic travel. So it may be that in his chosen role as 'official' state historian (his book was a continuation of Stow's *Annales*), Howes chooses to single out for posterity a 'pure' example of the recent vogue, one that is ennobled through being performed, as he tells us, by 'a Gentleman of an ancient Family ... and of good reputation', and with the blessing of King James and his court. It is ironic, then, that Lepton's ride exactly fits Moryson's category of 'cursorie journies', undertaken by men who merely 'make triall of their bodies strength' and have no interest in the serious challenges of travel.

Howes' decision to put Lepton's ride into the *Chronicle*, to make it in effect a piece of English history, raises in an acute form the issue of what such exploits ultimately signify. In what sense is this journey 'so memorable'? Is it because of its sheer oddity, or does it stand out as an exercise in gentlemanly bravura, the best that native courage and good horsemanship can produce? Howes must have chosen to believe the latter, and yet his recording of the episode yields what is essentially an intriguing item of gossip, revealing an ancestor of the eighteenth-century fads we glanced at in the opening chapter. It looks more like an item in the history of English eccentricity, and it provides a little insight into how the foundations of that history were laid. Despite the attempt to present the exploit as an exercise in sprezzatura (ending 'in as fresh and chearefull maner, as when he first began', and so on), Lepton's ride comes into focus only when we stop trying to see it (with Howes) as an autonomous example of courtly *virtù*, a self-evident demonstration of civilized accomplishment, and understand it as part of the court's participation in a fashionable game. If the late-Elizabethan surge in aristocratic gambling partly found expression in traditional wagers like Robert Carey's, it is also clear that by 1605 the vogue for travel stunts was determining the shape and character of courtly challenges. Lepton's exploit may have some precedent in the honour-contests of the early Tudor nobility, but the artificial and sublimely pointless to-and-fro of his itinerary looks like a new kind of charade, one that we are inclined to see as burlesque (or 'subversion') of traditional customs when it is offered by those excluded from patrician privileges, but which in the minds of the minor gentry making their way in the Jacobean establishment had evidently become a timely way to gain favour, make money or get noticed. John Chamberlain caught this mood rather better than Howes when he reported in July 1608, 'On Monday a gentleman wan a great wager for riding five measured miles (between Brainford and Kensington) twenty times over in lesse then five howres.'[25] But he is silent on the question – the one that Howes begs with his unstinting praise of Lepton – of how this sort of endeavour relates to the cultural priorities and standards of the time.

Fynes Moryson's criticism of stunts that are merely feats of endurance goes to the heart of a debate about sports and the value of physical activity (including the act of travel) that went on throughout the sixteenth century, as codes of behaviour for the nobility and gentry were hammered out in treatises and conduct books. In the early Tudor period, humanists emphasized England's cultural backwardness and the need to supplement the martial and gaming skills of the nobility with more refined pursuits. The cautionary tale of how '[i]n the Court of our King *Henry* the eight, a certaine great Peere ... could say, it was enough for Noblemans sonnes to winde their horne, and carry their Hauke faire; that studie was for the children of meaner ranke'[26] was frequently invoked against the dangers of philistinism, yet the nobility also had humanist warrant for their priorities, since it was accepted that sporting activity played a central role in ancient cultures, which even appeared to provide a precedent for their betting customs: as Richard Mulcaster pointed out in an influential treatise, in the classical world the '*athleticall* and gaming exercises, were in generall assemblies, to winne some wager, to beare awaie the prise, to be wondered at of the world'.[27] At the same time, those who defended sports like archery, wrestling and riding as an essential training ground for warfare felt the need to distinguish them from games pursued merely for 'filthye gaine', and increasingly warned the nobility to stay away from others, like football, that were unworthy of their station.[28] Physical activities were a key marker of social difference, and engaging in the right ones was regarded as vital to the creation of the rounded courtier. Yet circumstances were changing. The development of firearms, as J.R. Hale points out, 'had ruined war as a finishing school for the knightly character'[29] and reduced the status of those sports that used to support it; meanwhile, the growing belief in foreign travel as the means to complete an education had shifted the argument about physical activity into a new key. Travel was an arena in which it was, notoriously, more difficult to be sure of the exercise of virtue. Those who were in favour of it could avail themselves of a familiar pun and call it 'travail', serious labour or effort, and see it as an antidote to the idleness that, according to one mid-century writer, infected the nobility as it 'licentiously roames in ryot, coasting the streets with wavering plumes'.[30] But there was pressure on the advocates of travel, and on the travellers themselves, to demonstrate that going abroad genuinely bettered their understanding. Many were ready to agree with the scholar and diplomat Thomas Wilson that '[n]one are more healthfull, none more lustie, none more merie, none more strong of bodie, then suche as have travailed countries'[31], but it was also assumed that these benefits were nugatory unless they were used to pursue more significant forms of self-improvement. Those who were more sceptical about travel's advantages worried endlessly about where the undirected energies of the youthful tourist might lead him. It was an anxiety that could only be exacerbated by some of the ideological conflicts of the later sixteenth century.

In his polemical tract *The Schoole of Abuse* (1579), Stephen Gosson contrasted 'the olde discipline of Englande', with its emphasis on 'such maisteries, as eyther consisted in swiftnesse of feete, agilitie of body, strength of armes, or Martiall discipline', with 'the exercise that is nowe among us', which he says consists of effeminate pursuits like 'playing, pipyng, and dauncing.'[32] Gosson has no time for the argument that the old 'maisteries' have latterly been deployed into a vigorous tourism that will benefit mind as well as body; as far as he is concerned, English travellers have simply made sure that the 'abuses' of Italy are 'rife among us' (fol. 17). And as the Puritan assault on sports and pastimes intensified in the closing decades of the century, even Gosson's nostalgic view of the traditional athletic virtues was to be discarded. Richard Mulcaster and other moderate reformers defended physical games on health grounds, and promoted a humanist belief in exercise as care and development of the body, but Puritan radicals increasingly lumped all sporting activity and most of the performing arts with what they regarded as sinful pastimes and disorderly revel. We should not exaggerate the impact of this campaign on the physical training of young gentlemen, and to offset it there was, among other counsel, the influential opinion of James I that 'bodily exercises and games are very commendable, as well for bannishing of Idleness … as for making the body able and durable'.[33] But it seems clear that the long-running controversy about sports and recreation had a retarding effect on English absorption of the full humanist curriculum. As late as 1617, in a comprehensive attack on foreign travel, Joseph Hall made a revealing concession to his opponents: since, as he believes, going abroad cannot improve the mind, 'all the advantage it can afford us, must bee in those mixt abilities, wherein our bodies are the greatest partners, as dancing, fencing, musicke, vaulting, horsemanship; the only professions of the mis-named Academies of other nations'. And he reluctantly agrees that travel is necessary to acquire these skills because 'perfection in these qualities is thinner sowne amongst us, then some other-where'.[34] The defensive strain in these remarks is interesting: Hall would like to say that what Englishmen are deficient in isn't really worth having, or at any rate is overvalued in the 'mis-named Academies of other nations'. Henry Peacham implies the same in his backhanded observation that the French 'delight for the most part in Horsmanship, Fencing; Hunting, Dancing, and little esteeme of Learning and gifts of the minde'.[35] Neither man quite manages to separate self-improvement from the acquisition of these talents, but both comments suggest an ambivalence about the formal cultivation of such skills that was probably sharpened by Puritan polemic, and can be traced more generally to a problematic relationship between English culture and humanist ideals.

At the start of the seventeenth century, it was widely thought that the English gentry lacked cultivation in general: Peacham thought that most of them were concerned merely to 'follow the fashion, and to do just nothing', and Robert Burton agreed that 'amongst us the badge of gentry is idleness',[36] by which he meant that gentlemen were interested solely in hawking and riding to hounds. It was not only in Puritan discourse that idleness became synonymous with frivolous activity. Various academy schemes were proposed during James I's reign to address the challenge of fashioning the 'compleat gentleman' who could hold his own on the Continent, but none of them bore much fruit before the 1630s, and Randall Caudill suggests that within the circles who would have benefited there was little demand for such education beyond the informal facilities (dancing masters and so on) that were already available.[37] This carelessness about formal training can be seen as a mistaking of the humanist ideal of sprezzatura, the nonchalant display of skill that conceals effort and premeditation, that had been formulated in English by Sir Thomas Hoby's landmark translation of Castiglione's *Il Cortegiano*, published in 1561. In book 2 of Hoby's version, Duke Frederick, citing various sporting activities, declares, 'I will have oure Courtier therefore to do this and all the rest ... as a matter that is not his profession ... nor be acknowen that he bestoweth much study or time about it, although he do it excellently well.'[38] The cult of the amateur was central to Renaissance ideas of civilized courtliness, but when it is invoked by Hall to disparage the 'mis-named Academies of other nations' it becomes an equivocal excuse for the *lack* of English accomplishment, just as centuries later it would serve to explain why the country does not produce Wimbledon champions. In the same way that it was possible to rationalize England's geographical isolation by imagining it as a *locus amoenus*, a privileged refuge from the world, so the sense of inadequacy induced by the cultural prestige of France or Italy could be allayed by scepticism about the foreign tendency to overcultivate the physical arts. But the argument worked only up to a point, and the ambivalent responses of Hall and Peacham mirror a society that was neither fully at ease with humanist ideas about recreation and training nor able to ignore their importance for the development of a fully modern culture.

One result of this hiatus, I suggest, was the mad voyages, which all demonstrate an athleticism that is in some way perverse or paradoxical: either they insist that they are *not* the product of experience or practice (as in Ferris's declaration that he 'was never trayned up on the water'), or they are a bizarre application of a particular expertise, as in Lepton's equestrian feat or Will Kemp's dance over 120 miles of pot-holed highway. These exploits are by no means identical in motivation or circumstance, but they are all performances that turn the act of travel into a game and substitute a crazy inventiveness for the normal recreations of more self-confident cultures. It is interesting to compare the various antics already cited involving the tower of St. Paul's with the well-known story of a Spanish acrobat on the occasion of Edward VI's coronation. As the new king passed in procession through London in 1546, he witnessed this performance:

> There was a rope as great as the cable of a ship, streched in lengthe from the battlementes of Powles steple, and with a great anker at one end.... And when his Majestie approached neere the same, there came a man, a stranger, being a native of Arragon, lying on the same rope, his head forward, casting his armes and his legges abrode, running on his brest on the said rope from the said battlementes to the grownd, as it had been an arrowe out of a bowe ... [39]

The telling of this little story seems to link the virtuosity of the performance, its perfect control and grace, to the alien and mercurial nature of the performer: 'there came a man, a stranger, being a native of Arragon', descending *ab excelsis* to touch English soil. This was a *travelling* showman, and his skills, while not the kind to be emulated by the well-born, displayed a finesse that was evidently considered exotic and detained the king and his train 'a good space of time'. The foreign acrobatics at Paul's apparently became customary on big occasions: on the day before Mary Tudor was crowned in 1553, 'Peter a Dutchman ... stood on the weathercock of the steeple waving streamers' and after standing on one leg, knelt on it.[40] Significantly, however, these displays of gymnastic skill also drew a laconic comment from the courtier Edward Underhill: 'Att the coronasyone of Kynge Edwarde I sawe Poles steple ly att ane anker, and now she wearithe toppe and toppe-gallant. Surely the nexte wylbe shippwrake or it be longe.'[41] If he had lived to see Banks and his horse ascend Paul's tower half a century later, Underhill might well have decided that, culturally speaking, his prediction of disaster had been realized. What his remark actually anticipates, of course, is William Bush's 'experiment' with a flying ship in 1607, which gave visible shape to Underhill's sailing metaphor and, as we saw at the start of Chapter 1, only narrowly averted 'shippwrake' on the church tower at Lambourn. And it does so most tellingly because the later stunt seems to adopt something like the wry perspective that Underhill brings to the acrobats at Paul's, one that sees how physical and technical skills can be deployed into a rich and strange conceit. The incongruous use of Paul's steeple by a stranger was, said Edmund Howes in a later report,[42] 'good pastime' for King Edward and his nobles, but it could also stimulate more conflicted and original responses that would eventually find their correlative in some prodigious home-grown feats.

'Good pastime' in this context means time well spent, a productive moment of recreation. Howes read John Lepton's multiple ride to York in a similar light, and in so doing he affirmed the mad voyage as a characteristic English activity, effectively playing up the difference between native exploits and the more conventional rituals of other cultures. The imprimatur he gave to this particular escapade contrasts with the satirical attitude of the Gray's Inn students to 'strange Returns', particularly the 'Agilities' and 'Endurances' that they seem to treat as practical jokes or pranks belonging to a less sophisticated milieu – jest-book models of leisure activity that they claim to be replacing with games of verbal irony and wit (and with refined charades like their ship on the Thames). The students' modish view probably reflects European trends: as Peter Burke explains, Italian cities in the later sixteenth century set up academy-style discussion groups that went in for mock lectures and gave themselves parodic names like *Confusi, Immaturi* or *Incolti* (Uncivilised), encouraging a structured playfulness rather than the disorderly fooling of an earlier generation.[43] In this sense the Gray's Inn critique of the more prank-like stunts (like hopping up the stairs of St. Paul's) supports the argument that English culture lagged behind the Continent in embracing humanist ideas of recreation. One suspects, too, that Lepton would have come within their satirical frame for performing a journey no less ridiculous than the claim (in the lampoon quoted earlier) to have 'ridden through *Venice* on Horse-back Post ... or such like Hyperbolies'. Yet perhaps we should read these more fanciful hyperboles as a type of mock-encomium, which sees wit in what it pretends to scorn, and understand them as cousins of Howes' apparently wholehearted admiration. Like Edward Underhill, the law students have a sharp eye for absurdity, but they are also alive to the possibilities of paradox, as their own voyage on the *Ark of Vanity* shows. The unlikely boast of the returning traveller – riding through Venice and so on – might pander to English provincialism and ignorance (and perhaps encourage foolish pranks at home), but transposed into the elegant articles read to the knights of the order it also becomes an invitation to ingenious experiment.

## 'Madde voiages both by sea and land'

Both Samuel Rowlands and Ben Jonson imply that Ferris's voyage to Bristol kicked off an ambitious series of marine adventures in the two decades following, though it is unlikely that any of them benefited from official recognition or were seen as having comparable propaganda value. We know very little about these efforts, but references survive to several apparently single-handed rowing trips across the Channel and the North Sea, to Antwerp, Flushing and Calais; the most enigmatic is Rowlands' report of the 'woodden Whale, / Which unto *Callise*, did from Dover saile' sometime before 1612. The same sea route was followed in 1619 by one Bernard Calvard, who wagered that he could travel from Southwark to Calais and back in a single day in late July, and won his bet 'having almost an howre and a halfe to spare of his limited time, which was from brode day-light to sun-set'.[44] His exploit was more colourfully described by John Taylor in 1624:

With great expence, and peril, and much paine
He rode by land, and crost the raging Maine
In fifteene houres, he did ride and goe,
From *Southwarke* neere to *Callice*, too and fro.

His journey, says Taylor, 'Shewed us a memorable president, / In finding out a speedy worthy way, / For newes 'twixt *France* and *London* in one day'[45] – a claim that probably reflects Taylor's own later interest in purposeful projects like his voyage around the coast to Salisbury in 1623, undertaken to demonstrate the navigability of the river inland from Christchurch. Perhaps Calvard made a similar pitch to attract sponsors for the trip, for there was certainly interest in speedy communications at this date. Only a few weeks earlier, news of the controversial execution of the Dutch statesman Van Olden Barnavelt on 13 May had reached England from The Hague almost overnight.[46] Whether any of his backers would have seriously believed he was promoting better links with the continent may be doubted, though it is possible that the pursuit of such links encouraged some playful rehearsals in the form of the crossings we know about. Calvard himself was presumably trying to outdo his predecessors by combining a land journey with the cross-Channel voyage (a variant, we might note, on Bush's amphibious exercise 12 years previously). This later Jacobean moment does seem to have been crowded with rival ventures, particularly amongst long-distance walkers, and fortunately we have rather more information about the land-based wagers that it produced. In 1618 no fewer than three of London's professional writers were either engaged in or planning a journey northwards on foot, and their efforts form an intriguing group of interlinked projects.

The most celebrated of these expeditions is Ben Jonson's walk to Scotland, mainly because it produced the 'Informations to Drummond', an invaluable record of Jonson's table talk and assorted opinions compiled by his Scottish host William Drummond when the poet visited him at his home south of Edinburgh. Of the walk itself little was known until recently beyond indications that it was conducted as a wager: like Robert Carey, Jonson seems to have been collecting pledges for several months before his departure, and several contemporaries viewed the trip as financially motivated.[47] (The poet's contemporary portrait in Plate 3 was made at about this time.) Jonson told Drummond, however, that he intended to 'write his foot pilgrimage here, and call it *A Discovery*', and this may indicate a scholarly purpose as well. As Ian Donaldson points out, Jonson was familiar with the important chorographic work done by his mentor William Camden in a series of tours around England, and in electing to write about his trip, may have seen himself as supplementing Camden's observations about life north of the border. But two things had happened to complicate his attitude to the venture. One was the royal progress that James I had performed in the previous year, travelling to Edinburgh and back with an enormous retinue over a seven-month period. Jonson followed his monarch's route, taking advantage of road improvements made for the royal party, and travelling at an equally leisurely pace, accepting hospitality and making new social contacts as he went. This was an 'overgoing' of the royal route that could be seen to confirm Jonson's status as a prince of English letters. The other development was the publicity generated by his friend Thomas Coryat's walk to Venice in 1608 and the book he wrote about it (which Jonson helped to promote) and his subsequent trek into Asia. I shall discuss Coryat in more detail later; the important point here is that his travels had, almost singlehandedly, turned long-distance walking into a celebrity activity and an occasion for authorship, and while the rituals of many Jacobean gentry may have been undisturbed by his example, it was one that Jonson found stimulating and provocative. Its impress can be detected in Jonson's later description of his *Discovery*, which he claims was lost in the 1623 fire in his lodgings, as 'my journey into Scotland sung, / With all th'adventures' which, as Donaldson says, has about it 'a slight whiff of the burlesque'.[48] It was no doubt a very different kind of travelogue from *Coryats Crudities* (composed in verse, for one thing), but Jonson had probably learned something from Coryat's method, which showed a way of combining picaresque immediacy with a highly conscientious recording of local detail.

The walk to Scotland, then, could be seen both as a loyal reprise of his sovereign's journey and as a self-aggrandising parody of it, but this duality seems to have been grist to Jonson's serio-comic mill, as he embraced the conflicting forms of prestige that had recently accrued to the pedestrian wager and the northern journey. In flirting thus with the vogue for mad voyages, however, Jonson was confronted by what appeared to be a parody of his own venture, in the shape of John Taylor. We now know, from the recent discovery of an unpublished account of Jonson's outward journey by the poet's previously unsuspected companion, that he left London on 8 July 1618 – only six days before Taylor set off on his own walk to Scotland. This confirms that the two trips were being planned at exactly the same time, and since Jonson's intentions were common knowledge in London for many months before he departed, Taylor obviously understood that his journey would be seen as a rival venture of some kind. Was it intended to ridicule Jonson or steal his thunder? In the pamphlet he published about his journey, Taylor protested his innocence: 'whereas many shallow-brain'd Critickes, doe lay an aspersion on me, that I was set on by others, or that I did undergoe this project, either in malice, or mockage of Maister *Benjamin Jonson*, I vow ... that their imaginations are all wide' – an assurance that seems to be confirmed by the friendly meeting the two men had in Leith, where Jonson presented Taylor with 'a piece of golde ... to drinke his health in England'.[49] But it is likely nonetheless that complicated games were being played. Jonson told Drummond that 'Taylor was sent along here to scorn him', and he clearly meant to imply that influential people were responsible. The two men's peregrinations in fact seem to have been as entangled in the social politics of the court as the ventures of Robert Carey and Richard Ferris. Jonson made his excursion with the full approval and interest of King James, but it is quite possible that others at court saw an opportunity to have fun at Jonson's expense, especially if they thought his planned trip was guilty of *lèse-majesté* or if they had been offended by one of his blunt pronouncements on court morals. As for Taylor, he was perhaps a natural choice to mount a 'counter-voyage' to Jonson's walk. A demobbed soldier turned Thames sculler, he was one of the watermen responsible for ferrying the royal family and probably occupied a position at court rather similar to that of the pursuivant Ferris; moreover, his pamphlet writings since 1613 had given him a reputation as a controversialist that can only have added to his value as a potential thorn in Jonson's side.

Taylor and Jonson each had a history of court employment, though needless to say the latter would not have thought his work as a masque poet in any way comparable with Taylor's role as one of the watermen, nor did he regard Taylor's second career as a hack writer as qualifying him for entry to the privileged circles he himself moved in by virtue of his literary efforts. Nonetheless, Taylor was a popular figure at court, and his position there is a good example of the transitional state of affairs in which the elite still flirted with 'low' culture but were in the process of distancing themselves from vulgar entertainment (the same process that we observed with the Gray's Inn students' eschewing of pranks and practical jokes). Taylor's copious writings seem to have been patronized (in both senses) by his courtier acquaintances, and he was adept both at exploiting the support of the elite and at presenting himself, as Michelle O'Callaghan puts it, as 'a novelty – the unlearned labouring man who turned himself into a poet'. Taylor had carved out this role several years earlier in a series of pamphlets attacking Thomas Coryat (whose travels had been heavily backed by the court), whereby he sought 'to deconstruct the system of literary value that privileged the claims of a learned over an unlearned culture, and to set out the terms for valuing the labouring poet, the sculler, over the "overladen" prodigal wit, the scholar.'[50] At that point Taylor had no plans to trump anything other than Coryat's writings, but by 1618 he had both travel and a new learned rival in his sights.

Jonson's own standing at court presumably allowed him to set up his journey much as Robert Carey had done, as a wager between gentlemen, and to offer it to King James as a light-hearted act of homage, but Taylor's intervention, shadowing his own journey so closely, forced it into unwelcome association with a more demotic stunt. The Victorian critic who argued that 'it was as if, after a gentleman's chariot had set out in proper style on the north road, a costermonger's cart had been despatched in mischief to follow it',[51] over-simplified the class dynamics of the situation, but he captured the twin elements of emulation and parody that fuelled much of the vogue for travel exploits and in this case drew Taylor into playing the role of clown to Jonson's prince. In crude terms, Taylor needed a gimmick to draw attention to his own journey. Jonson had undertaken to walk all the way as a condition of the wager, but no other terms (such as a time-limit like the one observed by Robert Carey) seem to have been set. As travel bets went, it looked like a fairly conventional and open-ended challenge – if a rather arduous one for the heavily overweight poet – and Taylor was ready to cap it with something more particular and more ingenious. He undertook to walk to Scotland without 'carrying any Money to or fro, neither Begging, Borrowing, or Asking Meate, drinke or Lodging',[52] and (it seems) to return within a specified period – at any rate, he was back in London by October. His account of the trip was soon in print (the 1618 title page of *The Pennyles Pilgrimage* also states that it was 'Printed … at the charges of the Author') followed in 1619 by another pamphlet, *A Kicksey-Winsey*, in which Taylor berated all those who had refused to honour their wager agreements.[53] Jonson may have experienced a similar problem in claiming his winnings, if a laconic reference in his masque *News from the New World* is to be trusted,[54] but that was as far as he allowed such disputes to invade his literary work; and it is possible that the thought of competing on the bookstalls with Taylor's Scottish narrative and its disputatious aftermath was enough to discourage Jonson from publishing his own 'Discovery', which apparently remained in manuscript draft when fire tore through his lodgings in 1623. Our loss of that poem, however, has been compensated by the newly uncovered narrative of the outward journey, which demonstrates that for all Jonson's reluctance to be associated with Taylor's stunt, his journey into Scotland attracted a great deal of publicity and arguably epitomizes the overlap of popular and elite culture of which Taylor's career as court favourite has usually appeared to be a clearer sign.

Jonson's walk to Scotland has received a good deal of attention in recent years, particularly since James Loxley's remarkable discovery of the 'Foot Voyage' document, and I shall limit myself to a few observations. Ian Donaldson has suggested plausibly that the function of Jonson's unnamed companion, who appears to have been more than a servant, was to act as a witness to the poet's fulfilment of the conditions of the wager. Thus his account is essentially a log of the journey, testifying to the route taken and supplying a good deal of information about the extensive network of contacts made along the way. For our purposes, perhaps the most significant discovery about the journey to emerge from the 'Foot Voyage' is the amount it has in common with the well-documented exploits that I shall analyse in the next chapter. In particular, we catch numerous echoes of Will Kemp's dance to Norwich as he recounted it in the *Nine Dayes Wonder*, and at moments it is almost as if the writer of the 'Foot Voyage' is recalling the idiom of that famous account:

> Thence to Hogsdon, where a lunaticke woman met us by the way, and went dancing before us and a humorous Tincker of whom wee could not be ridd *etc.* There also three minstrels thrust them selves upon us asking whether wee would heare a merry song.[55]

The writer's role appears to have been the same as that of George Sprat, Kemp's 'overseer' who ensured that he danced all the way to Norwich, and he supplies occasional vivid details of how Jonson was assisted in his pedestrian labours, such as the information that early in the journey 'myne host Holland gave my *Gossip* a forrest Bill' (lines 14–15) – the standard infantry weapon with a curved hook mounted on a pole that Jonson probably used both for protection and as a walking staff. Later, the travellers were shown 'a little wheele … which drivinge it before you, would shew how many myles, poles or yards you went, and the just distance from towne to towne according to our measurd myles' (104–6), and subsequently they walked to Worksop with the inventor and 'his wheele, which hee drave before him to shew us the secreat and use thereof' (126–7). The vignette is graceful confirmation that Jonson was observing the terms of his wager even as he satisfied his curiosity about this device, and it is a germane addition to the topic of ingenious machines and their place in the mad voyage vogue that I shall take up in the next chapter.

The 'Foot Voyage' is above all major confirmation of Jonson's eagerness to exploit the vogue for wager journeys and thereby profit both financially and in terms of personal prestige, much as his erstwhile theatrical colleague Will Kemp had done in 1599. On arrival in Edinburgh he was escorted to the Mercat Cross in the city centre by the civic authorities, and all 'on their knees dranck the kings health, testifying in that place that he hadd performed his jorney' (436–7). Jonson then proposed a toast to 'the Bailief and Aldermen and the whole People their health they being so thicke in the street, that wee could scarce passe by them they ran in such thronges to have a sight of my gossip. The wyndowes also being full every one peeping out of a round hole lyke a head out of a pillory' (437–40). It is difficult to know how much of the excitement here was generated by Jonson's reputation as a writer or whether the city fathers promoted his arrival as some kind of envoy of the Scots' absent monarch, but there is other evidence in the narrative of Jonson's personal fame having spread well beyond the gentry circles that he cultivated in London and the provinces. A few days after crossing the border into Scotland, the poet was approached by a local landowner who 'tould my gossip that his sheerers, hadd made a great sute to him to have a sight of him. So hee walked up into the fieldes where was a number of them with a bagpipe, who no sooner saw my gossip, but they circled him and daunc'd round about him' (421–3). 'The image is captivating', as Loxley rightly declares; it is as vivid as anything in Kemp's famous account of dancing to Norwich, and rather more surprising – as Ian Donaldson says, these farmworkers 'would in all likelihood have been illiterate, and … would generally have heard little news about court or cultural affairs in London. Yet they are eager to welcome Ben Jonson, and to pay him homage in the fields; and dance, entrancingly, in a circle about him as their piper plays.'[56] If John Taylor sought to promote himself as a more popular and accessible poet than the supposedly elitist Jonson, he would seem to have had a formidable task on his hands.

Despite the relaxed pace of his journey and several detours to visit friends and local dignitaries, Jonson firmly observed the terms of his wager: James Loxley points to the moment when, travelling from Northallerton to Darlington, he and his companion made a two-mile detour to cross a bridge on foot rather than take the ferry across the Tees.[57] His punctiliousness would have been an example to Gervase Markham, another writer who was planning a northwards journey at this time, but who may well have come up with his own wager plan after noting an inconsistency in John Taylor's travel account. On reaching the Scottish border, taking a more westerly route than Jonson, Taylor crossed the river Esk, he claims, with the minimum of difficulty:

Without Horse, Bridge, or Boate, *I* o're did get
On foote, I went yet scarce my shooes did wet. (C4)

Many of those who defaulted on a wager with Taylor undoubtedly quibbled about whether he had fulfilled its terms, and they would have been able to point to a discrepancy in this instance, since the boasting couplet just quoted is flatly contradicted a moment later when he confesses (in prose) that he was 'well wet twise' (sig. D) after wading over the Esk and another river. Taylor's slippery way with the obstacles on his trip seems almost to invite the challenge taken up four years later by Markham, who in 1622 made a journey to Berwick on a single strict condition. According to the only surviving record of this trip, Markham pledged to cross all the rivers and streams he encountered by jumping over them and not using boats or bridges. He

did resolve with himselfe to undertake a longe paynfull Chargable and laborious Jorney which was to goe on ffoote from … London to … Berwicke and that … in his sayd Intended Jorney should nott goe over any apparente Bridge greate or smale whatsoever and … should nott … use dyrectlye or indyrectlye any boate, Shippe, or other Ingin for water more then an ordinarye Leape staffe or staffe to leape withal neither shoulde swyme any water whatsoever uppon which Jorney purposed and made knowne to diverse severall persons dyverse of the sayd persons weare desireous to deale with your sayd Subjecte uppon Bills of Adventure Concearneinge his sayd Intended Jorney … [58]

This tortuous piece of legal prose is found in the court documents dealing with the suit Markham brought against those of his sponsors who, like Taylor's, failed to pay up. Many of them were actors from the public theatres (most notably Thomas Heywood), and others from the circles in which Taylor also moved, and the latter's biographer suspects that this venture and Taylor's earlier walk to Scotland had similar sponsors.[59] Markham claims in his 1623 deposition that he resolved to make the trip 'about some ffyve yeares now paste', which suggests that it was conceived when Taylor and Jonson were planning or had embarked on their northward journeys. A distinct picture emerges from collation of these pedestrian feats with other Jacobean records, showing that by the second decade of the seventeenth century the travel stunt had become something of a game in literary circles, one which encouraged self-promotion, mutual encouragement and rivalry, and a taste for gimmickry. In the process, anxieties over breaching a patrician monopoly on adventure have mutated into a rather different argument about status and worth, one that reflects the participation of public figures in the vogue and is concerned about how that involvement might be interpreted.

These developments in some ways support, but in other respects substantially modify, the argument that Arthur Freeman offers in concluding his lively survey of 'Improbable Journeys', where he suggests that 'Ferris and Taylor stand for alien eras' and that between them 'lies a time of professionalizing and sophistication in stunting'. For him, Richard Ferris represents 'grave enterprise' in the wake of the Armada, whereas John Taylor gives us stylized parody and 'farce'[60], an argument that Freeman supports by drawing a specific contrast between the former's plain voyage and Taylor's bizarre exploit in 1619 with a brown paper boat – a vessel that was sustained, he tells us, by eight bulls' bladders blown up by various kinds of rogue who cannot be drowned (as the proverb had it) because they are destined to be hanged.[61] This kind of whimsy does seem to be a late-Jacobean development. It would, though, be equally easy to argue (if we ignore the court's involvement) that Ferris creates a jeu d'esprit that gives way to more pragmatic and serious projects in some of Taylor's other ventures: the voyage to Salisbury already mentioned, for instance, or his later attempts to promote inland navigation.[62] Taylor was expert in presenting these expeditions as travelogues, with diverting incidents and a certain amount of evocative description, and in this sense the mad voyage does become a professional venture in his hands. But the gap between his efforts and sixteenth-century stunts can be exaggerated: Freeman reaches his conclusion partly by overlooking the bets that Ferris made on his journey (he stresses its 'altruism'), and in other ways too the earlier mad voyages need to be rescued from a Merry England of timelessly innocent ventures. We shall see this applying particularly strongly to Will Kemp's dance to Norwich. Moreover, the strongly literary ethos of the Inns of Court in the 1580s and 1590s, with its taste for paradox and fantasy, was a direct stimulus to writerly games with travel and must have helped to shape a good number of ingenious bets amongst the wits of Elizabethan London. As we saw earlier, the mock-edicts in the Gray's Inn revels in 1595 are directed at a courtly and professional world where the travel stunt has evidently taken root and started to develop its own peculiar rituals. In doing so, moreover, it created a framework for the most radically experimental of the mad voyages, William Bush's extraordinary journey in the summer of 1607.

## Notes

1 Steven Mullaney, 'Strange Things, Gross Terms, Curious Customs: The Rehearsal of Cultures in the Late Renaissance', *Representations* 3 (1983), 48.

2 A.W. Green, *The Inns of Court and Early English Drama* (New Haven: Yale UP, 1931), 57; Noel Malcolm, *The Origins of English Nonsense* (London: HarperCollins, 1997), 124.

3 *Gesta Grayorum* (London, 1688), 49–50. Subsequent page references are to this edition.

4 Fynes Moryson, *An Itinerary* (1617; Glasgow: James Maclehose, 1907–1908), 1.426–8.

5 See Stephen Wright, 'Sir John Pakington (1549–1625)', *ODNB* 42.429.

6 Moryson, *Itinerary*, 1.426.

7 Malcolm's *Anecdotes of … London during the 18th century*, quoted in John Ashton, *The History of Gambling in England* (London: Duckworth, 1898), 154.

8 Lawrence Stone, *The Crisis of the Aristocracy, 1558–1641* (Oxford: Clarendon Press, 1965), 568; L.L. Peck, *Court Patronage and Corruption in Early Stuart England* (London: Unwin Hyman, 1990), 21.

9 John Harington, *Nugae Antiquae* (London: W. Frederick, 1769–75), 2.102.

10 F.H. Mares, ed., *The Memoirs of Robert Carey* (Oxford: Clarendon, 1972), 12.

11 See Fynes Moryson, *Shakespeare's Europe*, ed. Charles Hughes, (London: Sherratt and Hughes, 1903), xx. See also Moryson's *Itinerary*, 2.116–7.

12 Will Kemp, *Kemps Nine Daies Wonder, 1600*, ed. G.B. Harrison (London: Bodley Head, 1923), 13. See p. 83 below.

13 I.H. Jeayes, ed., *Letters of Philip Gawdy … 1579–1616* (London: J.B. Nichols, 1906), 118.

14 The special protocol governing an audience with the Ottoman sultan was to become better known through reports like William Biddulph's: 'When a man commeth to salute the great *Turke* … they are led betweene two by the armes, for feare of a stab … and when they returne, they goe backwards; for it is accounted a disgrace to turne their backe-parts to a great man' (*The Travels of Foure English Men* [London, 1612], 57).

15 R.B. Wernham, ed., *The Expedition of Sir John Norris and Sir Francis Drake to Spain and Portugal, 1589* (Aldershot: Gower 1988), liii.

16 *CSP Domestic* 2 (1581–90), ccxxiv. 50, 53.

17 Richard Ferris, *The most dangerous and memorable adventure of Richard Ferris* (London, 1590), A2. All references are to this edition.

18 The vicissitudes of Ferris's work can be tracked through the Privy Council records, which report him being 'verie violentlie used' in 1581 and 'assayled and hurt' 10 years later in trying to make an arrest (*Acts of the Privy Council*, ed. J.R. Dasent [London, 1896–1901], vols. 13.31, 22.53). In the two years prior to his adventure, and in the wake of the Spanish Armada, he was particularly busy carrying official letters regarding the muster of sailors and soldiers. See *Acts*, vol. 16 (London, 1900), 137–8 *et seq*.

19 Arthur Freeman, *Elizabethan Eccentrics* (New York: Dorset Press, 1978), 168–9. For a useful recent discussion of Ferris's voyage, see Michael L. Manous, 'You served God he set you free', *Early Modern Literary Studies* 6 (2007): online.

20 The authorities moved to protect Ferris from his own creditors by issuing a warrant stating that 'there are divers somes of money owing to him which he is not able to recover by suit of law by reasone of his dailie attendance in her Majesty's service', and requiring them to make sure he is reimbursed before demanding payment of debts presumably incurred in mounting his venture (*Acts of the Privy Council*, 21.361–2). Like many other wagerers, Ferris found it difficult to collect his winnings.

21 If this did happen, it may not have covered all of Ferris's costs in mounting his trip, since he was still in debt a year later (see previous note).

22 Alexandra Halasz, *The Marketplace of Print* (Cambridge: Cambridge UP, 1997), 195.

23 John Stow, *The abridgement of the English chronicle … continued … unto … 1610 by E.H.* (London, 1611), 446–7.

24 John Stow, *Annales … of England, continued by Edmund Howes* (London 1615), 806.

25 Chamberlain, *Letters*, 1.262.

26 Joseph Hall, *Quo Vadis? A Censure of Travell* (London, 1617), 29.

27 Richard Mulcaster, *Positions* (London, 1581), 51.

28 Lawrence Humphrey, *The Nobles, or of nobilitye* (London, 1563), B4v. On 'sport as a controversial form of English nationhood', see G. Semenza, *Sport, Politics, and Literature in the English Renaissance* (Newark: U. of Delaware Press, 2003), 13–16.

29 J.R. Hale, 'War and Public Opinion', *Past & Present* 22 (1962), 23.

30 Humphrey, *The Nobles*, sig.i.i (EEBO 82).

31 Thomas Wilson, *The Arte of Rhetorike* (London, 1563), fol. 16.

32 Stephen Gosson, *The Schoole of Abuse* (London, 1579), fol.16–v.

33 James I, *Basilikon Doron*, in *Works* (1616), 185.

34 Hall, *Quo Vadis?* 41–2, 44.

35 Henry Peacham, *The Compleat Gentleman* (London, 1634), 232.

36 Peacham, *The Compleat Gentleman*, 10; Burton, *Anatomy of Melancholy*, 2.68.

37 Caudill, *Some Literary Evidence of the Development of English Virtuoso Interests*, 366.

38 Baldassare Castiglione, *The Courtyer of Count Baldessar Castilio* (London, 1561), M2v.

39 J.G. Nichols, ed., *Literary Remains of King Edward the Sixth* (London: J.B. Nichols, 1857), ccxc.

40 Sydney Anglo, *Spectacle, Pageantry, and Early Tudor Policy* (Oxford: Clarendon Press, 1969), 322.

41 Edward Underhill's autobiography (1553), quoted in W. Jenkinson, *London Churches before the Great Fire* (London: Society for Promoting Christian Knowledge, 1917), 6.

42 John Stow, *Annales ... of England, continued by Edmund Howes* (London, 1615), 594.

43 Peter Burke, *Varieties of Cultural History* (Ithaca: Cornell UP, 1997), 91. Italian conduct manuals after Castiglione's emphasise the importance of humour in civilized life but increasingly caution against practical jokes.

44 Chamberlain, *Letters*, 2.255.

45 John Taylor, *The Scourge of Basenesse* (1624), C4v–5.

46 See Ivo Kamps, *Historiography and Ideology in Stuart Drama* (Cambridge: Cambridge UP, 1996), 141. A pamphlet about the execution was registered in London only four days later.

47 A letter written in June 1617, a full year before Jonson set off, noted that he 'is going on foot to Edinburgh and back, for his profit'. A garbled mid-seventeenth-century report referred to 'Ben Jonson ... goinge to Norwich & back againe upon adventure' and suggested that he tried to place a bet with Sir Francis Bacon. The confusion with Will Kemp's dance to Norwich is suggestive of the way his venture was perceived, and the story about Bacon offers a plausible context for the latter's witticism (as reported by Jonson himself) that 'he loved not to see poesy go on other feet than poetical *dactylus* and *spondaius*' (Donaldson, *Ben Jonson: A Life* [Oxford: Oxford UP, 2011], 34, 445, 29).

48 Donaldson, 26, quoting *Underwood* 43, 94–5. Donaldson's excellent chapter on the walk should be read in conjunction with the transcript of the account discovered by James Loxley ('My Gossip Joh[n]son his Foot Voyage and Mine into Scotland', in Jonson, *Works*, Electronic Edition), and Loxley's own report in *Times Literary Supplement*, 11 September 2009, 13–15.

49 Jonson, *Informations to Drummond*, 486, in *Works*, 5.388; John Taylor, *The Pennyles Pilgrimage* (London, 1619), A3, F3v; Donaldson, *Ben Jonson*, 45.

50 Michelle O'Callaghan, '"Thomas the Scholer" versus "John the Sculler": Defining Popular Culture in the Early Seventeenth Century', in M. Dimmock and A. Hadfield, eds., *Literature and Popular Culture in Early Modern England* (Farnham: Ashgate, 2009), 47, 53.

51 David Masson, *Drummond of Hawthornden* (London: Macmillan, 1873), 88–9.

52 John Taylor, *The Pennyles Pilgrimage* (London, 1618), title page.

53 A second edition of this pamphlet was published in 1624 as *The Scourge of Baseness*, in which Taylor brought his grievances up to date over non-payment on several subsequent wager-journeys.

54 '[P]erhaps he has not all in': Jonson, *News from the New World*, 144, in *Works*, 5.437.

55 Jonson, 'Foot Voyage', lines 7–9 in *Works*, Electronic Edition.

56 Donaldson, *Ben Jonson*, 41.

57 Loxley, 'My Gossip's Foot Voyage', 14; 'Foot Voyage', lines 280–81.

58 C.W. Wallace, 'Gervase Markham, Dramatist', *Shakespeare Jahrbuch* 46 (1910), 347. Markham provides a vivid economic rationale for the venture: having served as a soldier in Ireland and 'recyved dyverse greevous woundes' that have forced him to retire from active service, his large family and household expenses have made him 'desirous by some honest Indevor to rayse unto hymselfe some meanes whereon to lyve in his oulde yeares' (347). The journey was a challenging one for a partially disabled man.

59 Bernard Capp, *The World of John Taylor the Water-Poet, 1578–1653* (Oxford: Oxford UP, 1994), 20.

60 Freeman, *Elizabethan Eccentrics*, 187.

61 John Taylor, *The Praise of Hemp-seed* (London, 1620), 29–30.

62 See Capp, *World of John Taylor*, 110–12; and McRae, *Literature and Domestic Travel*, ch. 6.

# 3

# Two Prodigious Feats

This chapter is devoted to a close examination of two of the best documented of the mad voyages: William Bush's ingenious journey by ship, with which I opened this enquiry, and Will Kemp's famous morris dance to Norwich. The two exploits certainly illustrate the diversity of the vogue, but although one of them has endured in English cultural memory and the other has been entirely forgotten, there is some evidence that at the time they were regarded as equally remarkable feats of bizarre agility. They are related also, to each other and to ventures like Ferris's voyage and Jonson's walk to Scotland, by their reliance on provincial networks of support and wager agreements, and by the public reception their protagonists received as they battled to complete the course. That Kemp's dance was the one to be remembered had a fair amount to do with his prior fame, his talent for publicity and his association with Shakespeare, but it may also tell us something about the way in which the myth of English eccentricity developed in subsequent centuries. Before attempting a new reading of that celebrated stunt, however, I want to reclaim Bush's even more ambitious and elaborate venture from obscurity. To do so requires some preliminary historical excavation.

It was not only in the formal cultivation of athletic skills that England lagged behind Continental Europe. The nation's modernizers were anxious also to catch up with foreign developments in navigation and technical know-how, and this impulse seems to have left its mark on at least one of the English mad voyages. William Bush's versatile ship certainly reflects the international interest at this time in practical experimentation and the construction of ingenious machines. It invites comparison, for instance, with the Dutch inventor Simon Stevin's *zeil-wagen*, or wind car, described by Stevin's biographer as 'a kind of chariot equipped with sails, by means of which a party of 28 people including Prince Maurice were taken from Scheveningen to Petten along the shore of the North sea in two hours, the distance being fourteen Dutch miles'; he adds that 'this occurred probably about the end of ... 1600.'[1] (See Plate 5.) The eminent jurist Hugo Grotius, then still a teenager, took part in this expedition and reported that a 'short while ago we started to sail on land too: for we possess chariots, which ... fly over the plains with an incredible speed ... I was present when one covered in less than two hours fourteen of our miles.'[2] Other accounts claimed an even more impressive performance. Stevin could have seen a report of similar machines in use in China, to be found in Linschoten's *Itinerario* (1596), and the lively images of them in a 1593 Dutch atlas, but he had also met the author of the first printed account of the Chinese 'coches and wagons that goe with sailes', the Spanish missionary Juan Gonzalez de Mendoza[3] – then a prisoner of war at the Hague – and included him in the first outing of his wind car. Stevin (and William Bush) may also have known that there had been experiments in recent years with a similar device in Spain,[4] probably as a direct result of Jesuit observation of the Chinese landships. The latter are invariably described by European commentators as devices of great ingenuity: Mendoza praised the 'industrie and policie' with which they were constructed, and Linschoten their 'wheeles so subtilly made, that being in the fielde they goe and are driven forwardes by the winde, as if they were in the water'.[5] Mendoza also remarks that 'there be many in the Indies, and in Portugall that have seene them painted upon clothes, and on their earthen vessel that is brought from thence to be solde' (Parke, *Historie*, 22). Those ceramics were of course also being carried by the East India Companies to England and the Netherlands, so the old idea of the ship on land was given widespread currency by long-distance trading and voyages of discovery.

The Chinese landships were commercial vehicles, whereas Stevin's invention seems to have been a recreational toy similar to Bush's pinnace, though in this case one designed for repeated use: it was displayed to various dignitaries in succeeding years and a later engraving suggests that more than one vessel was built.[6] But John Wilkins, in his treatise on *Mathematicall Magick*, took the *zeil-wagen* as an 'eminently remarkable' example of 'Automata, *or Self-movers*', and regarded it as a potential cousin of the mills and similar engines he discusses in the previous chapter. In fact, he is moved to ask whether 'it would be worth the experiment to enquire, whether or no such a sailing chariot might not be more conveniently framed with movable sails, whose force may be imprest from their motion, equivalent to those in a wind-mill', and illustrates his concept with a drawing that looks like a courtly helicopter. (See Figure 3.1.) Wilkins sees the wind-chariot as an energy-saving device – 'The labour of horses or other beasts ... being artificially supplied by the strength of winds' – and thinks that the English gentry 'who live near great Plaines, and smooth Champions' should be investing in such experiments, 'for what could be more delightfull or better husbandry, then to make use of the *wind* (which costs nothing, and eats nothing) instead of *horses*?'[7]

The wind-chariot's fame lasted into the eighteenth century: more than 100 years later, Laurence Sterne borrowed Wilkins' sentiments in order to elaborate a lively controversy in *Tristram Shandy* (1760), where Dr Slop, inspired by seeing the 'celebrated sailing chariot' for himself, is convinced that for modern transport purposes it 'would be excellent good husbandry to make use of the winds, which cost nothing, and eat nothing, rather than

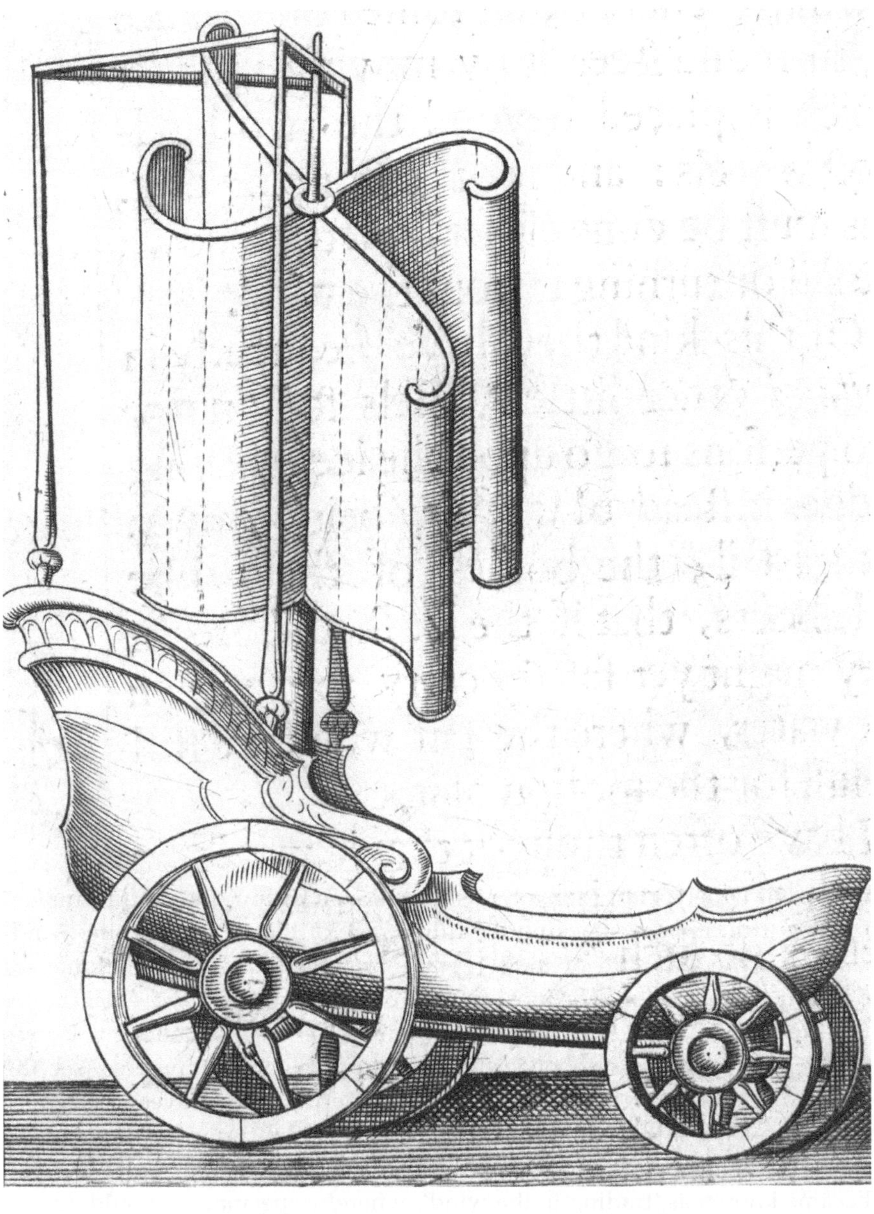

3.1 John Wilkins' design for an adapted wind-car, from *Mathematicall Magick* (1648). (Huntington Library, San Marino.)

horses', an opinion firmly rejected by Tristram's father who declares that 'it is the consumption of our products, as well as the manufactures of them, which gives bread to the hungry, circulates trade ... if I was a prince, I would generously recompence the scientific head which brought forth such contrivances; – yet I would as peremptorily suppress the use of them'.[8] This early example of environmentally sound technologies being blocked by conventional economic interests might be seen as an outgrowth of even earlier conflicts, for Stevin's contraption had from the beginning provided a focus for arguments about sound investment. After being satirized in

3.2 *Floraes Mallewagen*, by Crispijn van de Pas, 1637. (Rijksmuseum, Amsterdam.)

numerous Dutch prints soon after its invention, it became the central emblem in allegorical images attacking the tulip craze of the 1630s, with the wind-car like a modern ship of fools representing the 'airy trade or flutter' of disastrous speculation. The most famous of these images, *Floraes Mallewagen* (Figure 3.2), is an updated version of Brant's *Narrenschiff* conceit that uses Stevin's invention to symbolize the wrecking of Dutch commerce (see the small image on the right of the wind-car foundering in the waves).[9] As Simon Schama explains, the tulip mania, which at its height saw the most prized bulbs changing hands for fantastic sums, was an extreme result of what became known as 'trading in the wind', whereby speculators would deal in commodities that they did not yet hold or had not paid for – in other words, 'futures' trading, which became a virtual necessity in an economy dependent on the slow and uncertain delivery of long-distance cargoes, especially those carried by the newly founded *Vereenigde Oost-Indische Compagnie*. Stevin's wind-car offered to Calvinist commentators the perfect emblem of these speculative practices, especially insofar as the latter were less concerned with the actual profit to be made on commodities than with manipulating the market by betting on short-term price fluctuations. As we shall see, gambling and mad voyages were commonly associated in early-modern Europe, and

Stevin's invention could be read in Holland as an example of the vanity and opportunism that threatened 'sound money' and a godly conception of economic enterprise. The travel stunt was similarly greeted by satire in England, though rarely in this spirit of worldly piety. But Stevin's project had its own motives and purposes, and it was bound up with complicated attitudes to invention and experiment that help to explain why his device might have caught the imagination of English adventurers at the start of the seventeenth century.

Stevin was a working mathematician and engineer, who made a serious contribution to Holland's global enterprise with a treatise on navigation (translated into English in 1599 as *The Haven-finding Art*), and he may have envisaged profitable applications of his device; the frequency with which it was apparently demonstrated suggests that at the least it could have been a lucrative tourist attraction.[10] But Stevin is likely to have been interested less in his invention's popular appeal than in the approval and support of his employer, Prince Maurice of Nassau, who created an engineering school at the University of Leiden where Stevin taught mathematics and was Maurice's tutor and technical advisor. Centres of this kind, like the Emperor Rudolph II's scientific 'academy' in Prague and the late Medici court in Florence, were concerned to develop and exploit the latest research in fields like optics, astronomy and hydraulics, and the circle of experts that Henry, Prince of Wales, gathered at the Jacobean court from 1610 was a belated effort to emulate Continental developments. The science that was practised in these places was of many kinds, however, and the men who were drawn to them produced a startling mix of practical inventions, occult experiment and ingenious playthings. Most important for our purposes, the engineer was frequently called upon to be an artist-designer, creating spectacular effects like the fountains and automata for which Italian gardens were famous, or the pageant machinery required for courtly entertainments. Stevin's compatriot, Cornelius Drebbel, and the French garden designer Salomon de Caus both did work of this kind for the Stuart court, and it seems to have been at least partially in the role of impresario that Drebbel in 1621 constructed a submersible craft in which he made a voyage from Westminster to Greenwich. Contemporary accounts testify that the vessel could be steered underwater and remain submerged with its crew for several hours at a time, and such claims added to the reputation for technical wizardry that Drebbel had developed since he was first employed in about 1605 at the English court. Like Stevin, Drebbel was a respected engineer who designed hydraulic machines and munitions for the English navy, but he was also obsessed with the creation of mechanical marvels that were remembered long after his death. Drebbel's activities were pursued in a laboratory set up for him in Eltham Palace, and much remarked by foreign visitors, who seem to have been particularly impressed by wonder-working novelties like his perpetual motion machine or the 'virginals which played of themselves' when warmed by the sun.[11] These devices were part of a fashionable trend: mechanical curiosities were increasingly on display in

England's great houses, and were part of a culture of experiment that walked a fine line between recreation and purposeful research.

The fascination with ingenious machines can be seen on one level as 'pure' enquiry in an age of intense scientific curiosity, testing materials and hypotheses with little or no utilitarian purpose in mind. This may have been why Francis Bacon, when he wrote his science fantasy *New Atlantis,* was moved to include several of Drebbel's experiments (including his submarine) in the curriculum of Solomon's House, despite the disapproval he voiced elsewhere of 'fabulous Experiments, & Secrets, and frivolous Impostures for pleasure and strangenesse',[12] which he thought encouraged dilettantism and blocked a methodical approach to science. Bacon rejected the cult of marvels and insisted on the importance of rational investigation, yet as Lorraine Daston and Katharine Park have argued, the age of discovery had yielded a large new haul of natural marvels to be explained, so that exotic reports in the sixteenth century 'demonstrate a heightened sense of novelty and possibility' and new life was given to 'the long tradition of writing on natural wonders.'[13]. Furthermore, nature-defying engines were central to a classical and mediaeval tradition of natural magic that the Renaissance had revived and about which Robert Burton enthused as a salve for the melancholic mind: 'What so intricate and pleasing and pleasing withal, as to peruse and practise Hero Alexandrinus' works ... *de machina se movente*' (Heron of Alexandria experimented in the first century with steam power and hydraulics and was famed for his automata), or 'many such experiments intimated long since by Roger Bacon ... as to make a chariot to move *sine animali,* diving-boats, to walk on the water by art and to fly in the air'.[14] With the advent of humanism, these older schemes and experiments became part of a set of antiquarian interests and were taken up, in Italy to start with, by self-styled virtuosi or connoisseurs of the rare and marvellous. This 'aesthetic of rarity', as Randall Caudill terms it,[15] is to be found in much early-modern scientific collecting and experimentation. It promoted a new cult of wonders, a worship of the unusual for its own sake, one that some investigators opposed on the grounds that 'astonishment stifled inquiry'.[16] But it also fostered an interest in practical innovation and in the natural causes of unusual phenomena. This double response can be seen in much of the scientific writing of the period. William Bourne had provided a technical blueprint for Drebbel's submarine as early as 1578 in number 18 of his *Inventions or Devises,* a book whose running title (*Rare Inventions and Strange Devises*) nonetheless appealed to the reader's taste for wonders and concluded with a sketchy account of legendary machines 'which the common people would marvell at'.[17] Similarly, when Henry Peacham published the first edition of *The Complete Gentleman* in 1622, he included a chapter on geometry that reminds the reader of its uses 'in survaying your lands ... making your milles aswell for grinding of corne as throwing foorth water from your lower grounds' (77), as well as in developing the arts of warfare – all skills that Drebbel's work had advanced; but he prefaced these utilitarian applications with an account of ingenious devices known from antiquity and reportedly emulated by early-modern inventors in the courts of Europe. He cites Scaliger's *Exercitationes* (1557), no. 326, where

> he saith, he is able to make of his owne invention with no great labour, a ship which shall swimme, and steere it selfe ... by taking the pith of rushes covered over with bladders, or those thinne skinnes, wherein gold-beaters beate their leaves, and wrapped about with little strings of sinewes, where when a Semicircle shal set one wheele on going; it mooving others, the wings shall stirre and moove forward. (74)

The mix of practical experiment and aesthetic play evident here is also very apparent in the operation of Bush's ship, and although nothing else is known of its maker, who seems to have been an obscure provincial gentleman, he is evidently part of a trend that sought to increase English participation in these developments. Caudill suggests that the virtuoso taste for ingenious wonders is 'an attitude clearly at variance with professional Baconian and utilitarian inductive method' (3); but we might note that a year after Bush mounted his exploit, Francis Bacon made notes regarding the 'Foundac. of a college for Inventors'[18] – a project that remained unrealized but was to provide the seed of Salomon's House in *New Atlantis* (1624), for which he was to draw on Drebbel's work (considered outlandish at the time) in fields like refrigeration, optics and incubation. In practice the distinction between mechanical marvels and utilitarian enquiry was not always easy to preserve.

It was in fact often deliberately blurred. Jessica Wolfe has shown how many Renaissance technical treatises 'emphasize the trifling and playful quality of their work even when their inventions might possess some practical application.' They do this partly to redeem the mechanical arts from their 'low' associations by making them an exercise in sprezzatura and *serio jocum*:

> The mechanical operations and feats of legerdemain taught by technical treatises are, to use the sixteenth-century phrase, 'serious jokes' – tricks and puzzles that conceal metaphysical and epistemological questions. Rather than master a particular procedure or concept, the 'recreative' mechanical practitioner learns to master himself, the precise control of his instruments acting as a metaphorical and an actual tool for intellectual and moral discipline.[19]

Wolfe proposes a close analogy with courtesy theory, finding in both the conduct manuals and the fascination with technology a concern with artifice, cunning and deception. The interest in machines and devices becomes a branch of courtly *facilitá*, possessing 'the same kind of cultural currency as the verbal and physical pastimes practiced by Castiglione's courtiers' (72). This is a promising framework in which to examine the Bush project, and allows us to build on the earlier discussion of mad voyages that do not pose as technological feats but nonetheless offer themselves as strenuous modifications of (or alternatives to) courtly recreation.

## The Travels of William Bush

Bush's stunt, which occupied some four weeks in mid-summer 1607, apparently caused something of a stir in London and the Home Counties. On 27 September, just over a month after it was completed, the newswriter John Chamberlain reported to Dudley Carleton, his regular correspondent in Paris, that

> the greatest newes of this countrie is, of an ingenious fellow that in Barkeshire sailed or went over a high steeple in a boat all of his owne making, and without other help then himself in her, conveyed her above twenty miles by land over hills and dales to the river and so downe to London.'[20]

Chamberlain wrote this letter at the home of Sir Michael Dormer in Oxfordshire, and we can assume that during the autumn the story was a popular item of conversation in the houses of the local gentry, for several of them were involved in some way in Bush's feat. The flags adorning the pinnace were, according to Anthony Nixon, 'beautified with divers Coates of Armes', including those of two prominent Oxfordshire families, the Wenmans and the Harcourts, and along his route into London Bush was entertained at a number of gentry homes.[21] He seems to have been a well-connected young man. One of the moving spirits behind the project was William Essex, a Berkshire gentleman and former MP whose family seat of Lambourn Place was in the Berkshire village where the journey began. From Nixon's account it appears that the pinnace was built in the grounds of Essex's home, as it was from there on 20 July that it was 'brought foorth ... to proceede and passe forwarde in her journey' (Cv). Lambourn provided a convenient starting-point for the planned exploit, allowing Bush to combine a manageable journey over the downs with a longer voyage along the Thames, and perhaps Essex's standing in the small community overrode any objections to using the church tower as a temporary cable station – an expedient that in the event did considerable damage to the fabric of the building.[22] The two men may have been friends and neighbours; another, more interesting likelihood is that Bush was sponsored by Robert Harcourt, to whose sister Essex was married. The display of the Harcourt arms on the pinnace strongly suggests that Robert, a colonial adventurer who in the following year commanded an ill-fated voyage to Guiana, was an enthusiastic backer of Bush's travel stunt, and that the 'geny ... inclining him to see and to search out hidden regions' – as Anthony à Wood expressed it[23] – could also be stirred by a flamboyant rehearsal of the heroic journey. Essex and Harcourt were both in their early thirties, and they seem to have shared with Bush a taste for risky ventures. Essex is said to have dissipated a considerable inheritance, resulting in the sale of his ancestral home in Lambourn and other family estates in 1609, and Harcourt was to sell the manor of Stanton Harcourt in 1612 to raise funds for Guiana; he also invested in ironworks on another estate in Staffordshire. All three men, together with the 'divers other gentlemen of worth and worship' whose arms were flown by the ship, were part of a gentry community that was intrigued by ingenious technologies and the kinds of 'experiment' (to use Chamberlain's word) that they facilitated.

It is also possible that Bush's remarkable effort was designed as a fundraiser for the Guiana voyage. Well-planned stunts were capable of raising considerable sums, and the Harcourts could not count on material investment from government in a new Guiana venture. The latter had the blessing of the future Prince of Wales, who persuaded the King to give Harcourt his commission, but in official circles it had only limited support: the favoured region for English settlement was now Virginia, and after peace with Spain in 1604 the government was anxious to avoid conflict with that country over claims in the Orinoco region. Guiana was also closely identified in Jacobean minds with Sir Walter Ralegh, who was convicted of treason in 1603, and although in 1596 Ralegh had claimed the territory for the English crown in extravagant terms, his and subsequent expeditions had proved unable to make good on the promise that Guiana would yield more gold than Peru. A small colony was planted in 1604, but as James A. Williamson says, 'Guiana enterprises ... remained the speciality of the courtiers and country gentlemen',[24] and the Harcourts and their friends looked for support to the constituency around Prince Henry that was chafing at the restraints imposed by the Jacobean peace. Although only 13 in 1607, the prince was already the embodiment of a quasi-chivalric alternative to his father's irenic foreign policy, and he took a keen interest in military and naval affairs, so many young men with an appetite for foreign adventure and bold enterprises were attracted to his personal court at Richmond Palace. But while Henry encouraged the Guiana venture, he had limited resources with which to support it, especially as he was also strongly behind the rival project of Virginia.

In these circumstances, the Harcourts – three members of the family were to be involved in the Guiana voyage – would have been looking to their gentry colleagues to become 'adventurers' in the planned settlement: that is, not to be part of the expedition but to adventure their money in establishing and developing it. (The precipitate decline in William Essex's fortunes may well have been the result of his investing heavily in a project that brought little return.) The Virginia colony was being funded in this way, and one of its promoters described a system whereby some investors 'did underwrite to furnish three adventures in three yeeres', in other words promising to pay annual instalments, though he found that many of 'the greater sort' were unreliable in this respect.[25] The lack of dependable investment in Virginia led to the introduction of public lotteries in 1612 in order to sustain the colony. As we have seen, however, the greater sort had their own ways of gambling on a venture: Sir Robert Carey's winnings of £2000 on his Berwick walk in 1589 would, if he had been so minded, have enabled a substantial investment in a larger enterprise: compare the £3000 budgeted for each of the larger ships fitted out by Edward Fenton for an expedition in 1582.[26] It is not unlikely that Bush's spectacular voyage was mounted with numerous pledges from the same individuals and families that would be interested in the Guiana project, and this may have been one method of raising the funds immediately needed to launch the enterprise. My admittedly speculative scenario would have William Bush acting on behalf on a small syndicate rather than undertaking a wager for his own benefit, and it is quite possible that he was one of the 60 'Gentlemen and others' that Harcourt describes as joining the Guiana expedition.[27]

None of the contemporary descriptions of the Bush stunt declares that it was undertaken as a wager, but if it were not, this would make it virtually unique amongst the known examples of the mad voyage. The silence is not surprising: few of the developed narratives of journeys mention a wager, and none foregrounds it: we know that Richard Ferris and Thomas Coryat put out money on their ventures only from a ballad in the first case and an occasional poem and legal dispute in the second. But by the time Bush was building his pinnace, the practice of 'putting out' on a daredevil venture was thoroughly established, and the polite fiction that honour and prowess were the only things at stake was very much part of the game. Amongst the country gentlemen taking an interest in Bush, investment in chancy enterprises was often a way of establishing rank and status, and to be associated with a successful enterprise was desirable even if, as in the case of a wager, they would have to pay out as a consequence. So we would hardly expect Anthony Nixon to dwell on or even mention a financial element.[28] He does however describe Bush's careful attention to terms and conditions at the end of the journey, recounting his arrival at the Custom House quay in London, together with a boatload of 'sufficient witnesses', under cover of darkness in the early hours of Friday 14 August, to be met by four customs officials. Nixon implies that Bush was expected at the quay later that day but feared that 'the multitude of boates, and people might much annoy him' (E3v) if he attempted to land in daylight. At this point Bush rowed back to Brentford, set about refurbishing his vessel, and made his triumphal entry into London only four days later. The oath he finally takes at the Custom House on 19 August and the certificate he receives are apparently a ratification of what has already been attested in the previous week, and while Bush's delay in making his final entry is fully explicable in terms of wanting to put on a good show, the earlier arrival appears to be fulfilling a specific condition in a wager, which was perhaps to complete the journey within four weeks.

Whether or not Bush's voyage had a direct connection with the Guiana plan, it certainly looks like a product of the enterprising spirit found amongst those who were drawn to Prince Henry's circle. It may be significant that the chosen chronicler of Bush's exploit, Anthony Nixon, had recently been employed to promote another story close to the hearts of the prince's more militant supporters. Nixon's previous book, *The Three English Brothers* (1607), had related the adventures of the Sherley brothers, members of a Sussex gentry family who were out of favour with the English government because of their piratical exploits and their activities in the Middle East, where they were seeking to promote a crusade against the Ottoman Turks.[29] In that case, Nixon was almost certainly commissioned by one of the brothers to tell their side of the story and win public approval for their controversial deeds. Nixon was a hack writer who turned his hand to a wide variety of topics, and it is impossible to say whether he was singled out by Bush's backers as a likely scribe, but derring-do was food for his pen at the time (after the Bush pamphlet, he wrote one defending the role of English mercenaries in the Swedish wars), and he could be relied upon to render Bush's voyage as a story of resourceful and heroic preparation for the larger challenges facing England's navigators. The sententious vein that came so easily to Nixon added ballast to what looked like a jeu d'esprit, and helped to underscore the fact that the make-believe elements of this exploit were an intriguing reminder, especially for those in courtly circles or in touch with court gossip, of a highly symbolic moment in Prince Henry's initiation into public affairs.

Three years earlier, in March 1604, Lord Admiral Howard had presented the 10-year-old prince with a small ship built in the Chatham dockyard. Its builder, Phineas Pett, had been instructed to 'build a little vessel for the young prince Henry to disport himself in above London Bridge, and to acquaint his Grace with shipping and the manner of that element'. In his autobiography Pett recalled that 'the proportions and the manner of her garnishing ... was to be like the work of the Ark Royal, battlement wise': this was the great warship, originally built by Sir Walter Ralegh, that had led the Armada campaign in 1588 and saw action at Cadiz in 1596. Henry's scaled down version was a mere 25 feet long, but it was 'furnished at all points with ensigns and pendants', and when it had loaded guns and powder at the Tower, Pett sailed it down the Thames to Whitehall 'with multitudes of boats and people attending upon us. As we passed by Whitehall, I saluted the Court with a volley of small shot and our great ordnance, and upon the ebb, turning down again, we did the like, and then taking in our sails we came to an anchor right against the Privy Stairs.'[30] Four days later, the prince himself boarded the vessel, which 'then sailed as far as Paul's Wharf where the Prince baptized it the *Disdain* with a great bowl of wine.'[31] The name he gave his new ship expressed the martial enthusiasms and confidence in England's maritime future that were characteristic of his circle.

Bush's vessel was smaller still, perhaps little more than half this size, for he was able to row it with a single pair of oars, but it was designed to mount a very similar kind of performance, since it was dressed up to look like a miniature warship, complete with forecastle, masts and rigging, a rampant figurehead, and 12 cannon. It also flew 'the Armes of *England*' as well as 'pendents of rich Taffetie' (B4). Nixon's account of the ship appears to confirm most of the details in the woodcut on his title page, suggesting that this is not simply a generic image, but even if it were, the effect on readers of the pamphlet would be to affirm a link with the nautical traditions that many sought to revive. It was in fact a perfect emblem of the national project that Prince Henry, closely advised by Ralegh, was girding himself to undertake:

to rebuild the navy and reawaken the pioneering spirit of the Elizabethan navigators. Anthony Nixon's hyperbolic claim that Bush's achievement might surpass the great ocean-going ventures of England's past sailors similarly taps into the ambitions of the Prince Henry circle and offers his unlikely feat of navigation as an example of thoroughly modern expertise, avoiding the 'inextricable labyrinth of error' that Edward Wright, in dedicating a new edition of his *Certain Errors in Navigation* (1610) to the Prince, saw as awaiting a nation that remained deficient in maritime science (sig.¶2). Navigation, declares Nixon solemnly, is the 'quintessence' of the mathematical sciences, yet theory alone is not enough: 'without practise and experience it is unperfect. And how can perfection bee attained, but by making use & transporting from place to place ... ?' (Bv). Like Richard Ferris, who had asserted that others should follow his example 'the better to daunt the enemies of this nation', Nixon claims that the sportive occasion holds lessons for Bush's countrymen, for

> some may be drawn by example of his industrious indeavours, and labour to lay asyde, and shake of[f] the fruitles imbracements of Idlenes, and betake themselves to such necessarie experiments as may worthyly tend to praise, profit, or pleasure. (B3v)

Even this leaden pronouncement, however, makes clear that Ferris's spritely patriotism has given way to a more complicated idea of what constitutes 'necessarie experiments', and that Bush's stunt is a repository of some of the dreams and schemes that preoccupied court and gentry circles in the Jacobean years.

Nixon was presumably following a brief from the inventor when he represented his contraption as a vehicle for progressive ideas. He describes Bush as a kind of projector, a would-be scientific virtuoso, who 'framed and fashioned a Pynace by his cunning and skill Mathematique and Geometricall' and made it perform 'onely by his owne industry, and labor' (B2). The pamphlet claims to offer his exploit to practically minded people who are interested in 'the profitte of this Travellors labours' (A2), and to this end there is a certain amount of technical explanation, particularly of the means for getting the ship airborne – a system of pulleys 'and divers other engins that caused her (by one mans strength in her) without other helpe to mount up to the top of the ... Tower, and to descend againe to the ground at his pleasure' (B2v). Although we are not given the ship's dimensions, we learn that its two front wheels were four and a half feet tall and that the third wheel at the back 'turned in a frame of three foote highe' (B3v); more enigmatically, we are told of a fourth wheel that 'turned in her' and allowed Bush to propel the vehicle on land, presumably from the seat placed in the middle of the boat that he used when rowing on the Thames. The practical difficulties of completing the journey bulk large in the narrative, but it is not always clear exactly how they were overcome. The reader is initially promised a scientific perspective denied to the original spectators: for instance, we are told repeatedly that Bush's ship was an object of wonder and amazement, making the crowd 'captive to astonishment and admiration', but we are also assured that its journey

> is not performed, either by rashnes of chaunce, or strangenes of miracle, but according to certain universall precepts, or documents derived from the mathematicall fountains.... The causes therefore known, the wonder may cease. (Bv–B3)

This is disingenuous, however, since the written account is coy about explaining certain tricks, and anyone reading it to discover either how the ship was propelled on land, or how its guns were fired with 'no man neere them at their discharging' (B4), would have been disappointed. Nixon's sententious introduction prepares us for a lesson in new navigational technologies, but as it proceeds, his narrative appeals more to our appetite for magic and spectacle. Much of the description of the ship is essentially aesthetic – 'shee was orderly rigged with ropes and sailes, and in all poyntes had all manner of tacklings provided for her as fit and necessarie, as belongeth to a ship of her burthen' (B4) – so that what we are told is not so much how it worked as how it was able to represent a 'real' ship and so create an illusion for the spectators. As Bush got ready to commence his journey after descending from the tower, he made his ship 'passe too and fro in the church-yarde, as well to see that all things should be fit, and well appointed for his travell, as to content the people that stoode desirous to see the rest performed of that novell adventure' (C4). Similar performances were to be requested later in the journey: at Maidenhead, for instance, 'divers Knights and Esquires' requested 'that they might see the manner of his travell by land' before he proceeded on the Thames to Windsor (E2v–3). Nixon plainly suggests that their curiosity was satisfied by a theatrical show rather than an actual demonstration of the ship's functions, and even claims that Bush kept a technical trick up his sleeve in order to cope with the crowds slowing his progress. At one point, having lost time through a mechanical breakdown, he set off with a large gathering in attendance, and 'after hee had travelled almost three miles he practiced in his boate, *The concealed Arte for swift speed in running*. Which he performed with inexpected admiration, for in twelve score, he outran all the people twentie yardes' (D2v). This art remains as hidden from us as the secret of Drebbel's perpetual motion machine.

How seriously, then, are we expected to take the claim that Bush's ship is a useful invention for navigators and shipwrights, or an experiment from which others can learn? The question is a complicated one because it is bound up with shifting perceptions of the purpose and function of machines. Nixon's insistence that the vessel works and is built according to mathematical laws implies that it is some sort of technological breakthrough, offering a blueprint for the construction of similar mechanical devices, yet the story of Bush's adventure makes it clear that we are looking at a machine designed to create a single complex event. His ship transposes the results of research into play and seems to burlesque its own progressive implications: if its technology has any other applications, or indeed any practical uses at all, we are not told what they are. The pamphlet's epistle declares that Bush intends to give the public 'more profit and pleasure in matters of some other deepe performances' (A2v) – a promise apparently that his technical interests will yield further demonstrations; but it sounds more like a showman's boast than a scientific pledge. In this respect, Bush closely resembles the entrepreneurs who dazzled their courtly patrons with mechanical marvels. The fascination with machines in the sixteenth century predated the development of systematic thinking about the principles that governed them, and the growing obsession with waterworks, optical devices and collections of automata was very largely focused on their recreational functions and aesthetic appeal: what was interesting about these things was the way they appeared to cheat nature, and while their makers obviously followed theories and principles of design, there was before Galileo little attempt at the formulation of common laws underlying all mechanical operations. At a time when, for instance, a technical treatise on pumping devices described each machine individually without a clear statement of the basic principles that they share (even though this involved considerable repetition of operational details),[32] mechanical devices that could overcome natural limits were more likely to be assessed as single units than in terms of their conformity to fundamental principles. The products of virtuoso experimentation were offered primarily as examples of cunning and ingenious contrivance, products of the inventor's wit, and, as Jessica Wolfe suggests, their capacity to impress and deceive was analogous to the 'dissimulatory techniques' that courtesy theory prescribed 'as social and intellectual tools' for self-fashioning and personal advancement.[33]

In this respect, it is notable that Bush felt able to pursue a gentlemanly interest in technological novelty through the medium of the travel stunt, apparently without incurring a charge from his peers that his adventure was, in Fynes Moryson's words, 'base and ridiculous'. Rather than discrediting the customary travel wager with flamboyant contrivance, his exploit linked the fashionable concerns of a more mobile generation of young men by turning the gamble on a journey into a technical feat. Yet Nixon's pompous claims for the scientific rationale of the project do suggest that questions were in the air. The emphasis in so many technical treatises on wonder-working devices and the facility of their operation is part of the culture of sophisticated play that many critics have traced in the period, and it was a way of distancing the recreations of a leisured class from the mechanical concerns of the artisan. But the fashion for rarities and ingenious devices was also open to criticism. Natural philosophers had long warned that an obsession with mechanics could obstruct the highest kind of thought, and as we have seen, Bacon and others were ambivalent about the relevance of virtuoso experiments to the new methodical science they were advocating. When Anthony Nixon tells us that Bush's exploit 'hath drawne many mens humors and affections to concur in pleasure, and admiration' (B4v), he nonetheless anticipates that its seamless facility might provoke objections:

> And yet it may be that some superficiall shippe-wrights, or ungrounded Schollers in that Arte … will thinke this easy to bee performed, because they can say, they knowe it: But that will not suffice, because the sphere of knowledge doth infinitely exceed the limits of conjecture, or not deepe, and profound capacities … (B4v)

To illustrate his point, Nixon relates 'a merry report' he has heard about 'ships of sundry Nations, lying in harbour in faire weather', whose mariners engage in competitive 'feates of Activitie'. One 'nimble yonckster gets him to the very top of the foremast, and raysing himselfe bolt upright, turned around uppon his foote without any stay, challenging his *Antagonist* or any of the Nation to do the like'. But the young man who accepts the challenge,

> having turned scarce halfe about, fell downe, and … in his tumbling by good hap, caught hold of the shrowds: And as soone as ever he had a little recovred his spirits, being halfe dead for feare … he … with a loud voice dared his adversarie or any other of that Nation to doe the like: as though that which befell him by his error, he had done of very purpose … (B4v–C)

In the same way, Nixon argues, voyagers will boast of their exploits and exaggerate the dangers they have passed, pretending that 'they have done great things, and according to Arte … when indeede these shifts are but to shadowe their ignorance' (C). This recalls the Gray's Inn satire on lying travellers who stoke up the mad voyage vogue with stories of their bizarre adventures, and in defending Bush against the charge that his enterprise is mere legerdemain, a superficial trick, Nixon seems to be confronting the notion that there is something dishonest and exploitative about the venture. His story about the acrobatic sailors suggests a connection between the appearance of facile cleverness and a dysfunctional attitude to methodical training and the acquisition of skills: the climber who converts his error into a dazzling feat may be quick-witted, but he will never be a true expert. This was essentially Bacon's case against the dilettantism of the virtuosi, but Nixon turns it back on the putative critics of Bush's stunt, the 'ungrounded Scollers' who fail to appreciate his ship's contribution to science. It is they who are facile, he implies, and their lack of professional expertise leads to misguided criticism of experiments in naval technology.

Whether the Bush project really was controversial in these terms is now impossible to establish with certainty. But behind Nixon's elaborate analogies we can sense some of the insecurities about English accomplishment that were mooted earlier. Bush's ship looks like a determined attempt to emulate continental experiments, but the suspicion that it is merely a gimmick, a perverse deviation from serious scientific enquiry, feeds on old anxieties about national backwardness and unsteadiness. Just as returning English travellers perjure themselves in an attempt to 'shadowe their ignorance', so the fashion for travel ventures may be a giddy and slightly desperate response to insularity – not least when a gentleman tries to recreate the marvellous devices of European courtly culture on England's roads and rivers. Nixon's acrobatic metaphor might be invoked against the 'superficiall shippe-wrights' who resist new developments, but it suggests a more general problem of stubborn amateurism and misplaced ideas of sprezzatura. It also recalls, of course, Edward Underhill's remarks quoted earlier about the acrobats on the steeple of St. Paul's, which articulated a sense of incongruity that could only be sharpened when such stunts began to be mounted on less prestigious occasions and by home-grown adventurers in pursuit of profit. The 'shippwrake' that Underhill humorously predicted had come to pass, in conservative eyes, in many aspects of English tourism and adventure, and especially in the epidemic of wager-journeys that yielded the bizarre experiments we have been examining. Of all the mad voyages, Bush's stunt was the most obviously avant-garde, and Nixon exerts himself to dignify it with scientific credentials, but he is also well aware that its newsworthiness is that of an eccentric and logic-defying feat.

The criticism of superficial shipwrights may be shrugged off, but if Nixon's account is to be believed, Bush encountered more formidable opposition from another kind of waterman when he began the river journey at Streatley. Having prepared his vessel for the water after the shaking up it had received by road, he had no sooner put it on the Thames than he and his two companions were set upon by a group of bargemen, who 'wading in the water to the Pynace, with great violence haled, and pulled her up and downe, as if they intended nothing else but to have shaken her asunder' (D3v). Bush's attempts to remonstrate merely led to his being beaten up, and the bargees, their numbers now increased to 'tenne, or twelve persons', then redoubled their assault on his ship, as 'with great stones, hookt staves, and other weapons, [they] maliciously rent and spoiled her, and beat great holes through her … untill they thought they had sufficiently torne her for travailing any more' (D4). For Nixon this is typical mob behaviour, and his account probably exaggerates the damage that was done, but the episode is more intriguing than he suggests. Did Bush's embarkation, and the crowds it attracted, interfere with the bargees' work in some way? Or was the appearance of this miniature warship, so obviously a recreational toy of the leisured classes, enough to stimulate the fury of working men? Like some exotic bird descending amidst an indigenous flock, Bush's ship is an object of wonder to most of its audiences, but in this case amazement turns quickly into hostility, and we are left to wonder whether the result is merely gratuitous vandalism or whether the bargees interpret the project as some kind of threat or affront. Nixon's suggestion that they specifically intended to cripple the vessel, to prevent it going any further, may be an unwarranted gloss, and he offers no reasons why they should do so, but it is a more cogent idea than his general conclusion that the attack derives from 'the brain-sick resolutions of idle humors' which 'take pleasure in doing injuries' (D4). Bush's facsimile of an ocean-going ship was – as far as we know – an unprecedented interloper on the waterways of provincial and rural England (recall Nixon's assertion that most of the inhabitants of Lambourn 'never sawe shippe, or pynace before'). It was a device borrowed from civic and courtly pageants where the model sailing ship was a familiar sight, and a craft that, unlike the wherries and rowing boats used by Ferris, Taylor and other unnamed mad voyagers, had no conceivable function in the working environment of the river and coastal network. Nixon does not attempt to suggest, despite his advocacy of the ship as a progressive technology, that the bargees see this new-fangled device as a threat to their livelihoods, but it seems quite possible that they not only disliked its intrusion for the reasons just suggested, but were distrustful of any vessel whose purpose was not immediately apparent. Their violence superficially resembles the riotous behaviour that festive occasions could induce, as in the periodic vandalizing of London theatres by apprentices on Shrove Tuesday, or the fate of John Taylor's paper boat at the voyage's end in Queenborough 12 years later:

We to the Mayor gave our adventrous boat:
The which (to glorifie that towne of *Kent*)
He meant to hang up for a monument....
But whilst we at our dinners thus were merry.
The Country people tore our tatter'd wherry
In mammocks peecemeale, in a thousand scraps,
Wearing the reliques in their hats and caps.[34]

But the attack on Bush's ship – and on Bush himself – seems to have little in common with such celebratory dismemberment and souvenir-hunting, and if it sprang from the boisterous impulses of rural festivity, it nonetheless looks like an aberration, a piece of directed malice that is not part of a holiday game but seeks to end the game altogether.

This last episode remains somewhat opaque, but it does suggest that Bush's venture was capable of being read as deliberately exclusive – as a class-bound experiment that infringed on more mundane prerogatives. The social politics of what he was doing were evidently complex, even leaving aside the possibility that the stunt was designed to raise money for a Guiana voyage. Although the pinnace may have been a strange sight to rural folk, its maker's journey was an elaborate variant on something that seems to have been relatively familiar to provincial England by the early 1600s – the gentlemanly wager on an inland journey, like the walk to Berwick – and which could be seen as rehearsing or supporting a certain kind of authority over the terrain that it traced. Central to this process was the network of hospitality that Bush enjoyed in traversing a minutely observed route linked by the dwelling-places of prominent gentry, whose power of patronage within their own territories was thereby affirmed. Richard Helgerson has shown how chorography or surveying of land became a political act in this period, asserting 'local particularism and local prerogative' against royal claims to material possession of the kingdom, but what the surveyors' itineraries increasingly affirmed was the title of important families in each region, not common ownership of the land.[35] Recreational excursions and wager-journeys within England typically recapitulated parts of those itineraries, and the same pattern of reliance on gentry networks recurs in the exploits of less privileged adventurers like John Taylor and Will Kemp. The latter, as we shall see shortly, made particular use of these regional linkages to promote his cultural standing. Virtually all of the known wager ventures involving a journey within rural England took advantage of this patronage system, whatever the social class of the protagonist, and all could be seen as in some way rivalling the only established form of crowd-pulling rural journey, which was the royal progress. The more ambitious mad voyages may have been notable popular spectacles, but in significant respects they underwrote the interests of the gentry class whose lands they traversed.

In thinking further about what distinguished these unusual stunts from more conventional wager-journeys, it may be worth pursuing Helgerson's point and considering the distinction he makes between the 'weak' narrative of chorography, which was purely expository, and the 'strong' one of adventure, developed in accounts of exploration and discovery, that 'conferred authority on individual experience' (151). Many of the domestic mad voyages are a curious amalgam of the two, since they trace a journey over familiar territory, reiterating what maps and surveys tell us about the lay of the land, but do so in (mock) heroic and dramatic vein, turning reconnaissance into a symbolic act of conquest. Helgerson explains that the two genres, chorography and voyage narrative, emerged simultaneously in the 1570s and 1580s as complementary tools of geographical discovery, and it may be that the Bush project would have been inconceivable without the shaping influence of both ways of thinking about space and human claims upon it. All of the rural wager-journeys temper the strong narrative with the weak one; or, to put it another way, all of them rely on the conservative ground-plan of chorography to license and contain the extravagant act of travel. The relationship between the two remained unremarkable as long as the venture looked like a familiar custom practised by those who had brought it into being – a gentleman's walking tour, say, or a courtly challenge to traverse a route between two country seats. It became idiosyncratic once the strong narrative was the vehicle for aspirations that were novel or contested or frustrated in some way. I suggested earlier that the walk to Berwick might have been a substitute for the knightly adventures that a generation of courtiers were missing in the Elizabethan peace, and Robert Carey's example shows how the model came under strain when the legitimacy of the foreign expedition for which it substituted was questioned. This was only one of several ways in which the relationship between weak and strong narratives became unstable during the two decades that created the mad voyages. But the incongruity that was cultivated in the more flamboyant stunts, producing results as diverse as the ship on land, multiple rides to York and going backwards to Berwick, is dependent on that unstable relationship – on the way they parody or fantasticate a normal venture and make it strange, either as an involuntary demonstration of tensions and uncertainties in the culture, or as a playful search for a new kind of raison d'être. These are of course not straightforward alternatives: the one easily contains the other, for while the strong narrative allows the mad voyager to be in command of his own fate, it binds him to an eccentric course that is ambiguously related to serious accomplishment. This brings us to our second prodigious feat, Will Kemp's celebrated morris dance from London to Norwich in 1600.

## Kemp's Nine Days' Wonder

Will Kemp's extraordinary undertaking is the only one of the exploits noted by contemporaries to have attracted much subsequent attention, and it has been treated by modern critics as a solitary event, a feat without precedent or imitators, that is chiefly interesting for its minor role in English theatrical history and for the light it sheds on the intersection of popular culture and an emergent market economy at the turn of the century. These analyses are valuable for our purposes, but in fact the epic dance commemorated in *Kemps Nine Daies Wonder* (1600) has a number of revealing links with the ventures I have been examining. Kemp was certainly aware of participating in a tradition of travel exploits. On the fifth day of his journey, he tells us,

> I tript it to Sudbury, whether came to see [me] a very kinde Gentleman Master Foskew, that had before travailed a foote from London to Barwick: who, giving me good counsaile to observe temperate dyet for my health, and other advise to bee carefull of my company … departed leaving me much indebted to his love.[36]

The two evidently found much to talk about, despite the obvious differences between their projects, and Foskew's warning about 'company' suggests that the Berwick walk could attract the crowds of onlookers Kemp repeatedly describes as attending and sometimes obstructing his journey, and perhaps also drew unsavoury characters like the cutpurses who were caught on the second day of Kemp's dance and claimed to have laid wagers on his performance. Kemp was also concerned to control the message going out about his affiliations with other stunts: he claims to have published his pamphlet to counter the ballads and broadsides put out by a 'sort of mad fellows' during the four weeks it took to complete his dance – publicity that turned his exploit into a sensational news item and carried burlesquing titles like 'his desperate daungers in his late travaile' (3). One particular account, he says, described 'his entertainement to New-Market', a place Kemp claims never to have visited. At the end of the book he returns to the theme, with a plea to the ballad-makers to 'imploy not your little wits in certifying the world that I am gone to Rome, Jerusalem, Venice, or any other place at your idle appoint' (29). At this point, however, the complaint is an artful way of creating advance publicity for his next venture, which was indeed to dance across the Alps. Kemp warns the gossip-mongers that 'the great journey he pretends' is still an open proposition: 'I … am shortly God willing to set forward as merily as I may; whether I my selfe know not' (29), but he is clearly inviting his readership to see the new stunt as a rival to the favourite wagering journeys of English tourists to the Continent, in the hope of attracting investment in an audacious plan.

Kemp was probably the first to think of bringing the morris and the travel stunt together, but he may have faced some attempts to emulate his achievement. We have already seen that William Rowley referred to someone 'hopping from *Yorke* to *London*'. Taken literally, this seems as unlikely a feat as going backwards to Berwick, but 'hop' could mean 'dance' (as it still does in some quarters), and this is clearly what Kemp refers to when he tells Anne Fitton, the dedicatee of his pamphlet, that her kindness 'makes me … judge my hart Corke, & my heeles feathers, so that me thinkes I could flye to Rome (at least hop to Rome) as the olde Proverb is, with a morter on my head' (4). ('Hop' was also at this date a synonym for 'leap', making it a suitable verb for morris dancing.) The proverb he quotes meant 'to go on a fool's errand', and is Kemp's rueful acknowledgement of the ridicule that has been heaped on him in ballads about his journey, though it also implies that Anne Fitton's patronage has encouraged him to think about a more ambitious undertaking. Kemp did manage to reach Rome in 1601 (presumably not dancing all the way), but the trip did not bring the financial rewards he hoped for. Home-grown attempts to rival or outdo the Norwich dance may have been more successful: Dudley Carleton reported a few months later that near Witham in Essex (and close to Kemp's route) 'we met a company of mad wenches … who travelled from house to house … attended with a concert of musicians, as if they had undertaken the like adventure as Kemp did from London to Norwich'[37] – which suggests a similar dancing exploit; and it is quite possible that between then and 1609 (when Rowley reported it) someone attempted a more ambitious imitation over the 200 miles to York.[38] Morris dancing was a competitive activity at the turn of the seventeenth century – Ronald Hutton describes it as 'a new fashion … sweeping the nation's youth' – and in many areas it spawned touring teams of performers who vied for supremacy 'by displaying the remarkable physical stamina and dexterity which the dance demanded'.[39] There was regional rivalry as well: in a 1609 play a character declares that 'Hereford-shire for a morris-daunce, puts downe, not onely all *Kent,* but verie neare … three quarters of Christendome', and adds: '*Kemps* Morris to *Norwich,* was no more to this, then a Galliard on a common stage, at the end of an old dead Comedie, is to a *Caranto* daunced on the Ropes.'[40] The comparison aligns Kemp's dance with popular jigs in the theatre (an important connection for our purposes), and even in disparaging its memory, it recalls that his feat established a kind of benchmark for arduous performance. As David Wiles reminds us, to be a morris dancer 'was to be a species of athlete.'[41]

Kemp's decision to set off in February, on the first Monday in Lent, set the tone for his idiosyncratic effort. It was hardly a good time of year for road travel – in his account Kemp complains a good deal about the 'foule way … full of deep holes' in which 'sometimes I skipt up to the waste' (12) – but he may have been even more averse to the prospect of strenuous leaping in summer temperatures. It is also possible that his starting date was dictated by the closure of the theatres for Lent, though it is not clear that Kemp was attached to any acting company at the time, and his departure for the Continent soon after the Norwich stunt rather suggests that his abrupt break with the Chamberlain's Men in 1599, where he had been a principal shareholder and leading actor, had left him unemployed and in search of a profitable enterprise. He apparently found it by turning his special skills to the current vogue for travel exploits. Like Richard Ferris nine years earlier, he devised a journey that would be completed in stages over several weeks, but the wager he made on it probably included more specific conditions. According to his published narrative, with its eye-catching title *Kemps Nine Daies Wonder*, he undertook to cover the distance in exactly nine days of actual dancing – an adroit way of packaging the trip, since the expression "nine days' wonder", which was proverbial for the short-lived fame of anything new, here becomes the measure of Kemp's prodigious stamina and skill and ensures instead that his feat is remembered (as it has been). The journey, which covered about 130 miles, does seem to have been conceived in roughly nine stages, but on two occasions Kemp danced a short distance on a rest day in anticipation of the next stage, rode back to his lodgings and next morning took up the dance from the point he had reached. On the official ninth day, having reached the outskirts of Norwich, he rode into the city and obtained permission from the Mayor to delay his formal entry for three days, 'to the end that divers knights and Gentlemen, together with their wives and Children (who had beene many dayes before deceyved with expectation of my comming) might now have sufficient warning' and be there to greet him (22). George Sprat, the man 'appointed for my overseer', apparently had no difficulty with these arrangements, though he was punctilious in his duties: when he lost sight of Kemp in the crowds during the final stage in Norwich, he 'would not be deposed that I had daunst it' (25) and insisted on a repeat performance the following Tuesday. Clearly Sprat's job was to make sure that Kemp danced every inch of the way, but even his careful umpiring did not ensure that everyone who had bet on the enterprise actually paid up: in a now-familiar scenario, Kemp concluded his account of the trip with a complaint that having 'put out some money to have threefold gaine at my returne', some who took the wager had honoured it, but 'others I cannot see, nor wil they willingly be found, and these are the greater number' (27). He also gave notice that he intended to publish a 'cattalogue of al their names I ventur'd with', indicating those who had defaulted, though no such list survives. Still, he apparently did well enough out of the venture to feel that a Continental sequel was viable.

The dance to Norwich was a well-publicized stunt: we can be sure that it was widely advertised in advance, no doubt providing ammunition for the satirical broadsides that quickly started appearing, and although we have only Kemp's word for most of what happened in the course of it, his own claim to be separating fact from the balladeers' fiction was open to refutation by his overseer (unless he too is a fiction!) and numerous spectators, and like Richard

Ferris, he had little to gain from embroidering a narrative that bore witness to an attested feat.[42] This does not mean, of course, that the *Nine Daies Wonder* is a purely factual and objective account. Kemp's story is a careful piece of self-presentation that uses what he calls his 'blunt mirth' (4) to negotiate some complex cultural territory, and it needs to be read against what we know of both the general and particular circumstances in which he mounted his venture.

In February 1599, Will Kemp joined his fellow players in the Chamberlain's Men in signing the lease on the Globe, their new theatre on Bankside, and acquired a major shareholding in a profitable and growing enterprise. As the company's specialist in clown roles he was, with Richard Burbage, the most celebrated actor of his day, yet by the autumn of that year he had sold out his investment and left. It is generally agreed that his abrupt departure was a result of internal disagreement about the company's artistic priorities as it moved up-market, shifting away from popular traditions of improvisation and physical clowning to a more controlled and author-centred kind of theatre. In particular, the Globe's new regime meant an end to the jig, a short farcical sketch with music and dance that habitually concluded the day's performance in the public theatres, and the medium in which Kemp had first made his name. Jigs were notorious for their bawdy subject-matter and lewd dancing, and created a volatile mood in the playhouse, with a good deal of audience participation from the pit, that management decided was incompatible with respectable theatre-going. Yet despite his evident versatility as an performer – he created several of Shakespeare's earlier clown roles, and many scholars think that he was the first Falstaff[43] – Kemp remained closely associated with the jig: he published several of his own during the 1590s, and told Anne Fitton in the epistle to *Nine Daies Wonder* that he 'hath spent his life in mad Jigges and merry jestes' (4). He had been a solo performer long before he embarked on the Norwich dance, and honed his specialist clowning skills on the public stages; when he turned out on that February morning to begin his new venture, the spectators in London's streets may have found Kemp's leaping progress reminiscent of some of their favourite moments in the theatre. The morris dance was a key component of the stage jig, according to C.R. Baskervill, combining with courtly dances like the galliard to produce a mixed form in which performers were able to improvise freely; and as he danced through the streets, Kemp probably drew on the repertoire of moves he had developed onstage in order to give the watching crowds a taste of the skills that had made him famous. In this respect, while it may be true to say that Kemp's venture turned the traditional morris dance into a marketable commodity (he is certainly busking at this point), it also gave a free demonstration of something that had already been adapted to the commercial needs of the public theatre.

The notion of the 'traditional morris dance', in fact, needs examining more closely. Critics habitually speak of it as a mediaeval institution, or as the centrepiece of a immemorial folk culture, in ways that emphasise the novelty of Kemp's commercial initiative and turn the latter into a parable about the transformation of old values and customs by the market. But the morris was an early object of cultural mystification. Folklorists and modern practitioners still argue about its origins, with some attempting to trace the dance back to pagan rites, yet even this suspect anthropology has its origins in Puritan attacks on its 'heathen' and devilish qualities. Similarly, the view of morris dancing as a timeless constituent of English popular culture was fostered by specific developments in the early modern period that conferred upon it a symbolic role in social and religious reform. In fact, although its origins remain obscure, historians agree that morris dancing first arrived in late-mediaeval England as a courtly entertainment, and was incorporated into the revels and ceremonies of the early Tudor monarchs; thereafter, as courtly interest in it waned, processional morrises became a regular feature of civic and trade guild events. It was only in the sixteenth century that the morris dance began to be sponsored by local parishes to support fundraising events like church ales and became part of licensed festivities in town and country like May Day and the Midsummer revels. As it spread into the rural areas and grew in popularity, especially in the middle decades of the century, the morris was effectively installed as the beating heart of communal celebration and provided a vehicle for games and playlets featuring folk heroes like Robin Hood and the Summer Lord. Kemp taps into this festive mythology at several points in the *Nine Daies Wonder*, beginning with the title-page woodcut (see Figure 3.3) where he is shown wearing a shirt decorated with a vine pattern, and then introducing himself with a flourish as '*Cavaliero Kemp*, head-Master of Morrice-dauncers, high Head-borough of heighs, and onely tricker of your Tril-lilles'. By the time he did so, however, the cultural status and role of the dance had shifted. In the 1570s the reforming bishops had started to act against the carnivalesque elements in popular festivity that had developed under the old religion and were now deemed subversive of orderly worship and social stability. High on their list were activities containing 'scoffs, jests, wanton gestures or ribald talk',[44] and since morris entertainments had absorbed older rituals like the hobby horse dance with its knockabout elements, and regularly featured a capering fool and the seduction of a cross-dressed Maid Marian, they became an obvious candidate for proscription. The episcopal ban was never fully effective, since its implementation depended on the varying zeal of local authorities, but it led to a complex situation in the closing decades of the century whereby the growing popularity of morris dancing in the population at large coincided with the erosion or eradication of its customary holiday function. The morris was also a prime target in the growing Puritan campaign against games and pastimes. We owe one of the most vivid pictures of the dance in this period to the classic denunciation by Philip Stubbes of its performers 'with their baudie Pipers, and thundering Drummers, to strike up the Devils Daunce withal', and 'their handkerchiefs fluttering about their heades like madde men, their hobbie horses and other monsters skirmishing amongst the thronge'.[45] Like the Protestant authorities, Stubbes was particularly exercised by continuing violations of the Sabbath and infringements of church property – 'Then martch this Heathen company

3.3 Titlepage of *Kemps Nine Daies Wonder* (1600).

toward the Church and Church-yarde', he declared – but the vitality and enthusiasm of the dancers conveyed in his account were also being channelled into new recreational outlets as the old were denied them.

Church sponsorship had encouraged the dissemination of morris dancing into small towns and villages, and when that was withdrawn, people were faced, as John Forrest puts it, with 'the loss of a *sponsor*, the loss of a *place* to dance, and the loss of an *occasion* for dancing.'[46] Not every village could find solutions to these difficulties, and the church's action certainly contributed to the overall decline of the rural morris in the seventeenth century. But those that did manage to adapt created a novel phenomenon, one that provides an important context in which to view Kemp's project. The loss of venue and festive occasion led to the creation of rural touring groups who turned the morris dance into a money-making activity, and an occasion in its own right. Instead of attracting people to a celebratory focal point, as the old calendar holidays did, these tours took the dance out to small communities in a particular area, and were sufficiently lucrative to permit the employment of hired musicians. Forrest speculates that they were 'a significant income-producer in slack agricultural times',[47] and given the failed harvests and rural poverty of the 1590s, they could have made an appreciable contribution to local economies in the years before Kemp offered his own epic excursion.

Professional dance troupes had long existed in urban centres to service civic entertainments, and as the authorities in larger towns came under pressure to ban morris dancing, these performers may have travelled to the country houses of the gentry, but the first recorded example of a rural tour took place in 1589. By the beginning of the seventeenth century, 'morris-dance teams were perceived as representing specific villages'.[48] Touring provoked intergroup rivalry, and this in turn encouraged the evolution of morris entertainments, drawing in elements of country dance and leading to a formalisation of repertoire that probably made many of these touring performances look very like stage jigs: sexual comedy, suggestive dancing and the antics of the fool being only the most obvious elements in common. In his 'Entertainment at Althorp' (performed in 1603), Ben Jonson describes 'a morris of the clowns [rural folk] there about, who most officiously presented themselves', and their fool announces himself as 'the usher to a morris, / A kind of masque, whereof good store is / In the country here about.'[49] Kemp, who describes himself as 'best bel-shangles betweene Sion and mount Surrey' (5), was encroaching on spaces where his famous skills had some significant counterparts.

It is interesting in this regard to note Kemp's changing interaction with the onlookers as he moved out of the London area. At the start of his journey, he is mobbed by crowds in Whitechapel and the suburbs:

> My setting forward was somewhat before seaven in the morning ... and as fast as kinde peoples thronging together would give mee leave, thorow London I leapt: By the way many ... gave me bowd sixepences and grotes, blessing me with their harty prayers and God-speedes. (5–6)

The 'multitudes of Londoners' that come out to greet him so early on a winter morning are obviously drawn by Kemp's celebrity as a dancer and comedian, and they treat his exploit as an excuse for revelry, following him out of the city as if on one of their habitual holiday progresses (the Mile End road, says Kemp, is 'no walke without a recreation at Stratford Bow with Creame and Cakes'), and encouraging him to feast and carouse with them. He also suggests that many who followed him did so 'to make themselves merry, if I should chance (as many thought) to give over my Morrice within a mile of Mile-end' (6). To gainsay the sceptics, Kemp refuses all offers of drink, and paints himself in the narrative as an unwilling Lord of Misrule who, having given the people something to celebrate in the straitened days of Lent, dissociates himself from their revels and resumes the journey as soon as he has given 'my boone Companyons the slip' (7). But as he moves into the countryside and market towns on the way to Norfolk, Kemp is rather suddenly put on his mettle. Here he not only continues to attract crowds of onlookers, but also finds that he has regular dancing companions, since 'honest Country fellows' would hear his pipe in the morning and 'get up and beare mee company a little way' (12). He makes this sound like a spontaneous reaction, and we get a glimpse here, perhaps, of the morris's current popularity as an independent recreation. Countryfolk must also have been primed to respond to the familiar sound of touring morris dancers, whose bells, pipes and drums were easily heard, as John Forrest remarks, in 'an era when there were few loud sounds in the English countryside' (274); and their eagerness to join in when they heard Kemp's pipe could also indicate that they had advance warning of his special tour: in this prosperous part of England, even illiterate rural folk might well have heard his published jigs being read or sung, and relished the chance to dance a short distance with the legendary clown.

Kemp is genial enough about his newfound company, but in his narrative he cannot resist making competitive capital out of it, as with the case of the butcher who offers to accompany him from Sudbury to Bury (a distance of about 20 miles) but is forced to give up after half a mile, 'protesting, that if he might get a 100. pound, he would not hold out with me; for indeed my pace in dauncing is not ordinary' (14). (The butcher's exclamation may indicate that he had made a wager in which he stood to win rather less than £100.) He is not the only one who can't keep up with Kemp: a little earlier there is a fine comic sketch of two 'pretty plaine youthes' who insist on dancing with him in single file on the road to Braintree, until they come to 'a broad plash of water and mud', which Kemp manages to leap over only getting his ankles wet, while one of the youths

> took his jump, and stuck fast in the midst, crying out to his companion, come George, call yee this dauncing, Ile goe no further: for indeede hee could goe no further, till his fellow was faine to wade and help him out. I could not chuse but to lough to see howe like two frogges they laboured: a hartye farwell I gave them, and they faintly bad God speed me, saying if I daunst that durtie way this seaven yeares againe, they would never daunce after me. (12–13)

The point of these stories is to emphasise Kemp's superior prowess, and the fact that he is doing something unprecedented with the morris dance: as Max W. Thomas nicely observes, the 'durtie way' that he has danced 'seems to refer simultaneously to his method, his direction, and his road.' But if Thomas is correct in his deduction that 'the rural economy somewhat resented, or at least resisted, the "durtie" tricks of Kemp's commercial venture',[50] this is not because he is violating traditional custom but because he trumps (and sometimes humiliates) his fellow dancers with a prodigious version of their own pastimes, and in some instances at least, could be seen as trespassing on their professional turf. Although we cannot be sure that all these incidents happened as described, the picture that is created, of a rural populace ready to turn out and dance in the depths of winter, with no official holiday in sight, is very much in line with the developments we have noted. The loss of church sponsorship may not have detached the country morris entirely from its festive moorings (it continued to have a vital role at weddings, secular ales and suchlike), but it pushed it into significantly new initiatives.

We should be cautious, then, about seeing Kemp's dance to Norwich either as a commercial raid on unchanging popular traditions or as an attempt to recuperate a world that has been lost in the rampant market conditions of early modern London. Richard Helgerson has suggested that 'Kemp takes over the popular to make it the ground for a new kind of popularity, that of the popular celebrity, the famous entertainer',[51] but it might be truer to say that he uses the morris's new kind of popularity to try to recover or shore up the celebrity he is in danger of losing. Having been ousted from the Globe, he takes his special skills on the road in the confident expectation that he can ride the wave of a fashionable trend in popular culture. Morris dancing, like the theatre, was changing and evolving, but whereas modernization on London's public stages tended to exclude Kemp, the volatile conditions of play and pastime in the regions provided a fruitful venue for his audacious project. His reputation as a jig-maker and prodigious dancer preceded him, and an essential thread in his own account of the journey is the series of challenges like those already mentioned: invitations to dance that are invariably construed as contests in which his superior agility and stamina are demonstrated. But this is not just a question of seeing off a few yokels, however entertaining the anecdotes that resulted. Two of these episodes throw a more intriguing light on Kemp's enterprise than the comic moments we have just examined. First, when the unfortunate butcher admits defeat and pulls out on the road outside Sudbury, he is mocked by 'a lusty Country lasse' amongst the spectators who then challenges Kemp to dance a mile with her:

> I lookt upon her, saw mirth in her eies, heard boldnes in her words, and beheld her ready to tucke up her russet petticoate, I fitted her with bels: which she merrily taking, garnisht her thicke short legs.... The Drum strucke, forward marcht I with my merry Maydemarian: who shooke her fat sides: and footed it merrily to Melfoord, being a long myle.

Kemp's prose here is a burlesque of festive clichés, in which the 'merry' interlude has a mundanely realistic outcome: 'I gave her (besides her skinfull of drinke) an English crowne to buy more drinke, for good wench she was in a pittious heate.' Yet amid the rustic comedy, Kemp pays tribute to her skills: 'to give her her due, she had a good eare, daunst truely, and wee parted friendly.' Not only did she stay the distance, but she 'daunst truely', and Kemp's unsparing version of pastoral does not ridicule the country lass so much as disclose the unglamorous and workaday circumstances in which the rural morris was now flourishing. Was the Sudbury woman a leading figure in her village troupe? John Forrest says that this is one of the first references outside courtly circles to women dancing the morris – Maid Marion was always represented in summer revels by a transvestite man or boy – and, together with Dudley Carleton's report in the same year, cited earlier, of the 'mad wenches' going from house to house in apparent imitation of Kemp, it appears to be evidence of increased female participation in the rural morris as it became an itinerant and commercial activity. If women morris dancers were indeed a novel phenomenon, Kemp seems to take it in his stride, suggesting that he was aware of developments in the provinces.

The other episode takes place in Chelmsford two days before the Sudbury incident, when a teenaged girl (apparently a servant) asks to be allowed to dance with him 'in a great large roome', and insists on adopting 'the olde fashion with napking on her armes'; 'to our jumps we fell', Kemp reports, and '[a] whole houre she held out: but then being ready to lye downe I left her off'. The slightly ambiguous phrasing suggests that Kemp exhausted his partner but was himself extended by the encounter: he admits that 'the strongest man in Chelmsford' might not 'have done so much' (11). There were respectable precedents for women dancing the morris indoors, at court and in great houses, but they were rather distant ones for a servant girl in an urban middle-class home, and once again Kemp seems to be caught up in a fairly new trend. (His performances of the dance in stage jigs would obviously have been with boys or men in female roles). One critic suggests that the girl's preference for 'the olde fashion' means that she treats the dance 'as a frozen form, still limited by medieval rules', just as, in his view, the Sudbury woman represents a 'pure rural tradition' that is no match for Kemp's entrepreneurial design.[52] Yet both incidents suggest a challenge that is more mobile and versatile than this. The 'merry Maydemarian' is ready to take to the road, perhaps indicating some experience in the dancing processional entries that brought touring morris teams into each village, as evoked in a 1594 madrigal by Henry Morley:

Who comes here all along with bagpiping and drumming?
O 'tis the Morris-dance I see a-coming.
… see how trim they dance and trickly.[53]

Meanwhile, the Chelmsford girl's eagerness to pit herself against a famous theatrical exponent of the morris hardly suggests a timid confinement to traditional conventions, which in any case were mutating as they spread through the population. The new enthusiasts for morris dancing often lacked costumes and equipment of their own: Kemp has to lend bells to both partners, and the teenager's desire to wear napkins tied to the shoulders is presumably to permit her the same swirling movements that Kemp would obtain with the long dagged 'points' or scarves attached to his upper arms (see Figure 3.3).[54] These gladiatorial encounters have nothing to do with the fulfilment of Kemp's wager, but their inclusion in the narrative suggests that for him they were significant moments in the unfolding challenge of his journey.

Notably absent from Kemp's reporting of these encounters is what many of his readers might have expected or hoped for: the sexual suggestiveness that was central to his jigs and repeatedly condemned in the morris dance by its Puritan critics. He similarly avoids bawdy innuendo in another moment where the material seems to invite it. During the last stage of his dance in Norwich's streets, he accidentally treads on the skirt of a bystander, so that 'off fell her peticoate from her waste', to her immense confusion: 'now had she her cheeks all coloured with scarlet' (25). 'I was sorry for her', remarks Kemp, 'but on I went towards the Maiors.' The incident seems calculated to make the point that he is not the sly clown of the jig but the hero-traveller with greater things on his mind. In a similar way, the earlier episodes reveal the dancer who is ready to play with his audience but only in ways that promote his own virtuosity. Purging the morris of its licentious associations is just one of the ways in which Kemp gives his project (in the *Nine Daies Wonder* at least) a distinctly conservative cast. As we saw, he holds himself aloof from disorderly revel, portraying himself as the disciplined athlete rather than as a lord of misrule; he frames his journey with a civic send-off from London and an official welcoming reception by the Lord Mayor of Norwich, and along the way he aligns himself with the pillars of regional society: 'Sir Thomas Mildmay standing at his Parke pale, received gently a payre of garters of me: gloves, points, and garters, being my ordinary marchandize, that I put out to venter for performance of my merry voyage' (10). It is significant that this pledge by Mildmay, head of Chelmsford's leading family, is the only one to be identified by name, allowing Kemp to make his 'ordinary marchandize' redolent of a courtly, quasi-chivalric bond: gloves and garters, 'gently' received, are briefly transfigured by the exchange. Prominent local gentry like Mildmay often defended country festivities as important to social stability, and Kemp's bargain with him reaffirms the networks of rural hospitality and patronage that kept them alive. By so doing, he aligns himself with a 'traditional' English culture that was challenged by puritan reform, and insists that there is nothing socially disruptive about his mercenary venture.

Kemp no doubt knew that the morris tour 'was built on an old model, namely the tour of local villages by the May Lord and his liverymen ... prior to a church ale, to raise funds and meet costs' (Forrest, 270), and he taps into the mythology of such figures with his assumed persona of 'Cavaliero Kemp', the benevolent holiday monarch, and his increasingly charismatic progress towards Norwich. Nearing the end of his journey, he is mobbed on country roads by 'young men and Maydens ... at everie myles ende',

> One crying the fairest way was thorow their Village: another, this is the nearest and fairest way, when you have past butt a myle and a halfe: an other sort crie, turn on the left hand, some of the right hand: that I was so amazed, I knewe not sometime which way I might best take ... (21)

The dance to Norwich was the only one of the mad voyages to have a long afterlife in the public imagination, and this is surely because it was felt (without being examined too closely) to be the supreme enactment of a national institution – an idea never found to be incompatible with the oddity of the enterprise. (Kemp's personal celebrity may have helped to keep the story alive, but if he had walked or run to Norwich it would not have achieved the same effect.) For later connoisseurs of English heritage, the morris dance had its monument in Kemp, shorn of its farcical baggage and epitomized in a memorable display of endurance and flair. Yet, as with the inclusion of Lepton's ride to York in Edmund Howes' chronicle, we need to ask what the survival of Kemp's dance as popular history really signifies.

Recent criticism has resisted the sentimental or 'patriotic' view of Kemp's achievement and has tried to situate his venture in the enterprise culture that was gaining momentum in England at the turn of the century. This argument becomes more substantial, I think, when we revise the somewhat unhistorical assumption that Kemp was turning the 'traditional' morris into a commodity, 'dancing carnival into market' as Max W. Thomas pithily puts it, and acknowledge that the dance was already rapidly diversifying when he conceived the enterprise. A reasonable hypothesis is that Kemp noted the commercial popularity of morris dancing in the regions, and also saw that the current vogue for travel stunts provided a launchpad for his own idiosyncratic version of a morris tour. But we may wonder if Kemp's motivation was purely economic, as he pondered his options after leaving the Globe. The wagers he made on his journey were a test of skills that had been sidelined by his professional colleagues, and while he needed the money, he may have craved even more the prestige and the outlet for his creative energies that the stunt provided. It was a gamble in more ways than one, a risky career move, and in the event it did not improve his professional fortunes: his follow-up dance to the Continent was reportedly not a success, and although on his return he made a new start in the theatre, he died in poverty only two years later.[55] This is not to gainsay the fame that was garnered by his exploit, but not all the publicity was welcome, as his response to the ballad-makers shows, and when Ben Jonson revised his play *Every Man out of his Humour* for publication in 1600 (a quarto edition that came out at much the same moment as the *Nine Daies Wonder*), he spiced up his ridicule of the knight Puntarvolo's intended wager-journey to Jerusalem with a topical allusion to Kemp's stunt. 'Would that I had one of Kemp's shoes to throw after you', says Carlo Buffone to Puntarvolo[56] (whose addiction to 'returns and strange performances' proves fruitless), picking up on a detail of Kemp's trip that was apparently well-known before it saw print, and which in the published account represents a curious moment in the final moments of the venture. When his overseer George Sprat loses sight of him in the Norwich crowd, it is because for the only time on the trip (or so he claims), Kemp cheated:

> Passing by the Market place, the presse still increasing … on I went towards the Maiors, and deceived the people, by leaping over the Church-yard wall at S. Johns, getting so into M. Mayors gates a neerer way … (24–5)

'I must confesse I did not wel', Kemp admits as he tells us that he was forced to repeat the last stage three days later, but the shortcut nonetheless produced the venture's most tangible memorial:

> But now I returne againe to my Jump, the measure of which is to be seene in the Guild-hall at Norwich, where my buskins, that I then wore, and daunst in from London thither, stand equally devided, nailed on the wall. (25)

Kemp may have set a precedent: Thomas Coryat was later to hang his shoes in the church porch at Odcombe, and in 1618 John Taylor, in what was obviously by then a rather stale ritual, tried to get an unwilling Lord Mayor of York to buy his boat to put on permanent display.[57] The nailed-up shoes are testament to a wager successfully completed (even if a single pair is unlikely to sufficed for the whole journey), but what they much more potently symbolize is the leap that violated the terms of that wager. The point is made forcibly by the modern plaque that has replaced Kemp's shoes, located not in the Guildhall but on the wall that he is thought to have leapt over. Kemp pretends to tell us about his trespass in the interests of full disclosure, since his pamphlet is supposed to be setting the record straight, but in fact the story is organized to highlight the idea that his gigantic leap was an inspiration that could not be contained by mercenary priorities. It was, in exact terms, an eccentric move, deviating from the prescribed path of his dance, and when it quickly came to epitomize the journey, an important piece of the myth of English individualism was put in place. Looking at it in historical context, however, in relation to Kemp's recent exclusion from theatrical leaping, the growing controversy over games and sports, and his own venture into the competitive territory of the professional morris tours, we might ask whether his jump is not also a defiant, opportunistic response to the difficult cultural conditions in which a performer of his kind now found himself. In 1586, as a recognized jester in the service of the Earl of Leicester, Kemp earned five shillings for 'leaping in a ditch' to entertain his employer during a military campaign in the Netherlands;[58] by the end of the century, as a freelance jig-maker eking out his skills in trying his hand at the travel stunt, he felt the need to assert himself in ways that invited wonder but also a good deal of ridicule, not least from his erstwhile theatrical colleagues.

## Notes

1 G. Sarton, *Simon Stevin of Bruges* (Bruges: Saint Catherine Press, 1934), 282–3.

2 Quoted in R.J. Forbes, ed., *Principal Works of Simon Stevin* (Amsterdam 1966), 5.

3 J.G. de Mendoza, *The Historie of the great and mightie kingdome of China*, trans. R. Parke (London, 1588), 22.

4 Reported by Giovanni Botero in his *Delle Cause della grandezza … delle Città* (Venice, 1589), 309. This account first appeared in English in the 1606 London edition of Botero's book (18).

5 J.H. van Linschoten, *Discours of voyages into ye Easte & West Indies* (London, 1598), 40–41.

6 See the image on a map of China in G. de Jode's *Speculum Orbis Terrarum* (Amsterdam, 1593). R.J. Forbes mentions repeat performances on 17 May 1613 for the Elector Palatine, in 1621 for the Venetian ambassador, and in 1633 for the Queen-Dowager of France (*Principal Works of Stevin*, 6–7).

7 John Wilkins, *Mathematicall Magick* (London, 1648), 155–61.

8 Laurence Sterne, *Tristram Shandy*, ed. G. Petrie (Harmondsworth: Penguin, 1967), 135.

9 See Simon Schama, *The Embarrassment of Riches* (New York: Knopf, 1987), 363.

10 D.J. Struik claims that the trip was 'frequently repeated, certainly until 1790', and that similar devices were still in use when he wrote his book (*The Land of Stevin and Huygens* [Dordrecht: D. Reidel, 1981], 139).

11 L.E. Harris, *The Two Netherlanders* (Cambridge: W. Heffer, 1961), 189–95.

12 Francis Bacon, *The Advancement of Learning*, in M. Kiernan, ed., *The Oxford Francis Bacon*, vol. 4 (Oxford: Clarendon Press, 2000), 63.

13 L. Daston and K. Park, *Wonders and the Order of Nature, 1150–1750* (New York: Zone Books, 1998), 147.

14 Burton, *Anatomy of Melancholy*, 2.92–3.

15 Randall L-W. Caudill, *Some Literary Evidence of the Development of English Virtuoso Interests in the Seventeenth Century* (D.Phil. thesis, unpublished, University of Oxford, 1976), 220.

16 Daston and Park, *Wonders*, 292.

17 William Bourne, *Inventions or Devises* (London, 1578), 13–15, 99.

18 Draft dated 26 July 1608 (*Works of Francis Bacon*, 11.66). See J.C. Davis, *Utopia and the Ideal Society* (Cambridge: Cambridge UP, 1983), 123.

19 Jessica Wolfe, *Humanism, Machinery, and Renaissance Literature* (Cambridge: Cambridge UP, 2004), 71–2.

20 Chamberlain, *Letters*, 1.247. The exploit was still the subject of bemused gossip several months later: see Ch.1, note 52.

21 Anthony Nixon, *True Relation*, B4 and *passim*. Bush may have been one of a gentry family of that name based in Dilton, Wiltshire, about 40 miles from Lambourn. His family arms were also displayed on the pinnace. One of his name graduated from Eton in 1600. The exploit is described with an explanatory line-map in Katherine and Richard Bradley, 'William Bush – The Flying Boatman', *Berkshire Archaeological Journal* 71 (1981–82), 57–70.

22 'With regard to the effect of the exploit upon the fabric of the tower, it is to be noticed that the pinnacle at the north-east angle shows signs of seventeenth-century work…. [Restoration work in 1891–2 noted that] a crack in the north wall of the tower, nearly three and a half inches wide, went through the whole thickness of the wall, so that there must have been a tremendous pressure and strain on that side at one time' (John Footman, *History of the Parish Church of … Chipping Lambourn* [London: Elliot Stock, 1894], 108).

23 Anthony à Wood, *Athenae Oxonienses*, ed. Philip Bliss (London, 1815), 2.143.

24 James A. Williamson, *English Colonies in Guiana and on the Amazon, 1604–1668* (Oxford: Clarendon Press, 1923), 51.

25 Robert Johnson, *The New Life of Virginea* (London, 1612), F2v. See Chapter 5 for further discussion of the Virginia 'adventure'.

26 For his expedition to Guiana with two ships in 1610, Sir Thomas Roe raised just under £2000 (Williamson, *The English in Guiana*, 52).

27 Samuel Purchas, *Purchas His Pilgrimes* (Glasgow: James Maclehose, 1905–1907), 16.358.

28 It is hinted at in Nixon's insistence on Bush's 'care in a case of such danger, where he had so great a wager, as the venture of his life, in the performance of his undertaken voyage' (*True Relation*, C2v).

29 When a play about the brothers was quickly fashioned from Nixon's account, it was dedicated 'To Honour's favourites', a clear reference to those who found themselves 'cold and unactive' in the cautious world of Jacobean diplomacy. See my edition in *Three Renaissance Travel Plays* (Manchester: Manchester UP, 1995), 9–10.

30 W.G. Perrin, ed., *The Autobiography of Phineas Pett* (London: Navy Records Society, 1918), 21–2.

31 Roy Strong, *Henry, Prince of Wales, and England's Lost Renaissance* (New York: Thames and Hudson, 1986), 57.

32 See Agostino Ramelli, *Le Diverse e artificiose machine* (Paris, 1588), esp. ch. 29. A similar lack of conceptual thinking is still evident in John Bate's *The Mysteryes of Nature and Art* (London, 1634).

33 Wolfe, *Humanism, Machinery, and Renaissance Literature*, 14.

34 John Taylor, *The Praise of Hemp-seed*, 32.

35 Richard Helgerson, *Forms of Nationhood: The Elizabethan Writing of England* (Chicago: U. of Chicago Press, 1992), 137. He points out that by the seventeenth century 'chorographies become books where county gentry can find their manors, monuments, and pedigrees copiously set forth' (133).

36 *Kemp's Nine Daies Wonder*, ed. G.B. Harrison (London: Bodley Head Quartos, 1923), 13. All references are to this edition. I have slightly adjusted Kemp's confusing punctuation.

37 *CSP Domestic* (1598–1601), vol. 275, 93.

38 This expedition may also have links with the hopping competitions for prizes that John Heywood records in his proverb collection: 'Him that hoppeth best to have the ring' (*John Heywoodes woorkes*, London, 1566).

39 Ronald Hutton, *Stations of the Sun* (Oxford: Oxford UP, 1996), 268.

40 *Old Meg of Herefordshire* (1609), sig.B–v.

41 David Wiles, *Shakespeare's Clown* (Cambridge: Cambridge UP, 1987), 24.

42 Local records confirm the annuity for life that Kemp says was granted him by the Lord Mayor of Norwich.

43 This is much disputed, but the argument made by H.D. Gray has never been convincingly refuted, and nobody has come up with a good explanation for Kemp's denial in *Nine Days Wonder* that he 'delivered gifts to her Majesty', which Gray thinks refers to Kemp's pirating of *The Merry Wives of Windsor* ('The Roles of William Kemp', *Modern Language Review* 25 [1930], 266–9).

44 Grindal's Article 44, cited by John Forrest, *The History of Morris Dancing, 1458–1750* (Toronto: Toronto UP, 1999), 192.

45 Philip Stubbes, *The Anatomie of Abuses* (London, 1595), 107.

46 Forrest, *History*, 259.

47 Forrest, *History*, 269.

48 Forrest, *History*, 271.

49 James Knowles, ed., *The Entertainment at Althorp* (1604), in Jonson, *Works*, 2.409–10.

50 Max W. Thomas, '*Kemps Nine Daies Wonder*: Dancing Carnival into Market', *PMLA* 107 (1992), 519.

51 Helgerson, *Forms of Nationhood*, 229.

52 Thomas, 'Dancing Carnival into Market', 518–19.

53 Quoted in Forrest, *History*, 274.

54 Forrest notes that there is no documentary evidence for this being the 'olde fashion'; Kemp may simply regard it as a traditional substitute for the proper costume item.

55 Wiles, *Shakespeare's Clown*, 37–41.

56 Ben Jonson, *Every Man out of his Humour*, 4.5.118 (*Works*, 1.386); and see Bruce Boehrer, 'The Case of Will Kemp's Shoes', *Ben Jonson Journal* 7 (2000), 271–96.

57 John Taylor, *A Verry Merry Wherry-Ferry Voyage* (London, 1622), B7.

58 Wiles, *Shakespeare's Clown*, 32.

# 4

# Bills of Adventure

The fashion for travel exploits that erupted in the 1590s may have been a distinctively English phenomenon, but it did not confine its activities to domestic roads and waterways. Richard Ferris saw his heroic efforts matched, and possibly trumped, by rowing ventures across the North Sea to ports like Flushing and Antwerp, and we have already noted the dance across the Alps with which Will Kemp reportedly followed up his morris dance to Norwich. John Taylor also expanded his range of activity in later years to include continental destinations. Thomas Coryat, whose 1608 walk to Venice will be examined in the next chapter, was seen as one of the most flamboyant participants in the vogue, with the book of his travels being marketed as the record of a prodigious feat. Coryat was undertaking a genuine tour and not simply cashing in on the current craze, but it seems likely that some of the impetus for his epic walk came from the newsworthy exploits at home, which had turned the gamble on a journey into an idiosyncratic ordeal and created conditions favourable to Coryat's brand of showmanship. On his return from the Continent, Coryat hung up his shoes in the porch of the church in his home village, a memorial that recalled the preservation of Kemp's buskins at Norwich; and in the collection of mock-panegyric verses that prefaced *Coryats Crudities*, the account of his journey that was published in 1611, the many tributes to his durable footwear (one writer affirms that 'Twixt Venice and Flushing on foote he went / With one paire of shoes ere they were halfe spent'[1]) become ironic testimony to a thoroughly eccentric performance, one that aligns him not only with Will Kemp but with the unlikely travel 'experiments' noted by John Chamberlain and the students of Gray's Inn. (See Plate 4.) The wit who made this call in the prefatory verses –

Hang up his shoes on top of Powles,
Tyed to his name in parchment rowles,
That may be read most legibly
In Tuttlefields and Finsbury (60)

– knew that it would link Coryat's tour-de-force with exploits like hopping up the stairs of St. Paul's and Banks' ascent of the cathedral tower with his horse

Morocco, and Coryat himself seems to have relished the additional publicity that came from having his travels burlesqued in this way. The individualism that shines out of the *Crudities* made him a perfect exemplar of the new kind of tourist, but it also predisposed him to undertake his European adventure as a kind of stunt and to allow his peers to present it as an extension of the current vogue for mad voyages.

In one important respect, though, the domestic mad voyages were themselves inspired by foreign adventure, since most of them were structured as wagers on the 'putting out' model described in the previous chapter, a kind of bet that had been associated with overseas travel for decades previously. Fynes Moryson, we recall, suggested that 'this manner of giving out mony upon these adventures, was first used in Court, and among the very Noble men', and he claims that the 'long journy' performed 'with courage and discretion' was an admired part of their repertoire, distinguishing it both from 'ridiculous adventures' and, implicitly, from habitual betting 'upon a horserace, or speedie course of a horse, under themselves, yea upon a journey on foote' – the standard domestic exploits of 'Gentlemen in our Court'.[2] Moryson does not say (and perhaps did not know) when exactly the courtly wager on travel abroad began, but his remarks firmly associate it with a time when tourism was restricted to the upper classes and prompt us to look for its origins in the early Tudor period, even if evidence is lacking of aristocratic 'putting out' on Continental trips before the 1580s. As we shall see, however, the travel wager was by no means confined to courtly circles and had its origins in much earlier arrangements amongst pilgrims and merchants. Fynes Moryson is preoccupied with rescuing what he regards as a worthy custom from its debasement by the lower orders, but he cannot have been unaware that various types of gambling on long-distance journeys had long been a feature of commercial life and were given an impetus by the growth in overseas ventures of all kinds during the sixteenth century.[3] His assumption that an exclusive courtly ritual had been hijacked by 'men of base condition' is one we have already had occasion to question, and while the patrician wager on travel clearly was an important model for a number of adventurers in this period, it was itself shaped by wider developments in late-mediaeval Europe. The model for the kind of bargain involved in the mad voyages turns out to have surprisingly deep and diverse roots.

This chapter will examine the surviving evidence for wager-journeys beyond British shores in the early-modern period and consider their significance within the larger picture of English travel abroad as tourism and trade links expanded. The practice of betting on foreign journeys has never received more than cursory notice, presumably being regarded as trivial and incidental to the main purposes of travel, yet it is in many ways a useful barometer of changing conditions and attitudes, and provides a way of looking at some significant developments. Because wagers were a prominent feature of aristocratic play, they are part of the story of recreational travel in Renaissance Europe, but they also represented an important stage in the development of insurance practices and ways of thinking about risk. The hazards of moving around were obvious to all, but Europeans were slow to come up with ways to provide systematic cover against those hazards and for a long time questioned the morality of doing so: life insurance was banned in several countries, and even the provision of cover for commercial ventures, though its origins could be traced to marine insurances in the ancient world, had a tortuous history in mediaeval legislation. As we shall see, the private wager offered ways of underwriting a travel project in an environment that was struggling to develop ways of facilitating and indemnifying risky ventures.

At the same time, it is clear that by the late sixteenth century the 'bargain of return' was turning into an increasingly contentious transaction. A good deal of our information about its workings is derived from legal records, since those who took such bets often refused to pay up and were taken to court, and critics of travel often saw wagering as emblematic of the moral and physical hazards to which the tourist exposed himself. The wager on a journey abroad provided the occasion for numerous satires on the self-advertising traveller, of which this early Jacobean epigram by the playwright John Cooke is a representative example:

> *Ficus* was fat in body and in purse,
> And unto Sea is gone himselfe to purge,
> Some fifteene hunderd markes he did disburse,
> To receive three for one, a tempting scourge,
> To whip my Gallant up the surging seas,
> And daunce to Venice with a whistling winde ... [4]

Cooke's probably fictitious gallant owes something to Will Kemp's recent dance across the Alps and anticipates Coryat's walk to Venice a few years later, but it takes aim at a class of fashionable and improvident young men (1500 marks, or £1000, was more than 20 times Coryat's wager in 1608) who were widely regarded as giving foreign travel a bad name. Barnabe Riche sees the wager as enabling the excesses and follies of early Jacobean tourism:

> Heere comes a spruce fellow now ... Would ye knowe who it is? Mary sir, it is a *Traveller*, not of those sort that endevor their travels, but of purpose to growe into the hieway of Experience, for the better service of their Prince or Country: but of those whipsters, that having spent the greatest part of their patrimony in prodigality, wil give out the rest of their stocke, to be paid two or three for one, upon their returne from *Rome*, from *Venice*, from *Constantinople*, or some other appoynted place. These fellows in their journeying doe so empty themselves of the little witte they carried out, that they can make no better return than their mindes full fraught with farre fetcht follies, and their heades over burthened with too many outlandish vanities ... [5]

From vignettes of this sort we can build up a sketchy picture of adventurers who typically wagered three-for-one on European destinations but sometimes demanded higher odds on journeys to cities in the Middle East. But these vivid satires, numerous as they are, give a one-sided view of the wagering craze in early Jacobean England, and we need to dig behind them to get a proper sense of what such contracts entailed. What purposes did these wagers serve? What was their role in the expansion of English ventures abroad during the sixteenth century? And to what extent were they shaped by the habits and priorities of older forms of travel?

Traditional forms of journeying certainly left their mark upon the travel wager. One of the most ancient, Christian pilgrimage, might seem an unlikely stimulus to betting practices; yet in the process whereby the ritual journey to sacred shrines gradually gives way in northern Europe to cultural pilgrimage and recreational tourism, we can identify continuities that help to explain why wagering ventures took the form that they did. When William Rowley gives as example of a mad voyage 'the travell to *Rome* with the returne in certaine daies', we are looking at a stunt with venerable antecedents. English travel to Rome was a tradition that stretched back as far as the early centuries of the Christian Church, involving not only pilgrims but ecclesiastical officials and diplomats, and long before visiting Rome became hazardous for Protestants, there were guidelines in place to provide for the traveller's return or failure to do so. Legal agreements made by departing mediaeval pilgrims might stipulate the elapsing of a year and a day before a will was executed, or determine the period of time before a pilgrim's presumed widow could remarry. Of course, to invest 'the returne in certaine daies' with significance is strictly at odds with the high mediaeval conception of pilgrimage, which accords meaning only to the destination, the shrine or holy place towards which the journey is directed. The homeward trip is purely incidental. Yet in practice the pilgrim's return could be crucial to the fulfilment of his mission, as in the case of a penitential journey. Diana Webb reminds us that from 'the mid thirteenth century on, the inquisition of southern France imposed pilgrimages … on repentant heretics; they were told where to go, and required to bring back a certificate of performance from the church authorities at their destination.' The same was true of the secular courts in cities in late medieval Flanders, which had lists of approved destinations, including English shrines like Canterbury and Walsingham.[6] The custom existed in Rome itself during the 1580s, when it was imposed by the Jesuits on miscreants at the English College.[7] Voluntary pilgrims also expected and received certificates in what appears to have become a virtually automatic ritual. Fynes Moryson, describing his visit to Jerusalem in 1596, reports that the Franciscan friars 'gave to each of us freely and unasked (as it seems of custome) … a testimony under the seale of the Monastery, that we had beene at Jerusalem'. This sounds as if such documents had become standard souvenirs, along with the 'little stones' from the city's monuments that the travellers were also given. But Moryson adds that the friars 'for better credit' added to the certificates 'some remarkable signes of our faces and bodies' (*Itinerary*, 2.37), and it seems likely that this practice, which may have originated with the needs of penitents, took on a fresh significance with the advent of travel wagers. Another of Moryson's anecdotes indicates why some might have thought the identification procedure important: he relates that an English gentleman of his acquaintance, fearing a Turkish ambush on his way to the Holy Land, got cold feet about completing the last stage of his journey and 'returned into England without seeing Jerusalem … only carrying with him a counterfet testimonie and seale that he had been there, because he had put out much money on his returne' (1.461).

Pilgrimage appears to have provided the template for various kinds of speculation on a journey. By the sixteenth century, if not before, it became customary for Dutch pilgrims to leave a will containing a legacy in favour of a friend, stipulating that if they came back safely 'the friend would have to return double the value of the legacy',[8] and European archives reveal a variety of wagering agreements on journeys to religious destinations in late-mediaeval times. There is some evidence that these bargains provided a viable way of funding obligatory pilgrimages, where the offender needed money to make the voyage to a shrine and found a backer who would be able to claim his property and goods if he failed to complete the journey in the appointed time. One historian cites the example of an intending pilgrim to Rome who made a deferred sale of his house and goods (at a reduced price) in order to raise funds for the trip and to provide for his family during his absence, on the understanding that the sale would be cancelled if he returned and confirmed if he did not. The property is effectively the object of a wager on the owner's return, as was even more clearly the case in a contract where no money changed hands until he did so, at which point the owner would receive the purchase price without having to give up the house, while if he did not come back the 'purchaser' would get the house free.[9] It is not always clear from the records whether the expedition to cities like Rome and Jerusalem specified in such deals was a traditional pilgrimage or something more like cultural tourism, but as late as 1614 a dispute in Rotterdam about an architectural feature in Rome was settled by a journey thence that must have been presented as having a pious purpose, since the terms of the wager required it to be verified by the Pope himself.[10] (We shall return to the subject of papal responses to travel wagers.) In cases where the trip was not made purely for the purposes of wagering, secular and religious motives were no doubt often mixed, as they had been in *bona fide* pilgrimages for centuries. And while there were certainly constraints in mediaeval Europe on blatant gambling with one's salvation, they are visibly crumbling in announcements like the one made in Utrecht in 1518, 'that in the city of Bergen op Zoom a lottery shall be held for the needs of the holy church where one may win not only indulgences but also many other precious prizes'.[11]

Worldly transactions were certainly much in evidence during earlier periods of religious travel. John Evelyn, visiting the Continent in the 1640s, reported an old story that the founders of the Jerusalem church in Bruges in 1428, Italian merchant brothers who made several trips to the Holy Land to study the Holy Sepulchre church which served as their model, paid for its construction via 'divers great wagers' that involved walking between Bruges and Antwerp.[12] At about the same time as this alleged stunt, Lollard allegations of abuse included the claim that pilgrims borrowed excessively or even stole money for the journey; fifteenth-century advice manuals were full of information about exchange rates and reminders that a bed bought in Venice could be traded half-price on the return trip; there were contractual regulations governing some itineraries, like the provision that if a pilgrim bound for Jerusalem died on the sea passage from Venice half his fare would be refunded to his executors; and the quest for spiritual absolution became increasingly mixed up with the purchase of indulgences, eventually to the point where a vow of pilgrimage could be commuted by buying a dispensation from one's local church.[13] Another kind of speculation involved paying a professional pilgrim to make the journey on one's behalf, a practice that had its origin in wealthy patrons subsidising the travelling costs of their followers in order to benefit spiritually from their pilgrimage.[14] This sort of investment in a journey offered no financial reward, but it did involve a pecuniary gamble on personal salvation. Its only disadvantage, perhaps, was that one had to forgo the pleasures of the actual trip – a growing consideration as recreational travel became more common; and by the early sixteenth century the increasing prevalence of secular motives for long-distance journeys, which might include but not be confined to visiting Christian shrines, meant that the practical transactions involved in pilgrimage were ready to mutate into new forms of speculation on personal travel.

As traditional pilgrimage, then, shades into the cultural and educational tourism favoured by European humanists, and as itineraries begin to entertain what had to be seen as voluntary risks, the concept of gambling on a journey acquires a more material cast, and the travel wager appears to become entrenched in English practice. But it is worth searching a little further in mediaeval ideas of pilgrimage for the origins of the custom. The voyage of faith was in its earliest forms closely bound up with notions of endurance and ordeal: Celtic Christianity in the first millennium developed the concept of 'wandering for God', an indeterminate peregrination by land or sea that symbolised the essential homelessness of mankind on earth, and that seems to have served an early need for missionaries in post-Roman Europe. As monastic settlements grew, it was discouraged as a form of vagrancy, just as with the development of judicial systems, various forms of trial by ordeal, including the act of setting adrift, were abandoned as methods of punishment or of establishing truth. But the idea of the unpredictable journey that tests constancy and reveals God's purpose remained a potent one, as Chaucer's retelling of the tale of Constance shows, and it was a prime means of giving a Christian shape to the peripatetic motif in classical epic.[15] The Ulyssean hero becomes the knight-errant of mediaeval romance, and his venture is a test of the values of his culture. It is already taking the form of a wager in a late fourteenth-century poem like *Sir Gawain and the Green Knight*, where the challenge issued by the mysterious stranger to play 'a Christmas game' with the young knights of Arthur's court commits Gawain to a contract that must be fulfilled by a long and difficult journey. The 'beheading test' to which he is subjected seems to derive from ancient folklore, but Gawain's fortitude in meeting its conditions is ultimately less significant than the ethical challenge he faces in his temptation by Sir Bertilak's lady, for it is only by resisting her advances and being honest with the host that he is able to survive the return blow. Seth Lerer has argued that *Gawain* is influenced by an 'advisory literature' that 'geared itself to the establishment of social values for the European aristocracy', and the wager, which only Gawain of all the Round Table knights is ready to accept, turns his ordeal into a public performance and becomes a test of the ideals of gentility that were already being promoted in conduct manuals for the ruling class and those who aspired to join it.[16] In this way the poem affords a glimpse of mediaeval developments that would be important for the Tudor culture in which English tourism abroad took shape. Gawain's venture involves him in an elaborate game with seemingly impossible conditions, but it is also a test of character, of travel used well. Moreover, as R.F. Green points out, no one in the poem 'appears to regard the fact that the compact had been made in play as a reason not to honor it', and although mediaeval lawyers apparently grappled with the issue of whether 'joke' contracts could be regarded as actionable, one legal historian suggests that 'it never seems to have been argued … that wagering contracts were bad at common law, either on the ground of mere frivolity or on the ground that their enforcement was contrary to public policy'.[17] As we shall see, this did not prevent numerous later disputes in the courts over the enforceability of the 'bargain of return', but the wager on a journey seems nonetheless to have helped enable a spirit of adventure in English culture by providing a way of framing the hazards and challenges of contemporary travel, one rooted primarily not in the law but in the codes of honour operating amongst those who took advantage of foreign opportunities.

## Knightly Adventures

The monetary wager on a journey may have been one of a plethora of noble betting games, but its capacity to rehearse the travels of crusader and knightly pilgrim as a kind of formal game would have lent it a particular status in courtly circles. The favoured destinations of long-distance 'putting out' by men of rank later in the sixteenth century (and pursued well into the eighteenth) were all borrowed from the itineraries involved in those two activities: Rome, Jerusalem, Cairo, Damascus, Constantinople. Within the terms of an Arthurian honour code like the one found in *Gawain*, these were logical sites at which to test patrician virtue and prowess, and this archaic ideal clearly provided a useful container for the aspirations of the new tourism. It allowed travel to be reconceived as adventure, in a manner familiar from epic and romance literature but largely absent from the actual practice of the late-mediaeval

English nobility, a few soldiers of fortune notwithstanding. Crusades were effectively a thing of the past, despite a few attempts at revival, but the old expeditions could be playfully recuperated to give the rituals of knightly behaviour a new and fashionable context in which to operate. Whether long-distance wagers on this basis were undertaken with any regularity in the early sixteenth century is not possible now to establish, though Rome and Jerusalem were popular pilgrimage destinations and obvious candidates for a 'bargain of return'; my own belief is that the wager-journey to most of the Middle Eastern sites became an institution only after mid-century, when tourism was expanding and the cult of chivalry was revived at court after several decades of political and religious turmoil. But these exploits were constructed on foundations that had been laid in the fifteenth century, when chivalry ceased to be a practical system for martial training and became 'a social code for an aristocracy engaged primarily in civil occupations'.[18] The tilt yard and other chivalric pastimes largely replaced the battlefield as the proving-ground of honour, and the new-style chevalier had open to him a range of opportunities for peaceful foreign adventure.

We catch a glimpse of this transitional process in the eventful career of Sir Peter Carew, a Devonshire gentleman soldier who in the 1530s was attempting to make his way at court. In early Tudor England the Ottoman regime enjoyed considerable prestige: the antiquary John Hooker, in his Elizabethan biography of Carew, recalled the mood in 1535 when, after war began between the Ottomans and Hungary, 'the most common speeches in the court were of the great Turk, and of the royalty of his court, and what a mighty prince he was, and how that he had conquered the strong city of Buda, in Hungary; which so pierced the young lusty gentlemen of the court, that many of them were desirous to travel and see the same.' Hooker reports that Henry VIII 'did like well of their minds, but nothing liked to adventure them in so perilous a journey', and initially refused permission. When he relented, a group including Carew travelled to Venice, by sea to Ragusa, and reached Constantinople in 1541. The rest of the story sheds an interesting light on the ways in which venturing to such destinations often needed to be managed.

Although Carew's party carried a safe conduct from the Ottoman ambassador in Venice, nonetheless in Constantinople

> they were examined what they were, and what business they had there to do: who being loath to be known to be gentlemen, and that their travelling should be only to see the Turk's court, for so they might have put themselves in great peril, they alleged that they were merchants, and came to seek for alum, under which colour they remained there about six weeks, or two months, and in that time they visited the Turk's court, and saw him twice or thrice in his greatest royalty and glory'.[19]

Many a later visitor to the Ottoman world was to fall under suspicion of being a spy, and the expedient adopted on this occasion was apparently common practice: decades later Thomas Gainsford was still recommending to travellers 'this acceptable title of Marchant. For so I must tell you, that except you advise with your selfe for this denomination in many places of the world the excuse of curiositie will not serve your turne: For you shall be taken for a Spie, and a dangerous Hypocrite, such is the jealousie of Kingdomes toward wanton Travellers.'[20] As we shall see, another way of avoiding trouble was to claim to be travelling on a wager, and Carew and his friends might have done better to avail themselves of this device, for their cover was eventually blown: 'they, being not able to dissemble their own estates, were in the end had in great suspicion, and like to have been taken and apprehended, had not the French Ambassador stood their good friend, for he did not only advise them of the same, but, also helped to convey them away in a merchant ship.' Their appetite for adventure not yet curbed, they heard about the siege of Buda by a Hapsburg army and went off, via Milan, 'to see the manner of these wars'. On getting home, Carew entertained the court with his adventures, of which 'nothing was more liked than the description of the Turk's court and the manner of his wars'.[21] What is notable from this account is that despite the political perils of the visit, and the general belief that Turkish military power threatened the security of Western Europe, the gentlemen of Henry's court are ready to engage with this formidable culture as tourists and observers and adopt merchant dress only because they know that their curiosity about other people's wars might be misinterpreted. There is no hint in this account that England's knights see themselves as squaring up to an old enemy or gathering intelligence that might lead to military advantage.

It is tempting to conclude from this that Carew and his friends have entirely abandoned the crusading ethos of a previous age and are taking advantage of a new era of mercantile ties with the Ottoman world. Yet their military interests also suggest a complicated relationship to the chivalric ideals that were still strongly present in courtly rhetoric and had quite recently been invoked by Henry VIII to mobilise resistance to Turkish expansion. Crusading indulgences continued to be collected in England, and her knights were prominent in the Order of St. John (Carew's brother Philip was a member) of which the King was official Protector. Little came of renewed calls to holy war, but as Christopher Tyerman argues, in 'such an atmosphere crusading attitudes and aspirations circulated naturally', and the sixteenth century repeatedly bears witness to 'some survival of receptiveness to crusading sympathies amongst the vigorous classes.'[22] We need to ask what happened to these aspirations in the changing circumstances of Mediterranean travel after 1540, when the Order of St. John was dissolved and the funding it provided for crusades dried up.

There was a long tradition of knightly voyages to exotic regions that mingled stories of the crusades with travel for its own sake: Hakluyt assiduously collected several of the latter, including an early twelfth-century account of one who 'being of a good wit, and being desirous to increase and enrich the same with the best things … left his Countrey for a time, and … went through Egypt, and Arabia, and found out many things which he desired to his owne private contentment'.[23] The idea of travel as private recreation was thus not new at the start of the Tudor era, but it received a boost from cultural developments in the fifteenth century that saw humanist scholars and artisans on the move and fostered the idea that even official journeys offered opportunities for novel experience and diversion. Surviving narratives of diplomatic travel on the Continent from the early 1500s, though written according to strict conventions, reveal an appetite for sight-seeing and on occasion what J.R. Hale calls 'a strong atmosphere of holiday', reflecting the kinds of cultural stimulus and relaxation available in sophisticated urban environments.[24] Hale's examples are not English, and we shall need to consider later whether the relative insecurity of English travellers on the continent, especially after the Reformation, fostered the attitude that recreation abroad was often best regarded not as an amiable engagement with foreign communities but as a calculated gamble. Earlier I suggested that turning the act of travel into a game may have been part of an ambivalent English response to humanist ideas about recreation and physical accomplishment, and in the European arena it was to offer a way of negotiating some treacherous situations, as we shall see. But at the dawn of the early-modern period, and before serious debates about the moral and educational value of tourism had made much impression in England, the sport that was offered by opportunities to travel might well have been seen as 'the custome and usage of noble chivalry' that Caxton in 1484, voicing the perennial appeal to a golden age of nobility, approvingly contrasts to the practice of contemporary knights who prefer to indulge in idle pastimes and 'playe at dyse'.[25]

In comparable fashion, the impulse towards adventure was already emerging in late-mediaeval accounts of knightly pilgrimage that break with the strictly utilitarian guides to the holy places that preceded them. The chronicler of Sir Richard Guylford's visit to the Holy Land in 1506 devotes a considerable section of the narrative to the homeward journey, describing tempests and near-shipwrecks, and observes that Sir Richard makes these an occasion for piety and grateful commitment to further pilgrimage,[26] but the emphasis on his tribulations, like the rich accounts of city-hopping in Hale's analysis, creates a story whose logic and interest are almost entirely secular. By the late fifteenth century guide manuals for English pilgrims going to the Holy Land via Venice were offering advice on possible side trips on the way home (including dangerous landmarks like Mount Etna and Vulcano in the Aeolian Islands), and the oft-repeated observation that both Pliny the Elder and Empedocles fell victim to their curiosity about volcanoes merely fuelled the tendency to supplement a biblical geography with a map of classical sites that had to be visited. We get a glimpse of the continuities involved here in a surviving example of the standard legal formula used to draw up the terms of a bet on travel. First printed in 1590 but almost certainly ratifying a long-established practice, this document (in which the abbreviation I. is used like our modern X) stipulates that the traveller intending to go 'to the Cittie or towne of I. in the province or country, sometime called I. or to the place where the said City or towne sometime was scituate & stoode' shall be repaid an agreed sum within so many days of his return provided his journey is

> lawfully proved, shewed & declared or published ... by certificate or testamoniall under the seale of the said city or towne of I. or of the next city, towne, or place having a common seale, unto the place where the said Citie or towne of I was scituate or stood.

Some such *pro forma* could have been used equally by the pilgrim searching out biblical landmarks in the Middle East and by the tourist looking for classical ruins, and even the revealingly specific example of a certificate issued 'under the seale of the state of Venice in I.' points both to the northern humanist love affair with Italy, and to the package tours for pilgrims to the Holy Land that were organized by the Venetians until the closing years of the sixteenth century.[27] And while it is unlikely that voluntary pilgrims of an earlier period entered into many such agreements, it seems that the slippery business of proving a visit to legendary and vanished sites was one that was well established long before humanists went touring with a copy of Virgil in their hands. The pilgrim industry was adept at identifying elusive locations, like the exact site of St Paul's conversion or 'the stone from which St. George mounted his horse when he went to combat the dragon.'[28] These canny inscribings of the Middle Eastern landscape fed the imaginations of knightly travellers and pilgrims and greatly increased the number of 'authentic' sights and experiences that tourist guides were able to point out. This was particularly the case in Jerusalem, where the geography of Christ's ministry and passion had been carefully reorganized to provide a convenient tour and locations found to match almost every detail of the scriptural account.[29] Pilgrims did not always believe what they were told, of course, and Protestant resistance to literal claims and a more sophisticated attitude to evidence are increasingly apparent amongst sixteenth-century visitors to the Holy Land. But being aware of manipulation by tourist guides in Jerusalem did not prevent generations of travellers from having themselves dubbed Knights of the Sepulchre, despite Erasmus' withering satire on the practice, and obtaining a certificate to that effect.

In a number of ways, then, pilgrimage practices shaped the tourist experience in early-modern Europe, and provided for the emergence of the bet on travel by creating the need for verification and by setting up financial mechanisms to manage (or substitute for) the experience of the journey to holy shrines. We have noted also some evidence from the Low Countries of sixteenth-century pilgrims making deals of the 'putting out' variety, though this is much less likely to have happened in Reformation England, where the outlawing of religious travel meant that the fashion for wagers coincided with the growth of secular tourism. At the same time, Protestant travellers never lost their appetite for visiting sites associated with the biblical story, and could hardly help regarding such trips as a kind of pilgrimage; while the voyage to the Middle East, especially after Jerusalem fell to the Ottomans in 1516, fell into the category of glamorous risk. It was at this point, we may conclude, that the courtly game of gambling on travel found a congenial focus in the journey to the Holy Land, choosing to treat the expedition as a latter-day crusade or challenge to knightly honour. Most of the travellers who were made Knights of the Sepulchre by the Franciscans in Jerusalem would have taken home their certificates simply as a memento and not in order to win a monetary wager, but for many of them it was nonetheless evidence of an ordeal successfully completed. The Middle East was not a cosy destination for European tourists and pilgrims, who were particularly conscious that whatever 'was scituate or stood' in historical sites there had often been damaged or obliterated by forces they felt to be extremely hostile. Henry Timberlake declared in 1603 that 'the holy Land [bears] the name only and no more: for all holyns is cleane banished from thence, by those Theeves filthy Turkes and Infydells that inhabit the same', and he ordered his priorities accordingly: 'having my certificate sealed by the Quadrian, and a letter delivered unto me, to showe that I had washed my selfe in the River of *Jordan*, I departed from Jerusalem.' 'Shall I come backe againe and tell you of *Jerusalem*, *Tyrus*, and *Sidon?* alas they are but names,' lamented Thomas Gainsford, recognising that the evacuation of these cities' hallowed qualities by the infidel occupiers posed a special challenge to the traveller who sought to report a proper experience.[30] One implication of such remarks is that to produce evidence of having been there may be a necessary substitute for real engagement with the place, an admission that the game of verification is a way of structuring an uncontrollable or inaccessible experience so that the traveller returns with his honour intact. The won wager, the risky challenge overcome, the proof snatched from peril might all be demonstrations of the venturer's integrity, his capacity to meet a testing ordeal, but they also reveal something about the difficult English encounter with the foreign in this period, a difficulty that is rooted both in the contingent circumstances of Continental travel in this period, and in the ambivalence about recreation and practical education that I discussed earlier.

## Merchants' Wagers

The impulse to wager on a journey was also stimulated by the rapid expansion of international commerce, which was not as far removed from the courtly game of travel as Fynes Moryson perhaps wanted to believe. It has long been argued that the larger project of European exploration from Columbus onwards was conceived in quasi-chivalric terms, and as Richard Helgerson has emphasised, the commercial imperatives of the early voyagers were regularly clothed 'in the rhetorical (and sometimes in the literal) garb of chivalric knights'.[31] The dressing up of merchants as knights-errant was a favourite tactic of Elizabethan popular writers, for reasons cogently explained by Helgerson, but it reflects earlier developments within the cult of chivalry itself whereby speculative ventures came within the purview of the late-mediaeval nobility and gentry seeking new avenues of self-advancement. Diane Bornstein describes this as 'the mingling of chivalric and commercial interests that characterized the taste of a fifteenth-century knight',[32] and while England's was not a mercantile aristocracy in the manner of Italy or the Netherlands, neither did it affect the intense disdain for commerce so prevalent amongst the French nobility. Whether they were privateering on the high seas or leading expeditions to open new trade routes, England's knights pursued profit as much as glory and in so doing, must have found themselves increasingly inhabiting the same climate of risk and opportunity as the merchant classes. Certainly the gambling culture that emerged in the sixteenth century tended to link rather than distinguish the two groups. English merchants enjoyed betting on many of the same kinds of topics as the upper classes: the instances of merchants' wagers given by Gerard Malynes in his *Lex Mercatoria* (1622), such as a 'Wager upon a sonne or a daughter to be borne' or 'a Wager to run with another' are very similar to those that Fynes Moryson claimed were popular amongst gentlemen, while Malynes' further examples, '[t]hat such a Cardinall shall be elected to be Pope ... that the pope of Rome, or the Emperor, or any other great personage shall die within the yeare', or that 'such a town [i.e. under siege] is taken', recall the patrician betting habits of Renaissance Italy as well as the popular wagers made on the Antwerp Exchange.[33]

More significant, perhaps, is Malynes' conclusion that 'Wagers between Merchants are many times more done for sport and recreation than for gaine: for over great wagers are against good manners, and may concern a Merchant much in reputation and credit' (199). This strengthens the idea that the gambling ethos operating in the merchant community was not unlike the one to be found in aristocratic circles where the wager was a matter of honour and ostensibly not about making money. By the early seventeenth century it may have been quite normal for merchants with an eye on upward mobility to present their gambling practices as a gentlemanly diversion, but it would be wrong to assume that the 'playful' wager in these circles was simply a case of patrician values filtering down to the world of trade. It also sprang from the complicated workings of premodern commerce. Hazardous though it is to speculate about the *mentalités* that governed the conduct of mediaeval merchants, we know that their bargains were subject to tight regulation by canon and civil law and were made within a corporate ethos that understood competition in different terms from those of modern economics. Marketplace rivalry in mediaeval Europe, suggests Jean-Christophe Agnew,

> was commonly understood to be a contest between rather than among individuals, an assumption reflected in the long-standing and widespread diffidence toward speculative investment and fully negotiable commercial instruments. The market was a *place* and the trader was expected to make his ventures within it, not against it. The costly 'freedom' that towns and cities offered their merchants and craftsmen was, in many respects, a freedom *from* the hardships of what would now be called unrestricted competition.[34]

Guilds and urban fraternities offered, like courtly circles, a space for controlled play, and the wager on the sex of one's next child was simultaneously an affirmation of virility, social confidence and financial sufficiency. As Agnew puts it, a good deal of economic activity expressed 'an older commercial athleticism that put wit, honor, and manliness periodically to the test', and wagering on an agreed topic offered a way of speculating with spare capital that avoided restrictions on unlawful profiteering and at the same time celebrated the reciprocity of business relationships. The market was a network of kinship and acquaintance, as Alan Everitt explains, one in which 'commerce could not be impersonal. In the absence of banks a man's "credit" could only be what he was personally reputed to be worth in his local community'.[35] Malynes' claim that merchants' wagers were not about financial gain is largely the same polite fiction that was offered about bargains between gentlemen, but it makes the point that the commercial world placed as much importance on social ritual and performance as did the ruling elite.

The mediaeval statutes that regulated gambling and speculation at all levels of society were built upon important distinctions in Roman law, which banned 'the playing of games of chance (*alea*) for money or value' but made some allowance for 'games of skill and manly worth (*ludi virtutis*)' that could be played for limited stakes.[36] This provided the warrant for certain kinds of competition between men of status, whose recreations and contests were thereby distinguished from common gaming, and it is easy to see how it might offer a rationale for bets that involved an element of ordeal, a physical challenge or perhaps a major test of nerve, as in the wager on long-distance travel. For merchants, of course, the gamble on a journey could never be simply play, and the high stakes that were involved in more ambitious voyages led, as we shall see, to the kinds of bargain that may have occasioned Malynes's warning against 'over great wagers'. Such deals were to lend a topical edge, in the closing years of the sixteenth century, to Shakespeare's treatment of a popular story in *The Merchant of Venice*. Antonio's acceptance of the flesh-bond (in what Shylock calls 'a merry sport') confidently declares his worth and his willingness to put it to the test. But as Shakespeare's scenario also indicates, the playful wager could entail substantial hazards, and just as gentlemen might frivolously gamble away an entire patrimony, so the merchant was at risk of overreaching himself in a period of growing wealth and speculation. Investing in the fate of cargoes at sea, as Antonio effectively does in signing the bond, was probably the mediaeval merchant's earliest formal bargain with uncertainty, in the codes of marine insurance that emerged from Barcelona and Genoa in the fourteenth century; however, Shylock is not offering to insure Antonio and the latter is gambling on future returns, as all long-distance traders were forced to do. Malynes's distinction between sporting wagers and the unseemly pursuit of profit may be partly aimed at merchants who are tempted to ape the gambling habits of the nobility and bet excessive sums on trivial occasions, but his words also hint at the temptations to speculate offered by an expanding overseas trade, turning the custom of wagers into an unwarranted game with men's fortunes and the nation's prosperity.

Shylock's wager would not have been upheld in English or Dutch courts on the grounds that it offended against public morals, and less extreme bargains, such as bets on the life expectancy of a private individual, were often rejected for similar reasons, or because they were found to be frivolous. As an instance of the latter, Malynes states that a 'Wager laid who shall eate or drinke most, is unlawfull' (198). But the disputes over what constituted valid speculation went deeper than this. In his chapter on merchants' wagers, which Malynes says he is providing because 'divers Civilians have intreated' him to do so, he seeks to address a situation where the legal position was often unclear and the courts were struggling to deal with a growing number of challenges to wagering agreements. The civil lawyers were clearly troubled by an increase in what they saw as foolish or tasteless topics for a bet and insisted that 'all Wagers laid must be for honest causes' (197–8), but they also made a distinction, according to Malynes, between straightforward wagers on a particular event, in which he who predicts correctly wins his opponent's stake, and the more complicated kind of speculation that was involved in 'putting out' – '[w]here a thing delivered or by a covenant made with another person, the same is promised to be restored, and double, treble, and ten times the value thereof unto the partie with whom the Wager is made, if the matter in question or doubt do not take effect' (197). What seems to be at issue here is the complicated kinship of gambling and insurance in early-modern Europe, and the legal attempts in the later sixteenth century to put the latter on a more solid footing. Malynes introduces the topic by pointing out that 'matter of Assurances is comprised' under the heading *de Sponsionibus* ('Of Wagers') in previous legal writings. It is found there because in mediaeval jurisprudence no theoretical distinction was made between insurance and other ways of betting on future outcomes. While we now make a clear distinction between playing with risk and providing against unavoidable mishap, premodern commerce was slow to do so, and in an age before actuarial calculations, as Lorraine Daston suggests, a generalised conception of risk became 'the defining characteristic for a distinct class of legal agreements, the aleatory contract, thus combining such socially diverse practices as insurance, gambling, and annuities under a single heading, and emphasizing their similarity'.[37]

The overlap is plain in one of the principal financial devices used to underwrite commercial voyages, the bottomry 'loan', whereby a shipowner borrowed money to complete a voyage and pledged his ship as security. On successful completion he pays back the principal with interest – Malynes says that 'the use payed for the same is verie great, at 30, 40, and 50 *procent* … within so many daies after the voyage ended' (171); the lender can claim the vessel in the event of not being paid but does not get his money back if the ship is lost. More complicated than a loan, the arrangement is less than a proper insurance since it does not cover the risk to cargoes or compensate the merchant for loss of his ship. It is essentially a wagering agreement in which, as Samuel Marshall puts it, the one partner 'takes upon himself the perils of the sea, and the other compensates him by a share of the profits of the adventure'.[38] Contracts of this sort drew criticism from religious authorities, who regarded the lender's gains as usurious,[39] and lawyers responded by arguing that the hazards of commercial enterprise justified the profits accruing from loans and speculative investments. Malynes similarly insisted that bottomry was different from ordinary lending at interest, since the loan is '*Pecunia trajectitia*, because that upon the lenders danger and adventure it is carried beyond or over the seas,' whereas 'money letten at interest is delivered on the perill of the borrower' (171). The argument that one could put a price on risk was basically accepted by the early sixteenth century, when various forms of insurance became an established part of business in northern Europe (having been established in the Mediterranean countries two centuries before), but this did not mean that merchants abandoned the wager as a way of handling transactions, with some intriguing consequences in the expanding world of early-modern trade.

We can see how the kind of 'putting out' bargain summarised by Malynes might facilitate a risky maritime venture for which capital investment was otherwise difficult to obtain, and could offer limited guarantees to both sides. But it is also apparent that the terms of the wager ('double, treble, and ten times the value') may be only loosely related, if at all, to the material value of the goods in question. As such, it resembles the pilgrim's deferred 'sale' of his house – forfeit if he did not return – to someone prepared to fund his travels, that I cited earlier. The rewards are more like those of a lottery than a rational investment. This was clearly a problem for those who were attempting to regulate the insurance business and eliminate fraud and inappropriate speculation, but it reflected the habitual methods of risk-management that preceded the emergence of premium insurance, at a time when cover was provided instead by various kinds of monetary bond that usually took the nominal form of a loan. Insurance of some kind was clearly essential to the development of seagoing commerce, and the maritime loan can be traced from antiquity through refinements in mediaeval Europe like the bottomry system described above, but it remained a device that saw both parties gamble on outcomes rather than providing total security to the one insured. In fact, it was the lender rather than the borrower who was better able to minimise personal risk in these wager-like agreements, usually by spreading his investment: a venerable example for early-modern merchants was the Roman statesman Cato the Elder, who in Sir Thomas North's translation of Plutarch's *Lives* is described as

> a great usurer, both by land and sea: and the usurie he took by sea, was most extreame of all other.... He would have them to whom he lent his money unto, that trafficked by sea, to have many partners, and to the number of fifty: and that they should have so many ships. Then he would venture among them for a part only.... And thus he did not venture all the money he lent, but a litle peece only for his part, and got marvellous riches by his usury.[40]

North's forthright description of this much-admired figure as a usurer illustrates the moral dubiety that still attached to guaranteed profits, or the attempt to indemnify oneself against the workings of providence, and it may be that the model of the wager held its appeal for men of business partly because it foregrounded the role of chance in human affairs, which created a space for the exercise of what Agnew calls 'commercial athleticism', and implied a kind of equity that was tarnished by the broker's mercenary calculations.[41]

Moreover, when full-fledged insurance policies began to be issued in the fourteenth century, it soon became clear that they suffered from various practical limitations, such as the problem of proving the value of cargoes lost or verifying the circumstances of a robbery or shipwreck at a time when long-distance communications were very unreliable. To get around many of the disadvantages of formal insurance, merchants often disguised such deals as a wager, which meant that they could avoid the exceptions that might typically be raised by insurers and ignore legal restrictions on the percentage of any loss that was recoverable.[42]

Many of the early premium contracts drawn up in Italy and Catalonia were modelled not on a loan but on a contract of sale, because it was considered essential that the parties had a proprietary interest in the object at risk. The policy-holder had to be the owner of whatever was insured and effectively sold his interest in it to the insurer for the duration of the cover. This provision tied the premium to the value of a cargo and prevented speculation on risky ventures: it was designed to prevent insurance becoming a mere wager. However, the development of maritime commerce soon made such policies too restrictive, and by the end of the fifteenth century a common device in contracts was the insertion of a clause stating that the agreement between the parties did not depend on either having a proprietary interest in the uncertain event at stake, so that (for instance) someone putting down money on a commercial voyage would not have to prove that he owned the ship or its cargo in the event of either being lost. The clause was a realistic response to an increasingly complex commercial world, where traders and investors were not necessarily dealing with personally owned cargoes or vessels but still needed protection against risk, and it also made room for the speculative activities of a merchant fraternity playing on the exchange with spare capital, and catered to its taste for wagering on a variety of topics. (An example would be the betting on 'futures' that was stimulated by East-Indian trade, when the price of cargoes that might take years to arrive had yet to be determined.) Setting up insurance in the form of a wager – usually betting a fixed sum that would cover the 'insured' against a failed venture, but would be paid to the 'insurer' out of the profits of a successful one – offered a simple and congenial way of doing business. It relied of course on trust and the kind of face-to-face dealing that characterised the mediaeval marketplace, and as commerce became more impersonal, the blurring of the line between *bona fide* indemnities and speculative gambling by those with no material investment in a voyage was to be a source of increasing anxiety and led to various restrictions on wagering in the Mediterranean countries and subsequently in the Netherlands. Nonetheless, the wager was too useful to mercantile culture to be abandoned, at least until alternative financial instruments were fully developed and accepted. And merchants proved adept at masking its more profitable uses with the same mechanism that had originally been employed to purge insurance cover of wager-type speculation, by dressing their bargains as a contract of sale.

Let us take a specific example, from the private transactions that occurred within England's first joint-stock venture abroad, the Russia (later Muscovy) Company established in the mid-sixteenth century. A London grocer called George Stoddard, writing apparently in 1554 or 1555, recorded a bond into which he entered with one Francis Robinson:

> Fras. Robynson to G.S. 200$^{s}$ [shillings, i.e. £10] lent him in form following: that F.R. must gyve me 200£ for the sayde 10£ at my coming from Russer, wher one Inglys ship hath bene alredy, and yf I marre before I go thether, then the sayde Fransis must repaye me 20£ agayne, and I must give his wyffe a payer of sleves of velvet, but if I deye he must have it.[43]

This looks like a clear example of 'putting out', whereby Stoddard crafts an astute deal: first, his 'loan' of £10 will be repaid double if for any reason he cannot make the trip, and his only obligation will be a gift to Robinson's wife. This part of the transaction is designed to circumvent the usury statutes by masking a lucrative indemnity as a sale – an example of what one writer characterised as 'open divers contractes and bargaynes that are used to avoide usurye'.[44] But Stoddard's real harvest is to be reaped at the end of a successful voyage, when his original stake of £10 will be repaid twenty-fold. Such large odds seem to have been the preserve of merchants and must have involved more than simply wagering on an uncertain outcome. Francis Robinson would have taken Stoddard's money not so much as a gamble from which he might make £10, but as some kind of premium for carrying the risks of a venture from which he himself hoped to profit. In other words, both men were betting on a successful return and probably created what was later known as a 'non-gaming' wager as a vehicle for the enterprise. Robinson was a charter member of the Russia Company and may have owned one of the vessels or put money into goods to be exported to Russia.[45] We do not know what the formal contract, if any, drawn up between the two looked like, but Stoddard's own record presents it as a monetary gamble on his safe return and hints at a rationale for the odds of 20-to-1 in the fact that it covers a voyage to a difficult destination where, nonetheless, 'one Inglys ship hath bene alredy' – in other words, a risky venture for both parties but one offering each of them a potentially large return. We should look briefly at the background to this highly speculative bond.

The agreement between Stoddard and Robinson was made at a time when London's merchants were contemplating what was being talked up as one of the investment opportunities of the century. In 1553 an expedition of three ships under the command of Sir Hugh Willoughby had left the Thames in search of a north-east passage to Asia and the Spice Islands. They were armed with Sebastian Cabot's 'Ordinances' laid down for 'the mysterie and companie of the Marchants adventurers' in 'the discoverie of Cathay, and divers other ... places unknowen',[46] and although two of the vessels were lost when they were forced to winter in a Norwegian inlet and their crews, including Willoughby himself, froze to death, the *Edward Bonaventura* captained by Richard Chancellor managed to reach Archangel and, after an arduous overland journey to Moscow in mid-winter, established contact with the Russian emperor, Ivan IV (known as 'the Terrible'). On his return in 1554, Chancellor's adventures were widely publicised and within a year the articles of a newly formed Russia Company were being drawn up in preparation for a second voyage, which left England in May 1555. Stoddard must have been a member of that expedition, and while reports of the first venture had made clear the danger and difficulty that awaited a second voyage, they had also shifted attention from Cabot's hypothesis about the North-East Passage, which he was forced to admit had 'ministred matter of suspition in some heads, that this voyage could not succede for the extremitie of the North Pole, lacke of passage, & such like',[47] to the solid prospect of obtaining a share of Russian trade. As suggested, both the risks and the potential payoff are reflected in the odds of 20-to-1, and because so novel a venture was scarcely insurable in conventional terms, the merchants seem to have resorted to a familiar mechanism of wagering in order to enhance their investment in the project.

We can only guess at what precisely Francis Robinson expected from the deal, but some of Stoddard's other transactions show how he was able to profit from foreign ventures when he himself acted as the fixed end of the compass. His ledgers reveal that he supplied one R. Leds with 'a Dager' for which he will 'paye me at his comynge from Venys a nage or gelding which shalbe worth 40$^{s}$ at the leste'. This sounds like a shrewd bargain, and one perhaps driven by the traveller's urgent need for a weapon. Arthur Edwards, a merchant who went to Russia on Chancellor's ship, made a deal with Stoddard whereby the latter supplied him with a cash advance of £24.10s together with 'a sword gerdyl', 'a foullinge pease' and 'a spanyell', on the understanding that Edwards would bring back a stipulated number of sable and marten pelts as payment. Edwards also took to Russia '2lb whyt sheugar candy which he promised me woolde be sold ther for 30 Rubbylls or more a lb, so that he haythe promysed 8 frenche crownes of yt at the lest'.[48] Edwards's promise may have been a rash one, for the merchants who made the second voyage to Russia in 1555 were offered a fraction of this figure for a pound of sugar,[49] but Stoddard (as a grocer by profession) presumably saw an opening for trade in this commodity when he joined the 1555 expedition – which also included Edwards – and must have received acceptable compensation for his investment in the earlier voyage. Stoddard's ledger entries freely mix conditional wagers on the sex of a child or a future marriage with commercial gambles on foreign ventures, and in both he usually employs the mechanism of a sale, suggesting that it was his habitual practice to avoid the charge of excessive profiteering by presenting his speculative bargains as straightforward dealing in commodities.

At the same time, the trade in commodities was by no means always incidental. Stoddard's bargaining for sable and marten pelts reveals his awareness of them as luxury items, and his transactions appear to be an attempt to get round the rules on private dealing laid down by the joint-stock company. From the very start of the Muscovy enterprise, strenuous efforts were made to forestall unofficial trade: Cabot's ordinances had specified that merchants on the first voyage 'shall not make any shew or sale of any kind of marchandizes, or open their commodities ... without the consent, privitie, or agreement of the Captaines', and the articles of the Russia Company sought to ensure that individuals would not profit at the expense of the joint-stock operation.[50] The repeated warnings against private dealing during such ventures indicate that it was common practice to make money on the side, and in their contracts with Stoddard, Robinson and Edwards must have been in breach of their oath not to 'privately bargein, buy, sell, exchange, barter, or distribute any goods' for personal gain or for 'the private lucre, gaine, or profit of any other person'.[51] Unauthorised dealing carried its own kind of risk, but it was a gamble worth taking in ventures where opportunities abounded and unprecedented profits were dreamed of. As it happens, the animal furs that Stoddard coveted were a principal focus of this illicit traffic, and by 1560 the company was already reporting that high-quality pelts were in short supply because of it.[52] Private trade of this sort did not necessarily have anything to do with wagering, of course, but given the tendency to structure the 'bargain of return' as a commercial transaction, merchants and sailors who made such bets on long-distance travel had good reason to engage in a few deals of their own. Stoddard's case also suggests that the covert acquisition of prized furs was part of the challenge he and his business partner had devised, and raised the stakes in a way that made the gamble more attractive to both. It was inspired not only by the prospect of illicit trade, however: there was a clear model for the wager in the official methods of maritime funding, since the 'putting out' phenomenon in its pure form – shorn of any trade in material goods – closely resembled the 'bill of adventure' drawn up on behalf of investors in joint-stock operations like the Muscovy and East India Companies. In both the adventurer lays out a sum that will be multiplied in the event of a successful return, and the term 'bill of adventure' was regularly used in either case. One difference is that the articles of the commercial voyages generally specify that his share of the overall 'benefitt profit encrease and gaine'[53] will be paid to his executors or a nominated individual in the event of his death en route. Stoddard's private deal with Robinson, in contrast, stipulates that 'if I deye he must have it [the original outlay of £10]', as in other examples of the travel wager where the traveller gambles on his own safe homecoming. But it seems clear that the two provisions spring from a common entrepreneurial culture, even if we can also see why the private wager was increasingly treated with suspicion.

The East India Company records furnish some interesting evidence of wagering activity that met with official disapproval. In the commission drawn up for the second voyage in 1604, the prohibition of 'all unlawfull gameinge especialie dice play' by 'the poore ungoverned Marriners' is followed by a warning about

> the practise of divers in the last voyadge who to furnish them selves with money in that unthrifftie ymployment ingaged them selves to pay 3 for 1 upon their retourne, & thus haveing wasted their wage by such unthriftie meanes went aboute to laye a scandall upon the Companie, alledgeing they were oppressed by necessitie in the voyadge to enter into those excessive usurious contractes to mayntayne their lives.[54]

The first voyage in 1601–1603 was financed on a subscription basis, and the ordinary mariners were granted a share in the venture, equivalent to two months' pay, as well as a two months' advance on their wages so that they could provision themselves for the journey. Factors were promised a share of between £40 and £200 depending on their status.[55] The Company minutes allege, however, that some of its employees used monies advanced to lay wagers on their return, having complained that their regular pay was too paltry to provide a sufficiency. It is notable that this should have happened right at the outset of the East Indian venture, which suggests that those engaged in maritime trade may already have been accustomed to wagering on their participation in regular commercial voyages, like those of the Levant Company in the preceding decade. The East India directors appear to have granted the thirty-six appointed factors and crew a share in the enterprise partly in the hope of discouraging them from private trading during the voyage, but this merely prompted some of them to speculate before they left with the advances received. Evidently not everyone's financial hopes were realised, perhaps because of the perennial problem of getting wagers paid out, and the Company felt compelled to rebut the charge that participants had been driven to gamble in this way by low wages and a negligible return on their lengthy investment in the voyage. In calling their wagers 'usurious', it was falling back on the traditional moral objection to letting money breed, but the men who made these bargains would have taken the same view as Fynes Moryson in defending travel wagers, that it made sense to 'dispose of their money with their friends upon reasonable adventure of gaine, (which in absence they cannot otherwise dispose to profit)' (*Itinerary*, 1.429). Mariners, after all, had nothing to spend their money on while at sea and were away for years on an East Indies voyage. The Company was at pains to prevent its employees from making any profit at its expense, gradually tightening the rules until, in the commission for the eighth voyage in 1611, it instructed that factors and other minor officials 'att Bantam & elswhere' who were 'tradeinge for their owne particuler gaine with the greate neglect of ours' should be paid in situ only enough to cover their essential needs, with the rest of their wages 'paid in England to such as they shall consigne them unto'.[56] Similarly, no-one on board Company vessels was allowed to acquire more goods than would fit 'within his proportioned chest of allowance for this voyadge'.[57] It is hardly surprising that employees should have turned to other methods of profiting from the journey.

Ordinary mariners who were paid only a few shillings a month were hardly in a position to put out on a wager, and the Company's warning must have been aimed more at the factors, agents, pursers and ranking sailors who were paid upward of £4 a month and were granted a modest share in the venture that they were tempted to supplement by other means. This was nonetheless a notable extension of travel wagering to the middling and lower orders of English society, made possible by the growth of long-distance commerce, and it further tests Fynes Moryson's distinction, cited earlier, between the 'desperate actions for gaine' by 'men of base condition' who 'put out their money in Tavernes', and the 'long journy' performed 'with courage and discretion' by travellers of whom he approves. For while there was often no doubt an element of desperation in the attempts of East India Company employees to improve their fortunes, their voyages were hardly the 'ridiculous adventures' that Moryson detected in the vogue for travel stunts,[58] and like Stoddard's deals, the wagers they took out replicated in miniature the investment system used to fund the joint-stock venture.[59] The Company directors seem to have shared Moryson's dim view of working men's wagers, motivated principally by a distrust of any transaction associated with the voyage that did not feed their profits, but in many cases the claim that employees 'wasted their wage' may have been accurate only from the Company's point of view.

## Managing Risk

As we saw, the use of wagers by the mercantile community was bound up with the evolution of insurance in mediaeval and early-modern Europe, and it was initially indispensable to the type of cover that took longest to gain acceptance, which was life insurance. Betting on lives was one of the most popular topics of wagering, and in fact a wager on the survival prospects of public figures like a monarch or pope is commonly described as the only kind of life 'policy' in general use before the modern era.[60] Such bets were called 'insurances' by merchants in Renaissance Italy, and they tended to hold back the development of other forms of life cover, since gambling on lives raised some obvious questions about the morality, and perhaps the safety, of seeking to guess what providence had in store for other human beings and hoping to profit from the event.[61] Nonetheless, the risks involved in an expanding marine commerce generated the need to protect not only ships and cargoes but those who were moving them around, and there is evidence of insurance against capture by pirates being available by the end of the fifteenth century to Italian and Spanish merchants travelling overseas, as well as opportunities to insure the lives of one's debtors.[62] It was possible to buy insurance against the occurrence of plague in Genoa in the same period. Moreover, the sale of annuities to raise public funds in several European countries since mediaeval times[63] indicated a readiness to put a price on life expectancy that could be, and was, deployed into providing indemnities against personal risk.

Insurance of lives may have been treated primarily as a form of betting (which is essentially what it is), but by the sixteenth century it had become something more than a sporting wager, and in England at any rate, where life insurance was tolerated more readily than on the Continent, it seems to have been used by travellers in conjunction with 'putting out' to provide safeguards within what was otherwise a purely gambling venture.

The way this worked was clearly set out in 1622 by Gerard Malynes in his discussion of '[a]ssurances ... made upon the lives of men':

> A traveller undertaking a voiage to Jerusalem or Babylon, delivering out money payable at his returne, will providently assure a summe of money upon his life, either to secure some men that do furnish him with money to performe his voyage, and to put forth the greater summe, or to leave some meanes unto his friends, if he should die and never returne.[64]

This suggests that it was common practice to borrow money in order to increase one's wagering stake ('to put forth the greater summe'), and to repay the debt either out of winnings or through a life insurance policy in the event of non-return. It amounted in effect to a hybrid contract that indemnified the traveller and his backers against financial loss whatever the outcome, and might have offered another reason why travel wagering could be seen as a type of usury. Certainly it indicates that insurance was available for recreational travel abroad by the early seventeenth century. The scenario sketched by Malynes has points of contact with the pilgrim's practice, noted earlier, of framing wagers in a way that would look after the needs of those left behind, but it makes more sophisticated provision for the secular versions of the Middle Eastern voyage that emerged in the post-Reformation era, and in the process overrides the clause found in the standard form for life insurance that appeared in William West's much-reprinted legal handbook, specifying that a policy holder must be 'now in health and well, and meaneth not to travaile out of England'.[65] If this latter stipulation was made with would-be tourists in mind, it was one that had to yield to the demands of the emergent Grand Tour. As Malynes implies, insurance was an important adjunct to the wager not just as a means of enlarging the sum that the traveller could put out, but also because the journey itself might not be possible without it. Fynes Moryson tells us that the travel wager was a fundraising device: to finance the trip, prospective travellers borrowed against the money they expected to get from the bargain of return, and he points out that this is the only way those 'not rich by patrimony' can be 'inabled to that expence'. But such debts often needed to be guaranteed, so the traveller might be engaged in a complicated mix of borrowing, insurance purchase and gambling on anticipated returns in order to get his venture off the ground. It was a volatile type of portfolio, and tended to stoke the doubts of those who were sceptical about the value of tourism rather than reassure them that its risks had been safely assessed.

There is a sense in which the entire argument about voluntary travel in this period devolves on to the question of what kind of gamble it represents. To take a bet on a journey logically requires a calculation of the risks involved, and there is an element of this in the different rates of putting-out that were agreed (five-for-one on the adventurous 'voyage' to Constantinople may have been the highest odds available to tourists) and in the arguments that sometimes arose when bond-holders refused to pay up after a traveller's successful return. After walking to Venice and back in 1608, Thomas Coryat had to go to court to claim his winnings, and his indignant riposte to insinuations about 'the smalnesse and commonnesse of my Voyage' was to play up his dangerous trip through the Alps, where he risked falling into a 'Tartarean lake sixe times deeper then Pauls tower is high', and his ability in Italy 'to passe throgh that carnificina, that excruciating and excarnificating torture of the *Spanish Inquisition*'.[66] Coryat characteristically elaborates the element of ordeal, but as a measurement of the risks involved it remains rather impressionistic. His wager of approximately three-for-one (£40 put out to earn 200 marks, or just over £133) seems to have been fairly typical for ventures within western Europe, of which the Venice trip was probably the most popular, but in the Chancery dispute over Coryat's case (to which I shall return in more detail) we can see the difficulties involved in putting a price on adventure. The Yeovil merchant who took his bet evidently claimed that the journey had become routine, a known and negligible set of risks, and therefore not worth such a large payout, to which Coryat responded by pointing to the rigours of the Alpine road and the particular dangers faced by Protestant Englishmen in certain parts of Italy. The marine insurance industry had long had adjustable premiums for different destinations and seasons and political conditions,[67] so there were precedents for the kind of calculation needed to assess particular routes, but the attempt to use them, however loosely, in setting up travel wagers led to numerous challenges at law, and it brings to our attention some core issues within the long-running controversy in England about the value of foreign tourism.

The measurement of travel risks could never be an exact science, of course, but finding ways of predicting and averting them nonetheless preoccupied both insurers and the writers of guide books. Mediaeval Europe had arrived at a fair understanding of risk as something that could be quantified (for the purposes of issuing life annuities, for instance), but it lacked a *mathematics* of probability – something that, for reasons that are still much debated by historians of science, did not emerge until the 1650s.[68] Before this, the mathematical question of how to calculate odds was mainly tackled in relation to gambling problems such as the division of the stakes in an interrupted game of cards or dice. The commercial sphere worked with norms and averages established by collective experience, but it did not have the theoretical apparatus or statistical systems required to model economic or social outcomes. For the most part, probability remained the province of gambling rather than actuarial forecast, and the journey undertaken as a wager was a kind of dare against (vaguely conceived) odds. We should hardly expect it, then, to provide evidence of statistical thinking, even of an embryonic kind. And yet the background to the intellectual puzzle of probability – the problem of how to measure the likelihood of a particular outcome using relevant existing data – nonetheless had a real bearing on the emerging phenomenon of tourism. This is because the argument about the value of travel experience was part of a larger debate about the dependability of different kinds of testimony.

Travel, like gambling, is the deliberate courting of chance. Early ideas of pilgrimage had been strongly providential, ceding the role of chance or fortune to the will of God, to the point where the boat without oars or rudder is trusted to carry its passengers to their destined and appropriate end. In much the same way, dice were used as a means to divination or to obtain crude astrological forecasts.[69] These kinds of reliance on random outcome came to be seen as a misuse of God's hidden design, and like trial by ordeal were gradually abandoned. But the more radical shift to a secular understanding of contingency lay in the future, and early-modern Christian thought had no alternative to seeing accident and chance events as signs of the divine plan. Until the nineteenth century, Lorraine Daston suggests, the notion of 'genuinely random phenomena' was inconceivable, and European culture was slow to make the initial shift from a purely religious conception of chance to one that perceived the role of mathematics in the calculation of odds and possible outcomes.[70] Thus a mediaeval attitude to causality survived well into the Renaissance, encouraging a providential understanding of random events and fresh data, and it was reinforced in particular respects by the prestige accorded to ancient books. A 'probable' opinion, in this premodern context, is not one based on observation but one that has the weight of textual authority behind it, which is why, for instance, strong practical arguments against the existence of a north-west passage through the Arctic could be set aside by insisting that classical writers from Plato to Pliny 'affirme the continent of Asia, Afrike, and Europe, to be environed with the Ocean' (Hakluyt, *Principall Navigations* (1589), 613–14). It is also the reason why so many justifications of travel start by praising the 'painful travails' of ancient philosophers and church fathers across the known world to gather knowledge. Even under the pressure of sixteenth-century scepticism about the possibility of certainty, and the growing claims of empirical science, this reliance on textual witness did not break down entirely but mutated into practices like Jesuit casuistry – what later became known as probabilistic thinking, which offered a powerful tool for resolving issues of conscience by finding a 'probable' text that could be relied upon in the face of dissenting authorities. The objection from casuistry's opponents, as Ian Hacking reminds us, was that 'the probabilists would first of all decide on a course of action for its social and moral expediency. Then they would find some old text that could be interpreted as approval of that course of action' (24). But it is an objection to which all deductive reasoning from authority was becoming vulnerable, as observation, experiment and measurement came into conflict with received notions of what was 'probable' or most worthy of belief.

This was the dilemma of several Renaissance scientists, notably Galileo in his clash with the Vatican, and Hakluyt struggles with the same problem in trying to base the 'history of travel' on recent first-hand accounts without impugning the traditional authorities. It was also at the heart of the long-running controversy about Continental tourism and New World adventure, for the prime argument of those who condemned foreign travel was that it substituted an unreliable and morally perilous experience for the surer act of gaining knowledge through books. Those who defended excursions abroad insisted on the value of first-hand experience, and it gradually became clear to the majority of English people that a European tour backed by a good education was a desirable preparation for most careers. Tourism was a key part of the humanist shift towards practical training and civic awareness: young men needed to be exposed to the political and cultural life of other countries, and to their languages, in order to complete their education and turn them into useful servants of the state. At the same time, no one in the governing classes really believed that travel should do more than confirm the principles and axioms of a previous training and give the tourist some polish and range of reference. It was not supposed to be an inductive or life-changing experience. The fear that it might be usually gets expressed as hostility to the 'heady new-fanglenes' of European ways, or the typical view that the tourists who are 'at their way-going, both rich and discreet-like men; at back-coming, prooveth to be nothing else but fantasticke Fooles, Atheists, or superstitious monsters'.[71] Moralists were fond of quoting the tag from Horace about travel changing men's locations but not their minds, but the truth was that for such people transformation of any kind had generally negative implications. The argument about the value of travel raged for decades, because what was ultimately at stake was a question about what constituted ethical knowledge at a time of growing empiricism.

At the heart of humanist education is the idea of turning precept into experience, putting theory into practice, and a rhetorical training, as Arthur Kinney and many others point out, creates arguments that yield probabilities, likely truths that need to be tested in the real world, and be measured not by absolute standards (or prior authority) but by their utility in solving problems and dealing with actual situations. Travel was one of the most important of these tests, and yet many humanists worried about whether the contingencies of foreign experience could be coherently evaluated and used in these ways. Roger Ascham expressed this concern in an extreme form when he declared that '[l]earning teacheth more in one yeare, than experience in twentie: And learning teacheth safely, when experience maketh more miserable then wise.'[72] Everyone agreed that young men should not be let loose abroad without prior education, and the careful attempts of the guidebooks to distinguish good travel from bad sought to ensure that their precepts would contain and define the experience rather than be tested by it. A similar caution presumably informs Thomas Wilson's view that 'An Oration deliberative' is the most suitable to 'counseil my frend to travaile beyond the Seas', rather than a demonstrative praise of travel that inflames the imagination and the will.[73] Ascham, who was one of the most vociferous critics of English tourism abroad, phrased the issue in telling terms, for behind his raging at the iniquities of Italy in *The Scholemaster* one can detect his belief that the habits of the English gentry not only fail to set a good example but also make them particularly vulnerable to hazard. For young men to go to Italy in search of experience is a desperate gamble, he suggests,

> whan you doe consider, what mischeife they have committed, what daungers they have escaped (and yet xx for one, do perishe in the adventure).... A Father, that doth let loose his sonne, to all experiences, is most like a fonde Hunter, that letteth slippe a whelpe to the whole herde. Twentie to one, he shall fall upon a rascall [an immature deer], and let go the faire game.[74]

Like many others, Ascham thought the English were innocents abroad, and here he rephrases the travel wager in terms which remind the governing classes of their moral obligations and the real risks they run. Joseph Hall, in his polemic against travel *Quo Vadis?* was thinking along similar lines when he summed up the various claims for foreign travel:

> And now let us sit downe, and see what wee paid for this stocke, and count our winnings: What must our compleat Traveller stake downe for this goodly furniture of his Gentry? If not losse, danger; danger of the best part, if not all; a double danger; of corruption of religion, and depravation of manners; both capitall: And can we thinke these endowments so precious, that they should bee worth fetching upon such an hazard?[75]

Hall also found it apposite to repeat the well-known anecdote about 'a certaine great Peere [who] could say, it was enough for Noblemens sonnes to winde their horne, and carry their Hauke faire; that studie was for the children of a meaner ranke', inviting the riposte that 'then Noblemen must bee content that their children may winde their hornes, and carry their Haukes, while meaner mens sons doe weild the affaires of State' (29–30). His point in telling the story again is similar to Ascham's, that aristocratic travel fosters philistine habits rather than ameliorating them, because it distracts young men from the proper business of learning. For his part Ascham confessed that 'I am afraide, that over many of our traveilers into Italie, do not exchewe the way to *Circes* Court: but goe, and ride, and runne, and flie thether' (fol. 26) – an image that invokes the rhythms of gaming and sport as a ready means to perdition, and implicitly links the aristocratic love of gambling on leisure activities to the act of travel itself: an association that had in reality become a durable one.

## The Voyage of Italy

The polemics of Hall and Ascham do considerably less than justice to the important cultural exchange with Italy during the Tudor period. Early in the sixteenth century the presence of several notable Italian humanists in the English court stimulated a good deal of travel in the other direction, and after the hiatus of Henry VIII's rupture with Rome, and following his death, the flow of English visitors to Italy resumed – in particular to Padua, whose university offered a tolerant environment to northern Protestants and has been described as being virtually 'the graduate school for English humanism'.[76] But although Padua was an important training ground, particularly in medicine, it was also a place where the well-born could acquire a smattering of skills and, as at Oxford and Cambridge, leave without taking a degree, and for many English gentry and noblemen, this meant business as usual: university as a kind of finishing school for a year or two. As such, it was an environment calculated to encourage the gaming spirit, and the demands of being abroad would have stirred that spirit further.

The embryonic versions of the Grand Tour that the English upper classes started to take in the sixteenth century were an insurer's nightmare for numerous reasons, but the fact that they coincided with the Reformation and its consequences ensured that travelling in Catholic Europe was seen as involving, and often did involve, a recognized gamble on personal security that was distinct from the imponderable risks of bandits, bad roads and foreign food. This was particularly the case in Italy, from the start a prime destination for tourists. Venice and Padua were at different moments in the century places of refuge from the Protestant and Marian regimes in England, and the allegiances of any traveller were likely to be interrogated by the expatriate English community. Elsewhere in Italy, and for a time in Venice itself, the Inquisition made life increasingly perilous for non-Catholic visitors, with Spanish-controlled Naples and Milan in particular being very dangerous destinations. Meanwhile, tourists with Catholic friends or sympathies were doubly vulnerable: the development of the Elizabethan spy network under Walsingham and Burghley made every new encounter on foreign soil potentially compromising, and those regarded as susceptible to conversion might be specifically targeted by Catholic agents. It was widely thought, for instance, that the unfortunate John Mole, who as tutor to Lord Roos went to Rome in 1608 and was immediately thrown into an Inquisition jail where he remained until his death 30 years later, had been prised away from his charge because the latter was thought to favour the old religion. The young John Donne almost certainly visited Italy in the mid-1580s, and may have got as far as Naples where his Jesuit uncle Jasper Heywood was living in exile, but the trip was kept a close secret at the time.[77] The image of Italy as a land of poisoners and machiavels was shaped by relentless Protestant propaganda, but it was partly generated by a real threat. Ascham's *Scholemaster*, which did much to cement the myth of Italian villainy, was first published in the same year, 1570, as the Pope's excommunication of Elizabeth I, the opening salvo in Rome's efforts to overthrow the Queen and restore the Catholic Church in England. That campaign was a faltering one over the next decade, but it included repeated papal attempts to get Spanish backing for an invasion of England, and in 1578 Gregory XIII backed the expedition of the renegade Thomas Stukeley. In the same year the English hospice in Rome, which had long functioned as a sanctuary for exiled priests, became a seminary, and in its new incarnation as the English College became responsible for training missionaries to be sent into England. Reports regularly filtered back to England of young tourists falling prey to the Jesuits and being persuaded to convert, and while the *inglese italianato*, the Englishman corrupted by Italy, is another stereotype that was fed by anxiety and prejudice, the label also reflects awareness of the battle for hearts and minds that was central to Jesuit strategy. On the face of it, this is an extraordinary environment in which to lay playful bets on one's survival. But in the early 1580s we are confronted with an intriguing conjunction of historical data, and it invites us to ask more searching questions about who chose to travel on these terms and more broadly how the gamble of foreign travel was conceived.

In June 1580 the Jesuit priests Edmund Campion and Robert Persons arrived in England, prompting the government to recall all English travellers abroad, including students: families were required to give names of relatives then out of the country, and the travellers had to be back within four months. Only four months earlier the English ambassador to France had reported the opening of a new seminary in Paris designed to attract Scottish students, to 'instruct youth in their papistry, and to entice the meaner sort'; he added that 'divers gentlemen's heirs come hither weekly, and of other quality, who alter their religion'.[78] William Fennor offers a sharply prejudiced vignette of this process in a propaganda pamphlet, describing how English travellers are lured to the seminary at Louvain. Gentlemen with money are conned out of it by the Jesuits, while poor men are examined and if possible recruited by theological argument, but

> if this catch him not, they allure him with promises ... of some earthly crownes: the needy snake cannot chuse but nibble at this charitable baite, and rather then faile they will then venture a crowne or two, and with comfortable wordes tell him that if he continue he shall not want ... then dismissing him the house, they tell him it is no shame to begge and bid him be bold. Thus he that could live in his owne country by his honest labour, is converted, or rather by them perverted to an imprudent and shamelesse beggar.[79]

Fennor presents this process as a special instance of a general fear, that foreign travel, like gaming, turns men into vagabonds, and insinuates that the Jesuits are able to entice 'the meaner sort' with a devilish bargain, advancing money in order to create the prospect of 'earthly crowns' and thereby lead the traveller to perdition. There is no doubt that many tourists – and not just the meaner sort – found themselves in financial difficulties and thus vulnerable to this sort of persuasion. The circumstances of travel had changed in two crucially intertwined respects. While there had always been poor pilgrims on the road, their numbers and purposes were predictable and systems of hospitality existed to cope with them. And before the Reformation they moved through a landscape generally untroubled by doctrinal conflict. In the sixteenth century the world of mediaeval travel was disrupted both by a growth in numbers and by uncertainty about the status and intentions of many tourists, and this coincided with religious schism in some calamitous ways.

In July 1581, the Venetian ambassador in Rome reported that 'in Saint Peter's an English heretic attacked the priest officiating at mass, and endeavoured to snatch the Host … from his hands.… [H]e has confessed that he is one of several who have come into Italy for this very purpose.'[80] The 1580 edict recalling English travellers had been ineffective, a point that was rubbed in by a very different ruling from the Pope just over two months after the St Peter's incident. On 9 October, the English ambassador in Paris reported to Walsingham that

> The Pope, as I am told, has given severe orders that all Englishmen who shall come to Rome on 'bargains of return' are to be apprehended, imprisoned, and executed as felons. Some are upon this lately imprisoned, and others who last passed this way will be in great danger. The execution of this tyrannical order was offered to the English College there, but they refusing it the Inquisition has taken the matter in hand.[81]

The English College in Rome had three years earlier been placed under the control of the Jesuits, but it remained a place of call for Protestant visitors, who were allowed to remain in the city for eight days as pilgrims, and for that period were under the protection of the English cardinal. The College was clearly unwilling to be associated with a draconian policy that might affect a number of its visitors and lump them together with extremists. But the ambassador, despite condemning the order as 'tyrannical', is not apparently surprised by it, and it seems very likely that the Pope's edict was provoked in part by incidents like the one described, which Fynes Moryson condemned as the product of excessive zeal but which he feared might result from the Protestant tourist habit of attending mass 'as going to see a stage-play, or for curiositie, wherewith many are led' (*Itinerary*, 3.415). Attending such a spectacle, he implies, can lead to acts of bravado, and those acts lent fuel to the idea that English travel to Rome is excessively bound up with the making of dares or wagers. One wonders whether the unfortunate prisoners described in a letter from Nicholas Faunt to Anthony Bacon in March 1582 were victims of this policy: 'For LISTER and others in the inquisition at Rome, it will go very hard: but on EGLEBY and DUTTON there is like to be execution done, if already it is not.'[82]

The St Peter's offender was one Richard Atkins, whom the writer Anthony Munday reports as turning up at the English College in midsummer 1581 to rebuke his countrymen for the 'great misorder' of their lives, before going on to commit his fatal act. A Catholic account of the incident portrays Atkins as an illiterate fanatic, virtually unhinged by his heresy, who dressed himself in a cloak or scapular

> having the figure of a paire of gallowes sowed fast upon the same in redde clothe bothe on the backe and the brest, aswell for signification that he sought to be persecuted for the gospel, as for prophecie, that he should die upon the gallowes for his faith … professing that he came to that place purposely that he might be killed for Christ, and that he would from thence into Turkie if he could not attaine the same in Rome.[83]

Zealots bent on martyrdom were surely distinct from travellers negotiating the perils of Rome on a 'bargain of return', but the authorities may not have seen it like that, especially since the English were known for clumsy theatricality. Moryson, who is proud of his own ability to pass himself off as a foreigner, says that the 'craftie spies of Rome' can usually see through English attempts at disguise, 'as the muffling a man's face with his cloke, or the like', and he tells the story of the Englishman who tried to hide behind 'apparrell of so many colours, and so strange fashions' that 'he drew the eyes of all Jesuites and Romans upon him' (*Itinerary*, 3.412). The prospective martyrs best known to the Vatican were of course the Jesuits who undertook the English mission, and in 1581 reports were already filtering back to Rome of their hair's-breadth escapes and elaborate subterfuges. Persons and Campion had arrived in England in summer 1580 disguised as a swordsman and a jewel merchant, disguises that Dennis Flynn describes as offering 'a dash of chivalry that was ... exotically attractive to many who sympathized with the old religion'.[84] In November, Campion wrote to Cardinal Allen saying, 'I cannot long escape the heretics, they have so many scouts; I wear ridiculous clothes, often change my name, and so often read news' letters that Campion is taken, that I am without fear.'[85] Allen wrote approvingly of how would-be martyrs at the English College clamoured 'that they might have the lotte' and be selected for the mission: knowing that they could not expect 'worldly preferment or honour', they 'were much inflamed to hazard their person in the same spiritual adventure'.[86] But the Vatican became ambivalent about the English taste for risky escapades, as Robert Persons reveals in his report of later conversations with Clement VIII about the students in the English College who 'bragged much of their Martyrdome.... His Holinesse oftentimes told me that he was never so vexed with any nation on the world ... and ever now and then ... would put his finger up to his braine, signifying: that there stood their sicknesse: and so would most of the Court, when they talked of them, saying: the *English* were *indiavoluti*, and like words.'[87] Dicing with death had become, in these circles at least, a hallmark of English travel.

Clement's predecessor, Gregory XIII, who in 1581 renewed the bull of excommunication against Elizabeth I, enthusiastically promoted the English mission and paid the travel expenses of those who joined it, but from the start he had to deal with dissension in the English College and had good reason to be sceptical about the motives and character of some of its occupants. Atkins's claim to have been part of a conspiracy was not upheld at his trial, yet a similar incident took place in November 1581 in which an Englishman tried to strangle a priest officiating at Mass. If such behaviour was not the direct result of wagering, it nonetheless looked like the product of a mindset that was attracted to rash gambles on personal immunity. 'I was at *Pontius Pilates* house and pist against it', says Jack Wilton on his arrival in Rome in Nashe's *The Unfortunate Traveller*, immediately setting the tone of truculent resistance to the city's dangerous allure. Anthony Munday, who spent some time in the English College in 1579 and later testified against the Catholic priests he met there, catches the bravado of Protestant talk in England whilst defending himself against those who accuse him of having dabbled in Popery:

> These rash heads being in *England*, would doo many goodly matters at *Roome*, they would tell the Pope of his lascivious & unchristian life, the Cardinals of their Sodomiticall sinnes, the Friers of their secret jugling with the Nunnes, & the Preestes of their painted Purgatorie, their wafer God, and their counterfeit blood in the Challice: all this they would doo, nowe they are in *England*. But I doubt if they were at *Roome* … they would be as ready to doo any thing for the safegard of their lives, as I was.[88]

Yet Munday himself acknowledged the brave candour of Atkins at his trial and agreed with the official report that he went to his death 'with such firmness as to excite universal comment'.[89] This kind of behaviour was also being licensed by popular fiction of the Nashean kind in which reckless iconoclasm is made part of the English idea of the picaresque. In a prose narrative called *Haigh for Devonshire*, published in 1600, Henry Roberts recounts the fictional exploits of six West Country merchants in France, including a trip to Rouen in which one of them disrupts a Catholic procession and smashes the cross. This is described as a 'mad pranke' and lands them in jail for a while; our heroes go on to take merchants' revenge for losses suffered in Anglo-French conflicts and fit out six vessels to prey on French shipping. Roberts' story is pamphlet fiction, but it occupies the same cheap print marketplace as the accounts of Protestant martyrs in Rome, the tales of itinerant renegades like Stukeley, and – we might add – travel pamphlets like Kemp's *Nine Days Wonder* which it somewhat resembles in cocky assertiveness and mock-heroic manner.

Pope Gregory's strenuous reaction to bargains of return remains surprising at a time when he was preoccupied with the English mission and the creation of diplomatic and military alliances against Elizabeth's government. But it can probably be explained in part as a suspicion that the travel wager acted as a cover for other activities. In 1578 the Papal Nuncio in France indicated 'the Pope's desire to know who are the persons in the pay of the Queen of England in Italy'.[90] The English government lost no time in planting spies in the newly formed seminaries: among the earliest visitors recorded in the Pilgrim-Book of the English College in Rome on 10 March 1581 is Solomon Aldred, who soon after being granted a pension by the Pope became one of Walsingham's agents.[91] In April of the following year came a report of '[f]ifty Englishmen, as well Papists as Protestants taken in Rome and other places, for spies'.[92] The situation was complicated by the ambiguous reputation of the English residents in Rome. Cardinal Sega, appointed by the Vatican in the 1590s to investigate the chronic unrest in the English College, was convinced that the 'multitude of spies and traitors … sent out from England' helped to 'sow discord' there, and suggested that the College needed to be more careful in choosing candidates for seminary training.[93] When the English Jesuit Robert Persons took over as Rector in 1598, he suspected that many were enrolling as theological students more for the comfortable lifestyle than out of true vocation, and Sega argued similarly that many of the students coming to Rome were 'steeped with worldly thoughts, and accustomed to uncontrolled freedom'. A majority of graduates from the College did not undertake the English mission, and some of the alumni who remained in Rome were regarded by Sega as leading 'a wandering and unrestricted life' marked by 'irregularity and lukewarmness'.[94] It is not difficult to see why they might be suspected of providing an alibi for visitors who claimed to be travelling for pleasure or on a wager but were actually spies and informants.

A good example of the dubiety and confusion surrounding wager-travellers is the visit to Rome of a goldsmith by the name of Francis Ridelstone. According to the report of Walsingham's spy Charles Sledd, Ridelstone turned up in Rome in August 1579 claiming to have gone there on a wager, and carrying letters of introduction designed to help him obtain the 'certificate & seale of the cittye', which he needed with 'spedy dispache … by cause the daye of his retorne to London againe must of necessite be before Michelmas Daye nexte.' Ridelstone could have stayed at the English College, where under the rules 'poor pilgrims shall be retained for eight days': this was the old custom of the fourteenth-century hospice, ratified when it became the English College, and generally extended to all non-aristocratic visitors who were also protected by the English Cardinal for the period of their stay. Apparently choosing *not* to stay there, he nonetheless attracted the immediate attention of the College, and 'the next daye came Robert Parsons Jesuite' and two others 'to welcome Ridelstone as they said but they were porporslye sente to talke with him & to knowe the cause of his cominge thether, to undermine him & knowe what capasite he was of or whether he was a like name to a spye'. They 'exorted entreated & persuaded him to come to the englishe seminarye', meet the students, be instructed in religion, and renounce the Queen. Ridelstone seems to have resisted the pressure and left six days later; Sledd reported that '[o]f his departure grewe many wordes for that he had not confessed nor submitted himselfe to the Pope', nor did he comply with the 'requests & persuationes' of Persons and the others, 'wherfore his departure was not well disgested neyther taken in good parte by the said parties which … repented them greatly that they had not caused his imprisonment & for his sake thretned all suche Englishemen as should come thether afterwards'.[95]

Ridelstone's story illuminates the particular perils faced by Protestant travellers in Catholic Europe and particularly in cities where seminary training had been instituted: being suspected of spying for the English government, and falling victim to the Jesuit battle for hearts and minds. Yet we cannot see these tourists simply as victims of perilous circumstances. Ridelstone chose to make a stop in Milan, arguably the most dangerous city in Italy for Protestant visitors, part of his journey and perhaps part of his wager, and Anthony Munday, in justifying his trip to Rome in the early pages of *The English Romayne Life,* claims that various Catholic gentlemen in Paris urged him and his companion to go to Milan and offered to give them letters 'for our better welcome thether'. Wanting to emphasise that Catholic persuasion was not what decided him, Munday then declares that 'we thought, that if we could goe to *Roome*, and returne safelie againe into *England*, wee should accomplish a great matter, the place beeing so farre of, and the voyage so daungerous' (8). Munday is clearly availing himself of the vocabulary of the heroic gamble, even though his journey does not seem to have involved a monetary wager, and given his later notoriety both at home and in Rome, the brag indicates why the authorities might have had reason to suspect that any claim to be 'putting out' was a cover for other activities – whether it be Persons' suspicion that Ridelstone was a spy, or the uncertainty, which has persisted to our own day, about Munday's real reasons for going to Rome.

Munday also says that he wrote the book because 'a number have been desirous, to understand the successe of my journey to *Roome*, and a number beside are doubtfull, whether I have beene there or no', which was a common reaction to the vaunting claims of the traveller, especially if he were trying to claim on a wager. But we might note that Munday's more sober explanation for his trip, that he was impelled by 'desire to see straunge Countreies, as also affection to learne the languages' (1), is identical to that given by Charles Sledd: 'desyerous to learne languages & also to see the naturall enclynations and dispositions of strainge & forayne contryes withe their inhabytes'. Both men present themselves as having realised after the fact that their real mission was to expose, as Sledd put it, 'the Popes ... devices & polices which were first discovered to me in Rome' (214), or in Munday's words, 'the odd conceits and crafty jugglings of the Pope' (1). Yet however assiduous were Munday's subsequent attempts to destroy the English Mission by informing on his erstwhile contacts at the English College, and his claim that he pretended to be Catholic in order to 'undermine them and sift out their purposes', opinion has started to swing back to the old proposition that he set off on his travels as some sort of Catholic and may have enrolled in the English College as a sincere believer in the old religion.[96] The argument is not one that I can pursue here, but Munday's case illustrates the extraordinary difficulty of disentangling motives for travel at this time and suggests ways in which the picaresque adventure could act as a container for a variety of clandestine activities.

## Going to Constantinople

Journeying to the cities of the Ottoman world also had its considerable dangers and could require a fair amount of subterfuge, but over the course of the sixteenth century it was increasingly a magnet for the adventurous traveller and became perhaps the most prestigious vehicle for the bargain of return in late Elizabethan and Jacobean England. Whereas the wager on travel might incur a death sentence in Rome, in Constantinople and other Ottoman cities it seems to have been tolerated as a relatively harmless custom (or so the available evidence suggests) and became a challenge that generations of English gentlemen aspired to meet. The bet on a journey to Jerusalem or the Turkish capital was to be one of the early-modern period's legacies to Augustan and nineteenth-century tourism, alongside the more familiar foundations that it laid for the Grand Tour. This is not to say, however, that 'putting out' to these destinations was free of the questionable motives and purposes that became attached to wager journeys in Catholic Europe. On the contrary, as we shall see in the rest of this chapter and in one of the cases analysed in the next, the popularity of the bet on travel to cities in the Middle East made it a convenient cover for a variety of other activities.

I suggested earlier that travelling in Ottoman dominions became in the early Tudor court a kind of replacement activity for crusading, a ludic, quasi-chivalric impulse that eventually yielded the formal wager on these ambitious and high-profile ventures. As we have seen, there were precedents for such bargains in the financial arrangements made by pilgrims (to Jerusalem) and by merchants (who by the fifteenth century were actively trading in the Levant), but the wagering journey to Constantinople, Damascus or Babylon seems to have become a gentleman's game, and one that as the century wore on was played in some highly opportunistic ways.

Take the case of George Gifford, one of Queen Elizabeth's gentleman-pensioners (her ceremonial bodyguard) who for the entire decade of the 1580s sought the means and opportunity to make a trip to Constantinople. Gifford came from a family with recusant connections: his younger brother William went into exile in 1573 and eventually became Archbishop of Rheims, while his cousin Gilbert trained as a missionary priest in Douai and spent time at the English College in Rome before becoming involved in espionage and acting as a double agent in Walsingham's employ, most notably in the exposure of the Babington plot in 1586 (see note 93). George himself may also have been working for Walsingham as early as 1583: in that year he went to Paris and plotted with exiled Catholics to assassinate Elizabeth I, but it is possible that the scheme was being master-minded from London in an attempt to flush out those who were conspiring to put Mary Queen of Scots on the English throne. He was nonetheless named by the Babington plotters as a would-be assassin and was imprisoned for a time in the Tower, though he escaped prosecution.[97]

George Gifford eventually made his journey to Constantinople in April 1591, fully 10 years after the future navigator Thomas Cavendish, then enjoying a lavish lifestyle close to the centres of power, collaborated with fellow courtiers Thomas Perrot and Richard Skipwith in putting up £1000 to finance the venture. Their reasons for doing so are unclear: Cavendish's latest biographer speculates that while this was 'possibly a wager', the planned trip 'may have been a secret part of Walsingham's plan to revive the Levant trade'.[98] Cavendish's own foreign interests in the 1580s were in American colonization and then in girdling the globe, and if he sustained a Levantine adventure throughout those busy years it was most probably as a 'bargain of return' (Cavendish was an inveterate gambler) or as some sort of speculative enterprise in which he was a sleeping partner. As we have seen, wagering did not exclude commerce and could be a conduit or cover for it, as it could for espionage. The Turkey (later Levant) Company received its first charter in 1581, at the same time as the courtiers agreed to back Gifford's trip, but none of them was a member of the new joint-stock company that was given exclusive rights to trade within the Ottoman dominions. It is possible nonetheless that in the late 1570s Cavendish saw opportunities to make money in the Levant, since prior to the formation of the company, the Queen had petitioned the Turkish sultan to allow the trading privileges already granted to William Harborne and two merchants to be 'inlarged to all our subjects in generall'. Cavendish might well have been attracted by plans to revive the maritime trade with Chios and Crete that had figured largely in earlier English commerce in the Levant.[99] But it is hard to see how these prospects would have been advanced by sending a man like Gifford to Constantinople, especially after the company had been granted its exclusive charter, and it is equally unlikely that Cavendish would have remained interested in an Ottoman project while pursuing his oceanic ambitions in the eventful decade that followed.

Other evidence suggests that Gifford's prime objective was to cash in on an expedition fashionable in courtly circles. Shortly before Cavendish and his friends agreed to back the venture, Gifford was present at a gathering in the Earl of Oxford's lodgings where the talk turned to ways of making money. As part of his 1581 indictment of Charles Arundel and others for pro-Catholic activities, Oxford testified that

> a littell before Christmas [1580] at my loginge in westmester … George Gyfford talkinge of the order of livinge by mony and [the] dyfference betwien that and revenu by land, he [Arundel] sayd at the last if George Gyfford could make [i.e. scrape together] thre thousand pound he wowld set him in to a course whear he ned not care for all England and theare he showld live more to his content and wythe more reputatione then ever he dyd or myght hope for in England and they wowld make all the cowrt wonder to heare of them.

Gifford had been forced to sell some of his lands in 1579, and Oxford reports him as responding enthusiastically to Arundel's offer: 'whereat George Gyfford replyd gods blud Char[l]es whear is this.' Arundel 'answerd yf yow have thre thousand pound or can make it he could tell', and Gifford replied that 'he thought he could find the means to make thre thousand pound. that speache finished withe the cominge in of supper'. As Alan Nelson suggests, 'Dangerous conversation ceased when servants entered with food.'[100] The nature of Arundel's offer is unclear, though it presumably involved sharing the voluntary exile that he himself would shortly undertake. Gifford's own path was to be more tortuous, but the fact that within a few months he had secured backing for the Constantinople trip, and clung to the plan for the next 10 years whilst being drawn into various shady activities, makes it likely that profitable travel was what he had in mind in his response to Arundel's proposal. If the money he raised from Cavendish and his friends had been 'put out' on a voyage to Constantinople on a three-for-one wager it would have realized the £3000 required.[101]

Charles Arundel offered a more innocent account of the conversation at Oxford's table, declaring that

> I remember well beinge at the Earl of Oxfords lodgeinge in Westminster we fell in talke, of travel and travellers how a Jentill man that wold travel might live and after what sorte that had three thowsan powndes in his purse and my opinion was, that beinge but a private man no man liveid more gallantlie in the cort …

As Nelson says, 'Arundel softens the topic … into a discussion of travel',[102] but his phrasing ('how a gentleman that would travel might live') remains ambiguous. Only the most affluent nobleman would contemplate spending so much on a Continental tour, and Arundel seems rather to be talking about its potential financial benefits, diverting attention from the seditious idea that Gifford wanted money for a comfortable exile by suggesting that travel might be one way of living 'more gallantly in the court' (like Sir Robert Carey who boasted that his wager-journey to Berwick in 1589 'was worth to me two thousand pounds, which bettered me to live at court a good while after'). Perhaps the conversation that evening really was about wagering, although Oxford's insinuation that Arundel was tempting Gifford to disloyalty reveals once again the fraught contexts in which the bet on travel often operated. In December 1587, Gifford's cousin Gilbert was arrested in Paris and denied trying to recruit him to kill the Queen in 1583, claiming to have spoken to George only 'to tell him that his brother wished him to hasten his intended journey to Constantinople'.[103] Why William Gifford, then teaching at the seminary at Rheims, should have been concerned with the 'intended journey' is unknown, but his urging could only have increased suspicions that his brother wanted the money payable on a wager for treasonable purposes. When George Gifford finally reached Constantinople some three years later, in April 1591, Edward Barton, the English ambassador to the Porte, appealed to Burghley for protection against attempts to discredit him by people who 'made he knew not what surmises about Mr Gifford's voyage to Constantinople'. The speculation might have been about some kind of interloping commercial activity, but is more likely to have reflected doubts about Gifford's probity, as a suspected Catholic plotter and government spy. In all events, he remained in Constantinople for only eight days when, according to Barton, he 'was now ready to depart again'.[104] The quick turnaround, especially in a journey so long contemplated, suggests that Gifford had no reason to linger and was more concerned to meet the deadline on a bargain of return.

The final entry in this murky saga is found in the Privy Council records, where the financial aftermath of Gifford's journey can be traced. He had apparently acquired new or additional backers for his trip, for on 28 May 1590 he, together with Lord Chandos and one Nicholas Porter, entered into two bonds of £800 with the prominent London goldsmith Sir Richard Martin. One of the bonds carried a defeazance (provision for voiding the debt) 'that the said Mr. Gifford shal make a voiadge to Constantinople, and bring from thence trew certificat thereof', and Martin appears to have accepted that this obligation had thereby been discharged. But the other bond remained unpaid, and to recover his money Martin went to law. Gifford and his sponsors may have tried to argue that both bonds were taken out to enable the journey (which was probably the case), but since only one of the contracts appears to have been set up as a wager on safe return, Martin managed to convince the Privy Council that for the other he should be recompensed by all three men. In February 1592, Gifford and Porter were ordered to pay Martin £240 over the next two years, with Chandos making up the balance of the debt, and Gifford was restrained from collecting on any bonds (which may have included other wagers) that had been turned over as securities to his creditor.[105]

Gifford's standing in court circles had been precarious ever since his actions in the mid-1580s, and these legal rulings must have added to his woes. He continued to enjoy the support of Sir Walter Ralegh, who gave him employment at sea over the next few years (he took part in both the Guiana expedition of 1595 and the Cadiz raid in the following year), but prior to this he seems to have regarded the Constantinople trip as his best hope of retrieving his fortunes. Any plan to make money for a life abroad had presumably evaporated once he became a government agent, and as the decade wore on, any commercial motive in 1581 for going to Constantinople must have fallen away. In persisting nonetheless with the plan, Gifford seems to typify the generation of footloose young men who clustered around the centres of power and influence, lacking obvious means of advancement, trying to sustain an expensive lifestyle at a time when credit was scarce, and being tempted into the gambling culture that escalated in England after 1580. We cannot know whether Gifford was at all motivated by curiosity or a taste for wider experience, but his long fixation on the trip seems to have derived from narrower motives, the sort that lent fuel to the complaints by satirists and men like Fynes Moryson, cited at the start of this chapter, that the worthy challenge of long-distance travel had been debased by the self-serving enterprise of the new tourists. Despite these criticisms, however, the fashionable gamble on expeditions to the Levant proved to be a useful bargaining tool in the hands of more resourceful travellers.

There is some direct evidence that the travel wager was used to deflect suspicion or to conceal the true purpose or destination of a journey. In November 1589, writing to his brother Edward from Germany during his first continental tour, the future diplomat, Henry Wotton, reported a meeting 'with one Mr. Mallorie, who went with Mr. Candishe to Constantinople upon the *braveraria*, and is lately returned'.[106] This was the journey undertaken by Henry Cavendish in the same year, recorded in a narrative by his servant Fox that was not printed until 1940; its modern editor, noting that no reason is given for the trip, speculates that it was a buying or trading venture of some kind by Cavendish's mother, Bess of Hardwick, and points to the presence in inventories of a number of Turkish carpets at Hardwick Hall.[107] No doubt the travellers returned with goods and souvenirs (Mallory did have commercial interests in the Levant), but the picture is complicated by the discovery that

Mallory was in fact a last-minute replacement for Cavendish's cousin, the scholar Anthony Wingfield.[108] It seems much more likely that a journey 'upon the *braveraria*' is synonymous with the travel wager; the Italianate word looks like Wotton's own coinage from words like *bravo* and *bravare*, and the English 'bravery', with their connotations of vaunting or taking on a challenge. This early example of tourism to Turkey would then have been firmly in the aristocratic tradition of putting out, and Cavendish may not have had any other motive for the journey. But Wotton's response to his meeting with Mallory shows vividly how the patrician custom is losing its immunity to being appropriated and distorted. 'Him I closed withal,' continues Wotton, 'and persuaded that I meant to go very shortly the same voyage; and so I did.' What Wotton means, however, is that he pretended an interest in doing the same. 'I learned his advice, and he laid open unto me a large discourse of his travel, which I have treasured up to [my] good use' (1.230). In a later letter Wotton explains what his intentions had been:

> Concerning Constantinople, I had never any thoughts or inclination that way, but gave it forth among the English merchants in Nuremburg upon this reason, that they might satisfy themselves with opinion that I was gone that way, and I in the meantime cross up the country in secret; and my intent is not to be seen by them again till I come into Italy, because it might much endanger me, to have any know the time of my going thither ... [109]

It is clear from his correspondence that the ambitious Wotton took particularly seriously the injunction to travellers to observe political conditions abroad, as a preparation for his ambassadorial career. There are signs, in fact, that on this first journey he was already engaged in information-gathering for the English authorities, which helps to explain Wotton's ambitious itinerary in Italy, taking in difficult destinations like Naples and Milan as well as several visits to Rome.[110] On his first trip to the latter Wotton staged his own kind of *braveraria*, entering the city 'with a mighty blue feather in a black hat', so that 'I was reputed as light in my mind as in my apparel', and 'no man could think I desired to be unknown' (1.272). Wotton's stunt apparently worked, though Fynes Moryson (as we saw earlier) described a case of such exhibitionism having a less happy outcome. Moryson also opined that the *bona fide* tourist should 'have a chearefull countenance, as an argument of innocency, to free him from suspicion of ... being a spie' (*Itinerary*, 3.399), but it seems that some travellers adopted more inventive methods to avoid this danger.

Another such was Sir Henry Blount, who travelled to the Middle East via the Mediterranean in 1636. On arrival at Rhodes he went sightseeing and was

> taken for a Spy; for in *Rhodes* is no pretence of Merchandise for a *Christian*; and but that my excuse of going upon wager into *Egypt* seemed possible, I had here beene lost: yet in that *suspition*, some of them out of such a bravery, as I had once before found in their *Campe*, shewed mee the *Palace* or *Fortresse* of the *Grand Master* formerly, with the *Out-works*, and three great *deepe ditches* ... [111]

So convincing is this proof of his harmlessness, apparently – suggesting that the eccentric freelance traveller is an already familiar figure – that his interrogators are happy to show him classified sights. It was a useful ruse, for Blount was in reality an assiduous spy. When he reached Egypt, the restrictions placed on his movements at Alexandria 'made me suspect some notable defect in that harbour, which might hereafter, be made use off; whereupon I went the next day secretly, unto a high decayed peece of a *Turret*, upon the wall over that Haven, to take a considerate view thereof' (58). More than once his snooping landed him in a tight spot, and Blount repeats that the most effective way of extricating himself 'when they questioned my condition, & designe, which was often', was to

> give them severall accounts, as I noted the *Place*, and *Auditory*; still in effect to shew me borne *rich*, but falne to *povertie*, without any fault of mine; my friends all dead, and that having no abilitie for gaine, I had wager'd the small reliques of my fortune, upon a returne from *Constantinople*, and *Gran Cairo*: this though farre below my fortunes, yet passed with them for truth, and such a one, as embelleshed with fit circumstance, procured me esteeme, and compassion (103).

One notices the implication that showing an interest in fortifications and strategic matters is a mark of gentility ('to shew me borne *rich*'), and that well-born but hard-up young men travelling on a wager were a familiar and credible sight. Blount actively trades on the image of the spendthrift gallant that had become associated with such bets, and which Fynes Moryson saw as a sad reduction of a noble custom. Both men wanted to believe that the mercenary wager of modern times was beneath them, but each in his own way found it too useful to ignore. The 'bargain of return' played a minor but significant role in widening access to tourism, and Blount's opportunism is rather firmly put in perspective by the remark of the working man in Thomas Nashe's *Terrors of the Night*, published in 1594, who points out that 'such poore fellowes as I … cannot put out money to be paide againe when wee come from *Constantinople*'.[112]

## Notes

1 Thomas Coryat, *Coryats Crudities*, 75.

2 Moryson, *Itinerary*, 1.428.

3 Moryson does note earlier that 'this manner of gaine, had of old been in use among the inhabitants of the Low Countries, and the Sea-Coasts of Germany (and so it is yet in use with them)' (1.426). Cf. his discussion of wager-contests in the Netherlands in the writings gathered in Moryson, *Shakespeare's Europe*, ed. Charles Hughes (London: Sherratt and Hughes, 1903), 384.

4 John Cooke, *Epigrames* (London, c.1604), no. 39, C8.

5 Barnabe Riche, *Faultes Faults, and nothing else but Faultes* (London, 1606), 8.

6 See Diana Webb, *Pilgrimage in Mediaeval England* (London: Hambledon, 2000), 234. Penitential pilgrimage was commonly imposed on offenders in fifteenth century England (E. Duffy, 'The Dynamics of Pilgrimage in Late Mediaeval England', in C. Morris and P. Roberts, eds., *Pilgrimage* [Cambridge: Cambridge UP, 2002], 173–4). The extensive use of such penances by the Dutch authorities well into the sixteenth century is discussed by Jan van Herwaarden, *Between St James and Erasmus* (Leiden: Brill, 2003), ch. 5, esp. pp. 139–79.

7 In *The English Romayne Lyfe* (London, 1582), Anthony Munday itemizes 'trudging to the seven churches ... going into the dark vaults under the ground, or travelling on pilgrimage' (41) amongst the penances imposed.

8 Antoni Mączak, *Travel in Early Modern Europe* (Cambridge: Polity, 1995), 175. See also Titus Tobler, *Denkblätter aus Jerusalem* (Konstanz: Scheitlin, 1853), 569.

9 J.P. van Niekerk, *The Development of the Principles of Insurance Law in the Netherlands* (Kenwyn: Juta, 1998), 117.

10 van Niekerk, *Development*, 116.

11 van Herwaarden, *Between St James and Erasmus*, 96.

12 John Evelyn, *The Diary of John Evelyn*, ed. Austin Dobson (London: Macmillan, 1906), I.51. See M. Kirkland-Ives, 'The Adornes Family of Bruges and Holy Land Devotion', *Sixteenth Century Journal* 39 (2008), 1041–64. Lotteries were frequently held in the Netherlands for civic and charitable causes.

13 William Thorpe in a deposition of 1407: 'ofttimes divers men and women of these runners thus madly hither and thither into pilgrimage, borrow hereto other men's goods (yea, and sometimes they steal men's goods hereto), and they pay them never again.' E. Arber, *An English Garner* (London: Arber, 1877–96), 6.84; William Wey, *The Itineraries of William Wey* (London: Roxburghe Club, 1855), 4–5; *Informacion for pylgrymes unto the holy londe* (London, 1498), sig.b6; and H. Prescott, *Jerusalem Journey* (London: Eyre and Spottiswood, 1954), 51.

14 Jonathan Sumption, *Pilgrimage: An Image of Mediaeval Religion* (London: Faber, 1975), 298–9.

15 'The Man of Law's Tale', in *The Works of Geoffrey Chaucer*, ed. F.N. Robinson (London: Oxford UP, 1957), 63–75, and see the illuminating discussion of Constance's ordeal in V.A Kolve, *Chaucer and the Imagery of Narrative* (Stanford: Stanford UP, 1984), ch. 7.

16 Seth Lerer, *Chaucer and his Readers* (Princeton: Princeton UP, 1993), 88–9. Historians have argued that from their inception chivalric romances functioned as courtesy books aimed inter alia at the younger sons of knightly families who could not expect to inherit land and title. The hostility to such writing shown by humanist reformers like Roger Ascham may have been prompted partly by a sense that it continued to offer bad examples to the touring gentry of Tudor England, whose adventures he vociferously opposed (Jennifer R. Goodman, *Chivalry and Exploration, 1298–1630* [Rochester, NY: Boydell, 1998], 7–8).

17 R.F. Green, *A Crisis of Truth: Literature and Law in Ricardian England* (Philadelphia: U. of Pennsylvania Press, 1999), 320; and A.W.B. Simpson, *A History of the Common Law of Contract* (Oxford: Clarendon Press, 1975), 534. See Chapter 5, note 38 below.

18 Diane Bornstein, *Mirrors of Courtesy* (Hamden, CT: Archon Books, 1975), 45. Arthur Ferguson suggests that until humanism had taken root in England, a

gentleman hung on to 'those elements of chivalric idealism that served to lend dignity and meaning to his life' (*The Indian Summer of English Chivalry* [Durham: Duke UP, 1960], 225).

19 John Hooker, *The Life and Times of Sir Peter Carew, Kt.*, ed. John Maclean (London: Bell and Daldy, 1857), 15–19.

20 Thomas Gainsford, *The Glory of England* (London, 1618), 320. Gainsford offers a graphic example of what might happen if his advice is ignored: 'In the yeere 1605. amongst other Travellers, and searchers for novelties out of curiosity, a French Gentleman presumed to tell the artillery, and canons before the Tapinaw [in Constantinople], as they lay by the sea shore, which was taken for so great an offence, that he had a 100. blowes given him on the feete' (197).

21 Hooker, *Life and Times of Sir Peter Carew*, 19–21.

22 Christopher Tyerman, *England and the Crusades 1095–1588* (Chicago: U. of Chicago Press, 1988), 352–3.

23 Hakluyt, *Principall Navigations.* 1598 (Glasgow: James Maclehose, 1903–1905), 4.307.

24 J.R. Hale, ed., *The Travel Journal of Antonio de Beatis* (London: Hakluyt Society, 1979), 7, and see esp. 29–41.

25 William Caxton, epilogue to his translation of Ramon Lull, *Book of the ordre of chivalry* (London, 1484), cited by Bornstein, *Mirrors of Courtesy* (97), who quotes Lull's very similar comments about degenerate nobles in France in the thirteenth century.

26 *The pylgrymage of sir R. Guylforde knight* (London, 1511), fol. xli *et seq.*

27 William West, *The First Part of Simboleography* (London, 1603), Sect. 121, sig. I8. Two German visitors arriving in Venice in 1625 found that the pilgrim galleys had ceased a little over twenty years earlier (M. Margaret Newett, *Pietro Casola's Pilgrimage to Jerusalem* [Manchester: Manchester UP, 1907], 112).

28 Thomas Wright, ed., *Early Travels in Palestine* (London: Henry Bohn, 1848), 295.

29 See Samuel Chew's detailed account of English pilgrimage to Jerusalem in *The Crescent and the Rose* (Oxford: Oxford UP, 1937), ch. 2, especially pp. 75–95.

30 Henry Timberlake, *The Travailes of Two English Pilgrimes* (London, 1611), 37–8; Thomas Gainsford, *The Glory of England* (London, 1618), 30.

31 Richard Helgerson, *Forms of Nationhood* (Chicago: Chicago UP, 1992), 169.

32 Bornstein, *Mirrors of Courtesy*, 99.

33 Gerard Malynes, *Lex Mercatoria* (London, 1622), 197.

34 Jean-Christophe Agnew, *Worlds Apart* (Cambridge: Cambridge UP, 1992), 37–8.

35 Agnew, *Worlds Apart*, 37; Alan Everitt, 'The Marketing of Agricultural Produce', in Joan Thirsk, ed., *The Agrarian History of England and Wales*, vol. 4, *1500–1640* (Cambridge: Cambridge UP 1967), 557. Cf. the discussion of 'the kind of face-to-face commercial relationships' and direct bargains that obtained in the mediaeval marketplace, in Christopher W. Brooks, *Law, Politics and Society in Early Modern England* (Cambridge: Cambridge UP, 2008), 311–12.

36 van Niekerk, *Development of the Principles of Insurance Law*, 100.

37 Lorraine Daston, 'The Domestication of Risk', in L. Kruger et al, eds., *The Probabilistic Revolution* (Cambridge, Mass.: MIT Press, 1987), 240. Daston

emphasizes that this was a broad category, 'subsuming all agreements involving an element of chance … annuities, gambling, expectation of an estate, purchase of a future harvest or the next catch of a fisherman's net, insurance, and even risky business ventures all fall under this rubric' (238–9).

38 Samuel Marshall, *A Treatise on the Law of Insurance* (London: J. Butterworth, 1808), 738.

39 Bottomry developed out of the maritime loan, the most ancient form of cover and essential to the development of long-range trade, but criticized as a form of gambling even in classical times (see R. Brenner, *Gambling and Speculation* [Cambridge: Cambridge UP, 1990], 103). Maritime insurance was condemned as usurious by mediaeval popes because it was a form of investment 'that reaped gain without labor' (Daston, 'Domestication', 238) – a criticism that could readily be made of sedentary moneylenders who underwrote maritime ventures and charged a high rate of interest.

40 *The Lives of the Noble Grecians and Romans*, trans. Sir Thomas North (London, 1595), 383. Malynes describes a type of hybrid contract involving insurance that paid a virtually guaranteed 30 per cent interest on investment (*Lex Mercatoria*, 172).

41 Agnew, *Worlds Apart*, 37. The practice of framing insurance as another kind of contract may also, as James Franklin suggests, have had something to do with 'the conceptual difficulty of isolating a risk as a thing in itself' (*The Science of Conjecture* [Baltimore: Johns Hopkins UP, 2001], 274), so that although in practice late-mediaeval commerce was able to set premiums for specific maritime routes and variable rates for winter and summer, these were based on experience and observation rather than actuarial calculation.

42 van Niekerk, *Development of the Principles of Insurance Law*, 159.

43 National Archives SP 46/185, fol. 28, printed in Hubert Hall, *Society in the Elizabethan Age* (London: Sonnenschein, 1892), 53–4.

44 Thomas Wilson, *A Discourse upon Usury* (London, 1572), fol. 99v. Wilson's examples are mostly merchants' transactions that involve excessive profiteering and suggest a kinship with Stoddard's deals: e.g., 'I come to an other man, and borrowe forty pound of him for three moneths, and do promise to geve his wife a gown of satine, or an amblyng gelding for his or her ridinge, without any expresse covenaunt in writing, this is playne usury, although for his lendyng, hee dothe not receive anye thinge that is paide by number, weight or measure. Yet forasmuche as he receiveth a value above the principall, he is an usurer' (fol. 102v–103).

45 T.S. Willan, *The Muscovy Merchants of 1555* (Manchester: Manchester UP, 1953), 27, 120. Robinson was an exporter of woollen cloth, one of the prime commodities for which English merchants sought new markets after 1550 (T.S. Willan, *The Early History of the Russia Company, 1553–1603* [Manchester: Manchester UP, 1956], 3). Stoddard's role may have been to facilitate the sale of cloth and to invest the proceeds in goods brought back from Russia, principally furs, wax and naval stores, on which there were large profits to be made. See Willan, *Early History*, 52–3.

46 Hakluyt, *Principal Navigations*, 2.195, 212.

47 Hakluyt, *Principal Navigations*, 2.204.

48 Hall, *Society*, 53. Another of Stoddard's deals saw him supplying warm clothing to a Russia merchant in exchange for '3 sabylls of the very best … or to paye me at his return … 20£' (52). 'As for sables and other rich furres' commented a

company memo, 'they be not every mans money' (Hakluyt, *Principal Navigations*, 1.383). Stoddard was getting his sable pelts at a bargain price.

49 Hakluyt, *Principal Navigations*, 2.291.

50 Hakluyt, *Principal Navigations*, 2.200, 283ff.

51 W.S. Page, *The Russia Company from 1553 to 1660* (London, W. Brown, 1911), 12.

52 Raymond H. Fisher, *The Russian Fur Trade, 1550–1700* (Berkeley: U. of California Press, 1943), 200.

53 Bill of Henry Bridgeman for the 'fourth voyadge to the East Indies' (1608), in G. Birdwood and W. Foster, eds., *The Register of Letters of the ... Company ... trading into the East Indies* (London: Quaritch, 1893), 272. This volume is usually known as *The First Letter-Book of the East India Company, 1600–1619.*

54 Birdwood, *Register of Letters*, 53–4. I am indebted to Richmond Barbour for this reference; see also his 'Corporate Praxis and the Legacy of Privateering: The Jacobean East India Company', *Clio* 41 (2011), 1–29, esp. p.14.

55 *CSP Colonial, East Indies, China and Japan, 1513–1616* (1864), 110–11 (Court Minutes for 6–18 November 1600); see also John Bruce, *Annals of the Honorable East-India Company* (London: Black, 1810), I.131.

56 Birdwood, *Register of Letters*, 418.

57 Birdwood, *Register of Letters*, 344.

58 Moryson, *Itinerary*, I.428–9.

59 Compare, with the typical private wager, this agreement made with an investor who joined the first voyage: 'for his entertainment in the voyage, £100 for his expenses, and £200 for an adventure; if, on his return, the profits of the voyage yield two for one, he is to have £500, if three for one £1,000, if four for one £1,500, and if five for one £2,000' (*CSP Colonial*, 107: Court Minutes for 8 October 1600).

60 Lorraine Daston argues that 'insurance on lives was closely associated with bets on the life of a third person until the latter half of the eighteenth century', and that '[a]ll ordinances regulating insurance prior to 1681 that mention life insurance prohibit it and usually prohibit bets on lives in the same clause.... Life insurance remained illegal in France until 1819' ('The Domestication of Risk', 239, 256).

61 Wagers on lives were banned in Genoa and Barcelona in the fifteenth century and in the Netherlands in 1571. See F.E. de Roover, 'Early Examples of Marine Insurance', *Journal of Economic History* 5 (1945), 197.

62 See R.S. Smith, 'Life Insurance in Fifteenth-Century Barcelona', *Journal of Economic History* 1 (1941), 57–9; he also points out that in the port cities of Genoa and Barcelona masters insured their pregnant slaves and husbands their pregnant wives.

63 Franklin, *Science of Conjecture*, 276, 269.

64 Malynes, *Lex Mercatoria*, 149.

65 West, *Simboleography*, Sect 664 (Qq5). Malynes says that working out a rate for life insurance depends on 'whether aged or young ... of disposition gentle or quarrelsome, a traveller or a dweller' (160).

66 Thomas Coryat, *Coryates Crambe* (London, 1611), A3v, D4.

67 De Roover, 'Early Marine Insurance', 189–94.

68 For a succinct summary of the issue, see Gerd Gigerenzer et al, *The Empire of Chance: How Probability Changed Science and Everyday Life* (Cambridge: Cambridge UP, 1989), 1–13. F.N. David suggests that in Italy during the sixteenth century 'among mathematicians the knowledge of how to calculate a probability percolated', leading to Galileo's work on games of dice (*Games, Gods and Gambling: A History of Probability and Statistical Ideas* [Mineola, NY: Dover, 1998], 62).

69 Ian Hacking, *The Emergence of Probability* (Cambridge: Cambridge UP, 1975), 50, and *passim* on the prehistory of these ideas.

70 Lorraine Daston, *Classical Probability in the Enlightenment* (Princeton: Princeton UP 1988), 10.

71 W.H., *The Reformed Travailer* (London, 1606), sig. B.

72 Roger Ascham, *The Scholemaster* (London, 1571), fol. 18.

73 Thomas Wilson, *The Arte Of Rhetorique* (London, 1553), D4. See Arthur Kinney, *Humanist Poetics* (Amhurst: U. of Massachusetts Press, 1986), 58–9.

74 Ascham, *The Scholemaster*, fol. 18v–19.

75 Hall, *Quo Vadis?* (London, 1617), 46–7.

76 K.R. Bartlett, *The English in Italy, 1525–1558: A Study in Culture and Politics* (Geneva: Slatkine, 1991), 34.

77 See Dennis Flynn, *John Donne and the Ancient Catholic Nobility* (Bloomington: Indiana UP, 1995), 170–71.

78 *CSP Foreign*, 14 (1579–80), 168.

79 William Fennor, *Pluto his Travailes* (London, 1612), 15–16.

80 *CSP Venetian*, 8 (1581–91), 16 (29 July 1581).

81 *CSP Foreign*, 15 (1581–2), 335.

82 Thomas Birch, *Memoirs of the Reign of Queen Elizabeth* (London: Millar, 1754), 1.21.

83 Munday, *English Romayne Life* (London, 1582), 72; *The Copie of a Double Letter* (Rheims, 1581), 9.

84 Flynn, *Donne and the Ancient Catholic Nobility*, 98.

85 *CSP Domestic* 6 (1580–1625), vol. 27, Addenda, 24.

86 William Allen, *An Apologie and True Declaration … of the two English Colleges* (Rheims, 1581), fol. 83v–84.

87 William Watson, *A Decacordon of Ten Quodlibeticall Questions* (London, 1602), 128. Cf. Sir Robert Cotton's disparaging remarks about English Catholics: 'most certaine it is, that the people of this Isle exceed the *Romans* in zeale of their profession; In so much that in *Rome* it selfe, I have heard the *English* Fugitives taxed by the name of *Pichia pelli Inglesi*, Knock-brests, *id est*, Hypocrits' (*Cottoni Posthuma* [London, 1651], 125–6).

88 Nashe, *Works*, ed. McKerrow, 2.280; Munday, *English Romayne Lyfe*, 47.

89 *CSP Venetian* 8 (1581–91), 17 (5 August 1581).

90 *CSP Rome* 2 (1572–8), 537.

91 *Records of the English Province of the Society of Jesus, ed. Henry Foley (London: Burns and Oates, 1875–1883), 6.550.*

92 *CSP Domestic* 2 (1581–90), vol. 153, 50.

93 *Records*, ed. Foley, 10. Sega further noted that 'nearly all the ringleaders in sedition are of those who have been admitted immediately after their arrival from England, and for the future, none should be received, but after examination and sifting' (59). The notorious double agent Gilbert Gifford had been part of the first intake of trainee priests in 1579, and was expelled the following year for fomenting conflict in the English College.

94 *Records*, 60, 66.

95 Charles Sledd, 'A general discourse of the Popes holynes devices', in *Miscellanea: Recusant Records*, Catholic Record Society 53 (London: Catholic Record Society, 1961), 219–21.

96 Donna B. Hamilton, *Anthony Munday and the Catholics, 1560–1633* (Aldershot: Ashgate, 2005), 39–40.

97 See the lively and informative account by Mathew Lyons, 'Dreams of Escape – George Gifford: Courtier, Con-Man, Conspirator', at http://mathewlyons.wordpress.com/2011/10/03/dreams-of-escape.

98 Susan M. Maxwell, 'Thomas Cavendish', *ODNB*, 10.645–9.

99 See Hakluyt, *Principal Navigations*, 5.176, 167–8. As Robert Brenner shows, those with money to invest in overseas enterprise were ready to combine interests in Mediterranean commerce, Far Eastern trade and Atlantic privateering (*Merchants and Revolution* [Princeton: Princeton UP, 1993], 19–20).

100 Alan H. Nelson, *Monstrous Adversary: The Life of Edward De Vere* (Liverpool: Liverpool UP, 2003), 203, citing National Archives SP 12/151/42. fol. 96.

101 In January 1581, Gifford participated with at least one of his future creditors, Sir Thomas Perrot, in a Whitehall tournament where Oxford was awarded the prize, but he may have avoided looking for backers amongst his friends in the Earl's inner circle after its fracturing had highlighted the dangerous opinions and lifestyles of so many of its members.

102 Nelson, *Monstrous Adversary*, 204, citing National Archives SP 12/151/43. fol. 95.

103 *CSP Domestic* 2 (1581–90), vol. 208, 240. This was the report of the English ambassador in Paris, who was trying to get Gilbert released.

104 R.B. Wernham, ed., *List & Analysis of State Papers Foreign*, vol.2 (July 1590–May 1591) (London: HMSO, 1969), 470.

105 *Acts of the Privy Council*, 22 (1591–92), 281–4.

106 Henry Wotton, *The Life and Letters of Sir Henry Wotton*, ed. L.P. Smith (Oxford: Clarendon Press, 1966), 1.230.

107 David N. Durant, *Bess of Hardwick* (New York: Atheneum, 1978), 153. The narrative of the journey was first printed in *Camden Miscellany* 17 (3rd Series, vol. 64), as 'Mr. Harrie Cavendish his Journey to and from Constantinople, 1589, by Fox, his Servant', ed. A.C. Wood (London: Royal Historical Society, 1940).

108 D.J.T. Trim, 'Henry Cavendish', *ODNB*, 10.619.

109 Smith, *Wotton*, 1.256.

110 See Smith, *Wotton*, 1.287. In October 1592 Wotton wrote Lord Zouche to tell him, 'I think to cross the Genovesato and Dukedom of Milan. Few are likely to know of that, for those parts grow dangerous' (1.290). The Inquisition was particularly active in Naples and Milan, and the limited protection given to English visitors to Rome was not available there. Cf. Moryson, *Itinerary*, 1.399 on the need for silence in going to Rome.

111 Henry Blount, *A Voyage into the Levant* (London, 1637), 30–31.

112 Nashe, Epistle to *The Terrors of the Night*, in *Works*, ed. McKerrow, 1.343.

# 5

# Gambling, Wagers and the Law

The monetary wager on a journey of some sort had become a familiar device in England by the late sixteenth century, and the structured bet seems to have been a common element in the somewhat disparate collection of exploits that various contemporaries lumped together as 'mad voyages' or 'experiments'. This is not to say that they were linked in people's minds only by this mercenary aspect, since offbeat adventure and the intriguing challenge attracted attention in their own right and the plenitude of both in this period came to be perceived as a distinct vogue. Nonetheless, these wagers were the product of a situation in which gambling was on the increase and taking new forms as economic activity intensified. Historians have tended to focus on the explosion of upper-class betting in the late Tudor and Stuart period: as Lawrence Stone observes, playful transactions in patrician circles after 1580 were characterized both by 'the extraordinary range of subjects for betting' and by a 'phenomenal rise in the stakes'.[1] We have also seen, however, that the wager was not the preserve of aristocrats and gentry: it had long been a feature of merchants' bargains, and bets made in taverns on a foot race or a foreign conflict were hardly a recent invention.[2] But the association of travel with gambling and financial risk was becoming more complicated and multifarious by the final decades of Elizabeth's reign, encouraged by a speculative environment in which the 'adventuring' of money was essential to the enterprise of overseas traders, colonists and privateers. In what follows I want to explore some of these developments a little further, in particular looking at the different forms that the 'bill of adventure' might take, and the ways in which they helped to shape the experience of travel in the period. An important source of information here is the record of litigation over wagers and pledges of investment in projects like the Virginia Company, and three cases that reached the Chancery courts will be examined in some detail. They include the legal dispute that arose after Thomas Coryat's return from Venice in 1608, one that Coryat himself did his best to publicise but which has never been seriously investigated; doing so enables us to construct a more accurate picture of the transaction he made and to consider afresh the relationship between Coryat's wagering agreement and his commitment to recreational travel.

Just as the wager-journey to Rome in the later sixteenth century was affected by political and doctrinal issues, so the risks involved in the voyages on which trade and colonization depended were having to be calculated and met in new ways. We can see these adjustments at work across a range of speculative overseas ventures. Take the complicated relationship of the wager to forms of insurance, discussed earlier. Marine insurance had evolved since the late Middle Ages to meet the seasonal conditions and particular challenges of merchant traffic in northern waters, and we might have expected that life insurance, which was not prohibited in England as it was elsewhere, would have been available to meet one of the most formidable hazards facing seamen who were engaged in voyages to the eastern Mediterranean. Nabil Matar has shown that as early as 'January 1584, there was a money collection in London to redeem sixty English captives among the Muslims.... So numerous were the Englishmen in North African captivity that by 1598, the Spitals Sermons, preached on the Monday and Tuesday after Easter from a special pulpit at St. Mary Spital outside of Bishopsgate, were becoming closely identified with church collections for ransoming "prisoners of the Turk or other heathens."'[3] It is interesting that in France, where life insurance *was* banned after 1570, an exception was made for travellers 'intending to sail in pirate-infested waters', and Geoffrey Clark notes that the 'very real danger of being captured by Turks in the Mediterranean and either sold into slavery or held for ransom made this a prudent investment'.[4] Yet when Gerard Malynes itemizes the 'verie words' used to describe the hazards covered in most English insurance policies, '*Of the Seas, men of Warre, Fire, Enemies, Pirats, Rovers, Theeves*', his concern is entirely with ships and cargoes, not with the vulnerability of those on board, and I have found no evidence of underwriters making insurance specifically against such capture available in England.[5] The ransom collections made in London were in effect a remedy for the lack of formal cover, and they may well have been required to rescue travellers who had put out money in a bill of adventure. The fact that working sailors were making wagers on the earliest voyages of the East India Company makes it probable that these bargains were already a feature of the Levant trade in the previous decade or so, and gentlemen embarking as privateers in the Mediterranean often staked what fortune they possessed on participation in such voyages. There were few (if any) ways in which either group could provide against perils to the person. William West's much-reprinted legal handbook included a specimen life insurance policy for the first time in 1603 (his *pro forma* is dated 1596), which required that the insured 'meaneth not to travaile out of England' – a stipulation that remained in subsequent editions up to 1647. As we saw earlier, the prohibition on foreign travel must have been lifted in the Jacobean years, since Malynes in 1622 tells us that the wager-traveller to 'Jerusalem or Babylon ... will providently assure a summe of money on his life' as security for loans obtained to enable the trip.[6] Yet the Barbary captive was in an awkward position, since payout on such insurance depended on his presumed demise, and the policy would probably have been seen by his creditors as a more reliable source of reimbursement than anything a returning prisoner was likely to have to his name. English travellers in pirate-infested waters, whether wagerers or not, were taking a gamble on personal safety that relied on the goodwill of their neighbours at home rather than the protection of an insurance policy – one that in any case might have been denied to those who took to the Mediterranean as would-be plunderers themselves. Fortune, not Prudence, was their ruling deity.[7]

Gambling encroached on the world of travel in other ways as well. In the 1560s England experimented for the first time with lotteries, which were well established in the Low Countries as a means of funding public works. One historian has found evidence of English and Scottish participation in a lottery at Bruges in 1446, and we can assume that traders across the narrow seas regularly enjoyed a flutter in the more liberal economic climate of the Netherlands.[8] When the lottery eventually reached England in 1568, however, it was something of a flop: the Queen had hoped to raise £200,000 for England's harbours and other projects, but ticket sales realized less than 10 per cent of that figure. Five proclamations were needed to galvanise interest, and a large number of blanks had to be put in the draw. An additional enticement to punters was the provision 'that every person adventuring their Money in this Lotterie, may have ... libertie in comming and departing to and from the Citie of London, during all the time of the reading of the same Lotterie, untill their last adventure be to them answered', an allowance that also promised freedom from 'any molestation or arrest' to any offender not accused of a major crime.[9] This rather exceptional lifting of the normal restrictions on personal movement (under the vagrancy laws) was a harbinger of the mobility that would become irresistible in later decades, particularly from the countryside into the cities, and it is possible that the 1568 lottery offered the first officially sanctioned opportunity in England for domestic tourism that was not linked either to pilgrimage or to attendance at civic celebrations.

The lukewarm response of the English public to the first state lottery may have been due to unfamiliarity with the concept of public gambling, or simply to the high price of tickets, which cost 10 shillings, and suspicions were probably reinforced by conservative religious warnings about the dangers of tempting providence. As we saw earlier, the idea of betting on an uncertain event could be seen by Christians as potentially impious, a frivolous tampering with God's will, though divination by lot was sanctioned by the Bible and used in mediaeval Europe for serious purposes like selecting magistrates and dividing lands among several heirs. Church Fathers like Aquinas had made space for the role of chance in God's providential order and were not opposed to all forms of monetary gambling. In post-Reformation England, however, the issue took on a new urgency. Puritan teaching insisted that God determines 'the outcome of all randomized events both in divination and in gambling',[10] so the latter came under renewed attack: as James Balmford put it in 1593, 'making God an umpire, by playing with lotterie, must needs be a sinne', and the Puritan divine William Perkins warned that 'seeing the use of a lotte is a solemne act of religion, it may not be applied to sporting', by which he meant 'games of meere hazard', such as dice-play, which are 'matter of stirring up troblesome passions ... and so they distemper the body and mind'.[11] This was a common complaint at the time about the effects of gambling on the populace, and it must have resonated with the city fathers, who reacted to the holding of private lotteries in 1604 and 1606 (the latter set up by an Italian merchant to raffle surplus stock) with a petition to the government in January 1607 for a ban because of the 'great clamour and tumult daily made by servants and apprentices', and begging that 'none should in future be permitted within the City'.[12] But the authorities were swimming against the tide: unlike the occasional state lotteries of the previous reign, these commercial enterprises were clearly popular with ordinary citizens, despite various charges of malpractice and chicanery, and they tapped into the 'adventuring' culture of early seventeenth-century England in ways that are revealing about the perils and opportunities that it offered. To illustrate this, I want to look first at a vivid contemporary document of events in the severe winter of 1607–1608 and then at the simultaneous beginnings of English settlement in North America.

In his pamphlet *The Great Frost* (1608), commemorating a nationwide freeze that lasted almost four months, Thomas Dekker invents a dialogue between a London citizen and a countryman from Yorkshire, in which the latter claims to have come to the capital to see the frozen Thames with his own eyes, and to 'drink a pinte of sack in the Tavern that runs upon wheels on the river' (A4). After testing his credulity with a reference to William Bush's exploit the previous summer, the citizen entertains the visitor with stories of the 'wylde youthes and boyes [who] were the first Marchant-venturers that set out to discover these cold Ilandes of Ise upon the River' (A4v), but the countryman finally admits to another motive for his journey, having heard 'strange report of a certayne Lottery for Plate, of a great value, here in London' (C2v), and that 'the people flie thither like Wild-geese'. The citizen sardonically confirms the rumour: 'You may well say like Wild-geese: for some of them prove such Goose caps by going thither, that they leave themselves no more feathers on their backs then a Goose hath when she is plucked.' He continues with a lively sketch of the scene:

> About the doores multitudes still are crowding ... Everie mouth is balling out for lots, and every hand thrust out to snatch them: both hands are lifted up, the one to deliver the Condemned shillings, the other to Receive the papers of life and death. And when the papers are payed for ... what praying is there in every corner, that God would (if it bee his will) send them good fortune. How gingerly! doe they open their Twelve-pennie commoditie! ... But when he findes within but a pale peace of paper, Lord, how he sweares at his owne folly ... and cries a plague on the house.... Yet when hee hath emptied his bosome of all this bitternesse, the verie casting of his eye upon a goodly faire Bason of silver, so sweetens the remembrance of his lost money, that to it he falles againe ... (C3v–C4)

The countryman responds with a variation on the citizen's earlier voyaging metaphor: 'But amongst all these Land Rovers, have none of them the lucke of men of warre, to winne rich prizes?', and is told that 'the making of one, is the undoing of an hundred.... These doe all suffer shipwracke, and the sea swallowes the spoyle.' The alignment of lottery prizes with the spoils of piracy looks like an easy joke, and certainly the shipwreck metaphor is a very common one in writing about the hazards of London existence at this time, but in this case it lights up a world of hardship and insecurity in which the speculative ventures of the day were seen by those with little to lose as a means to improve their fortunes. Dekker's pamphlet draws a clear connection between the suffering of both town and country, the cessation of trade in the harsh conditions, and the exaggerated hopes invested in the raffle just described, and the countryman's analogy reminds us that the crews of privateering ships were drawn from the same straitened communities and preferred the major risks of a potentially gainful voyage to the privations of home, even though such ventures were the 'undoing' of a large proportion of mariners. In this economic climate, lotteries had an obvious appeal to entrepreneurs and punters alike, despite the objections of civic and religious leaders, and it was only a matter of time before they were pressed into supporting an actual overseas project.

At the very moment that the intrepid youth of London were venturing on the ice of the Thames, and the exceptional cold had otherwise brought the country virtually to a standstill, the settlers at Jamestown, the first permanent English colony in the Americas, were struggling to survive their first winter on a new continent.[13] In each case, hardship highlighted class interests and divisions. In Dekker's pamphlet the countryman complains that amidst the rural dearth in England '[r]ich men had never more money, and Covetousnesse had never lesse pittie: there was never in any age more mony stirring, nor never more stir to gette mony' (B3v), while the citizen comments ironically, '[i]f it be a Gentlemans life to live idely, and doe nothing, how many poore Artificers and Trades-men have beene made Gentlemen then by this Frost' (B2v). Meanwhile, on the other side of the Atlantic the gentleman colonists, who numbered fully a third of the original party, were poorly suited to the hard work of building a settlement in the wilderness, and were in many cases more interested in searching for the gold and other minerals that they had been assured were present in Virginia. By the end of the first winter many of them were dead, and the rock samples they sent back to England to be assayed turned out, in an echo of Frobisher's pyrites fiasco 30 years earlier, to be worthless. As the colony was replenished in the following two years, however, lessons did not appear to have been learned. Its commander Captain John Smith complained that the Company was still sending out settlers 'more fit to spoyle a Commonwealth, then either begin one, or but helpe to maintaine one', and denounced 'our gilded refiners' (the goldsmiths brought over by Newport in 1608) who 'with their golden promises, made all men their slaves in hope of recompense. There was no talke, no hope, nor worke, but dig gold, wash gold, refine gold, load gold.' For Londoners going to the theatre and reading pamphlets like Dekker's *Great Frost*, this was already the stuff of satire, for the hugely popular play *Eastward Ho!*, staged in 1605 and going through three quarto editions in the same year, had provided a lampoon of Virginian delusions in the foolish knight Petronel Flash, an epitome of the feckless gentleman adventurer seen by many as undermining the colonial effort. In the play, Sir Petronel's voyage to Virginia gets no further than the Isle of Dogs, in an acerbic comment on colonial failures up to that date, but the disproportionate number of 'poore Gentlemen ... libertines, and such like' going to Jamestown became a pressing issue for Company officials, who soon came to realize that they needed more skilled artisans and experienced manual workers. As John Smith saw it, the gentry were importing a service culture that was wholly unsuited to the task in hand, for 'those we write labourers were for most part footmen, and such as they that were Adventurers brought to attend them ... that never did know what a dayes work was'.[14] The resulting dysfunction and social strife, according to the promotional writer Robert Johnson, meant that 'the poore Colonie seemed (like the Colledge of English fugitives in Rome) as a hostile Campe within it selfe'.[15] In the event, though, Jamestown would be rescued not only through better planning and investment but also by resort to the kind of speculative devices that had become an enabling part of contemporary voyaging.

The subsequent story of the formation of a joint-stock company, the colony's reinvention in a blaze of publicity in 1609, and its tribulations in the following two years, is too well-known to need retelling.[16] What matters for our purposes is that in 1612, despite strenuous fundraising efforts and recruitment drives, the Virginia Company's finances remained precarious, and the directors decided to seek royal permission to hold a lottery. Although the number of declared investors had been expanded by the 1609 campaign, a steady stream of bad news from Jamestown meant that support was drying up, and a number of prominent subscribers were accused of reneging on their commitments. In his promotional tract Robert Johnson attacked the parsimony of these men 'of the greater sort' (F2v), claiming that because so many have let the Company down, the 'few willing mindes' bear all the burden. A lottery was therefore needed to raise funds for the colony, and Johnson defended it as suitable 'for the publike service of most commendable actions, wherein no man being compelled to adventure lots further then his own liking, and being assured of direct and current dealing' (F3v). His model was clearly the public lotteries held in the Netherlands rather than private Jacobean affairs like the 1608 raffle discussed above, and he urged citizens to invest in what was in essence a national project. Even if they did not win anything, they would have the satisfaction of knowing they had contributed to a worthy cause. In this sense Johnson reframes the lottery as a kind of subscription system, but one that because it requires the purchase of a ticket makes it impossible to withdraw from the deal. This became explicit in the lottery held in 1616, for which the following inducement was offered to the public:

> And whosoever ... shall adventure twelve pounds ten shillings or upward, if he please to leave & remit his Prizes and Rewards, bee they more or lesse, the Lottery

> being drawne out, hee shall have a bill of Adventure to *Virginia*, for the like sum he adventured, & shall be free of that Company, & have his part in Lands, & all other profits hereafter arising thence, according to his adventure of twelve pounds ten shillings or upwards.[17]

In other words, the mere purchase of lottery tickets at the stipulated amount constituted an investment, from which benefits could flow once the buyer had surrendered the right to any prizes he might win in the draw. The Company directors must have decided that repackaging the game of chance as a commercial opportunity would appeal to a certain type of player, and build closer relationships between the organization and wealthier members of the community. But there was irony in the fact that only a few years earlier they had turned to public gambling precisely because of the difficulty in raising such investment.

The reality was that standing lotteries to raise money for Jamestown had only mixed success. Tickets were expensive (from 2s.6d. to 5s. as against the shilling charged in the 1608 private lottery), and negative reports of life in the colony continued to circulate. Whatever the reasons, public response to each of the proclaimed draws in London was sluggish, often leading to their postponement, although 'running' lotteries in the provinces, which operated on an immediate 'lucky dip' basis rather than a single grand draw on a set date, and had much cheaper tickets, were considerably more popular and effective. By 1616, the Company was in the difficult position of trying simultaneously to reinvigorate the standing lottery and to get reluctant investors to honour their pledges. Another of the inducements offered reveals a canny two-handed approach:

> Whosoever is behinde with the payment of any sum of money, promised heretofore to be adventured to *Virginia*, if hee adventure in this Lotterie the double of that sum ... he shall be discharged of the foresaid summe so promised ... and of all actions and damages therefrom arising, and have also the benefit of all Prizes and Rewards ... due by reason of the like sum which he shall bring in, and yet notwithstanding, if after the Lottery drawne, he list to remit al his said Prizes and Rewards, he shall have a bill of adventure to *Virginia* for the said entire summe ...

We saw that the minimum payment required for such a bill was £12.10s., which not coincidentally was equal to the annual contribution pledged by most individual investors. When the Virginia Company took several of those investors to court in 1612 for defaulting on their commitments, its plea was that they had undertaken to 'adventure and lay Down towards a newe supply to bee sent for the reliefe of the said Colonie in Virginia the some of seaven and thirty pounds and tenn shillings at least ... the said some to bee paid in three yeares' – that is, in annual instalments of £12.10s.[18] If we assume that such persons were typically a year in arrears, they were now being invited to spend £25 or above on the lottery, have their debt forgiven, and either to keep any prizes they won or to have that sum invested in the stock of the company.

The offer was shrewdly calculated to allow adventurers to save their honour by having a flutter, albeit an expensive one, and at the same time give them a second chance to pursue a sound investment. Whichever option they chose, the Company would receive an injection of funds that was proving difficult to attract by the usual means.

We do not know how successful this latter ploy was, but it suggests an awareness of how to tap into the wagering inclinations of merchants and gentlemen and coax them into serving a more systematic business plan. The invitation to forgo prizes in favour of a stake in the Company turns the lot into a piece of venture capital, whose potential returns are directly linked to the fortunes of the colony, and it is implicitly offered as a superior course for the serious speculator, the man of affairs who treats hazard as something more than the workings of chance. It would not have escaped such investors that they were being manoeuvred into doubling their stake, but the Company was cleverly appealing to their gambling instincts whilst suggesting that the true adventurer looks for something more than a win on a raffle. In doing so, it reclaims risk from the opaque process of the lottery, in which judgement and imagination can play no part, and prompts the player to bring those qualities to a set of more intelligible hazards.

The churchmen who promoted the Virginia colony from the pulpit would have approved. As already noted, radical preachers reserved their special ire for 'all such Games and Playes as merely consist upon blind hazard and doubtfull chaunce': these, declared one in 1586, 'are flatly by us (as unlawful) rejected and condemned'.[19] But the same writer moved on to offer a cautious allowance to other recreations where 'to the winning and obteyning of the victorie, honest industrie of the minde helpeth more, then any blind casualtie or chaunceable hazard', and bad luck may be 'amended and refourmed by Arte and cunning' (F4). A few years later James Balmford was prepared to 'consider whether exercise of wit doth sanctifie playing with lotterie, or playing with lotterie make such exercising of wit a sinne' (A6v), and although he embraces the latter proposition, he is clearly aware of the alternative's appeal. William Perkins in 1608 noted the common distinction between games of 'wit or industry', and of 'hazzard' (bk.3, 121), but was more interested in their interaction, whereby 'hazard beginnes the game, and skill gets the victorie: and that which is defective by reason of hazard, is corrected by witte' (123). Such arguments provide the basis for a defence of risky enterprise, of 'adventure' in all its senses. They support the growing stress on adaptability and engagement with a multifarious world. I suggested in the last chapter that Jesuit casuistry, which sought textual authority for a 'probable' outcome to an uncertain event, offered support – not least in the vexed argument about the value of travel – to the idea that books were a better guide to conduct than learning from exposure to worldly accident. But the Protestant rejection of ecclesiastical authority meant that the appeal to old texts lost much of its cogency, and the space for individual initiative, for exercise of wit, was necessarily increased.

An engaging minor example of such initiative was shown by the 12-year-old John Ogilby, future translator of Virgil and Aesop and author of atlases, who, in a variation on the ransom collections for Barbary captives, bought winning lottery tickets that enabled him to deliver his father from debtors' prison.[20] And a number of religious institutions were able to overlook the strictures on 'blind casualtie' and see their way to a pragmatic investment: for instance, the clergy of St Mary's, Colechurch 'agreed to adventur sixe poundes of the proffitt of our churche stocke in the lottrey for the plantacion of Vergenya and what benifitt shall hapen thereby shalbe for the good of our church'.[21] They, and others, were able to tell themselves that their lots were purchased in a noble cause, even though there were many who thought that betting on Virginia was anything but honest industry of the mind. For his part the Spanish ambassador, nervous about the Company's designs on North America, refused to see the lottery as genuinely enabling the Jamestown settlers and called it 'a generall kynde of begging', adding that the colony 'was maynteyned but by these shifts, which could last but a yeare or two'.[22] He was right about the role of money thus raised in sustaining the colony, though wrong about its durability, for in fact lotteries were crucial to the survival of Jamestown throughout the second decade of the seventeenth century, providing, as John Smith declared in 1621, the 'reall and substantiall food, by which Virginia hath been nourished'.[23] Yet what they provided was subsistence, not development, and by 1620 they had exhausted their usefulness. A royal proclamation on 8 March suspended the lotteries used by those 'intending to deduce a Colony, and to make a Plantation in Virginia', noting that they 'doe dayly decline to more and more inconvenience'.[24] Just as English maritime policy needed to adapt to new conditions, so the types of financial adventuring that were used to pursue overseas initiatives were being tested by economic and social developments in Stuart England.

## Varieties of 'putting out'

As we have seen, the bill of adventure could take many forms, and American voyages invited particular kinds of speculative investment. Although it is not inconceivable that one of the 'wits of England', as Robert Johnson called them, men 'of unsettled braines' who 'wander from coast to coast' (*New Life*, F4v) might have undertaken a voyage to Virginia as a bargain of return, depositing a sum on departure and betting on a quick fortune made in the colony's putative goldfields, this became less likely once the business of settlement was fully underway. Most of the colonists who returned to England in Jamestown's early years had not planned to do so, not at least in a way that could be captured in a contract, and I have not found evidence of anyone 'putting out' on a wager to America in the way people did to Europe and the Near East. Nonetheless, there is a family resemblance between the contracts being made to finance the Jamestown colony and the wager agreements examined in earlier chapters, one that becomes apparent when we examine the legal records in which many disputes over financial adventures are aired. In the 1612 case mentioned above, where the Virginia Company brought a case against several defaulting investors, it alleged that

> manie of the said Adventurers out of a Careles or Covetous Disposicon have not only refused to send in theire said adventures at the tymes dew … but being required and sent unto for the same moneys some of them doe make slight and dilatory aunsweres and others doe utterly denie and refuse to pay the same unles they shalbee thereunto by lawe Compelled … [25]

The Company had taken the step of bringing the case direct to the Court of Chancery 'for the avoiding of multiplicitie of suits at the Comon lawe' (38), and implied they had warrant for this in the King's special interest in and support for the Jamestown project. The directors may have wished to pre-empt the appeals to Chancery that were routinely made by debtors trying to overturn rulings against them in the Common Law courts. One of the defendants, Sir Thomas Mildmay, answered the charge by professing ignorance of the terms of the royal charter that approved the 1612 lottery and that spelt out the obligations of those who had pledged support. Mildmay's name and those of his co-defendants were on the charter document, yet he claimed that he had been approached privately 'three yeares … past or more' by Sir Robert Mansfield and invited to 'adventure in the said Plantacon'. Having been assured that

> the said mony would be imployed for the benefitt and profitt of the adventures, this defendant condiscended unto the request of the said Sir Robert in hope of receiving benefitt by his adventures accordinglie.

Mildmay admitted that he did 'subscribe his hand unto a booke', but had subsequently learned that there had been 'noe profitt yealded or given up' to any of the adventurers and none expected within 20 years. He also alleged 'that the treasurer of the said mony intendeth … to make profitt and advantage to him selfe and not any such generall good' (*Records*, 40). It is a curiously contradictory defence, on the one hand insisting on consideration of the 'generall good' and on the other claiming the right to renege on the deal if it did not deliver him a personal profit.

Despite the obvious holes in his argument, Mildmay took refuge in the implication that this was essentially a private agreement between men of honour and rank; not a wager, since he expected a more or less guaranteed return, but a pledge on terms that had turned out to be misleading and which he argued should exempt him from any obligation in law. Not only had Sir Robert's assurances of a profit turned out to be baseless, but the treasurer's alleged misappropriation of funds had discredited the entire project. Another defendant, Sir John Sammes, made the further claim that 'the greate somes of mony amountinge to £8000 or thereabouts which have bene gotten by the lottarie and intended to have bene used and disbursed in and about the buisines and plantacon of Virginia have not beene imployed nor bestowed accordingly' (47–8). Whether these claims had any substance or not, they look in this context like special pleading, and indicate that these men saw their 'adventure' as one ruled by a code that was conveniently selective in its use of the law.

Let us compare this case with a rather different one heard in Chancery a few years later. In July 1624, Sir Richard Conquest, a senior member of an ancient Bedfordshire family, brought an action against his cousin George Conquest to dispute a debt of £30 that George was seeking to recover from him.[26] The money being claimed was the payout on a wager journey to the Middle East that had apparently been completed some four years before. Both sides testified that one Thomas Fynett, described as 'gent.' in one of the court documents, had elected to make the trip and that Sir Richard had agreed to receive £10 from Fynett as the latter's stake in a 3-for-1 wager on his return. (George Conquest later took over the bond and assumed responsibility for collecting on the debt: it was after he threatened to take his cousin to court that the latter launched a suit in Chancery to have the debt set aside.) In his answer to Sir Richard's suit, George claimed that he himself had made a similar wager with Fynett, who 'did tell this defendant that he purposed to make a voyadge or iourney from England unto Babylon or Bagdatt in Caldea'. (Ancient Babylon and modern Baghdad were often assumed to occupy the same site in Chaldea [Mesopotamia].) Whereupon George agreed 'to accept and receave of the said ffynnett the some of £10 and to become bounde to give and paye unto him the said ffynnett £30 att his … retorne', which 'this defendant bona fide did doe and performe accordinglye'. George admitted that, 'beinge a well wisher to the said ffynnett', he also persuaded his cousin and others 'to accepte and take of the said ffynnett some moneys to paye him 3 for one at his retourne', but insisted that he did not try to prescribe the amount to be wagered. He also denied Sir Richard's claim that 'he much encouraged your orator with serious affirmations that he verily thought the sayd vyage to bee soe dangerous that it was altogether unlikelie that the sayd ffynnett showld ever retorne from thence into Ingland agayne'. Apparently neither plaintiff nor defendant had any qualms about what a safe bet meant in this instance. Like the defaulting investors in the Virginia Company, Sir Richard claimed that a betrayal of expectation nullified the legal claims upon him, and again like them, sought to show that the entire transaction was tainted by the actions and motives of other players.

Conquest's wager that the deadly perils of travel would work to his advantage was a less edifying gamble than the one undertaken by the Virginia knights, who were risking their money on overcoming comparable dangers. But in each case, the financial adventure turned out to be an uneasy fit both with the realities of overseas enterprise and with the requirements of law. Sir Thomas Mildmay and his colleagues found themselves in a project that belied their hopes of quick reward and saddled them with unwelcome debt, while the Conquest case reveals some of the messy complexities of travel that a 'sporting' journey might seem designed to sidestep or overlook. As one of very few known examples of the travel wager that we are able to examine in any detail, it is worth exploring a little further.

Sir Richard Conquest, we recall, took Thomas Fynett's wager of £10 but on the latter's return from Baghdad was unwilling to pay him the £30 due under their agreement. In his submission to Chancery he offered various reasons for this, including a doubt about whether the journey had actually been performed:

> After such tyme as … the sayd ffynnett had taken upon him to goe the sayd vyage and did make shewe therof accordinglie, [he] afterwards within three or foure monthes at the most did make retorne agayne into Ingland as he sayd from Babylon (albeit your orator never had any certen informacon or intelligence that he was there in deed) … the tyme was so shorte that your orator did not beleive that it was possible that any man could make so greate a vyage & retorne in so little tyme

Fynett had apparently neglected to acquire a testimonial of his visit, if indeed he ever reached Baghdad, then under Ottoman control and a more distant and challenging destination than Constantinople, the favoured goal of enterprising Jacobean tourists to the region. But if Sir Richard was prepared to swallow his incredulity on this point, he was less forgiving about what he claimed to have discovered after taking the wager. What had been presented as a simple 'bargain of return', he alleged, was in fact a more elaborate scheme to make money out of unsuspecting backers:

> And thereupon the sayd George Conquest & ffynnett did compounde and agree that the sayd George Conquest having beene a marchant that used to trafique into Turkey and those countries nowe adjoyninge towards Babilon should be ymployed by the sayd Thomas ffynett in the puttinge forth of divers somes of money for … profitt and gayne

The two men, 'so much the better to countenance and give creditt to these dealings', agreed 'that the money so to bee putt forth or disposed of for that use showld bee taken to bee the proper money of the sayd ffynnett and of noe other person', and thus 'George Conquest himself would seeme to take money of him the sayd ffynnett & in outward shewe showld agree to paye three poundes for everie pound upon his retorne'. The aim of this subterfuge was supposedly 'to drawe the more customers to deale with the sayd ffynnett in taking of money of him upon the sayd vyage as was pretended'. In truth, Sir Richard asserted, each 'putting out' bet that Fynett made was actually financed by his cousin George, who was using his knowledge of the region to create an ingenious confidence trick.

Sir Richard may have suspected that he was not only the only punter to be advised that Fynett was unlikely to complete the journey, but all George Conquest needed to do, arguably, was to let general paranoia about the Turkish threat magnify the odds against a safe return, whilst withholding from potential backers his own more realistic assessment of the risk, based on his experience as a former trader to Ottoman lands. If his cousin's charge is accurate, George Conquest and Fynett were exploiting people's wary fascination with eastern travel to collect multiple pledges and turn a modest financial outlay into substantial earnings. George vigorously denied the accusation, but in presenting his side of the story, he described a complicated negotiation with Fynett which confirmed that the latter had indeed 'ymployed' him to finance the trip. He testified that, having taken the initial wager of £10, 'the said ffynnett having as he said putt out all his moneye upon that voyadge did earnestly entreate this defendant to lend him £100', offering to pay him back 'at his retorne from the place aforesaid £200 for the said £100', on the understanding that if he died en route George would not be repaid. This is a pattern we have encountered before, whereby the putting out of wager money is enabled by a loan that in turn (and in theory) will be repaid out of the returning traveller's winnings. George also declared that he gave Fynett a horse worth £10 'ffor which the said ffynnett did agree to paye to this defendant upon his said retorne £28' – a deal resembling the transactions that were part of George Stoddard's Russian wager-agreements in the 1550s, discussed in the previous chapter.[27] Indeed, the large sum of £200 that Fynett is said to have promised in repayment is the same amount that Stoddard expected from the Muscovy expedition, and while it is not the impressive return of 20-for-1 that the latter expected on his merchant wager, it still represents a very handsome profit on the loan; and this raises the question of what exactly was involved in Fynett's Middle Eastern trip. Was it simply a tourist venture, or was commerce of some kind involved? Was our traveller, like George Conquest, a younger son of the gentry who went into trade? Or was the claim that he needed £100 for the journey a smokescreen to deflect attention from a joint scheme – courtesy of George's money – to put out on multiple wagers and reap an impressive profit?

At one level, Sir Richard's indignation was naïve, since betting on travel to adventurous destinations was always a profit-seeking enterprise, but he clearly felt that being misled about the source of Fynett's £10 and his chances of survival violated the necessary conditions of a wager between men of honour. We may wonder, however, what kind of adventure he imagined Fynett was undertaking. Did he really believe that a journey to Baghdad had been undertaken only for sport and curiosity, and would a more complicated purpose for the trip have changed his perspective on the wager-agreement? A curious hiatus in the Chancery documents may help to address these questions.

George Conquest in his answer to the suit is quite specific about Fynett's destination, describing it more than once as 'Bagdad also called Babylon' and locating it in Chaldea (Mesopotamia), and Sir Richard's charge against his cousin was that as 'a marchant that used to trafique into Turkey and those countries nowe adjoyninge towards Babilon', he 'delte in the sayd martes to his owne use … and therin used the name of the sayd ffynnett onlie & made showe of takinge the like marte himselfe only to bee a setter on of your orator'.

George's chicanery is thus directly linked to his commercial interests in Asia Minor. Yet immediately before making this inference, Sir Richard states that Fynett's intended journey was 'beyond the seas unto Babylon in Egypte', and he repeats the phrase later in the document. There was nothing wrong with his geography: he might well have read of this particular Babylon in George Sandys' recently published account of his travels, where it is described as

> the ruines of the old Citie adjoining to the South of *Cairo*, called formerly *Babylon*, of certaine *Babylonians* then suffered to inhabite by the ancient *AEgyptian* Kings … said to have bene built by *Omar* the successor unto *Mahomet*; but surely rather reedified by him then founded, having had in it such store of Christian Churches as testified by their ruines.

Different places called Babylon were fairly easily confused, not least because a generation of religious controversy had for many Englishmen identified the name with Papal Rome. But how did the two locations come to be mixed up in the careful phrasing of a legal document? It is possible that the error was made by the Chancery clerk who transcribed the deposition, but much more likely that Sir Richard in composing or dictating his testimony fastened on Babylon in Egypt as a natural destination for the private traveller. One of George Sandys' observations of the place made clear its appeal to pilgrim-tourists:

> Besides here is a little Chappell dedicated to our Lady: underneath it is a grott; in which it is said that she hid her selfe when pursued by *Herod*.[28]

This is squarely in the tradition of biblical locations pointed out to pious travellers for centuries and absorbed into the cultural sightseeing of early-modern times, and it is most likely the place that Gerard Malynes had in mind when he gave the example of 'a traveller undertaking a voiage to Jerusalem or Babylon, delivering out money payable at his returne'.[29] It was also one from which a tourist might plausibly return within four months since it need not involve much overland travel, and it is possible that George Conquest initially let his cousin believe that a wager journey to Babylon in Egypt was what Fynett had in mind, in order to win his confidence and distract attention from their more complicated designs in Mesopotamia.

Be that as it may, Baghdad was not a likely destination for the recreational traveller in 1619–20. (In his suit of July 1624 Sir Richard said the journey had been mooted 'aboute ffive yeares since'.) There were of course notable sites in the region: in 1615 Thomas Coryat passed through Ur ('where *Abraham* was born'), somewhat to the south of Babylon, and in the following year, writing from India, he declared his intention on the return trip of seeing 'ancient *Babilon* & *Nymrods* Tower, some few miles from *Nineve*, & in the same the Sepulcher of the Prophet *Jonas*, spacious and goodly'.[30] A few others, like the Reverend John Cartwright on his tour in 1611 and William Lithgow in the same year, were similarly drawn to Mesopotamia's ancient ruins, but the overriding interest of the region for English visitors was political and commercial.[31] Coryat could not have been unaware of the diplomatic efforts by some of his countrymen to secure an alliance with Persia and divert the silk route away from Ottoman territory, for he personally encountered two of them, Sir Robert Sherley and Sir Thomas Roe, during his travels.[32] He would also have witnessed the controversy before his departure from England over Sherley's petition to James I 'that his majesty should admitt genttilmen to adventure in fassion of trade' with Persia. This initiative was strongly opposed by both the Levant and East India Companies, but the king initially supported it, and according to the Venetian ambassador Sherley won permission 'to go to the Persian Gulf with three vessels with people who desire to trade there'. The plan was eventually scotched, but after Sherley had left the country early in 1613, one of his presumed supporters was reported as being ready to 'go for Persia, and many gentlemen go with him and adventure greatly with him'.[33] Their adventuring, needless to say, was commercial, and perhaps military, given the Sherley brothers' role in promoting conflict between Persian and Turk, and nobody less intrepid than Coryat would have contemplated sight-seeing in Mesopotamia in the years following when the Shah was preparing to invade Ottoman territory (he eventually captured Baghdad in 1624).[34] This was the volatile theatre into which Fynett planned to venture and with which George Conquest was already acquainted, and it is difficult not to suspect that their association in the wager agreement was linked to some kind of commercial activity, probably of the 'interloping' sort so deplored by the incorporated trading companies.

In May 1618 a short-lived truce between Persia and the Ottomans freed up the movement of goods across borders, with the Venetian ambassador in Constantinople reporting that '[t]he last letters from Aleppo announce that a very large caravan had arrived there from Bagadet bringing 100 packs of silk' and other goods.[35] Did business opportunities of this sort help to stimulate the Conquest-Fynett arrangements? There is no hard evidence to link either man to Mesopotamian trade at this date, but a plausible explanation for the trip is otherwise lacking. If an attractive gaming wager was all that they sought, there were much easier and more obvious destinations (like Babylon in Egypt). Thomas Fynett may have been the cousin of John Finet, a senior court official under James I and himself an energetic traveller on state business.[36] The agreement that he made with George Conquest must have been predicated on a lucrative venture, since he would surely not have agreed to repay a loan at 100 per cent interest (£200 for £100 outlay) unless he was expecting to use the money to generate substantial profits. (In reality, George may simply have given him £100 to conduct trade and expected a good return on his money.) This looks very much like Stoddard's deal with Robinson, as already suggested, set up as a private wager in order to avoid the restriction on usurious profits. Sir Richard alleged in his suit that his cousin was as a Turkey merchant accustomed to dealing 'for his owne private excessive gayne', and if George was instrumental in setting up and financing Fynett's wager-agreements he may have driven a hard bargain on the loan of £100, not to mention the nearly 300 per cent return he expected on the 'gift' of a horse to Fynett. Sir Richard suspected that George 'was to have all the advantage and benefit therof which might bee so gained upon the retorne of the sayd ffynnett', but his own assertion that George was 'ymployed' by Fynett to raise money for the trip suggests a more complex bargain. So does George's claim that after his return Fynett was unable to pay his £200 debt and that he, George, was left trying to recover money both from the traveller and from his own cousin. Unless Fynett was really a tourist and was rash enough to assume that he would be able to raise the full sum from his wager winnings (Sir Richard may not have been the only punter reluctant to pay up), it looks as if the venture failed to yield the profits expected from trade of some kind and left George with no choice but to take over some of the wager debts and try to recoup some of his investment in the project.

The dispute dragged on for several years, and its outcome is unknown. Sir Richard appealed in 1624 to the Chancery judges to cancel the bond and so forestall George's threat to sue him for 'the sayd whole some of thirtie pounds within a verie shorte tyme' – George's patience clearly being exhausted, but a move which his cousin protested 'is against all equitie & conscience.' Sir Richard sounds here a familiar note in Chancery proceedings, which were frequently undertaken in an attempt to overturn judgements in the Common Law courts or (as in this instance) to forestall cases being tried there. Chancery was an equity court presided over by the Lord Chancellor that dealt particularly with contracts and property rights and adopted a more flexible approach to questions of debt and breach of promise.[37] Private individuals increasingly sought redress there for what they considered harsh or unfair rulings at common law, and as contract issues grew more complex the discretionary approach of the equity court was important in shaping a procedure to deal with difficult cases. But this was perceived as challenging the status of the common law courts, and by late Elizabethan times there was conflict between the two jurisdictions, which sharpened after the turn of the century with the rivalry between the new Lord Chancellor Ellesmere and Sir Edward Coke, a common law judge who was to become Lord Chief Justice. The dispute concerns us here insofar as it flared up briefly over the issue of wagers when the 'bargain of return' was generating a number of legal disputes.

Sir Richard Conquest doubtless hoped to get a sympathetic hearing in Chancery for the argument that his cousin had misrepresented the wager proposal, and a ruling that there was (in legal terminology) no proper 'consideration' for the debt of £30. (A.W.B. Simpson defines consideration as the doctrine that 'the legal effect of a promise should depend upon the factor or factors which motivated the promise.'[38]) That an outstanding bond for £30 existed was not in dispute, but Conquest claimed that to enforce it was against reason and conscience. The defendants in the Virginia Chancery case made the same type of argument. The aleatory element in wager contracts clearly raised a number of problems for the common law courts, not all of which could be resolved simply by reference to the wording of an agreement. Yet, as Simpson argues, it was 'in connection with wagers that the common law first recognized the doctrine that a promise was good consideration for a promise [i.e., that betting on an uncertain event was a reciprocal promise to pay up, binding on both sides] so that wagering contracts so far from being anomalous have in fact been the source of an important contractual doctrine.'[39] One can also see in many common law proceedings the trace of precedent deriving from a forerunner of the travel wager, which was the pledge to perform a devotional journey. We have already noted this custom and its contractual trappings in Dutch practice, and its pre-Reformation usage in England can be inferred from legal formulae such as 'if he go not to Rome by such a day, that his estate shall be void', or analogies like the stipulation that someone inheriting land conditionally 'ought to shew that the condition is performed' just as (citing a fifteenth-century case) a man 'ought to shew that he went to Rome, because it is a precedent condition'.[40] This standard usage evolved naturally with the growth of secular travel bargains: a 1625 argument was that 'a conjectural day of payment is not good, as at Mich[aelmas] after the return of such a one from Rome', which shows the influence of actual wager contracts with explicit deadlines for payment. Contrast this with an earlier judgement (1603) that still reflects pilgrimage practice, finding that a repayment of a debt 'cannot be hastened on request. As if I am bound to you that I will go to Rome, or Jerusalem, &c. In ... all such cases, the obligor has any time in his life to do it.'[41] But if the law was able to draw on a long history of travel practices to illustrate and support its findings in other areas, it was less comfortable dealing with the disputes arising from actual travel wagers.

The surviving cases in the common law reports usually involve the obligor or debtor being taken to court by the returning traveller in order to compel payment of a wager. Most commonly the defendant argued that no proof of the journey being completed was forthcoming, or that there was insufficient or no notice given of the traveller's return, thus violating the terms of the bond. A clutch of cases in the 1580s, the first decade in which the bargain of return seems to have been fashionable, challenged legal interpretation in a number of ways. One Edmund Mullineaux was taken to court in 1588 for reneging on a typical 'putting out' agreement, and asserted that the plaintiff had not reached Rome as claimed. The court was exercised over the issue of whether it could adjudicate on what happened abroad, one opinion being that 'le matter est parcel triable & parcel nemy' – in other words, it could adjudicate on the traveller's return to England but not his arrival in Rome. Serjeant Gawdy thought however that the two matters 'sont accouples per un conjunction en le conditōn', so if one was not triable the whole case must fall. At about the same time, another wagerer to Rome brought a suit to claim his winnings, and was able to back it up with a 'testimonial south les seals de several grand persons vivants al Rome', but its authenticity was challenged ('il dit fortasse cest testimonial est counterfeit'), and the view was taken that the case should be referred to a jury, since 'en cases doubtful le verdict de 12. homes fait sufficient proofe'. A similar argument was made in the case of *Clement v. Browne* (1587–88), where the plaintiff submitted a testimonial 'under the hand of the Duke of Venice', but 'this was held to be no sufficient proofe', and arbitration by jury was recommended.[42] (Juries at this time could be recruited on the basis of expertise, particularly in mercantile matters, and might be people with appropriate knowledge of foreign places.) As time went on the courts grew impatient with some of the defendants' attempts to avoid their obligations and were more ready to rule on international wagers. In a case about a disputed trip to Venice, the judges accepted the plaintiff's testimony and ruled that 'where part is to be done within the realm, and part out of the realm, the plea ought to be triable within the realm'.[43] And in 1594, the King's Bench overturned a Common Pleas judgement in a case where one Griffin undertook to 'pay to Spencer a hundred pounds within one month after notice of his return from Constantinople in Istria'. Griffin had argued that he wasn't given such notice and won an initial ruling, but the King's Bench declared crisply that 'when the defendant saith he had no notice, this is a confession *ver nient dedire*' – a tacit acknowledgement – 'that he had not paid' a lawful debt, and decided for the plaintiff.[44]

As these examples show, the disputed travel wager was the occasion of a fair amount of legal argument, though the common law courts generally found for the plaintiff where there had been a clearly reciprocal agreement between two parties, one who travels and the other who takes his 'putting out' bond.[45] Matters could become more complicated when there were others involved in the transaction, as we have already seen in the Conquest case, for while it was possible, and probably quite common, for a third party to put out money on someone's voyage[46] (either instead of or as well as the traveller himself), his role could create difficulties of interpretation if he were also making a loan of some kind or could be accused of colluding with one or other of the main players. We shall shortly examine the latter problem in the court proceedings that resulted from the wager journey to Venice of Thomas Coryat in 1608. That case, like Sir Richard Conquest's, was heard in Chancery, and was part of the trend to take cases to equity hearings in the hope of a more favourable decision. By the end of the sixteenth century, this had become a common enough tactic with travel wagerers to attract the critical attention of the Master of the Rolls (and soon to be Lord Chancellor Ellesmere), Sir Thomas Egerton. Contract law in general seems to have drawn his scrutiny at this time, and he was alert to the ways in which merchants made deals among themselves, particularly in foreign trade, advising that he 'likes not of these letters of policy upon assurance of adventures used among merchants. But if any case come before him in that kind, he refers the same to be ended amongst merchants, to whom the same course is best known.' Unless they involved fraud, Egerton wanted such matters settled by the merchants' courts that were still a separate jurisdiction. But he recognized that the wagering methods of the merchants had crept into general practice, when shortly afterwards he declared that he 'does utterly reject all bills exhibited to be relieved touching these marts of going to Venice and paying three for one upon return and such like mart bargains. My lord will relieve no party in such case; in like case it is of letters of mart, letters of policy, and of concealments.' That is, Egerton put the bargain of return in the same category as licensed piracy, merchants' speculative ventures and various kinds of sharp business practice; and at about the same time, in dismissing a plea relating to an allegedly shady transaction in which he finds both plaintiff and defendant 'lewd and dishonest', he took a similar line on travel wagers: 'So does my lord proceed in … adventures or marts from Venice or Constantinople, let it fall out of which side it will, practice, fraud, or deceit, all is one. My lord will leave them together to the common law and there shift for themselves.'[47]

Egerton's comments suggest considerable impatience with the vogue for bets on travel, and a hardening conviction that the disputes they gave rise to had no place in the equity courts. His determination to exclude these cases as far as possible from Chancery hearings is the more striking given his role as the defender of equity: as Christopher Brooks indicates, he 'held that, except in the case of usurious contracts, he would not intervene to overthrow a bargain merely because it was foolish', and in the legal notes quoted above made 'a pioneering attempt to lay down guidelines for the general application of equitable discretion.'[48] Moreover, some of his observations reveal a solid concern for the rights of those who have ventured money and been denied recompense: he was reported as declaring that 'where a man has lent his money *bona fide* or otherwise laid out his money and by … malice and malignity … be held out of his money against his will, my lord will allow such a man good damages'.[49] Egerton was evidently concerned to prevent the misuse of the equity courts, and his view may well have been conditioned by the spectacle of plaintiffs in Chancery seeking, often on a technicality or via devious arguments, to avoid their financial obligations. His readiness to detect 'practice, fraud, or deceit' in the travel wager might also have been sharpened later by proceedings like the Conquest suit in Chancery and the case brought against the most celebrated English tourist of his day, Thomas Coryat.

## Thomas Coryat in Court

Coryat made his famous pedestrian journey to Venice and back in the summer and early autumn of 1608.[50] Before he left he wagered £40 on the trip, and in terms of the 'bill of adventure' he drew up with Joseph Starre, a Yeovil linen-draper, he was to receive 200 marks, or £133.6s.8d., on his return. The original bill has not come to light, so we do not know whether a deadline was set or whether Coryat had to produce a testimonial of his visit, though we can be confident that he would have thought to obtain one from Sir Henry Wotton, then ambassador in Venice, to whom he bore letters of introduction and from whom he claimed to have received 'many great favours'. On his return to England in early October, Coryat apparently lost no time in claiming his winnings, but there his troubles began. Starre refused to pay up, and according to Coryat lodged 'a certaine Bill … into the Chancerie against mee shortly after my arrival in England' to have his debt 'nullified or qualified'. This bill too has disappeared, but part of Coryat's answer to it, from which I have just quoted, survives because he printed it in *Coryats Crambe* (1611), a pamphlet that followed hard upon the *Crudities*, the narrative of his European journey. Coryat apparently sued Starre in the Common Law courts, and his antagonist's response was to seek relief in Chancery. The case was heard in late May 1609, and the documents of the court proceedings then and in July of the same year tell a tangled story.[51]

In his Chancery suit Joseph Starre, like Sir Richard Conquest, claimed that there had been collusion against him between two co-defendants, Thomas Coryat and someone called Richard Rowe. (Like Starre, Rowe was a Yeovil man, and as we shall see, the two men appear to have had long-standing financial dealings.[52] Coryat came from the nearby village of Odcombe, and may have preferred to wager with local men who were well known to him rather than with his fashionable associates in London.) Starre implied that Rowe was in fact the prime mover in taking Coryat's wager, claiming that he himself merely agreed to stand 'suritye' for half the amount (100 marks) that Rowe would have to pay Coryat on his return. Under this agreement, Starre agreed that he was 'bounde with the saide Rowe to the defendant Corryet in a bonde of CC markes to paie to Corryet at his returne from Vennice a 100 markes'. But he denied that it was a joint wager, and complained that 'the saide Corryet beinge come from Vennice he by agreement and composicion with Rowe dothe not impleade Rowe for the saide 200 markes', and was instead pursuing Starre for payment. Did the contract spell out Rowe's liability clearly, or did it allow for creative interpretation?[53] Whatever the case, it seems that Starre was holding Coryat's £40, perhaps as security for his earlier pledge, and therefore could be held liable for the full wager. He may have assumed nonetheless that Rowe would pay the full 200 marks as a debt of honour, and it looks as if the realization that this would not happen persuaded him to bring his own pledge of 100 marks into the equation. In a second transcript of the Chancery hearing on 22 May, which is essentially a copy of the first, a few words are added that look like an exercise in damage limitation: Coryat 'dothe not impleade Rowe for the saide C markes *but the plaintiff onlie ffor wch cause and for that the plaintiff is willinge to paie Corryett the saide C markes*' (my italics).[54] The additional words apart, note that Starre no longer claims that Rowe owed the full 200 marks: he presumably asked his counsel at some point to make sure that an acknowledgement of his own liability for half the debt was inserted into his plea, in the hope that this gesture would obviate his contractual responsibility for all of it. The court was not impressed, however, and ordered Starre to accept the bond and pay Coryat the full sum.

That might have been the end of the matter, but apparently 'composicion' was still at work. Just over a month later, Richard Rowe's counsel came back to court to report that, while the bill had indeed been assigned to Starre for payment, the latter had then allied himself with Coryat to 'laye the burthen of the said bondes of CC markes upon the saide Rowe'. Perhaps Coryat now agreed with Starre that the real debt was Rowe's, or was simply looking for the most likely way of getting his money, but Rowe offered a very different account of the original deal, claiming that he was

> drawen in by the said plaintiff's perswation and that the plaintiff was the principall agent with Corryat in the premysses and the said Rowe had never any bill of adventure delivered unto him nor ever sawe any.

He added that this 'is confessed by the said Corryates Aunswere to the plaintiff's bill', though if so, the admission was not included in the section of the answer that Coryat chose to publish. Was Rowe, like Sir Richard Conquest, invited to participate in a transaction that was none of his making and about which he then got cold feet? Presumably his counsel would not have made a claim that could be disproved by a written statement currently before the court. The surviving documents in the case do not resolve this conundrum, but a possible explanation emerges from the records of a later legal dispute between the two men, one that demonstrates again the entanglement of wager agreements in this period with other forms of financial transaction.

In June 1619, 10 years after the Coryat case, Richard Rowe launched an action in Chancery against Joseph Starre, apparently disputing the latter's claim of an unpaid debt. The details of the case need not concern us, but the arguments mounted on both sides do shed some light on their earlier dealings and Coryat's role in them. Rowe testified that Starre had lent him 'the some of twenty pounds upon interest beinge a great usurer & one that letteth out much money upon interest', and Starre does not deny this characterisation, responding with a claim that 'Rowe for 'twenty yeeres or there about ... was never out of this defendants debte one moneth'. Rowe's own deposition does suggest that his financial dealings were complicated, involving various debts and bonds to cover them; he described himself as a yeoman but appears to have been active in local business and dependent on creditors like Starre. He claimed to have repaid 'all the interest' he owed Starre, but the latter used the occasion to dredge up an old debt, informing the court that he, 'the defendant paide for the complainant to one Mr Thomas Corriat amountinge unto seaventy pounds or thereabouts about three yeeres last past as he remembreth.... At which tymes to his best remembrance there was due from the saide Complaynant Rowe the some of fforty pounds of currant English money uppon sundrey accompts'.[55] Starre was hazy about the passage of time, but he clearly recalled the amount Rowe owed him: 100 marks is approximately £70. What is interesting is his further assertion that Rowe already owed him £40 when the wager agreement was made. This is the same amount that Coryat put out before his journey, and Starre may have had a particular reason to recall this debt if it became tied up in some way with the wager. Did Starre perhaps see an opportunity to recover his £40 by taking Coryat's bond and binding Rowe into an agreement to pay out the wager if and when Coryat returned? It would seem a potentially risky move for an experienced moneylender, especially if he had to sweeten the deal by offering to stand surety for half the amount that would be due to the traveller. It was also not an arrangement that stood to yield Starre any financial profit. But taking Coryat's bond, apart from giving him ready money, might have appealed to the instinct for 'sport and recreation' that Gerard Malynes says informed many merchants' wagers[56], and at the same time it tightened his hold over Rowe in the event of Coryat's return. As the later case shows, Starre had not forgotten this particular debt 10 years later.

Chancery was sufficiently impressed by Rowe's claims in the Coryat case to order that the evidence be reviewed before its previous ruling was implemented, and the Master of the Court appointed to do this reported a week later that 'the proceedings at common lawe upon the bond in the said order mentioned should stay untill the plaintiff procure a hearing in this court of the matters complained of by his bill'.[57] Rowe had claimed that Coryat assigned the original bill to Starre 'or to some other to his use whoe doe offer to put the saide bondes in sute in the name of the saide Corryate against Rowe': it is not clear what the subject clause here ('some other … doe offer') refers to, but presumably the court was inclined to believe that Coryat was party to this new action or it would simply have reaffirmed its earlier judgement against Starre. Halting the 'proceedings at common lawe' meant that both this latter suit and the earlier directive to Starre were put on hold, so Coryat's change of tactic was apparently counterproductive. There is no record of a further hearing, however, so this flurry of claim and counterclaim may have produced an out-of-court settlement.

In the parts of his answer to Starre's original suit that he preserved (and probably revised) in the *Crambe*, Coryat works up a fine head of steam about the 'miscellanie of diabolicall falsehoods' that his adversary has perpetrated, and promises to demolish each of Starre's 'fained objections' to paying the debt. Here at least he is in no doubt about who owes him money (though he does agree that Starre's debt was 'a hundred markes … according to his Band', so perhaps Rowe eventually paid the other half). But no details of the original agreement are offered, and in the event Coryat confines himself to an indignant rebuttal of Starre's alleged insinuations about 'the smalnesse and commonnesse of my Voyage', which were obviously intended to cast doubt on the validity of the wager. This would have been a shrewd move on Starre's part, for travel in many parts of western Europe was no longer considered exotic or likely to yield interesting discoveries, and the three-for-one wager to Venice was liable to devaluation through its very availability to tourists.[58] But Coryat was making the trip the hard way, walking a good part of the distance, and travelling alone, which explains his typically grandiloquent response:

> Can he justly call this a small and common Voyage to passe almost Two thousand miles by land? To expose ones body to such a world of imminent dangers both by Sea and Land as I did? to passe those stupendious mountains of the snowie Alpes … & after the consummation of my travels to be thus opposed by a Vilipendious Linnen Draper?[59]

Starre's attempt to belittle Coryat's journey was an admission, in the end, that he had effectively entered into a wager agreement with him: just as Sir Richard Conquest allowed himself to be drawn in by an assurance that the journey to Mesopotamia was unlikely to be completed, so Starre hoped to get out of his pledge by asserting that going to Venice was not worthy of a bet. By using such arguments both men confessed their subscription to the logic of a gambling contract.

It is usually assumed that Coryat got his money in the end, though it may be that his friend Christopher Brooke was referring to other, more successful wager-agreements when he declared that Coryat spent 'the three for one you got / At your returne' on printing his book (*Crudities*, 1.57). By the time Coryat printed his hyperbolical answer to Starre's 'most scandalous, contumelious and hybristicall Bill' in the book's sequel, the case must have been settled or abandoned, and there is a curious disjuncture between his exuberant attack on 'my crafty and versute adversarie' and his prefatory confession that 'my Plaintife hath not as yet given me his consent to publish' the same, which Coryat rather enigmatically declares he has been 'commaunded by Authoritie to Print.' What this suggests is that Coryat's answer had been circulating amongst those responsible for the collection of 'Panegyricke Verses' that prefaced the *Crudities* (perhaps drawing a laugh and a commission from Prince Henry himself[60]) and was now being added to that select group of printed jeux d'esprit, in a literary game that Starre himself was being invited ironically to endorse. Coryat may also have had an eye on his next journey in protesting his adventurous credentials. In the epistolary prefaces to the *Crudities* he is careful to advertise his next excursion to Constantinople and the Holy Land, promising 'to impart many memorable things ... after the end of my next journey' (1.15); he probably hoped to secure better wager terms for the trip to the Levant (five-for-one to Constantinople was not unknown), so it was in his interests to make clear that he had more than justified the smaller odds on a walk to Venice. In the event, Coryat abandoned any wager agreements made for the second journey when he pressed on to India, instead of heading home from the Levant like his companion Henry Allard and every other tourist to the region. It is possible, though, that his new-found celebrity at court and in London's legal and artistic circles after the Venice trip eventually secured him a degree of financial support for the new venture that made a wager unimportant. He had always before him the plan to write a new book about 'farre more memorable matters' in far-off places, and he may have been encouraged to think that next time he would not have to publish it himself.

Coryat's pedestrian feats were a watershed in English recreational travel, creating unprecedented publicity for the act of long-distance walking for pleasure or a bet – a custom that was already part of patrician culture but which thereafter, aided by the enduring popularity of the *Crudities* over the next two centuries, became a fixed part of the English reputation for eccentricity. To make the point in these terms, of course, is to imply that what endured above all was Coryat's reputation as an obsessive showman – the self-styled 'Odcombian Leg-Stretcher' – and that his travels created a model for outlandish adventure by lone Englishmen that has lasted to this day. It is true, I think, that *Coryates Crudities* did more to preserve the idea of the 'madde voiage' as an English speciality than any of the contemporary stunts or wager journeys discussed in earlier chapters, excepting Kemp's dance to Norwich with which Coryat's walk was repeatedly compared by the authors of the 'Panegyrick Verses'. And the reading pleasure the book gave to later generations was a passport to a freer, more subjective and individual concept of travel that in turn licensed numerous pedestrian exploits in eighteenth-century England, and still sustains the national instinct for unusual adventure that I discussed in my opening chapter.[61] It is not my intention, however, to reinstate Coryat's old reputation as a buffoon, however much his own tactics may have encouraged this image of himself. There is a good case for saying that his journey also created a blueprint for a major part of the Grand Tour, and that publication of the *Crudities* led directly to the appearance of a series of serious travel memoirs by writers like George Sandys, William Lithgow and Fynes Moryson. Coryat's own commitment to making a full and proper tour of his chosen route is never in doubt, but he understood that there were few precedents for his venture amongst provincial gentlemen of his type, and none that had seen print or yielded much social recognition. To get noticed in courtly and London circles, Coryat needed (or found it easiest) to play up his own idiosyncracies, and the currently modish travel stunt offered him an attractive outlet for them. But it did so because Coryat's temperament was at odds with many of the rules governing the orthodox tour of Europe and was bound to confront many of the assumptions about what made for beneficial travel. He brought to his travels a set of gifts, or quirks, that did not undermine his serious purposes so much as create a fresh perspective on how they might be achieved. His journey, as preserved in the *Crudities*, was a watershed in the nation's adventuring because it helped to transform people's understanding of what travel might be about.

It was the 'Panegyrick Verses' above all that created and promoted the idea of Coryat's trip as a mad voyage, relentlessly burlesquing his mode of travel, ridiculing his appearance, and highlighting the more bizarre moments of his progress across Europe. The 100-odd pages that the poems occupy have been extensively discussed in recent years, often in preference to studying Coryat's own narrative, and for my purposes the searching analyses of Katharine Craik and Michelle O'Callaghan leave little to add.[62] As these critics remind us, Coryat was thoroughly complicit in the game of assembling the prefatory material, proudly boasting about how much of it there was, despite his equal insistence on the worthy goals of his voyage. O'Callaghan asks the obvious question: given the claims made by Coryat for its educational value, 'why was he so willing to collude with his seeming detractors and make himself the object of their laughter?' Her persuasive answer is that much of the mockery is complex in its effects: 'Laughing at Coryate does not take place within the forms of satire, as such, but rather within the ludic forms of the mockencomion' (120), which represent the traveller as an object of wonder and admiration amidst all the ridicule. This is not to deny that scorning Coryat and representing him as a ragged vagabond was also a device whereby the wits asserted their own urbanity and social superiority, but he himself seems to have appreciated that the fantasticating introduction they supplied was an effective way of preparing the reader for a different kind of travel narrative. The wits offered various light-hearted hints of humanist precedent, such as Laurence Whitaker's commentary on the title-page image of Coryat flanked by personifications of France, Italy and Germany, the latter vomiting on his head:

These be the three countries with their Cornu-copia,
That make him as famous, as Moore his Utopia. (*Crudities*, 1.xviii)

Did Coryat's readers pick up from this a reference, as O'Callaghan puts it, to 'the front matter to More's *Utopia*'? 'The prefatory letters and verses to the *Utopia*', she points out, 'identified More's account of this "philosophical" city as an intellectual game which allowed its participants to play with the idea of travel, opening it to more speculative viewpoints' (128). And if so, how did they read the conflation in these lines of More's *lusus* with the Rabelaisian hint of a fantastic voyage to lands of licensed excess and indulgence? The game being played in Coryat's front matter certainly indicated that they would find in his narrative rather more than was prescribed by the numerous published guides to good travelling practice.

Coryat's complicity in burlesque extended well beyond his orchestration of the prefatory material, of course. It is immediately apparent in the overwrought description of his sea-crossing to France (1.152: another Rabelaisian moment), and a similar linguistic extravagance invades the narrative at regular intervals thereafter. He also took every opportunity to offer himself as protagonist in (and not infrequently victim of) the more colourful incidents of his journey. Coryat's self-dramatisation was entirely new to English travel writing and quite foreign to the priorities of the humanist advice manuals, but it had a kinship with the methods of picaresque adventure fiction, which had been staple reading fare in England for two generations before he undertook his journey. Even if Coryat was not tempted at the time to model his response to challenging moments on the agile conduct of characters like Nashe's Jack Wilton in *The Unfortunate Traveller*, he did avail himself of the anecdotal vigour in such tales when he came to write up his own experiences. There seems to have been something inevitable about such mimicry (intentional or not) at a time when English travellers abroad were discovering how to exploit the opportunities opening before them. We saw in the previous chapter how the 'mad prank' of popular fiction found its analogue in some notorious exploits in Rome, and in the year that Coryat published the *Crudities*, a story circulated about the young Lord Roos, nephew of Robert Cecil, disgracing himself in a manner that could have been modelled on Jack Wilton's travesty of a tourist itinerary in Nashe's tale ('I was at *Pontius Pilates* house and pist against it'). Approaching the town of Sluys in the Netherlands and reportedly driven by his Catholic sympathies, Roos threatened 'to do a very homely piece of work, exposed himself repeatedly in the town, and on seeing the Protestant church "shouted that he was going to perfume the sanctuary"'.[63] Nothing so unsavoury tarnishes Coryat's narrative, but he more than once disregards the guidance of the advice manuals in matters of discretion and crafts lively vignettes like his theft of votive offerings in a church at Brescia and his theological altercation with a Venetian Jew, from which he had to be rescued by Sir Henry Wotton.

The transgressive moments in the *Crudities* are the ones we tend to recall, partly because of their fabliau-like shapeliness but also because Coryat so obviously sees them as a proving ground of his calibre as a traveller. The brio with which he relates these episodes declares his investment in travel experience as a good in itself, experience made meaningful in large part by its courting of risk and openness to experiment.[64] That cultural touring could be, and should be a source of pleasure and fulfilment was rarely denied by humanist commentators, but their anxiety to contain and shape the experience, to leave as little as possible to chance, meant that even the most affirmative guides, like Hermann Kirchner's oration with which Coryat prefaced his own narrative, could never conceive of it as personal adventure. The wits who in the 'Panegyricke Verses' turned Coryat's journey into a madcap expedition were often tilting at the straitlaced moralism of the travel primers as they made fun of their hero, but they were abetted by the traveller himself, who pursued the conventional agenda of the tourist (sights, contacts, knowledge-gathering) with a zeal that yielded startling and occasionally revelatory results.

Coryat's 'Odcombian' performance was a sophisticated contribution to the vogue for mad voyages, but we need to look behind his loquacity and self-display for the most significant results of his personal pilgrimage. Take the tirade against Joseph Starre, from the section of his Chancery submission published in the *Crambe*, where he protests his achievement in managing 'to passe those stupendious mountaines of the snowie Alpes' and overcome the danger of being 'precipitated into a very Stygian *Barathrum* or Tartarean lake sixe times deeper then Pauls tower is high' (D3v–D4). Coryat seems more interested here in being verbally dazzling than in conveying the reality of the experience, and his bombast does not suggest that the wager journey has significantly enlarged his powers of observation or cultural sympathies. Yet his actual account of the Alpine passage is one of the most searching pieces of narrative in the *Crudities* (as I have argued elsewhere[65]), as Coryat struggles to describe an unprecedented ordeal without recourse to the standard commonplaces and analogies that appear in his Chancery statement and which were so often used by early-modern travellers to deal with novel experience. This is one moment where the tourist genuinely loses his bearings (as conservative critics of travel feared he was always liable to do) and gropes for a way of conveying his terror and disorientation, and his account is much richer for it. It shows, I think, that Coryat's longing to do something extraordinary – to make his own live contribution to the tradition of the fantastic voyage – was linked to a talent not just for self-dramatisation but also for adaptation and discovery, something that was particularly apparent in his later eastern travels, where with his remarkable facility for languages he was able to transpose himself into alien cultural situations in a way that, as Jonathan Gil Harris argues persuasively, went well beyond mere disguise or ventriloquism.[66]

Irrespective of such moments, however, Coryat gave contemporaries ample warrant for seeing his adventures as a mad voyage, and observers of the current vogue might have noted the ways in which he copied the strategy of other exploits. The comparison of his European tour with Kemp's dance to Norwich was made in several of the prefatory verses, and invited by Coryat himself when he hung his shoes in the church porch at Odcombe, and like Kemp he used the publication of his account to advertise his next trip. More surprisingly, perhaps, Coryat's enterprise recalls in key respects that of Richard Ferris some 20 years before – the venture that effectively inaugurated the popular craze for travel stunts. As we saw in Chapter 2, the pamphlet account of Ferris's voyage around the south coast of England was described on the title page as 'published' by the traveller himself, a highly unusual move for someone of his social station and resources, and while there is no reason to believe that Coryat had this lowly precedent in mind when he paid for his large volume to be printed, it does suggest that his initiative owed less to recent developments in the Jacobean book trade (as some critics have proposed) than to the particular set of conditions in which the two ventures were conceived. Both men were operating on the fringes of a courtly world in which the travel venture was an established recreation, and an occasion for betting, but which had not traditionally seen any value in encouraging wider participation in its rituals. Coryat and Ferris both exploited their connections to that world in mounting their ventures, and each then took the initiative in publishing an account of what he had done. In her excellent analysis of the cultural milieu in which the *Crudities* saw print, Michelle O'Callaghan argues that the book 'is the product of the transactions between the print marketplace and a patronage economy',[67] and much the same could be said of Ferris's pamphlet, which seems to have been an entrepreneurial effort made possible by the sponsorship of court dignitaries and officials. It may be that neither man had any alternative but to fund his own project: Ferris because in 1590 there was no precedent for writing up such exploit (and possibly none for the stunt itself), and Coryat because nobody had ever before published a long travel memoir in England. By 1611, the book trade had taken up the mad voyage, though patronage may still have been involved if Robert Harcourt and his friends backed publication of Nixon's account of William Bush's exploit, as suggested earlier. But Coryat wanted his trip to be taken seriously, to be dignified by its appearance in print, at the same time as being willing to exploit aspects of the current vogue for the sake of publicity. It was a careful balancing act that required both Prince Henry's blessing and the ironic attention of the city wits, and the result was a book clearly distinguished from the cheap print narratives of other 'bargains of return', and one that harkened back to the origins of the mad voyage in courtly entertainment rather than emulating the commercial stunts of the Jacobean years.

There is one puzzling aspect of Coryat's expedition that may have a bearing on the issue of patronage and its relationship to enterprise. Nobody has ever been able to explain what was meant by the following comment in a letter of recommendation for Coryat that the lawyer Richard Martin addressed to Sir Henry Wotton in his capacity as ambassador to Venice:

> One thing by way of preoccupation I would intreat of your Lordship, that if any of your Intelligencers should give advertisement of any traffiquing or merchandising used by this gentleman at Naples, your Lordship would rather interpret it as done collaterally or incidentally by way of entertainement, then finally for any gaine; being determined (besides his experience) to returne for other things a very beggar. (*Crudities*, 1.378)

The reference to Naples is curious, for nothing in the surviving records indicates that Coryat ever meant to go anywhere near the city. Peace with Spain in 1604 had made it easier to visit southern Italy, and Naples was certainly on the itinerary of English travellers, but unless the original wager agreement prescribed a much longer tour of Italy (could this have been what Starre meant in disparaging the 'smalness and commonnesse' of the journey Coryat actually made?), we have to presume either an error or a transaction made *with* someone in Naples. The letter was reproduced in full in the *Crudities*, so a slip is unlikely. Martin's cryptic remarks are chiefly arresting, of course, for the suggestion that Coryat might have been involved in 'traffiquing' of some kind. The idea seems quite at odds with his declared programme, his mode of travel, and a restless curiosity that devoured sights and objects but seemed interested only in making writerly capital out of them (unless they were illicit souvenirs like the votive offerings he purloined in Brescia). There is no reason to doubt Coryat's determination to 'returne … a very beggar', since he obviously prided himself on his thrift and ability to survive on very little, and when Martin advised him to 'carry with him, discretion and money', he may have been no more careful about the latter than he was about the former. But it is worth remembering that Coryat's image as a threadbare vagabond owes a great deal to the wits who sustained the running joke in the 'Panegyricke Verses' about his single pair of shoes and ragged shirt, and that in this respect as in others, the collective burlesque of his journey may be masking its more sober and material elements.

Coryat may have had no desire to traffic on his own behalf, but could he have intended to do so for others? Martin apparently sought to reassure Wotton that whatever business might be contracted was not some kind of 'interloping' trade but one in which Coryat would be acting as honest broker. Coryat could hardly have been anyone's idea of a merchant or factor, but he might have been considered a useful agent in the one field where his particular interests coincided with the contemporary movement of goods. This was the growing trade in antiquities and fine arts, and other objects of curiosity. As Randall Caudill points out, by the early 1600s 'English gentlemen increasingly emulated the practice of the European Renaissance collectors who had been thriving for over a century'. Coryat often refers in the *Crudities* to earlier English visitors to Italy, many of whom, as Caudill puts it, had come 'to regard foreign travel as a means to assemble their own collections of curiosities'.[68] Sir Henry Wotton, who was something of a connoisseur, became a discerning guide in Venice to such visitors and facilitated their acquisition of paintings, sculpture and other valuables, and he seems to have helped Coryat to find his way around the city's treasures (*Crudities*, 1.332). And although Coryat lacked the means to acquire valuable things for himself, he was well aware of the consuming interest in collecting amongst the court and London circles in which he moved. When Richard Martin tells Wotton that any transactions by Coryat will be 'done collaterally or incidentally by way of entertainement', the clear inference is that he would be acting on instructions from some employer, most likely an aspiring collector of rarities back home. Coryat was certainly acquainted with such men and their interests, as we see from his later message to the distinguished antiquary, Sir Robert Cotton, in one of his letters from India, about his discovery in Anatolian ruins of 'a very curious white marble head of an ancient Heros or Gyant-like Champion', adding that 'to this head wil his [Cotton's] best antiquities whatsoever veyle bonnet.'[69] This vaunt Coryat was ready to put to the test, since he had carried this relic all the way to India and clearly intended to bring it home to England.

Coryat gives no indication in the *Crudities* of having actually dealt in precious objects during his European tour, but the book is suffused with his admiration for rarities and what he calls 'witty fabrics and inventions', and he displays a remarkable eye for detail as well as a prodigious appetite for copying out inscriptions and epitaphs (which as he ruefully acknowledged had earned him the appellation of 'tombstone traveller'). Coryat told Prince Henry that he hoped to encourage his courtiers 'to travel into transmarine nations, and to garnish their understanding with the experience of other countries', and stressed that previous descriptions of Venice 'reporteth not halfe so many remarkable matters as mine doth ... of the antiquities and monuments of that famous Citie' (*Crudities*, 1.2–3). He clearly hoped that his exhaustive coverage of such things would cement his place in the progressive circles around Prince Henry, and he anticipates the view of Henry Peacham that although ownership of 'rarities' is not within everyone's means, 'the profitable necessitie of some knowledge in them' is vital. 'Sure I am,' says Peacham, 'that he that will travell, must both heed them and understand them, if he desire to bee thought ingenious, and to bee welcome to the owners.'[70]

We may also detect here, however, a strain of dilettantism. Coryat himself is at moments uneasily aware of the potential ridicule that an obsessive interest in rarities might attract, and in his poem in the 'Panegyrick Verses' Peacham tilts at numerous curiosities and 'toyes not worth the viewing', to which 'the rude vulgar so hastily post in a madnesse'. What he itemizes are domestic attractions like Drake's ship and 'the sword of valiant Edward' (*Crudities*, 1.114), but when he declares that these are nothing to Coryat's 'shooes so artificially tanned', the ironic inference is that the fruit of Coryat's foreign travel is merely further trivia. As Randall Caudill points out, there were many who believed that the frivolous chase after curiosities was a prime symbol of the folly of travel, and Peacham in his chapter 'Of Antiquities' had to admit that ancient remains were 'so extremely affected and sought after' that 'digging and carrying' had been banned in several European countries; he added that it was 'not enough for an ingenuous Gentleman to behold [them] with a vulgar eye'.[71] In the eyes of travel's critics, there was more than one way to turn it into a mad voyage, and Coryat's attempts to cater to fashionable taste, in helping to fuel the collecting mania of subsequent generations, added to – if they also qualified – his enduring reputation as an obsessive 'leg-stretcher'.

## Notes

1 Stone, *Crisis*, 568.

2 Moralists opposed to gambling saw the rot setting in early: Gilbert Walker declared at mid-century that 'it is not yet xx. yeres agone sins al that sought their living that waye [in 'crafty play'] as then were few in number … nowe such is the misery of our tyme … that of only dycerse a man myght have halfe an army, the greatest nomber so gayly bee seene, and so full of money that they bash not to insinuat themselves intoo the company of the hiest, & loke for a good hour to creepe into a gentleman's room of the privuie chamber' (*A Manifest detection … of Diceplay* [London, 1552], B2v–3). The tavern wager no doubt proliferated in step with the growth of gaming.

3 Nabil Matar, *Islam in Britain 1558–1685* (Cambridge: Cambridge UP, 1998), 6. 'During the Jacobean period … British ships were relentlessly pursued, captured or sunk by the Muslims: between 1609 and 1616, it was reported that 466 English ships were attacked and their crews enslaved' (6).

4 Geoffrey Clark, *Betting on Lives: The Culture of Life Insurance in England, 1695–1775* (Manchester: Manchester UP, 1999), 15.

5 Malynes, *Lex Mercatoria*, 150. The 1603 edition of West's *Simboleography* uses the same wording and stipulates coverage of 'all other perils and fortunes … to the hurt of the said goodes' (sect. 663, sig. Qq5).

6 See above, pp. 120–21.

7 Compare the poem prefacing Sir Thomas Herbert's *A Relation of Some Yeares Travaile* (London, 1634):

> No sooner welcome home from travel, then
> Cosen, thou dost put forth to Sea agen;
> Ist not enough t'have ventur'd life and goods,
> But good name must be stak't … Is the die cast, must
> At this one throw all thou hast gained be lost?
> The Worlds a Lott'ry; He that drawes may win:
> Who nothing ventur's, looks for nothing … (A3v)

8 C. L'Estrange Ewen, *Lotteries and Sweepstakes* (London: Heath Cranton, 1932), 27, and see Schama, *Embarrassment of Riches*, 309–10, on sixteenth-century lotteries in Antwerp and Middelburg.

9 Broadside advertisement of 'A very rich Lotterie generall' (London: Henry Bynneman, 1569).

10 D.R. Bellhouse, 'A Analysis of Puritan Casuistry', *International Statistical Review* 56 (1988), 67.

11 James Balmford, *A short and plaine dialogue* (London, 1593), A6v; William Perkins, *The Whole Treatise of the Cases of Conscience* (London, 1608), 122–3.

12 Quoted in Ewen, *Lotteries and Sweepstakes*, 69.

13 Recent climatic research has shown that the Jamestown settlers arrived in the early stages of an extended drought in Virginia, one that was compounded by 'that extreame frost, 1607' when winter arrived (W.S., *The Proceedings of the English Colonie in Virginia* [Oxford, 1612], 20). The 1607–1608 freeze in England was the first of several in the seventeenth century as Europe's 'Little Ice Age' intensified. Cf. *Purchas His Pilgrimes*, 1.757, 760.

14 John Smith, *Travels and Works of Captain John Smith*, 2 vols., ed. E. Arber and A.G. Bradley (Edinburgh: John Grant, 1910), 2.486–7.

15 Robert Johnson, *The New Life of Virginea* (London, 1612), sig. C. The parallel he draws seems to acknowledge his readers' awareness of English enterprises abroad tending to sabotage their own interests.

16 A vivid recent account may be found in Lorri Glover and Daniel Blake Smith, *The Shipwreck That Saved Jamestown* (New York: Henry Holt, 2008), chapters 2–7.

17 C. L'Estrange Ewen, *Lotteries and Sweepstakes*, 80.

18 *Records of the Virginia Company of London*, ed. S.M. Kingsbury (Washington: Government Printing Office), vol. 3 (1933), 36.

19 L. Daneau, *A Treatise touching Dyce-play and prophane Gaming* (London, 1586), F3.

20 Robert C. Johnson, 'The Lotteries of the Virginia Company, 1612–1621', *Virginia Magazine of History and Biography* 74 (1966), 262–3.

21 Johnson, 'The Lotteries of the Virginia Company', 264–5.

22 Ewen, *Lotteries and Sweepstakes*, 76.

23 *Records of the Virginia Company*, vol. 1 (1906), 451.

24 *Records of the Virginia Company*, vol. 3 (1933), 434-5. There was also a contradiction, doubtless embarrassing to some, between Jamestown's strict gaming laws, promulgated between 1610 and 1612, and the need for public gambling in England to sustain that virtuous regime.

25 *Records of the Virginia Company*, vol. 3 (1933), 38.

26 National Archives C2/33. The case is briefly referred to in Stone, *Crisis*, 568.

27 Like some of Stoddard's transactions, this may be the device of disguising a bet or loan as a sale to get around restrictions on usury.

28 Sandys, *A Relation*, 135.

29 Malynes, *Lex Mercatoria*, 149.

30 Thomas Coryat, *Traveller for the English Wits* (London, 1616), 11; *Mr Thomas Coriat … from Agra* (London, 1618), C2v.

31 George Manwaring, who was part of Sir Anthony Sherley's mission to Persia in 1598, reported that 'Babilon' was 'a place of great traffic with merchants' of many nations ('A True Discourse', in E. Denison Ross, *Anthony Sherley and his Persian Adventure* [London: Routledge, 1933], 192). Cartwright described his journey in *The Preacher's Travels* (London, 1611), and Lithgow his in *Rare Adventures & Painefull Peregrinations*, (1632; Glasgow: MacLehose, 1906), 178–81.

32 Coryat met Sherley by accident in the Persian desert and was looked after in India by Roe, who sent an agent to Persia shortly after Coryat's death.

33 Cited by I.H. Jeayes, ed., *Letters of Philip Gawdy … 1579–1616* (London: J.B. Nicholls, 1906), 174.

34 See H. Inalcik and D. Quataert, eds., *An Economic and Social History of the Ottoman Empire, 1300–1914* (Cambridge: Cambridge UP, 1994), 246–7; and A.C. Wood, *A History of the Levant Company* (Oxford: Oxford UP, 1935), 48.

35 *CSP Venetian*, 15 (1617–19), 213.

36 See Roderick Clayton, 'John Finet', *ODNB* 19.596–7. The family was of Italian descent and the name an unusual one. See William Berry, *Pedigrees of the Families of the County of Kent* (London: Sherwood, 1830), 449. John Finet may have been involved in transactions similar to those of his presumed cousin, since in July 1621 Richard Boyle, Earl of Cork made a note: 'To remember to send Sir John ffynnett ten peeces for Mr John Chapman now gone to Turcky' (A.B. Grosart, ed., *The Lismore Papers* [London 1886], 2.21). Finet, Boyle and Chapman moved in the same court circles, and the money may have been paid as part of a wagering agreement.

37 '*Chancerie* … is the court of equitie and conscience, moderating the rigour of other courtes, that are more straightly tyed to the leter of the lawe' (John Cowell, *The Interpreter* [London, 1607], N3). See Brooks, *Law, Politics and Society*, 312–18.

38 Simpson, *Common Law of Contract*, 321. His fuller definition is 'that liability should only be imposed for breach of promise when there existed some reason apart from the promise for saying that what the defendant had promised to do ought to be done' (273).

39 Simpson, *Common Law of Contract*., 534.

40 *English Reports* 73, p. 866 (Brook's New Cases, 44), citing a 1506 case; *English Reports* 79, p. 1259, a case heard in 1626. (These and following cases are cited from the online archive HeinOnline.org.)

41 Bothy's Case, Mich.3 Jacobi (*English Reports* 77, p. 299). Note also one of the standard legal definitions of impossibility: 'En nature, come a vaer a Rome en un jour' (*English Reports* 81, p. 1197).

42 Cf. *Gould v. Death* (*English Reports* 81, p. 476).

43 *Hales v. Bell*, Trin. 39 Eliz. (*English Reports* 123, p. 658).

44 *Spencer v. Griffin*, 36. Eliz, Easter term (*English Reports* 78, p. 322).

45 Though such cases continued to be the subject of quite intricate debate, as in the 1610 case where one Sturgis brought an action against Dean to claim £10 owed to him after his return from Jerusalem. The court was exercised by the question of whether his proof of being there should be produced as part of his bill or

whether it was enough that he had shown it to the defendant. A majority on the bench supported the latter, but Justice Coke dissented, arguing that 'a man might return from a place, when he was not at the same place, as if he had been near the place, or in the skirts of Jerusalem' (*Sturgis v. Dean*, Hillary 8 Jacobi: *English Reports* 123, p. 813).

46 See, for example, the *Hales v. Bell* case cited above, where Bell was contracted to pay Hales £40 'within fourteen days next after the return of one Russel into England, from the City of Venice' (*English Reports* 123, p. 658).

47 The quotations in this paragraph are from a collection of Egerton's notes made c.1598–c.1602, Cambridge University Library Ms. Gg.2.31, ff.437–478v, printed in W.H. Bryson, ed., *Cases Concerning Equity and the Courts of Equity 1550–1660*. 2 vols (London: Selden Society, 2001), I.294, 296, 308.

48 Brooks, *Law, Politics and Society*, 315.

49 Bryson, *Cases Concerning Equity*, 307.

50 See Michael Strachan, *The Life and Adventures of Thomas Coryate* (London: Oxford UP, 1962), and for a vivid recent account of the circumstances in which Coryat conceived and performed his journey, see Richmond Barbour, *Before Orientalism*, 115–32.

51 National Archives C33/115 (fol.818 [22 May] and fol.1029 [1 July]).

52 'Richard Roe' was of course a familiar legal fiction (like John Doe in modern American usage, and dating back to mediaeval English practice), but another Chancery document to be cited shortly proves that Rowe was a real player in this court drama.

53 It may have been a complicated document, since the court records suggest that one of Starre's relatives was involved in betting on Coryat. His deposition mentions a 'bill of adventure of Thomas Starre' which he asks to have assigned to him. The Christian name is unlikely to be a slip for his own, since it is corrected from 'William' to 'Thomas' in the first transcript and is reproduced in the second.

54 National Archives C33/116, fol. 820.

55 National Archives C2/JASI/R15/70. Starre reiterated that he had 'paide for the debte of the saide Complaynant to one Thomas Coriatt aforesaid the some of threescore and tenn pounds which the Complaynant never satisfied this defendant nor any parte thereof neither was it accompted for within the saide former accompts when the saide mortgage was made to this defendant'.

56 Malynes, *Lex Mercatoria*, 199.

57 National Archives C38/14, listed in IND 1/1880, No. 611, fol. 31v.

58 At the outset of his travel memoir, George Sandys declares that he is passing over his journey through France and 'the lesse remote parts of *Italy*: daily survaide and exactly related' (*A Relation of a Journey begun … 1610* [London, 1615], 1). Of course, Coryat's copious narrative published four years earlier helped him considerably to make this statement.

59 Thomas Coryat, *Coryates Crambe* (London, 1611), D3v–4.

60 Other, perhaps more likely candidates for this 'Authoritie' are Lionel Cranfield, future Lord Treasurer, who managed Coryat's finances and helped to promote the *Crudities*, and Sir Edward Phelips, Coryat's patron and a senior courtier, who as a Somerset man might have taken a local interest in the case.

61 Witness the recent retracing of Coryat's European travels by Tim Moore, who followed his route in an old Rolls Royce Silver Shadow, as recounted in his book *Continental Drifter* (London: Abacus, 2002).

62 Katharine A. Craik, 'Reading *Coryats Crudities* (1611)', *Studies in English Literature* 44 (2004), 77–96; Michelle O'Callaghan, *The English Wits: Literature and Sociability in Early Modern England* (Cambridge: Cambridge UP, 2007), ch. 5.

63 BL Harl. MS 7002/199–202, quoted by J.P. Feil, *Sir Tobie Matthew and his Collection of Letters*, unpublished diss,, U. of Chicago, 1962, 72). Roos had been converted to Catholicism by Tobie Matthew. On his role in the detention of his tutor John Mole by the Inquisition, see p. 126.

64 Cf. Moryson, *Itinerary*, 3.8: 'the fruit of travell is travell it selfe.'

65 Anthony Parr, 'Thomas Coryat and the Discovery of Europe', *Huntington Library Quarterly* 55 (1992), 593–6; *Crudities*, I.216–22.

66 Jonathan Gil Harris, 'Becoming-Indian', in Henry S. Turner, ed., *Early Modern Theatricality* (Oxford: Oxford UP, 2013), 442–59.

67 O'Callaghan, *The English Wits*, 103.

68 Caudill, *Development of English Virtuoso Interests*, 131–2.

69 Thomas Coryat, *Thomas Coriate Traveller for the English Wits* (London, 1616), 44.

70 Henry Peacham, *The Compleat Gentleman* (London, 1634), 104–5.

71 Peacham, *The Compleat Gentleman*, 107–9; Caudill, *English Virtuoso Interests*, 26.

6

# Orpheus in the Underworld

In a recently discovered poem addressed to Ben Jonson about his 'travelling a foote into Scotland' (the 1618 walk from London to Edinburgh discussed in Chapter 2), the illustrious writer's wager journey is subjected to the same mock-heroic treatment that Jonson and his friends had meted out to Thomas Coryat in the 'Panegyrick Verses', invoking a classical exemplar appropriate to the poet's calling:

Thrice worthy Poett of this halfe blest Ile
ile call the[e] *Orpheus*, for thy sweeter stile
And *Orpheus* for thy courage, though he went
downe to hell darke, thou hast the like attempt
. . . . . . . . . . . . . . . . . . . . . . . . . . . . . . . . . . .
Thither went *Orpheus*, but who can saye
he tooke the paines to foote itt all the waye
Perchance he thought itt paine enough to ride
thou there out goest him ... [1]

Its author was presumably aware of Jonson's epigram addressed to his young friend William Roe at the outset of a European tour, which treats a similar theme in less jocular fashion, anticipating the moment 'when we, blest with thy return,' shall declare

'This is that good Aeneas, passed through fire,
Through seas, storms, tempests, and embarked for hell
Came back untouched. This man hath travelled well.'[2]

Jonson's poem is not without a hint of playful hyperbole, though it carefully avoids burlesque, enacting Roe's safe delivery from peril in a seamless enjambement that sets up the assured final clause. The Virgilian analogy is mock-epic on its best behaviour, both witty and sincere. The eulogy inspired by his own walking trip is clumsy by comparison, more like some of the less polished panegyrics about Coryat the leg-stretcher, but its use of the underworld motif has an irreverent and combative note that catches something of the spirit of Jonson's Scottish venture. The tribute to the poet's Orphic voice, for instance, has a sting in the tail, for after he has been enjoined to 'play such streines as many yeares agoe / Drew listening sticks & stones', Jonson is urged to send home those who are flocking after him 'by looking backe / As *Orpheus* did his dead *Euridice*'. This archetypal example of breaking the rules laid down for travel would doubtless have appealed to the learned poet-walker, especially given the crowds that we now know pestered his journey as they did those of other wagerers[3]. More generally, Jonson had a complicated attitude to the claims that were made for travel, and the blessing he confers on William Roe's journey stands in oblique relation to his treatment of the subject elsewhere in his work. But no writer in this period was more interested than Jonson in the travel wager and its implications, and he alone both undertook a 'mad voyage' of his own, recognizably part of the vogue for such things, and produced a major piece of creative writing about one of these extravagant adventures.

'On the Famous Voyage', the controversial poem that concludes Jonson's *Epigrams,* was probably completed three or four years before he started to plan his Scottish journey, and may well have been conceived at the time of his involvement in the publication of *Coryates Crudities* in 1610–11, for which he provided a memorable prose 'Character' of the author. Jonson's affectionate burlesque of Coryat's mode of travel describes him as 'An Engine, wholly consisting of extremes, a Head, Fingers, and Toes ... set a going for Venice', and he was to make wry fun later of his own gargantuan walk when a character in his 1620 masque *News from the New World* recalls that 'one of our greatest poets – I know not how good a one – went to Edinburgh o' foot, and came back.'[4] There is nothing to suggest that Jonson saw any great difference between Coryat's wager-journey and his own, though he no doubt believed that he would produce a worthier literary record, and his readiness to engage with travel 'experiments' is also evident, though in more ambiguous form, in the poem he produced between these two walking ventures. In this chapter, I want to look again at this troublesome epigram, placing it in relation to other uses of the travel exploit in Jacobean writing and trying to assess Jonson's artistic purpose in writing it.

'Famous Voyage' is no longer a neglected work, following some substantial critical attention to it in recent years, yet it remains one that puzzles and repels many of its readers. Despite the resonant title, the venture it describes takes place entirely within London: a short but harrowing boat trip up the Fleet river, the city's largest tributary stream, from its exit point into the Thames as far as Holborn Bridge. Long regarded by Londoners as an urban blight, by the late sixteenth century the lower reaches of the Fleet had become an open sewer, with numerous privies built out over the water, and clogged with refuse from the butchering trade and industries like tanning and milling. Probably the only small boat traffic to use even a small part of this unsavoury waterway would have been that conveying prisoners to the water gate of the Fleet prison. In Jonson's poem, the decision to navigate the Fleet Ditch (as it was commonly called) is apparently the result of a tavern wager, one made moreover in the poet's own drinking haunts, for we are told that the protagonists

6.1 Titlepage of Richard Brathwaite's *A solemne ioviall disputation* (London, 1617), thought to represent a gathering of the 'Sirenaical gentlemen' at the Mermaid tavern. (Huntington Library, San Marino, California.)

At Bread Street's Mermaid, having dined, and merry,
Proposed to go to Holborn in a wherry (37–8) [5]

The Mermaid tavern was where the 'Sirenaical Gentlemen', as Coryat called them, met once a month, and where the project of writing mock-encomia for the *Crudities* was very probably conceived. (See Figure 6.1.) This regular gathering of self-appointed wits was clearly not averse to the fashion for wagering stunts, and it is quite possible that Jonson's poem was inspired by an actual adventure dreamed up in one of their lively dinners. The poem's narrator tells us that the prospective venturers hatch their plan 'in worthy scorn / Of those that put out moneys on return / From Venice, Paris, or some inland passage' (31–3), but their scorn appears to be entirely competitive, impelling them to emulate or overgo the more bizarre exploits also mentioned here, like the journey 'backward ... to Berwick' (35) and a recent feat of rowing across the North Sea to Antwerp (40). This is not the disdain felt by Fynes Moryson for 'base and ridiculous adventures' but a brash assurance that they have come up with an even more inventive stunt. One of the voyagers, we learn, has put out money 'to take at his return from hell, / His three for one' (27–8), and a provocative suggestion that this makes him the 'greater man' of the two seems to draw on the same reserves of irony that fuel Jonson's self-deprecation in the masque quoted in the previous paragraph. The issue raised by the wager, in fact, is whether it is simply a target of the poet's more comprehensive scorn, or whether Jonson sees it as a positive vehicle for the kind of enquiry he pursues elsewhere in the *Epigrams*.

Here the issue of what primarily motivates the exploit becomes significant. The densely specific narrative of 'Famous Voyage' pinpoints not only the tavern setting of the wager but also the weather conditions that influence the participants' choices:

It was the day, what time the powerful moon
Makes the poor Bankside creature wet it' shoon
In it' own hall (29–31)

During a spring tide, the south bank of the Thames was commonly flooded out, and among those directly affected were the prostitutes who operated there outside city jurisdiction. That going to Holborn is an alternative to visiting the Bankside whores seems to be confirmed at the end of the poem when, as they near their destination, the voyagers are told that 'Madam Caesar, great Proserpina, / Is now from home. You lose your labours quite' (180–81). ('Madam Caesarean' is named as a brothel-keeper in *The Alchemist*, and the Holborn district was another centre of prostitution.) Nonetheless, the voyagers receive a testimonial from a trio of local residents 'to witness of their action' (191): the conditions of the wager have been met, even as they return 'without protraction' (192) – an ingenious final pun which presumably registers sexual disappointment as well as haste to collect their winnings. Perhaps no journey, even the most pointless or single-minded, is entirely without ancillary objectives, but the question of motive in this case does have a bearing on how we read the poem. Most critics have found the prostitution theme to be consonant with the tawdry setting of 'Famous Voyage', and Andrew McRae has shown specifically how it ties in with the sexual imagery that pervades the poem.[6] The most recent discussion by Michael L. Manous, however, claims that to read the poem's narrative as being about a search for sex is to ignore or diminish the significance of the wager, and thereby to misinterpret Jonson's artistic purposes.[7]

Manous argues that critics have failed to appreciate the structural role of the wager-journey in generating the poem's meaning, and that this has contributed to the difficulties they have had in understanding the relationship of 'Famous Voyage' to the rest of the *Epigrams*. Rather than seeing it as a lapse of taste and judgement on Jonson's part, or as a deliberate travesty of his procedure earlier in the sequence, we should read the poem as completing the constructive design of the *Epigrams* with an ordeal that proves the moral heroism of the protagonists, as they negotiate the hell of London's underworld and discover that the 'path to true virtue in life' requires an engagement with all its dangers and deformities. From this perspective, 'Famous Voyage' faithfully expands on the message of the epigram to William Roe, and uses the narrative form to create a Lucianic fantastic journey in which wisdom is reached through a disorienting set of challenges. This reading of the poem pits the voyagers' determination to fulfil the terms of the wager against the temptations they encounter on the way, such as Madam Caesar's brothel. The logistics of the enterprise offer some support to this view. One commentator has pointed out the 'absurdity' of the proposed itinerary: if the goal were simply to reach the bordello in question, even 'quite drunk young men could stagger to Holborn from the Mermaid … in about twenty minutes'[8] – a challenge that might have encouraged them to stage the kind of foot-race popular amongst London's sporting gamblers. As it is, the ordeal of rowing up the Fleet Ditch is the point of the exercise, and the poem's narrator speaks for the diners who compare the project to the epic ventures they find in their favourite authors:

No more let Greece her bolder fables tell
Of Hercules or Theseus going to hell,
Orpheus, Ulysses; or the Latin muse
With tales of Troy's just knight, our faiths abuse.
We have a Shelton and a Heyden got,
Had power to act what they to feign had not. (1–6)

In Jonson's poetic scheme, of course, the facile distinction between acting and feigning opens the wager and its cultural milieu to stringent scrutiny, for it exposes the shallow confidence that drives contemporary enterprise, and promises that the 'bolder fables' of ancient travel to the underworld will in fact provide a prism through which to view this particular mad voyage. The introductory section of the poem is built out of a set of mordant parallels between ancient and modern, fable and actuality, that underlines the brash vulgarity of the present: in London's hellish underbelly, 'Arses were heard to croak instead of frogs', and 'Furies there wanted not: each scold was ten'. But as the parallels multiply, the mock-heroic idiom threatens to deflate both classical archetype and its tawdry modern equivalent, and there is a revealing shift of register in what follows:

And for [instead of] the cries of ghosts, women and men
Laden with plague-sores and their sins were heard,
Lashed by their consciences, to die affeard. (16–18)

For a moment we glimpse a Christian inferno beneath the Lucianic jesting, and the stakes are correspondingly raised on 'th'adventer' that Shelton and Heyden undertake, turning their travesty of classical voyages into an encounter with the desperate conditions of the urban underworld. The narrator quickly regains his jaunty manner as he moves into 'The Voyage

Itself' and proceeds to describe the wager, but this cannot erase – and in fact merely reinforces – the impression that the voyagers are like tourists in a disaster zone. The wager is indeed central to our understanding of the poem, but does it facilitate a voyage of discovery, a genuinely revelatory ordeal, or is it a venture contaminated by the frivolous priorities of the age?

In order to address the implications of this question more fully, I propose to widen the enquiry to look at some other literary examples of the travel exploit in this period, beginning with Jonson's own treatment of the phenomenon elsewhere in his work. Wager-travellers crop up in two of his early plays, and in both cases are ridiculed: Amorphus, the fashionable gallant who 'hath now made the sixth return upon venture' in *Cynthia's Revels*, and the eccentric knight Puntarvolo in *Every Man out of his Humour*, who 'deals upon returns and strange performances' and is determined to put out £5000 on a voyage to Constantinople. Yet neither is simply a buffoon: Amorphus is a charismatic and quick-witted charmer, whose skills are thrown into relief by the hapless Asotus seeking to imitate him, while Puntarvolo, 'wholly consecrated to singularity', is a quixotic figure who retains a certain dignity in his obsessions. It is worth noting also that Jonson takes the trouble to provide a detailed exposition of the terms of Puntarvolo's wager which, for all its absurdity (including the provision for his dog and cat to make the journey), is one of the most precise accounts we have of how these agreements were set up. As so often in his work, Jonson conjures the suspect allure of what he is satirising, and draws his audience into the logic of real-life transactions.[9] In *Volpone* (1606), Sir Politic Would-Be is obviously drawn as an epitome of the foolish traveller, but his rejection of the 'idle, antique, stale, grey-headed project / Of knowing men's minds and manners, with Ulysses' (2.1.9–10) – the hackneyed definition of respectable tourism – strikes an equivocal note. On the one hand, it emphasises his thraldom to fashion, and to his wife's 'peculiar humour' to "do" Venice; on the other, it captures the kind of impatience with conventional prescription that animates so many of the mock-eulogies to Coryat. If the wits in the Mermaid circle paid lip service to the traditional notion of self-improving travel with its strict guidelines, they clearly had more flexible ideas about what foreign adventure might entail, and the versatile Peregrine in *Volpone*, who disguises himself as a merchant to get the better of Sir Pol, would have been closer to their image of the fully equipped traveller.[10] Jonson seems to have been wary of the claims made for tourism: the epigram to William Roe pointedly emphasises the importance of his safe return, and he was to discover some of its perils for himself when he accompanied Wat Ralegh to the Continent in 1612–13 ('Famous Voyage' was probably written or revised just after this trip). But his approach to satire, influenced by his reading of Lucian and Erasmus, leads him to see the obsession with travel as an opportunity to explore some of the paradoxes of contemporary enterprise.

It was a view he shared with some of his fellow dramatists, on the evidence of the collaborative play *Eastward Ho!* (1606), where Jonson, Chapman and Marston give a particular twist to some of the standard themes of citizen comedy. Once again we have the foolish knight bent on travel, in this case Sir Petronel Flash, who has invested all his resources in a voyage to Virginia and is drawn into a scheme to mortgage his new wife's lands in order to raise further funds. The usurer Security who plans to take his bond comments ironically: 'Who would not sell away competent certainties to purchase, with any danger, excellent uncertainties? Your true knight venturer ever does it' (1.1.131–3). And he defends his own kind of 'putting out' – lending at large rates of interest – by comparing it with the risky practices of the merchant adventurer who

> complains and says, 'Traffic is subject to much uncertainty and loss.' Let 'em keep their goods on dry land, with a vengeance, and not expose other men's substances to the mercy of the winds, under protection of a wooden wall … and all for greedy desire to enrich themselves with unconscionable gain, two for one, or so; where I, and such other honest men as live by lending money, are content with moderate profit – thirty or forty i'th'hundred, so we may have it with quietness and out of peril of wind and weather, rather than run those dangerous courses of trading, as they do. (2.2.75–83)

Security's argument cleverly deflects the charge of 'unconscionable gain' away from its usual target (the usurer) onto England's expanding maritime activity: he allies himself in effect with the conservative critique of speculative ventures and long-distance trade that drew in luxury goods. His prudential ethic is not unlike that of the goldsmith Touchstone and his industrious apprentice Golding, who embody the citizen virtues of thrift, sobriety and hard work, in stark contrast to adventurers like Flash and Seagull who gamble on the prospect of quick riches in Virginia. The argument is oddly contradictory, however, since the usurer trades on the needs of those who must borrow to fund risky projects. Security wants nothing to do with voyages that might put his money in jeopardy, but he is quite willing to exploit Sir Petronel's need for ready cash. Touchstone, in contrast, insists that 'as for my rising by other men's fall, God shield me!' (1.1.37–8), yet as a goldsmith he is probably also a moneylender, and just as his self-righteous tone grates on the listener, so his cautious citizen ethic is increasingly seen to be inadequate to the realities of London's enterprise culture. The key figure here is Touchstone's other apprentice, Quicksilver, a well-born younger son whose limited means and expensive tastes have forced him to take up a trade. He and Golding are initially set up as antithetical characters, prodigality versus prudence, but in the play's closing stages this opposition is interestingly complicated. Quicksilver joins the Virginia party, which is immediately wrecked on the Isle of Dogs, and he ends up in jail. Meanwhile, the virtuous Golding goes from strength to strength, finally becoming an alderman, yet he wins the audience's approval not by his rectitude and new-found status but by the stratagem he adopts to deliver the apparently penitent Quicksilver from prison. By pretending to be arrested himself, he draws Touchstone to the prison so that the latter will hear Quicksilver's repentance, an extrovert display of singing that persuades Touchstone to order his release. Whether Golding himself is actually persuaded by Quicksilver's performance is not clear, but his deception of Touchstone is a step towards the kind of trickster behaviour that Quicksilver claims in his ballad to be putting behind him. As Jill Ingram suggests, the latter's 'bravado supplies a model of risk-taking economic practices helpful to more conservative characters such as Golding', so that the theme of the reformed prodigal is qualified by an emerging emphasis on adaptive wit.[11]

In a perceptive essay on religious conversion in city comedy, Alizon Brunning suggests that Quicksilver's repentance 'is brought about by his shipwreck and near-drowning experience', but adds: 'His spiritual journey towards salvation is brought about by his thwarted attempt to reach the promised land of Virginia. Quicksilver's rite of passage is an antitype of those later exiles whose voyage to America was seen in terms of divine deliverance.' There is a suggestion here of grace earned through adversity, but Brunning's 'antitype' more closely resembles what Elizabeth Chesney calls a 'counter-voyage', the humanist deconstruction of heroic ventures that she traces in writers like Rabelais and Ariosto.[12] In this play the Virginia expedition is consistently seen as foolish, and its premature end is sardonically observed in Lucianic fashion by Slitgut, who climbs the pole at Cuckold's Haven to 'discover from this lofty prospect what pranks the rude Thames plays in her desperate lunacy' (4.1.18–20). A burlesquing description of the expedition's demise, it is implied, is all it deserves. But the antitype of a providential landfall is not necessarily disillusionment with the idea of adventure. That Quicksilver's repentance is a charade is surely confirmed by his buoyant confidence after the shipwreck, when he assures Flash, 'I hope I have some tricks in this brain of mine shall not let us perish' (4.1.190–91). This is 'the plot of roguery', as Anne-Julia Zwierlein puts it in another valuable essay in the same volume, that survives after the plot of adventure (Flash) and the plot of increase (Security) have failed, and it signals the playwrights' ambiguous endorsement of the hero's witty journey through the play.[13] Virginia may have been a fool's errand, but Quicksilver has made the inauspicious voyage serve his own purposes, so that it is not so much a cautionary lesson as a spur to fresh enterprise. As it happens, the plot of roguery dominates the use of the 'counter-voyage' or travel exploit in Jacobean literature, and it is examples of this that we now turn, before tackling further the question of what Jonson hoped to achieve with his underworld venture in 'Famous Voyage'.

## The Plot of Roguery

Rogues loom large both on the early-modern stage and in the non-dramatic prose of the period, but I want to concentrate on their role in the busy itineraries of Thomas Dekker's popular tract *Lanthorne & Candlelight* (1607). Dekker, like Jonson, was obviously intrigued by the 'experiments' that proliferated in the vogue for mad voyages. As we saw earlier, he noted William Bush's 'rowing over steeples by lande in a wherry' in a 1608 pamphlet, and seems to have been mildly obsessed with the showman Banks' ascent of St. Paul's tower with his horse Morocco, referring to the stunt no fewer than five times.[14] In *Lanthorne & Candlelight*, however, Dekker reframes the travel exploit and wager as updated versions of 'cony-catching' enterprise, not necessarily to discredit them but certainly to sharpen the focus they provide on contemporary social practice. For instance, he describes a complicated scam in which a well-dressed fraudster visits a goldsmith to borrow £40 in silver for a few days. He explains that he 'is very shortly ... *To travel to Venice*, to *Jerusalem* or so' (the formula makes it clear this is a wager-journey) and does not wish to spend his existing savings of £40 in gold coins (which will be usable as foreign currency), but will hand them over as security for the loan. The goldsmith willingly accepts, 'knowing the pawn to be better than a Bond', but is subsequently fleeced when the gold is secretly substituted with a pile of shillings and the fraudster absconds with the £40 he borrowed.[15] The vignette is interesting for the glimpse it affords of the context in which many loans and speculative deals were made (goldsmiths being a prime source of credit[16]), and of the suspicions of cheating that clung to the financial bargains of would-be wager travellers – who, as we have seen, might be either victims or perpetrators of malpractice.

Dekker touches even more directly on the mechanism of the travel wager in his portrait of the Woodpecker, another confidence trickster who 'deals altogether upon Returns (as men do that take three for one, at their coming back from Jerusalem, etc.)' – though in this case 'putting out' involves taking advantage of ordinary gamblers. When the Woodpecker finds a game of dice in progress, he tempts the players with an additional incentive, showing them

> a Jewel, a Clock, a Ring with a Diamond, or any such like commodity. He notes him well that commonly is best acquainted with the dice, and hath ever good luck. To him he offers his prize, rating it at ten or fifteen pound, when haply 'tis not worth above six, and for it he bargains to receive five shillings or ten shillings, according as it is in value, at every hand, second, third, or fourth hand, he draws. By which means, he perhaps in a short time makes that yield him forty or fifty pound which cost not half twenty. Many of these Merchant venturers sail from Ordinary to Ordinary, being sure always to make saving Voyages ... (229)

The irony is that these 'venturers' less resemble the traveller taking a gamble than the creditor who accepts his bond, spreads his risk and makes a virtually guaranteed profit. In drawing an analogy with the tourist's bargain of return, Dekker's cony-catching story takes a swipe at the prodigals who bet on their travels, but the more compelling analogy is with those who exploit them, who 'take three for one' in the sense that they accept the wagers of young men who are risking their fortunes on an excursion. A more subtle effect of the story is to rehearse the argument about the legitimacy of commercial transactions that disguise a lucrative (or extortionate) sale as a wager. The 'prize' offered to the hapless dicer, after all, is little different from the goods offered to needy travellers by merchants like Stoddard and Conquest, in the cases discussed in previous chapters, for which they expected recompense well exceeding their worth. Dekker presents these sketches, which must be based in part on actual swindles, as opportunistic by-products of an enterprise culture, one that as it sought greater profits and developed its own systems of regulation (joint-stock company rules, bills of adventure, and so forth) inevitably spawned the marginal dealing and sharp practice that he finds mirrored in the everyday traffic of Jacobean London.

As this implies, Dekker's portraits of urban chicanery are not presented simply as aberrations from honest enterprise, but as the result of a transformed commercial world. Historians of the rogue literature in this period find many of its sources in the growth of vagabondage and lower-class mobility in Tudor England, though there is considerable argument about whether it offers a sociologically accurate portrait.[17] What is clear is that the detailed portrayal of criminal fraternities in these writings, while alarming and titillating early-modern readers with the routines of 'a strange and sinister underworld',[18] also held up a mirror to the wider society, demonstrating that, as Robert Greene put it in the early 1590s, 'all conditions and estates of men seeke to live by their wittes, and he is counteth wisest, that hath the deepest insight into the getting of gaines'.[19] A decade and a half later, Dekker is writing about city fraud with the same clear-sighted view of human transactions that we find in Jacobean city comedy, one that has absorbed the truth of Greene's observation and portrays its consequences with an ambiguous relish. Dekker's tricksters have learned to 'put out' in a newly devious way, one not dictated by the face-to-face dealings of merchants who contracted wagers on trust, but relying on the opaqueness that was characteristic of metropolitan exchange.

We should not exaggerate the novelty of this, of course: the long history of finance is full of argument about the morality of speculative transactions, and 'putting out' was a term for the usurer's activity before it became a way of describing the bargain of return. Dekker himself often takes his cue from an older satiric tradition, as in his portrait of 'The Gull-groper': 'an old Money-monger' whose 'whole felicity [is] to fill his bags with gold and silver' and draw improvident gentlemen into his clutches. This is the familiar terrain of Tudor complaint, but Dekker populates it with an intrigue that recalls the vagaries of some of the wager agreements we have examined. Like the Woodpecker, the money-lender ('*Signior Avaro*') is a frequenter of taverns where gaming is going on, though he claims to be there 'only for the company, and to converse with travellers'. He soon identifies a gentleman on a losing streak and offers him 'a hundred pound or two' to keep gambling, and when that is gone the trap closes: the victim ends up having to 'confess a judgment for so much money, or for such a manor or lordship, three times worth the bond forfeited, to be paid or to be entered upon by him, by such a day, or within so many months after he comes to his land' (228–9). The loan that enabled a wager, or which was necessitated by having invested all available funds in a wager, was a common part of the bargain of return, as Fynes Moryson testified (witness also the complicated transaction between George Conquest and Thomas Fynett), and Dekker's phrasing of the usurer's strict terms, requiring 'three times the bond forfeited', might have prompted Jacobean readers to reflect on the risks of a 'putting out' bet that technically offered the reverse – a *return* of three-for-one – but which was fraught with hazard and often involved young men selling their lands or disposing of what Sir Henry Blount called 'the small reliques of my fortune' (*Voyage*, 103). Throughout *Lanthorne & Candlelight*, Dekker stretches the cony-catching formula to cover the speculative devices of Jacobean finance and suggest some of the ways in which they have become central to English enterprise and 'adventure', in both senses of that word.

In much of the earlier cony-catching literature the entrepreneurial idea is embodied in bands of vagabonds like the 'whipjacks' or 'Fresh-Water Mariners' whose ships, declared Thomas Harman in 1566, 'were drowned in the Plain of Salisbury' (a laconic use of the ship-on-land trope) and who 'will run about the country with a counterfeit licence, feigning either shipwreck, or spoiled by pirates ... demanding alms to bring them home to their country'.[20] Dekker part-plagiarised this account in *The Belman of London* (1608), which mostly follows Harman's emphasis on the working-class rogue, but the book also has the urban centre of gravity that Dekker found in Robert Greene's pamphlets, and in maintaining this emphasis in the sequel *Lanthorne & Candlelight*, he gives an elaborate twist to the theme of vagrancy and the device of the forged document. Two groups of stories about roving tricksters widen the canvas to include regional England, the traditional haunt of the canting crews, but they involve plots that are hatched in London and show the countryside being subjected to the gravitational pull of the capital. As Andrew McRae suggests, London's 'irrepressible expansion ... was steadily reorienting patterns of traffic across the nation', and what he has to say about changes in commercial trade is also applicable to other kinds of regional travel. 'Traffic', he points out, 'was assuming unsettlingly new shapes', partly because as it grew it became increasingly impersonal, with long-distance trade replacing the intimacy of the local market.[21] Inland tourism followed in the wake of the traders, taking advantage of the expanding network of roads, and bringing strangers and their schemes into provincial communities. In a variety of ways, traditional 'putting out' – the conditional bargains made between people who know each other – was being modified by economic developments, and Dekker's rural rides are undertaken by mobile opportunists from the capital who know how to exploit this changing landscape.

In the first group of tales, one of these travellers is introduced with a theatrical flourish:

> There is yet another Actor to step upon the Stage, and he seems to have good skill in Cosmography, for he holds in his Hand a Map, wherein he hath laid down a number of Shires in England, and with small pricks hath beaten out a path, teaching how a man may easily (though not very honestly) travel from Country to Country, and have his Charges borne (256).

His twin brother, Dekker tells us, specialises in cheating innkeepers, to whom he brings 'counterfeit letters of commendations'. These peregrinations anticipate John Taylor's 'moneyless' walk to Scotland 10 years later, right down to his ability to persuade landlords to give him free bed and board, but Dekker is unwilling to see them as sincerely motivated or entitled to the traditional rural hospitality that Taylor was able to call upon. His adventurers are able to disguise themselves as gentlemen (like the adaptable knaves in several of Greene's pamphlets), and treat their outings as a kind of sport:

> He that undertakes this strange journey, lays his first plot how to be turned into a *Brave man*, which he finds can be done by none better then by a *Trusty Tailor*.... Out of the City (being mounted on a good gelding), he rides upon his own bare credit.... And you must note, that this *Hotspur* does never set upon any places but only such where he knows by intelligence there are store of *Gentlemen*, or wealthy farmers at the least (256).

This *picaro*'s closest relatives may appear to be the witty rogues of prose fiction or stage comedy, but his mock-heroic nickname ('Hotspur') perhaps points more directly to Dekker's strategy. The scenario here is a travesty of the patrician custom of inland journeys undertaken as a challenge, like Robert Carey's walk to Berwick or John Lepton's ride to York, that relied on hospitality at county seats along the way and reinforced the ties of honour and friendship between members of the gentry. At the time Dekker was writing, of course, such ventures were losing their exclusiveness with the growth of domestic tourism and, more to the point, were subject to parody and burlesque by the enthusiasts for travel stunts: the journey 'backward to Berwick' was a notorious example. So by offering his own example of burlesque, in the 'strange journey' of the bogus gentleman who rides out from London to conquer the provinces, Dekker subtly alludes to the vogue for travel exploits without having to draw explicit parallels or make it the object of his satire. As with his use of the foreign travel wager as analogy, it is a rhetorical resource that allows him to shine a playful light on wider issues of social and economic change.

Dekker's use of the strange journey as an investigative device finds itself at full stretch, however, in a final group of travelling scams that touch on his own trade as a writer. Here he creates a set of variations on the theme of fraudulent publication, involving plagiarism, literary theft and outright forgery, and describes how the protocols of the expanding book trade might be exploited by unscrupulous operators. His chapter on '*Falconers*' has the title 'Of a new kind of Hawking, teaching how to catch Birds by Books' (234) – a description with all sorts of ironic resonance for the writer of a commercial cony-catching pamphlet. We are told of one of the Falconers that 'having scraped together certain small parings of wit, he first cuts them handsomely in pretty pieces, and of those pieces does he patch up a book.' This he prints 'at his own charge', and having made a list of his intended victims, separately creates 'so many Epistles as they have names, the Epistles Dedicatory being all one, and vary in nothing but the titles of their patrons' (237). His stratagem is similar to that of the less inventive rogues who will buy up 'any old Book ... that lies for wastepaper and is clean forgotten, add a new-printed Epistle to it, and with an Alphabet of letters which they carry about them, being able to Print any man's name for a Dedication on the sudden, travel up and down most Shires in England, and live by this Hawking' (237–8). Another group is the 'Fraternity of wandering Pilgrims' who visit country gentlemen pretending to be authors seeking a patron and produce a pirated collection of writings ('witty Inventions … copied out by stealth') with a mocked-up dedication to each of their victims, who 'receives it, and thinking it to be a work only undertaken for his sake, is bounteous to the Giver, esteeming him a Scholar' (239). It is difficult to assess the historical veracity of these portraits. Dekker works quite hard to persuade us that such deceptions actually took place, with rich circumstantial detail about the involvement of stationers and printers, yet there is little evidence to corroborate them, and they may function more as a kind of parable of developments in the book trade that exploited credulous readers, not least of which was the growth of various forms of what we now call 'travel writing'.

Dekker was himself no stranger to plagiarism, and he knew only too well that patrons needed to be flattered into supporting the efforts of commercial authors. Acutely aware of his place in an increasingly crowded literary scene, he was quick to characterise his London rivals, the scribblers and poetasters who 'every new moon (for gaine onely) make 5. or 6. voiages to the *Presse*',[22] as an urban rabble matching the vagrant bands in the countryside. We are left to infer that the same hacks also provide the material fed by the 'wandering Pilgrims' to their unsuspecting dupes. Other writers keen to defend their credentials expressed themselves in similar terms. Two years earlier Richard Carew prefaced his translation of a French treatise on Herodotus with a warning that 'there are so many theeves lying in the way, and so many pirats in this our paper-sea (as wel sea-dogs as land critickes) it cannot be that any mans writings should safely travaile into any country without safe conduct, nor arive at any coast without a convoy'.[23] It is ironic that Carew should have cribbed part of these remarks from another translator, John Florio, but he applies them rather pertinently to the defence of an ancient author whom he regards as a sounder guide to exotic places and customs than contemporary travellers' tales.[24] His resort to the imagery of perilous travel, like Dekker's stories of itinerant impostors, is designed to warn readers that a culture of serious writing is threatened by the 'voyages' of literate rogues.[25]

If the counterfeit licences carried by Thomas Harman's 'Fresh-Water Mariners' bear a family resemblance to the bogus certificates produced by tourists to claim on their wagers, the epistles forged by Dekker's wandering pilgrims are more like a metaphor of the alleged abuse of the press by returning travellers, who claimed the authority of print for their lying tales. Complaints in this period about the proliferation of cheap print were not of course solely aimed at travel accounts, but as James Helfers points out, the 'flurry of exploration at the end of the sixteenth century produced a large amount of ephemeral literature',[26] and the same period saw the first published examples of personal narratives by people with no claim to be educated writers. The English reading experience of travel over the next two decades or so consisted largely of such material. The landmark atlases and collections like Hakluyt's *Principal Navigations* reached a fairly small audience, and even for those who could afford them or had access to them, the handsome folios floated on a sea of small books that treated foreign adventures, real and fictional, as stories, and contextualised them with rough compendia of exotic geographic lore that had been part of a hearsay tradition for generations. Alexandra Halasz's shrewd assessment of the role of cheap print in the literary marketplace applies with particular force to travel material: 'The pamphlets' ephemerality associates them with the orality of gossip, their printedness with the authoritative texts that they materially resemble. Yet it is their printedness that allows them to circulate like gossip.'[27] This is what tormented the writer Richard Brathwaite, who pauses near the start of a high-minded defence of learning to dismiss the interlopers:

> Here by way of digression let me touch the ridiculous labours, and unfruitful travailes of such who passe the Alpes, trace uncoth places, Desarts, Promontories; for what end Heaven knowes, save onely to wrest out a fantasticke behaviour of superfluous wit, or to comment on others travailes by way of dirision: These are such as upon their returne, publish what they have seene …

One of his probable targets here is Thomas Coryat, whose Asian adventures were in the news in 1614 and had just provided John Taylor with an excuse to publish a string of jocular assaults upon the absent traveller. Brathwaite has no time for this kind of literary flyting and spells out his quarrel with contemporary travel writers, who instead of providing a responsible 'materiall discourse' about foreign places are more interested in demonstrating 'an exquisite straine of wit, purchased by a little fruitlesse travell: they insert frivolous occurrents, borrowed, or (it may be) invented by their owne phantasticke braines. These misse the marke a good Traveller should aime at.'[28] But his words also conjure up the boastful and mendacious traveller in London's taverns who feeds the press with stories and feeds off those already published, and his fretting over 'ridiculous labours' and 'fantasticke behaviour' surely hints too at the more calculated performances engendered by the vogue for travel exploits, which has infected the behaviour of tourists and reduced the 'relation of a journey' to a packet of sensational news.

Brathwaite's sweeping critique encompasses most of the writerly engagement with travel during the Jacobean period: even a text like *Lanthorne & Candlelight* is caught in its toils, arguably, for Dekker's itinerant fraudsters are figures of suspect glamour whose witty deceptions provide the plot of his narrative. The cony-catching and rogue literature had always been ambiguously poised between reportage and fiction and could certainly be accused of feeding an appetite for ingenious tales. But Brathwaite's argument also touches on a kind of 'travel writing' that openly mixed fantasy with topical satire (it is an ingredient of Dekker's pamphlet we have not yet mentioned), and one of its most popular forms was the burlesque journey to (and from) Hell.

## Diabolical Travels

As Jonson reminds us in the opening lines of 'Famous Voyage', the imaginary visit to the underworld had a long classical pedigree, and humanist writers had revived Lucian's use of it as instructive entertainment and turned it into a tool of moral enquiry. Their serio-comic methods were largely shunned by the authors of Tudor complaint and morality drama, but made a significant reappearance in later Elizabethan and Jacobean literature as writers sought greater tonal variety and satiric penetration. Dekker's most sustained engagement with the infernal theme was in *Newes from Hell* (1606), which carried out Thomas Nashe's unfulfilled promise in *Pierce Penilesse* to write 'the returne of the Knight of the Poste' from his mission to the nether regions. Nashe had made the burlesque invocation of Hell into a kind of literary rallying-cry (Dekker's was only one of several responses to it), and his edgy, colloquial writing was an inescapable influence on a whole generation of satirists, making it difficult to revert to the purely homiletic note of Tudor complaint. Dekker's explicit embrace of a serio-comic mode in *Newes from Hell* (the book's second edition is described on the title page as 'Done in earnest: Discovered in Jest'[29]) shows him working in the same vein, treating the voyage to the underworld as a picaresque adventure that takes in parts of the standard European tour (deftly sketching the vices of France and Italy) and discovers that Hell is a looking-glass world for Londoners: 'It is an *Empire,* that lyes under the *Torrid Zone* … farther off then the *Indies*: yet to see the wonderfull power of *Navigation,* if you have but a *side-winde,* you may saile sooner thither, than a married man can upon St: *Lukes* day to Cuckolds haven' (C4–v).

This parody of the advice manuals for tourists stands in complex relation to the Renaissance argument about what constitutes a responsible discourse of travel. Brathwaite was prepared to allow some latitude to 'Relations Feigned' that 'include an excellent meaning', and named Homer's epics as a prime example because they avoid 'any scurrulous Affectation' – by which he meant the impiety and lack of gravity he and other commentators found in much of Lucian, features of his work that made him a dangerous model to writers in a sceptical and irreverent age. 'The liberty of these times', he declared, 'perswades some too easily to *Lucians* arguments.'[30] The implication is that, although Lucian would not be translated into English for another 20 years, his ideas and methods had infected popular discourse in ways not anticipated by his humanist champions. Brathwaite's remark appears to be aimed at what one critic calls the 'low ludic tradition' that emerged from Nashe's efforts (in response to Gabriel Harvey) to 'unsettle the dichotomy' between popular and elite forms of writing,[31] and which could be seen as producing texts as various as Coryat's travel writing, Dekker's pamphlets and the 'narrative' epigram that Jonson appears to parody in 'Famous Voyage'. But behind his anxiety about the fashion for Lucian's 'arguments' and their supposed effect on truthful discourse lurks a larger issue regarding Jacobean uses of the fantastic voyage, one that poses the question of whether some of its most ambitious exemplars are able to be ethically constructive in the manner of their humanist models.

The issue at stake here is hinted at in the trope of *mundus inversus* that Dekker plays with in his invocation of an '*Empire,* that lyes under the *Torrid Zone*', which links the classical journey to Hell to early-modern fascination with sub-equatorial exploration and discovery. One of the most remarkable works to reflect that interest appeared a year before Dekker published *Newes from Hell*. Joseph Hall's Menippean satire *Mundus Alter et Idem*, a product of the author's Cambridge years that was published in 1605 without his consent, narrates a journey to an antipodean world that offers Europe a grotesquely distorted image of itself. Its protagonist is Mercurius Britannicus, who sails on the ship Phantasia to discover, as Richard McCabe puts it, 'the four suspiciously familiar nations of Crapulia (gluttony), Viraginia (women), Moronia (folly), and Lavernia (deceit)'.[32] Hall's learned fantasy is thoroughly aware of its classical and humanist forebears, and the voyage it describes to 'Terra Australis', the unexplored great Southern Continent on contemporary maps, has a formal early-modern parallel in Thomas More's tale of landfall in the same hemisphere. Like *Utopia*, it was in the original Latin a considerable success on the Continent. These linkages, however, merely highlight the contrast between the two works. *Utopia* offers a sharp critique of the European status quo, but it proposes an idealistic alternative; like Montaigne's essay *Of Cannibals*, it uses the discoveries to shake readers into thought about the implications of a different way of living. Hall's book sets out to portray a bleak dystopia: the regions described by Mercurius are savage caricatures of European society, leavened by a fair amount of Rabelaisian humour but holding out little hope of worldly reformation. Not coincidentally, Hall was a strident critic of recreational travel and adventure: his satire is a lesson in the folly of ranging abroad, where the only discovery to be made is of the universality of human vice, rather than seeking fulfilment in a world of mind and spirit. Yet its method is very different from that of, say, Roger Ascham's jeremiad against Italy in *The Scholemaster*. Hall makes it clear in his annotations to the text of *Mundus Alter* that he is working within the conventions of *lusus ingenii* and is concerned to locate his attack on travel within the same philosophical matrix that produced the more optimistic narratives of More and Erasmus.

As J.M. Wands explains, Hall is deeply indebted to Lucian's *True Story* for the overall conception and many of the details of *Mundus Alter*, and his evident awareness of *Utopia*, and behind it the discussion of an ideal society in Plato's *Republic*, is balanced by marginal references to classical writers, Aristophanes and Lucian prominent among them, whose stance 'disputes the central assumptions of Plato's work, specifically that people will necessarily be wise, self-controlled, or just'.[33] Hall's Calvinist view of the human condition impels him to refute a proposal that the *mundus inversus* idea had made conceivable: that in a world 'upside down', on the other side of the line, may be discovered a society ruled by quite different, and better, values and preconceptions. In his scheme, rather, it is one where the vices of the known world are magnified and its more egregious trends made to look dangerously absurd. For all his scorn at the folly of travel, Hall (like Robert Burton) was clearly fascinated by geographical speculation about the southern continent, but the almost complete lack of concrete information about Europe's terrestrial 'underworld' made it a blank canvas on which he could project his particular view of civilisation.

*Mundus Alter* is a vital text in the English tradition of the fantastic voyage, one that anticipates Swift in important ways, and it seems to have been recognised from the start as a combative contribution to the genre. John Milton (who had his own quarrels with Hall) launched an intemperate attack on the book in 1642, calling its author 'this petty prevaricator of *America*', who has 'rambl'd over the huge topography of his own vain thoughts' and returned with 'nothing but a mere tankard drollery'. This he contrasted with

> [t]hat grave and noble invention which the greatest and sublimest wits in sundry ages, *Plato in Critias*, and our two famous countrymen, the one in his *Utopia*, the other in his *new Atlantis* chose, I may not say as a field, but as a mighty Continent wherein to display the largenesse of their spirits by teaching this our world better and exacter things, then were yet known, or us'd.[34]

Milton does considerably less than justice to Hall's intricate design and refuses to recognise his moral purpose in the book, which was to turn his culture away from the path of folly. The jibe about being a 'prevaricator of *America*' apparently accuses Hall of a shifty preference for an antipode on which he can write his prejudices over a commitment to the colonial project in New England. This zealous criticism oversimplifies the relationship of *Mundus Alter* to More's *Utopia*, which Milton chooses to read as a blueprint for reform; it might be argued, rather, that Hall's overt satire ultimately refers us back to the much more enigmatic irony in More's discovery of another world, one that also uses Lucianic paradox to sow doubts about the ideal society he is describing. Nonetheless, *Mundus Alter* does feel like a thoroughly Jacobean work, one in which the humanist vision takes on a dark hue, reflecting the multiple challenges and anxieties of the new century. While fantastic travel was to regain in the 1620s and 30s some of the scientific optimism present in *Utopia* (a recovery that yielded Bacon's *New Atlantis* and several fictions about a voyage to the Moon), its discursive role in the preceding two decades – which also corresponded with a surge in travel 'experiments' and speculative ventures – was to be much more ambivalent about innovation and development on a variety of fronts.

*Mundus Alter* was aimed at a university audience, but soon attracted the attention of London's writers: before long it was being translated into English by John Healey, whose racy adaptation appeared in 1609 as *The Discovery of a new World*. Healey's version rewrites the *Mundus* in a Nashean idiom that replaces the allegorical severity of the original with an exuberant attack on contemporary vice, one that is more obviously in tune with literary fashion but which dispenses with most of Hall's erudite humanist scheme. The learned joking is replaced by a looser, more colloquial humour that adapts many of the original's targets to fit the expectations of a vernacular readership. As a result, Hall's defamiliarising parody of social evils, with its recondite Latin nomenclature – one of the elements that lends his antipodes some kinship with More's, despite their differences – yields to a recognisable Jacobean milieu of fools and knaves and shrewish women (with place-names like 'Shee-landt', 'Asse-sex' and 'Gossipingoa'), and Healey's marginal comments point up Jacobean parallels to many of the exotic features of Hall's Antarctic world. In this respect, Healey's *Discovery* is typical of a tendency in English satire to domesticate the radical ideas that it courted with the use of serio-comic techniques. We can see this happening already in some later Tudor examples of utopian writing, where the visit to a topsy-turvy world, as in Thomas Lupton's *Siuqila. Too good, to be true* (London, 1580) and Mendax's trip to 'Terra Florida' in William Bullein's *Dialogue of the Fever Pestilence* (London, 1564), works almost entirely on the principle of subtraction: these are environments defined by an absence of the social abuses that characterise contemporary London. As Lawrence Manley suggests, the effect of this is to 'mirror the *status quo* in perfected form' rather than to prompt constructive engagement with an alternative possible reality; the fantastic voyage discovers nothing new because the 'utopias of late-Tudor writers were … but shadows or projections cast by a power structure which had come to seem ineradicably real.'[35] Writing a generation later for the same popular readership reached by those texts, and without the utopian option, Healey prefers to tame the grim discoveries of Hall's original into something more like the 'plot of roguery', giving his readers a narrator-traveller who is more involved in the scenes he witnesses, and a landscape familiar from the literature of vagrancy and cony-catching.

Nowhere is this clearer than in Healey's reworking of a passage in which Mercurius detects traces of 'a certain Welsh vocabulary' in the vernacular of thieves, which he thinks 'originated from the unknown travels of our countrymen' (Wands, 107). Hall seems to be glancing at Hythloday's speculation about the origins of the Utopian language, but Healey (as Richard McCabe points out) glosses his version with a very different allusion:

> Of this language there is an excellent exact discoverie made in *Thomas Deckers Bellman*, but in his *Lanthorne and Candle-light*, he hath outstript all the world for variety of knowledge in Canting.[36]

This is a reference to the opening chapter ('Of Canting') of *Lanthorne*, which looks like the start of a conventional rogue pamphlet, and it is telling that Healey should single out this feature of the book rather than Dekker's attempt at a more exotic fiction. In *The Bel-Man of London* (1608), Dekker reveals a pageant of urban and rural villainy through the eyes of the city's nightwatchman, but *Lanthorne & Candlelight*, described on the title page as 'The Bell-mans second Nights-walke', adds a more hectic tour of London and the provinces by the Devil's emissary Pamersiel, sent from Hell to undo the damage to diabolical interests done by the Belman's first patrol, which had 'looked into the secrets of the Best trades that are taught in Hell, laying them open to the broad eye of the world, making them infamous, odious and ridiculous'. If this corrective teaching goes unchecked, report Satan's spies, Londoners will become reformed citizens and 'Hell will have no doings' (224). The fears of the 'Satanical Synagogue' turn out to be groundless, of course, for as soon as Pamersiel arrives in the city, he finds himself a defenceless tourist at the mercy of rapacious tradesmen. Forced by them to buy an expensive suit, he commences his survey of London as 'an accomplished gallant', which naturally gives him access to most of the city's dark corners, and also provides cover for his wearying surveillance ('riding up and down the Country') of the itinerant swindlers already discussed.

This is a scenario obviously rich in comic possibilities, yet Dekker does relatively little with it. For much of the narrative Pamersiel drops out of sight and is not obviously a witness to the travelling scams, so an opportunity is lost to exploit the gap between the orthodox perspective of the Belman and the subversive one of the Devil's emissary. As Pamersiel prepares to return to Hell, 'having filled his Table-books with sufficient notes of intelligence', he meets the Belman, who asks him 'what discovery of *Land villainies* he had made in this *Island voyage*', whereupon 'the *Mariner* of *Hell* opened his chart' and 'shewed how he had pricked it ... where he put in ... where he went ashore, what strange people he had met', and the Bellman then proceeds to make 'a perfect Map' out of Pamersiel's data. That map is Dekker's book, which the author says 'he hath set out in such colors as you see, though not with such cunning as he could wish' (260). The admission is a writer's conventional apology for the shortcomings of his narrative, but it also implies a question about what the Belman's map might simplify or leave out because of his particular angle of view. Dekker seemingly intended to use the devil's adventure as a sort of 'counter-voyage' to the Belman's inquisition, substituting for the latter's previous crusade a less didactic tour that would draw in the reader and provoke a livelier response. Yet in the event he holds back from giving the 'strange journey' its head, perhaps uncertain about how far to tap into the devil's ambiguous appeal. The plot of roguery in *Lanthorne & Candlelight* does elicit a degree of admiration for its ingenuity, but Dekker is careful to keep it episodic, a series of self-contained vignettes, rather than allowing a diabolical mad voyage to reveal that beyond or beneath the Belman's 'perfect Map' lies a bewildering maze.

Dekker was also a playwright and knew about the capacity of the theatrical vice figure to disturb an audience's moral bearings, but it was his contemporary Ben Jonson who made the stage play that realised the Lucianic potential of the devil plot. Jonson was dismissive in the prologue to *The Devil is an Ass* (1616) about Dekker's contribution to the genre of the devil play, but it is rarely if ever noted how closely the visit from Hell in his drama is modelled on the early scenario in *Lanthorne & Candlelight*. In *Devil*, a junior fiend called Pug petitions Satan to be allowed a sabbatical on Earth, and in what ensues we repeatedly witness Pug's ineptitude in trying to orchestrate mischief in

London or be a match for the vices he finds there ('Hell is a grammar school to this!'). The joke is pivotal to Jonson's plot, and Dekker could profitably have used something like it to control and shape our reactions to his cony-catchers. The scenario in *Devil* recalls the moral relativism of *The Alchemist*, although the swindlers in this play have none of the charisma of Face and Subtle, and there is no theatrical satisfaction to be had out of their escape from retribution. Pug however is out of his depth not only with the villains, but also in the romantic plot involving Wittipol and Frances Fitzdottrel. His inept intervention in their budding relationship, tipping off Fitzdottrel about Wittipol's courtship of his wife, becomes an ironic comment on the limitations of conventional morality, since it threatens to short-circuit the genuine dilemma that faces Frances as she tries to choose between an unworthy husband and a sympathetic suitor. Pug is a helpless witness not only to the amoral city and its enterprise, but also to the ethical perplexities that assail admirable characters and reveal within them a capacity to change and grow.[37] In earlier plays, Jonson uses playful strategies to complicate our response to his entrepreneurial villains; here, it may be argued, he creates a plot that fully honours the humanist plan to deploy ludic methods in the quest for self-improvement and a greater moral awareness.

At roughly the midpoint of his career, then, Jonson was more inclined than some of his fellow writers to use serio-comic resources in a cautiously affirmative way, and he turned his attention to the travel exploit during the second decade of the seventeenth century in ways that suggest a more thorough engagement with its implications than he revealed in his earlier portraits of the modish traveller. Jonson's readiness to make literary capital out of Coryat's walk to Venice, and his playful testimonial to William Roe as a latter-day Aeneas, demonstrate a relish for the games that could be played with the fantastic voyage, and his own walk to Scotland was a kind of licence he granted himself to treat the fashionable wager-journey as a creative adventure, one that might add something enduring to the literary record. Between the composition of Coryat's 'Character' and his own expedition, however, Jonson completed the formidable poem that concludes his *Epigrams*, and in the event (since his 'journey into Scotland sung' did not survive) this was to be his most fully developed treatment of the travel wager, an essay in mad voyaging that epitomises many of the quirks and contradictions in the vogue we have been examining. Whether it can be seen as a fundamentally positive version of the fantastic journey in the humanist tradition of such things is the most difficult critical question posed by 'On the Famous Voyage'.

## London's Acheron

Recent criticism of the 'Famous Voyage' epigram has seen itself as challenging the squeamishness of earlier generations of readers and not allowing its rebarbative subject-matter to discourage a serious assessment of Jonson's purpose and achievement. In the 1980s and 1990s this determination was assisted by the enthusiasm in parts of the literary academy for the work of Mikhail Bakhtin and a consequent focus on the 'lower bodily stratum', together with much talk of carnival and transgression in early-modern texts. These approaches now look rather dated, though they did help to produce what is still the most substantial and compelling discussion of 'Famous Voyage', by Andrew McRae, who finds 'a strangely subversive vitality' in the poem that discloses, like the emphasis on the physical in Bakhtin's Rabelais, a 'triumphant, festive principle'.[38] McRae shows how 'prevailing discourses of civic description', like John Stow's, tended to ignore the urban underworld that Jonson explores so thoroughly; like Dekker's Bellman, perhaps, they offered a 'perfect Map' of the city that left out its most intractable elements. In the Fleet Ditch exploit, Jonson creates another version of the counter-voyage, and what it discloses for McRae is a 'radically divergent spaciality' that, for all its sordid confusion, 'also fosters a distinctive creativity'. McRae sees the poem as analogous to *Bartholomew Fair*, probably completed at much the same time as 'Famous Voyage': both evince Jonson's 'ambivalence towards the realm of popular culture', but both are 'vibrantly grotesque, and pregnant with significance for the city as a whole' (197–8). This reading of 'Famous Voyage' is powerfully responsive to Jonson's vision of the city's underbelly and the poetic craft that articulates it, and it is probably the critical account that comes closest to describing and accounting for the poem's particular tone. Yet a certain vagueness hovers around claims of a 'distinctive creativity' to be found in its degraded ordeal, and it is hard to see that the voyagers make the kind of humanising discovery vouchsafed to Adam Overdo at the end of *Bartholomew Fair*: he realises that he is 'flesh and blood' and acquires humility and a measure of wisdom, but they simply make it through an appalling experience and win an unlikely bet.

Nonetheless, as indicated earlier, the wager-journey in the poem has been defended recently as a morally significant venture and a means by which Jonson brings the *Epigrams* to an unorthodox but fundamentally affirmative close. Michael Manous makes the case in another closely-argued analysis that takes issue with McRae for downplaying the wager but also finds a 'carnivalesque example' in 'Famous Voyage', through which, he suggests, we might 'receive a lesson in human living'.[39] This essay grounds Jonson's treatment of the wager firmly in his understanding of the Menippean tradition and sees it as a humanist use of Lucianic methods to portray 'the human quest to triumph over and amidst moral deformity' (57). The argument is a welcome attempt to bring the poem within the frame of Jonson's Lucianism (a task avoided in Duncan's excellent study) and to re-engage with the old critical problem of its relationship to the rest of the *Epigrams* volume. Yet within his historically informed and scholarly reading, Manous is also reliant on Bakhtinian ideas, quoting with approval the Russian critic's assertion that 'adventures of truth on earth take place on the high road, in brothels, in the dens of thieves', and so on, in line with the valorising of 'festive deformity' (57) that revisionist criticism of early-modern culture has found so compelling.

It seems to me that this approach can be sustained only by developing a new kind of resistance to the poem: rather than being shocked and repelled by its scatology like earlier generations, modern critics are determined to look past, or through, its deliberately provocative evocation of filth and discover a salubrious cultural message. Hence the repeated tendency of commentators to misjudge the tone of the poem: vitality there may be aplenty in 'Famous Voyage', but 'truth', 'wisdom' and 'understanding' (*pace* Manous) are not terms that spring immediately to mind to characterise what the protagonists gain from the venture, and it is not clear that Jonson wanted the reader to feel the kind of immunity from contamination that has tempted critics to discover a festive principle at work amidst so much squalor.

Here Jonson's ludic handling of the trope of the underworld journey needs considering more closely, and a final comparison with Dekker's methods may be useful. In the latter's *Newes from Hell* the Knight of the Post, wearying of his European tour and 'having ... gotten Table-talke enough by his Travell', proceeds to 'the banckside of *Acheron*', where Charon is plying his trade like a Thames waterman, and the familiar analogy with London's underworld is given a slant that directly anticipates Jonson's pungent handling of it in his poem. Charon's breath is so noisome that the 'Sea-cole furnaces of ten Brew-houses, make not such a smoke, nor the Tallowe pans of fifteene Chaundlers (when they melt,) send out such a smell' (F3). 'As touching the River', comments Dekker,

> look howe *Moore-ditche* shewes, when the water is three-quarters out, and by reason the stomack of it is over-laden, is readie to fall to casting, so does that [i.e. Acheron], it stincks almost worse, is almost as poysonous, altogether so muddie, altogether so blacke: In taste very bitter, (yet to those that knowe howe to distill these deadly waters,) very wholesome. (F3v)

Moorditch was a notoriously stagnant drain just outside the city walls. Dekker's savage joke about London's brewers is serio-comic method at its most intense: there is no mistaking his determination to observe and document a grim urban reality. The metaphoric vehicle (Moorditch) becomes the tenor of the comparison, as Acheron struggles to match its horrors, and in the process the fiction recedes. Jonson's literary procedure is very different. Compare the assault on the reader's sensibilities as his voyagers turn into the mouth of the Fleet river:

> In the first jaws appeared that ugly monster
> Yclepèd Mud, which, when their oars did once stir,
> Belched forth an air as hot as at the muster
> Of all your night-tubs, when the carts do cluster,
> Who shall discharge first his merd-urinous load. (61–5)

This too leaves little about London's polluted waterways to the imagination, and the ensuing voyage pushes on into a veritable storm of excrement, dead animals and waste products. Yet as these lines already suggest, the poem's challenge is not just to our appetite for documentary detail. If we misjudge its tone by looking too hard for moral heroism or Baudelairean *nostalgie*, it may be because the irreverent manner in which Jonson treats his material makes it difficult to get a steady critical perspective on what he is trying to do.

Following the mock-heroic introduction that disposes of Greece's 'bolder fables' of underworld travel, Jonson switches in 'The Voyage Itself' to burlesque of Spenserian romance ('I sing the brave adventure of two wights') that creates a flexible but consistent tonal framework for the rest of the poem. He establishes this in a sequence (lines 61–86) heavily reliant on hyper-metrical feminine rhymes, which sustain the comic air needed to avoid capsizing the Spenserian vehicle with so much unsavoury material. The 'ugly monster / Yclepèd Mud' is announced in this dallying way (emphasised in the near-homonymic jingle of 'monster / once stir'), so that its true nature is confirmed only with 'merd-urinous load', as we land on the heavy end-stop concluding one half of the only decasyllabic couplet in a 20-line sequence. (Even this pungent phrase is a linguistic joke, with its principal vocatives spelling out the word m-u-d.) This is surely where many readers' difficulties with the poem have begun, with the incongruous match of levity and filth, but I would argue that this unease is a necessary result of Jonson's radical burlesque and should not be rationalised into perceptions of 'festivity'. After entering the Fleet, the voyagers 'make their famous road / Between two walls', on one of which

Hung stench, diseases, and old filth their mother,
With famine, wants, and sorrows many a dozen,
The least of which was to the plague a cousin.
But they unfrighted pass ... (70–73)

Once again, as in the introductory lines (16–18), Jonson sounds a diagnostic note amidst all the graphic detail, and it subjects the basic premise of heroic ordeal – the challenge to be 'unfrighted' by the experience – to sharp scrutiny: is this moral courage, or are the voyagers simply indifferent to evidence of social distress? Do they assume that 'old filth' is produced by the poor and deprived and, like them, can safely be ignored? The comedy takes on an aggressive and patrician air as orders are given to the demoralised crew:

'Back!' cried their brace of Charons; they cried 'No;
No going back; on still, you rogues, and row.'
'How hight the place?' A voice was heard: 'Cocytus.'
'Row close then, slaves.' 'Alas, they will beshite us.'
'No matter, stinkards, row!' (87–91)

There is a danger here, obviously, of proposing too earnest a reading of this and similar passages, but the tension between burlesque manner and social realities is something that Jonson has deliberately contrived.

The concept of ordeal that informs the classical journeys to the underworld of Aeneas and Orpheus is founded on the idea of abstinence, of resistance to temptation and an ability to remain focused on a larger goal. It is an idea that only superficially resembles the liberal belief that saturation in the seamy side of life may be an educative experience and make one a better person. Insofar as the wager is central to the poem, it involves a steadfast shunning of all the 'creativity' that Bakhtinian criticism wants to find in London's underbelly, and the only wisdom it delivers is akin to the disillusionment that critics of travel said was bound to be the result of venturing abroad. Being 'unfrighted' in this context means remaining aloof to the potentially transformative effects of travel. This idea was, as I suggested earlier, implicit in the 'bargain of return' and was a paradoxical ingredient in all the mad voyages: namely that, as apparent affirmations of the act of travel, they also subordinated curiosity and knowledge-gathering to the objective of completing a challenge, all the more so when the exploit was a particularly dangerous or bizarre one. In practice, of course, the wager journey was not always so narrowly conceived. Jonson himself on the walk to Scotland made numerous detours to visit friends and acquaintances, and presumably declined to make a bet that would (like John Taylor's) require him to be single-minded about reaching his destination. Will Kemp, too, managed to have (and to record in writing) experiences that had little direct bearing on his wager, and Thomas Coryat saw no conflict between his image as an eccentric 'leg-stretcher' and his determination to learn as much as possible from his travels. Yet in 'Famous Voyage' there is no hint of the wager being an educative experience for the voyagers, or of the ordeal being personally meaningful in any way.

Every commentator notes that Jonson's normal practice in the *Epigrams* is to make the act of naming one of approbation, as in the address to William Roe; those who are condemned or despised remain nameless, like the 'Something that Walks Somewhere' of *Epigram* 11. The naming of Shelton and Heyden as the Fleet Ditch voyagers is usually interpreted as a partial exception to this rule since they are not obviously admirable characters, though it has also encouraged the idea that the mock-heroic treatment of their efforts is not entirely satirical and may after all endorse the wager-journey as a moral victory. But a more significant departure from Jonson's usual practice is surely that he is not here speaking in his own voice. It is the narrator who declares at the start that 'We have a Shelton and a Heyden got, / Had power to act what they [the ancient poets] had not' (5–6), and the brutally pragmatic view that antiquity 'brought the poets forth, but ours th'adventer' (20) is clearly set up for ridicule. The protagonists themselves, however, are not required to carry the burden of Jonson's praise or blame. There is probably little to be gained from seeing them as lampoons of recognisable contemporary figures like the astrology writer, Sir Christopher Heyden, or Thomas Shelton, the translator of Cervantes, as Peter Medine has proposed, and the poem's Shelton is more plausibly identified with the character described by John Chamberlain as one of a group of 'fools or buffons' on the fringes of the court.[40] As this implies, it is worth retaining a sense of the poem's subject being initially generated by the rituals of the Mermaid circle, which may well have extended to an actual wager involving drinking-companions with these or similar names. But in fashioning such an experience or conceit into the finished poem, Jonson creates a ship of fools whose occupants are oblivious to the implications of their hectic voyage. The act of naming in this case merely emphasises that the protagonists are empty celebrities, whose fame is bought cheaply and instantly in an age that values only the sensational and the bizarre.

Notwithstanding his doubtful identification of the voyagers, and a somewhat solemn reading of the poem's manner, I think Peter Medine is broadly correct in identifying the satiric target of 'Famous Voyage' as 'the age itself' (98), indicting its vulgarity and false priorities, its neglect of true learning and its perversion of scientific endeavour. And in making the mad voyage do this kind of work in his poem, Jonson seems to be compelled by anxieties and convictions not far removed from those that shaped Joseph Hall's dystopian vision in *Mundus Alter*. In some ways, 'Famous Voyage' is very close to the sardonic literary game played in Lucian's satires, which lack the moral optimism that the humanists grafted onto his ludic scheme. Jonson was thoroughly attuned to the Erasmian serio-comic project, as Douglas Duncan has shown, and he was ready to deploy it both in the underworld plot elements of *The Devil is an Ass* and in his other engagements with wager travel. But this poem seems to be the product of a more sceptical attitude to human progress and achievement, one that turns to the mad voyage to question his culture's direction of travel.

As we saw, Shelton and Heyden imitate the real-life wagerers in obtaining solid witness of their unlikely feat, and in lines which probably represent Jonson's final revision of the poem, their ordeal receives even more tangible recognition from the city:

In memory of which most liquid deed,
The city since hath raised a pyramid.
And I could wish for their eternized sakes,
My muse had ploughed with his that sung A-jax. (193–6)

The 'most liquid deed' that all London was talking about in 1613 was the New River project, a newly completed scheme to pipe water from the Hertfordshire hills into the northern suburbs of the city, and the pyramid is almost certainly the Water House or cistern that was built at New River Head near Sadler's Wells to receive and distribute the new water supply, and officially opened on Michaelmas Day with 'excellent Musique ... and with speeches and other pleasant entertainements'.[41] By wickedly co-opting the symbol of this grand engineering feat for his own imaginative project, Jonson appears to disavow the idea that progressive schemes of this kind can have a significant impact on the way we think about the city. Rather than be a poet laureate and sing of the modernising efforts of the city fathers, Jonson chooses to puncture the belief that the New River scheme is really an answer to the fouling of London's natural waterways, despite one of its aims being to flush them out. And his reluctance to embrace this technocratic 'adventer' is compounded in the last two lines, where the narrator's wish that he could have rivalled Homer in celebrating the deeds of his voyagers – ploughing with the muse that sung of Ajax and Ulysses – is overlaid with a more contemporary reference through the mocking emphasis of the couplet rhyme.

The writer who 'sung A-jax' in Jonson's day was Sir John Harington, whose 1596 treatise *The Metamorphosis of Ajax* combined an historical account of privies (known as 'jakes' to the Elizabethans) with details of his own development of an improved model. Jonson, who was generally disparaging about Harington, insinuates that he would be an appropriate muse to tawdry adventurers like Shelton and Heyden. But Harington's improved privy, like the New River scheme, had the potential to make a real contribution to the quality of urban life, and both specifically respond to the sort of planning crisis and health hazard represented by the Fleet Ditch. Jonson was fond of claiming that the mechanic arts compromised the imaginative reach of the genuine writer, and his poem is not seeking an answer to moral or physical pollution outside the minds and consciences of his readers. But by opening London's own Acheron to public gaze in this poem, Jonson inevitably initiates a kind of dialogue with texts like Harington's, and in the end effectively acknowledges that his own purposes *have* forced his muse to plough a similar furrow. After all, Harington also meditates on the relationship between creativity and filth, and on the kinds of profundity that are desirable in these matters, in ways that comment obliquely and proleptically on Jonson's enterprise. After describing his invention, with its 'false bottome which shall have a sluce of brasse to let out all the filth … close plaistered, al about it, & renced with water, as oft as occasion serves', Harington then wittily anticipates the Jonsonian objection that 'there is no depth in the invention: for it is nothing but to keepe downe the ayre with a stopple & let out the filth', and

> for depth in the invention, I affecte it not (for I would not have it in all above two foote deepe.) And though the proverb is the deeper the sweeter, that is to bee intended in some sweeter matters, for the deeper you wade in this, you shall find it the sourer … [42]

– an observation that is amply confirmed by Jonson's poem.

In reading 'Famous Voyage', we should avoid the error Milton made in interpreting Hall's *Mundus Alter* as a gratuitous exercise ('a mere tankard drollery'), notwithstanding the poem's scabrous content and Jonson's refusal to sound a note of constructive reform. He uses the current vogue for mad voyages to bring about this deliberately discordant ending to the *Epigrams*, I think, because he had a grasp of its literary analogues in Lucianic satire and saw that it acted as a metaphor for the conflicted priorities of Jacobean society. It was easy enough, as other critics had done, to attack the fashion for stunts and wager tourism as frivolous, but Jonson seems to have been intrigued by the ludic content of these ventures and saw that they could be used for a variety of creative purposes. He certainly ironises the 'heroic' claims of the mad voyage in the pungent venture of Shelton and Heyden and in the brash assertions of the poem's narrator, but as we saw earlier, he also availed himself of the charisma attaching to the long-distance traveller in his own journey to Scotland and in his playful endorsement of Coryat. The range of response is not surprising, for Jonson played the game of travel with the same love of paradox that infused the literary voyages of writers like Thomas More and Rabelais. In doing so at the moment when the trope of the fantastic journey assumed a literal shape in the fashionable travel stunt, Jonson became the most searching commentator we have on the curious phenomenon of the mad voyage.

## Notes

1 This poem by 'I. Johnston' was first printed by Mark Bland in 'Ben Jonson and the Legacies of the Past', *Huntington Library Quarterly* 67 (2004), 397. Its author may have been John Johnston, a Yorkshire cleric whose family came from the same Annandale region in Scotland from which Jonson claimed descent (see William Dugdale's *Visitation of the County of Yorke* [1859], 6). Jonson does not appear to have met Johnston on the outward journey, according to the narrative discovered by James Loxley, but may have visited him on the return trip.

2 'To William Roe', Epigram 128, in Jonson, *Works*, 5.186–7.

3 In Pontefract, Jonson and his companion had a very similar experience to Kemp's in Norwich: 'wee tooke a by way to escape the crowd and staring of the people yet a swarme of boyes and others crossd over to overtake us, and pressed so upon us, that wee were fayne to present our pistols upon them to keepe them backe' ('Foote Voyage', 218–20).

4 *Coryats Crudities*, I.16; Jonson, *Works*, 5.437.

5 All references are to Colin Burrow's recent edition in Jonson, *Works*, 5.190–98. I have preferred the spelling of the names of the voyagers found in the 1616 Folio.

6 Andrew McRae, '"On the Famous Voyage": Ben Jonson and Civic Space', in A. Gordon & B. Klein, eds., *Literature, Mapping, and the Politics of Space in Early Modern Britain* (Cambridge: Cambridge UP, 2001), 190–92.

7 Michael L. Manous, 'An Eagle's Wing and a Vulture's Wing: Poetic Journey and Wager Journey in Jonson's "Famous Voyage"'. *Ben Jonson Journal* 15 (2008), 54–78.

8 Katherine Duncan-Jones, 'City Limits', *Review of English Studies* 56 (2005), 260.

9 *Cynthia's Revels*, 1.3.27–8; *Every Man Out of his Humour*, Characters, 15, and 4.3.31–41 (Jonson, *Works*, 1.463, 1.254, I.364–5). For more on Puntarvolo and the Constantinople wager, see my article 'Going to Constantinople', *Studies in Travel Writing* 16 (2012), 1–13.

10 If Sir Henry Wotton is caricatured in the foolish knight, as has long been suggested, there are perhaps traces of his aptitude for the *braveraria* in Peregrine too: see pp. 136–7 above.

11 Jill Ingram, 'Economies of Obligation in *Eastward Ho!*', *Ben Jonson Journal* 11 (2004), 22.

12 Alizon Brunning, '"Thou art damned for alt'ring thy religion": The Double Coding of Conversion in City Comedy', in D. Mehl et al, eds., *Plotting Early Modern London* (Farnham: Ashgate, 2004), 152; Chesney, *Countervoyage*, 5–6 and passim.

13 Anne-Julia Zwierlein, 'Shipwrecks in the City: Commercial Risk as Romance in Early Modern City Comedy', in Mehl, *Plotting Early Modern London*, ch. 4.

14 Thomas Dekker, *The Great Frost*, A4; on Banks, see Andrew Duxfield, 'That Horse that Runnes ... ', *Notes & Queries*, 252 (2007), 264–5.

15 *Lanthorne & Candlelight*, ch. 11, in Arthur Kinney, ed., *Rogues, Vagabonds & Sturdy Beggars* (Amherst: U. of Massachusetts Press, 1990), 254. Subsequent references are to this edition.

16 See Stone, *Crisis of the Aristocracy*, 531–7. 'Sixteen goldsmiths ... are known to have made loans to peers' between 1580 and 1620 (533). In this period scriveners 'began to accept long-term deposits from a variety of investors and to put the money out in a series of short-term loans in their own name' (537), so presumably money put out (i.e. deposited) by intending travellers was then put out in turn (as a loan at interest) by these brokers.

17 See Arthur Kinney's lively introduction to his *Rogues, Vagabonds & Sturdy Beggars*, and for recent debate, C. Dionne and S. Mentz, eds., *Rogues and early modern English Culture* (Ann Arbor: U. of Michigan Press, 2004).

18 Agnew, *Worlds Apart*, 66.

19 *The Defence of Cony-Catching* (London, 1592), quoted by Manley, *Literature and Culture*, 351. For a useful discussion of these 'structural analogies between in-law and outlaw society', see Manley, *Literature and Culture*, pp. 341–55.

20 Kinney, *Rogues*, 128.

21 McRae, *Literature and Domestic Travel*, 214–15.

22 *Lanthorne & Candlelight*, epistle, A3 (not included in Kinney ed.).

23 Henri Estienne (trans. R. Carew) *A World of Wonders ... touching the Conformitie of ancient and moderne wonders* (1607), Epistle, ♦3-v.

24 See the preface to John Florio, *A Worlde of Wordes* (London, 1598). The writings of Herodotus made a serious attempt to distinguish rumour from firsthand observation and were infinitely superior in method to *Mandeville's Travels* and indeed to most contemporary accounts of Africa and the East, but powerful conventions of tale-telling blocked full appreciation of the fact.

25 Alexandra Halasz interestingly compares Dekker's 'phobic' conception of the literary marketplace with John Taylor's embrace of an enterprise culture in selling subscriptions to his travel pamphlets: 'The entrepreneurial model of discursive production that emerges parodically in Dekker's *Lanthorn and Candlelight* is staged in "positive" terms in the subscription scenario', where 'writers and readers alike are inscribed within an entrepreneurial logic – the inevitability and necessity of "adventures upon return"'(*Marketplace of Print*, 200).

26 James P. Helfers, 'The Explorer or the Pilgrim?', *Studies in Philology* 94 (1997), 162.

27 Halasz, *Marketplace of Print*, 3.

28 Richard Brathwaite, *The Schollers medley* (London, 1614), 8–9.

29 Published as *A Knight's Conjuring* (London, 1607).

30 Brathwaite, *The Schollers medley*, 31, 34.

31 O'Callaghan, 'Thomas the Scholer', 49, 52.

32 Richard A. McCabe, *Joseph Hall: A Study in Satire and Meditation* (Oxford: Clarendon, 1982), 74.

33 J.M. Wands, *Another World and Yet the Same* (New Haven: Yale UP, 1981), xxvi.

34 John Milton, *Complete Prose Works*, ed. D.M. Wolfe (New Haven: Yale UP, 1953), 1.881.

35 Manley, *Literature and Culture*, 117–19. On 'subtraction' in satire, see Wands, *Another World*, xxxiv–v. Both Wands and McCabe offer excellent analyses of the relationship of Healey's text to Hall's.

36 John Healey, *The Discovery of a New World* (London, 1609), 221. See McCabe, *Joseph Hall*, 322–3, and More, *Utopia*, ed. Logan and Adams, 77–8.

37 For more on this, see my introduction to the play in Jonson, *Works*, 4.465–74, and Helen Ostovich, 'Hell for Lovers', in *Refashioning Ben Jonson*, ed. J. Sanders et al (Basingstoke: St Martin's Press, 1998).

38 McRae, 'On the Famous Voyage', 195.

39 Manous, 'An Eagle's Wing', 71.

40 Peter Medine, 'Object and Intent in Jonson's "Famous Voyage"', *Studies in English Literature* 15 (1975), 100–104; Chamberlain, *Letters*, 2.14.

41 Edmund Howes, *The Abridgement of the English Chronicle* (London, 1618), 543. Jonson's allusion to the New River project was first proposed by Ian Donaldson.

42 John Harington, *A new discourse of a stale subject, called the Metamorphosis of Ajax* (London 1596), G8v, H4v. Earlier, Harington declares that just as 'scholars do daily seeke out new phrases, & metaphors … Magistrats may aswel now as hertofore, devise new orders for cleanlines, & wholesomnes' (D6v). Harington's point is supported by Nicholas Breton, *Crossing of Proverbs* (London, 1616), 'P[roverb]. The deeper the sweeter: C[ross]. Not in a foule hole' (A5).

# Afterword

'When is travelling mad?' asks the philosopher Ian Hacking in an absorbing study of the phenomenon of fugue, a mental illness that leads to compulsive wandering in an amnesiac state and which has historically, for relatively brief periods, assumed epidemic proportions in particular societies.[1] Hacking's prime example is 1890s France, but he also considers examples of deranged wandering in classical Greek myth and as far afield as colonial Malaya. Nobody has ever proposed that fugue was an observable phenomenon in early-modern England, although the stories of roaming madness and its cure in ancient Greece caught the eye of Robert Burton in writing *The Anatomy of Melancholy*, and anxieties about vagrancy and frivolous tourism were both liable to create a moral panic in conservative minds. The rogue literature of the Tudor-Stuart period fashioned a colourful myth of wandering bands out of the unsettled conditions in the late sixteenth century that released traders, demobbed soldiers and the destitute on to England's roads, and helped to construct a geography of the London underworld that amply fulfilled Alexander Barclay's intuition of the metropolis as the harbour or destination of the ship of fools. Hacking's question was certainly current in this period, and it was always liable to be aimed at travel activities that rejected old constraints on mobility and encouraged what looked like mindless compulsion in those undertaking them. Jonson played humorously with this idea in his description of Coryat as an engine wound up and pointed at Venice, while the more severe critics of recreational travel could only have seen the rash of exploits that William Rowley called 'madde voiages' as confirmation of its deranging effects.

It is also apparent, however, that Rowley's designation of the craze had (and was intended to have) other resonances, for in a period when the debate about the value of travel was endless, amounting almost to a rhetorical *topos* in its own right, the mad voyage inserted itself into the argument in novel ways. On the one hand, it specialised in parody and burlesque of what was regarded as 'real' travel; on the other, its protagonists could be seen to conquer space and distance and overcome physical challenges in a fashion that credited them with a minor version of the status accorded to prestigious global adventurers like Drake and Cavendish. Nixon's write-up of William

Bush's exploit and Coryat's self-promotion in the *Crudities* are the most colourful examples of this. In the terms offered by the anthropologist Mary Helms, the extraordinary journey brings kudos to its skilful executant, even – or perhaps especially – when it is a ludic endeavour.[2] These were sophisticated developments that intrigued urbane observers like John Chamberlain and the Gray's Inn students, who seem to have grasped that they were exercises in folly of a different, more strategic kind.

From our vantage point, these travel exploits look less like a brief collective madness than early evidence of a chronic condition, since what contemporaries perceived as a local epidemic in fact anticipated many idiosyncratic treatments of adventure in later centuries. The popular notion that English eccentricity is bred in the bone owes much to hardy perennials like the long-distance walking stunt and a predilection for unusual escapades, and my demonstration that these activities are first cultivated not in the wager-books of eighteenth-century London clubs but in the taverns and town houses of Renaissance England might seem to reinforce this trans-historical reading of the national character. This is a topic that our wariness about racial and cultural stereotyping teaches us to avoid, even in a formulation as beguiling as Michel Foucault's statement that in the post-Renaissance era the English temperament 'was easily explained by the influence of a maritime climate, cold, humidity, the instability of the weather; all those fine droplets of water that penetrated the channels and fibers of the human body and made it lose its firmness, predisposed it to madness.'[3] The climatic theory that informs this observation is certainly out of favour nowadays, yet we might note that Foucault closely echoes a remark by Sir Philip Sidney (as reported by Fulke Greville in his biography of the poet) about his countrymen's difficulties in developing effective maritime policies:

> His opinion being that *Ilanders* have the air and waters so diversly moving about them, as neither peace, nor war, can long be welcome to their humors, which must therefore be govern'd by the active, and yet steady hand of authority. Besides he observed the Sea to have so naturall a Sympathie, with the complexions of them she invirons, as be it in traffique, piracie, or war, they are indifferent to wander upon that element; and for the most part apter to follow undertaking chance, than any setled ends in a Marchant-traffique.[4]

The paradoxical proposition that England's insular state compromised her performance as a maritime power is one that Richard Hakluyt also wrestles with in the prefatory epistle to the *Principal Navigations*, where he deals with the charge that the nation's sailors prefer privateering and short-term heroics to a sustainable plan of colonisation and trade.[5] This was, of course, one area where erratic conduct was decisively corrected in the subsequent acquisition of a global empire, though the claim that Britannia rules the waves has undoubtedly continued to feed the ambitions of single-handed yachtsmen and some of the recent maritime stunts that I outline in my opening chapter. In the more idiosyncratic of these exploits, the spirit of Richard Ferris's voyage in the wake of the Armada victory is alive and well.

In Chapter 2, I sought to trace the possible origins of such idiosyncrasy in late-mediaeval perplexities about national identity and the belated and piecemeal reception of humanist ideas. This is difficult territory to explore: the evidence is elusive and fragmentary, and I would not want to claim that the mad voyages are testimony to entrenched habits and quirks of behaviour later identified as typically English. There are signs of an emergent individualism and a strengthening sense of agency in the more ambitious tourists, but those who undertook the travel stunt in all its forms did not yet have recognized models of unconventional behaviour to follow. Their theatre of activity was an experimental one, however much it utilized established devices like the wager on a journey, and it was shaped by volatile forces. As we saw, the customary walk to Berwick was thrown into the melting pot by changing circumstances, and when commentators included wagers to Venice or Constantinople in the category of the mad voyage, they were tilting the hackneyed argument about the value of travel in a new direction. For while the bargain of return might still offer the satirist a way of labelling such trips as frivolous or wrong-headed, the wide-ranging lists of travel stunts made by observant critics like Jonson and Rowley describe a cultural playground in which tourism abroad has become part of a new kind of game, or gamble. The cult of the mad voyage to which these writers ambiguously subscribe is a liminal moment in English travel, moving beyond the anxieties of the Tudor moralists but not yet ready for the spacious recreations of the Grand Tour. It may have met a psychological need in a generation for whom mobility in nearly all its forms was either something new or a greatly expanded set of opportunities and dangers, and a challenge to settled restrictions and ideas of identity. In this, as in so much else, the early-modern period is one of transition.

Nowhere was this more true than in England's capital city. Most of the travel exploits I have been discussing either took place within London (the numerous 'experiments' noted by John Chamberlain) or had their starting point or destination there, and seem to have been stimulated by the urban dynamic that generated so many images of the city as a lure to adventurers, like the description of Pimlico as an '*inchanted* Iland' to which all readers of a 1609 pamphlet are encouraged to navigate, or William Fennor's account of a debtors' prison that he calls a 'voyage made to an infernall Iland, long since discovered … where many men lie winde-bound sometimes foure or five yeeres together'.[6] These images, and many others like them, feed off the popularity of travel accounts to give areas of the early-modern city a fantastic and slightly dangerous aspect. At this historical moment, when the city was growing rapidly, Londoners were struggling to comprehend the space they inhabited and the dangers and possibilities of urban experience, and the mad voyage was both a ready metaphor for their excited bewilderment at social conditions and (for some) a new and flamboyant vehicle for their aspirations in a challenging environment.

The varied kinds of enquiry required to address these issues mean that a single disciplinary approach is unlikely to come up with an adequate explanation for the mad voyages. Previous scholarly interest in the topic, such as it is, has inclined towards a literary focus on the mad voyage because of the availability of narrative accounts, the particular fame of performers like Kemp and Jonson, and the affinities of the vogue with fictions of fantastic travel. Yet what we find in imaginative writing is the mad voyage as metaphor, pressed into the service of a larger argument or vision, and not a documenting of social practice. A related point can be made about the written accounts of individual stunts, which in several cases were performed with a view to being described in print and by that means to reach a wider audience. But the way a text represents or otherwise uses an event is not the same thing as the event itself, and we need to remain aware of the difference. Will Kemp and William Bush with his versatile ship attracted large crowds as well as a subsequent readership, and although the pamphlets in both cases tend to present the spectators as a nuisance, impeding the progress of the lone hero as he battles towards his goal, this is obviously itself a kind of literary gloss, which rationalises the muddle and excitement and sweaty endeavour of the occasion and obscures one set of meanings even as it imposes another. The easy way out of this, of course, is to say that these events have no existence outside the texts that represent them, but to do so is to discount the truth that the actual stunts generated their own meanings while they were being performed, and effectively to render them no more real than, say, an episode in *Don Quixote* or Nashe's *Unfortunate Traveller* which is made to signify by linguistic and literary conventions. This would still leave us with a collection of texts to look at, but make it impossible to ask important questions about the events they represent.[7]

My final chapter attempts to show how creative writers made use of the vogue to explore the Jacobean zeitgeist and thereby articulated a particular phase of the early-modern transition: one in which the anxieties of the new century were uppermost in their minds and temporarily eclipsed the optimism that can be found in humanist uses of the fantastic voyage in early Tudor times, and which was to be rediscovered in scientific fictions of extraordinary travel later in the seventeenth century. But this too is a partial picture. The Jacobean years saw the greatest elaboration of the travel exploit, making it a ready vehicle for satire and the critical fictions of writers like Jonson and Joseph Hall, but the promoters and executants of many a stunt would not have shared their scepticism, nor would the crowds that we know were drawn to these exploits have automatically tailored their responses to a particular cultural mood.

That said, the role of literature in shaping perceptions of what mad travel could accomplish is one that needs further exploration, for we still lack an authoritative study of the tradition of speculative voyage literature in English that stretches from More's *Utopia* through Bacon's *New Atlantis* and Godwin's *Man in the Moone* to Swift and the eighteenth-century flood of 'Gulliveriana'.[8] The tradition does not end there, obviously, since fantastic travel is central to utopian writing and science fiction in the nineteenth and twentieth centuries, and remains a potent idea in several areas of contemporary writing, and of course in film. But this is to stray into areas well beyond the reach of this study. A more manageable terminus for my enquiry might perhaps be found in Augustan England, with the preservation of Thomas Coryat's memory by tourists and bibliophiles that ultimately saw the *Crudities* reprinted in 1776. By then, what John Taylor described as 'Coriatizing',[9] blending fiction and self-promotion with reportage, had entered the mainstream of travel writing and provided a congenial script for individual adventurers that was to be elaborated by later generations of English writer-travellers. It may be that such writing domesticated the impulse to mad adventure, providing for it an acceptable cultural channel that in modern times, as well as swelling the travel sections of bookshops, has made the travel stunt a popular feature of the heritage industry, as seen in recent re-enactments of Kemp's dance and Coryat's walk.[10] On the other hand, these events attest to the survival of the spirit of *serio jocum* that animated Renaissance interest in the fantastic voyage and developed out of Lucian's travel satires a set of inspirational literary experiments. The contemporary ludic impulse perhaps sustains the dream of those influential texts.

## Notes

1 Ian Hacking, *Mad Travelers: Reflections on the Reality of Transient Mental Illness* (Charlottesville: U. of Virginia Press, 1998), 51.

2 Mary Helms, *Ulysses' Sail: An Ethnographic Odyssey of Power, Knowledge, and Geographical Distance* (Princeton: Princeton UP, 1988), ch. 3.

3 Michel Foucault, *Madness and Civilisation: A History of Insanity in the Age of Reason*, trans. Richard Howard (New York: Pantheon Books 1965), 13.

4 Fulke Greville, *Prose Works of Fulke Greville*, ed. John Gouws (Oxford: Clarendon Press, 1986), 92.

5 Richard Hakluyt, *Principall Navigations … of the English Nation* (London, 1589), epistle, sig.*2v.

6 *Pimlyco, or, Runne Red-Cap* (London, 1609), A2; William Fennor, *The Compters Commonwealth* (London, 1617), B–B2v.

7 Bruce R. Smith's comments on May games and other popular rituals are apposite here: 'For such performances the vocabulary of literary criticism lacks a term, in large part because the events themselves lack verbal substance. … Middle and early modern English describes such events as "games," as varieties of play as opposed to work, or as "gests," as "deeds" or "exploits"' (*The Acoustic World of Early Modern England*, 136). Several of the mad voyages have a complicated affinity with that kind of traditional 'performance'.

8 See the five collections published under this title by J.K. Welcher and G.E. Bush Jr (Gainesville, FL: Scholars' Facsimiles and Reprints, 1970–74).

9 Taylor, *Pennyles Pilgrimage*, E2.

10 See Ch. 5, note 61. Kemp's dance was re-enacted in 2008 by comedian Tim FitzHigham. For more details of these and other re-imaginings of the two exploits, see their protagonists' Wikipedia entries.

# Bibliography

## Primary Sources


*Acts of the Privy Council of England*. Ed. J.R. Dasent. London: HMSO, 1896–1901.

Adams, Thomas. *Mystical Bedlam*. London, 1615.

Allen, William. An Apologie and True Declaration … of the two English Colleges. Rheims, 1581.

Anon, *Gesta Grayorum*. London, 1688.

Anon. *Informacion for pylgrymes unto the holy londe*. London, 1498.

Anon. *Le Prince d'Amour … with a Collection of several ingenious poems and songs by the Wits of the Age*. London, 1660.

Anon. *Old Meg of Herefordshire*. London, 1609.

Anon. *Pimlyco, or, Runne Red-Cap*. London, 1609.

Anon. *The Copie of a Double Letter*. (Attributed to Robert Persons.) Rheims, 1581.

Anon. *The pylgrymage of sir R. Guylforde knight*. London, 1511.

Anon. 'A very rich Lotterie generall'. London: Henry Bynneman, 1569.

Arber, E. *An English Garner*. London: Arber, 1877–96.

Ascham, Roger. *The Scholemaster*. London, 1570.

Avity, Pierre d'. Trans. E. Grimstone. *The Estates … and Principallities of the World*. London, 1615.

Bacon, Francis. 'Certain considerations touching the plantation in Ireland', in J. Spedding et al, eds, *The Works of Francis Bacon* (Boston: Brown and Taggart, 1860–64).

——. *The Advancement of Learning*, in M. Kiernan, ed., *The Oxford Francis Bacon*, vol. 4. Oxford: Clarendon Press, 2000.

Balmford, James. *A short and plaine dialogue … concerning the lawfulnes of playing at cardes*. London, 1593.

Barclay, Alexander. *The present Boke named the Shyp of folys of the worlde*. London, 1509.

Bate, John. *The Mysteryes of Nature and Art*. London, 1634.

Beatis, Antonio de. *The Travel Journal of Antonio de Beatis*. Ed. J.R. Hale. London: Hakluyt Society, 1979.

Best, George. *A True Discoverie of the late voyages of discoverie ... by the Northweast*. London, 1578.

Biddulph, William. *The Travels of Foure English Men and a Preacher*. London, 1612.

Birch, Thomas. *Memoirs of the Reign of Queen Elizabeth*. London: Millar, 1754.

Blount, Henry. *A Voyage into the Levant*. London, 1637.

Botero, Giovanni. *Delle Cause della grandezza ... delle Città*. Venice, 1589.

Bourne, William. *Inventions or Devises*. London, 1578.

Brant, Sebastian. *The Ship of Fools*. Trans. Edwin H. Zeydel. New York: Columbia UP, 1944.

Brathwaite, Richard. *The Schollers medley*. London, 1614.

Breton, Nicholas. *The Good and the Badde*. London, 1616.

——. *Crossing of Proverbs*. London, 1616.

Bullein, William. *Dialogue of the Fever Pestilence*. London, 1564.

Burton, Robert. *The Anatomy of Melancholy*. Eds T.C. Faulkner, N.K. Kiessling and R.L. Blair. Oxford: Clarendon Press, 1989.

*Calendar of State Papers, Colonial, East Indies, China and Japan, 1513–1616*. Ed. W. Noel Sainsbury. London: Longman, 1864.

*Calendar of State Papers, Domestic*. Eds R. Lemon and M.A.E. Green. London: Longman, 1856–72.

*Calendar of State Papers, Foreign*. Eds A.J. Butler, S.C. Lomas, A.B. Hinds and R.B. Wernham. London: Longman, 1863–1950.

*Calendar of State Papers, Rome*. Ed. J.M. Rigg. London: HMSO, 1916–26.

*Calendar of State Papers, Venetian*. Eds H.F. Brown and A.B. Hinds. London: HMSO, 1894–1911.

Camden, William. *Annales: The True and Royall History of ... Elizabeth Queene*. London, 1625.

——. *Remaines concerning Britain*. Ed. R.D. Dunn. Toronto: University of Toronto Press, 1984.

Carey, Robert. *The Memoirs of Robert Carey*. Ed. F.H. Mares. Oxford: Clarendon, 1972.

Cartwright, John. *The Preacher's Travels*. London, 1611.

Castiglione, Baldassare. *The Courtyer of Count Baldessar Castilio*. London, 1561.

Cavendish, Henry. 'Mr. Harrie Cavendish his Journey to and from Constantinople, 1589, by Fox, his Servant'. Ed. A.C. Wood. *Camden Miscellany* 17 (3rd Series), vol. 64. London: Royal Historical Society, 1940.

Chamberlain, John. *The Letters of John Chamberlain*. 2 vols. Ed. N.E. McClure. Philadelphia: American Philosophical Society, 1939.

Chapman, George. *The Poems of George Chapman*. Ed. P.B. Bartlett. London: Oxford UP, 1941.

Chaucer, Geoffrey. *The Works of Geoffrey Chaucer*. Ed. F.N. Robinson. London: Oxford UP, 1957.

Cooke, John. *Epigrames*. London, 1604?

Coryat, Thomas. *Coryats Crudities*. [London, 1611.] Glasgow: James Maclehose, 1907.

——. *Mr Thomas Coriat to his friends in England … from Agra*. London, 1618.

——. *Thomas Coriate Traveller for the English Wits*. London, 1616.

——. *Coryates Crambe*. London, 1611.

Cotton, Robert. *Cottoni Posthuma*. London, 1651.

Cowell, John. *The Interpreter*. London, 1607.

Daneau, L. *A Treatise touching Dyce-play and prophane Gaming*. London, 1586.

Davies, John. *Epigrammes and Elegies*. Middleborough (false imprint), c.1599.

Dekker, Thomas. *The Great Frost*. London, 1608.

——. *Newes from Hell*. London, 1606.

——. *A Knight's Conjuring*. London, 1607.

——. *A Strange Horse-Race*. London, 1613.

——. *Lanthorne & Candlelight*. London, 1608. In A. Kinney, ed., *Rogues, Vagabonds, & Sturdy Beggars*. Barre, MA: Imprint Soc., 1973.

*English Reports* (legal records). HeinOnline.org.

Estienne, Henri. Trans. R. Carew. *A World of Wonders … or A Preparative Treatise to the Apologie for Herodotus*. [1566]. London 1607.

Evelyn, John. *The Diary of John Evelyn*. Ed. Austin Dobson. London: Macmillan, 1906.

Ewen, C. L'Estrange. *Lotteries and Sweepstakes*. London: Heath Cranton, 1932.

Fennor, William. *Pluto his Travailes*. London, 1612.

——. *The Compters Commonwealth*. London, 1617.

Fenton, Roger. *A Treatise of Usurie*. London, 1611.

Ferris, Richard. *The most dangerous and memorable adventure of Richard Ferris*. London, 1590.

Florio, John. *A Worlde of Wordes*. London, 1598.

Gainsford, Thomas. *The Glory of England*. London, 1618.

Gawdy, Philip. *Letters of Philip Gawdy … 1579–1616*. Ed. I.H. Jeayes. London: J.B. Nichols, 1906.

Gosson, Stephen. *The Schoole of Abuse*. London, 1579.

Greville, Fulke. *Prose Works of Fulke Greville, Lord Brooke*. Ed. John Gouws. Oxford: Clarendon Press, 1986.

H., W. *The Reformed Travailer*. London, 1606.

Hakluyt, Richard. *Principall Navigations … of the English Nation*. London, 1589.

——. *Principal Navigations*. 2nd ed., 1598. Glasgow: James Maclehose, 1903–1905.

——. 'Discourse of Western Planting'. 1584. Ed. E.G.R. Taylor. *The Original Writings & Correspondence of the two Richard Hakluyts*. London: Hakluyt Society, 1935.

Hall, Joseph. *Quo Vadis? A Censure of Travell*. London, 1617.

——. *Mundus Alter et Idem*. London, 1605.

Harington, John. *A new discourse of a stale subject, called the Metamorphosis of Ajax*. London 1596.

——. *Nugae Antiquae*. 2 vols. London: W Frederick, 1769–75.

Harvey, Gabriel. *Letter-Book of Gabriel Harvey, 1573–1580*. Ed. E.L.J. Scott. London: Camden Society, 1884.

Healey, John. *The Discovery of a New World*. London, 1609.

Herbert, Thomas. *A Relation of some yeares travaile begunne anno 1626*. London, 1634.

Heywood, John. *John Heywoodes woorkes*. London, 1566.

Higden, Ranulf. *Polychronicon*. Trans. J. Trevisa. London, 1527.

Hooker, John. *The Life and Times of Sir Peter Carew, Kt*. Ed. John Maclean. London: Bell and Daldy, 1857.

Howes, Edmund. See Stow.

Humphrey, Lawrence. *The Nobles or of Nobilitye*. London, 1563.

James I. *Basilikon Doron*, in *The workes of the most high and mightie prince James*. London, 1616.

Jode, G. de. *Speculum Orbis Terrarum*. Amsterdam, 1593.

Johnson, Richard. *The most pleasant history of Tom a Lincolne*. London, 1631.

Johnson, Robert. *The New Life of Virginea*. London, 1612.

Jonson, Ben. *The Works of Ben Jonson*. Cambridge: Cambridge UP, 2012.

Kemp, Will. *Kemp's Nine Daies Wonder*. Ed. G.B. Harrison. London: Bodley Head Quartos, 1923.

Linschoten, J.H. van. *Discours of voyages into ye Easte & West Indies*. London, 1598.

Lipsius, Justus. *A Direction for Travailers* London, 1592.

Lithgow, William. *Rare Adventures & Painefull Peregrinations*. 1632. Glasgow: James MacLehose, 1906.

Lucian of Samosata, *Works*. Trans. A. Harmon. London: Heinemann, 1921–25.

Lull, Ramon. *Book of the ordre of chivalry*. Trans. W. Caxton. London, 1484.

Lupton, Thomas. *Siuqila. Too good, to be true*. London, 1580.

Malynes, Gerard. *Lex Mercatoria, or The Ancient Law-Merchant*. London, 1622.

Mendoza, J.G. de. *The Historie of the great and mightie kingdome of China*. Trans. R. Parke. London, 1588.

Milton, John. *Complete Prose Works*, vol.1. Ed. D.M. Wolf. New Haven: Yale UP, 1953.

More, Thomas. *Utopia*, Eds G.M. Logan and R.M. Adams. Cambridge: Cambridge UP, 1989.

Moryson, Fynes. *An Itinerary*. 1617. Glasgow: James Maclehose, 1907–1908.

____. *Shakespeare's Europe: Unpublished Chapters of Fynes Moryson's Itinerary*. Ed. Charles Hughes. London: Sherratt and Hughes, 1903.

Mulcaster, Richard. *Positions*. London, 1581.

Munday, Anthony. *The English Romayne Lyfe*. London, 1582.

Munster, Sebastian. *A briefe collection ... of strange and memorable thinges*. London, 1574.

Nashe, Thomas. *The Works of Thomas Nashe*. Ed. R.B. McKerrow. London: A.H. Bullen, 1904–10.

*National Archives* (UK): Chancery documents C2/33, C33/115, C33/116, C2/JASI/R15/70, C38/14, IND 1/1880.

Nixon, Anthony. *A true Relation of the Travels of M. Bush*. London, 1607.

North, Thomas. *The Morall Philosophie of Doni*. London, 1570.

Peacham, Henry. *The Compleat Gentleman*. London, 1634.

Perkins, William. *The Whole Treatise of the Cases of Conscience*. London, 1608.

Pett, Phineas. *The Autobiography of Phineas Pett*. Ed. W.G. Perrin. London: Navy Records Society, 1918.

Plutarch. *The Lives of the Noble Grecians and Romans*. Trans. Sir Thomas North. London, 1595.

Purchas, Samuel. *Purchas His Pilgrimes*. Glasgow: James Maclehose, 1905–1907.

Puttenham, George. *The Arte of English Poesie*. London, 1589.

Ramelli, Agostino. *Le Diverse e artificiose machine*. Paris, 1588.

*Records of the English Province of the Society of Jesus Ed. Henry Foley. London: Burns and Oates, 1875–1883.*

*Records of the Virginia Company of London*. Ed. S.M. Kingsbury. Washington: Government Printing Office, 1906–33.

Riche, Barnabe. *Faultes Faults, and nothing else but Faultes*. London, 1606.

Roberts, Henry. *Haigh for Devonshire*. London, 1600.

Rowley, Samuel. *When you see me, you know me*. London, 1605. Ed. F.P. Wilson. Malone Society: Oxford UP, 1952.

Rowley, William. *A Search for Money*. London, 1609.

S., W. *The Proceedings of the English Colonie in Virginia*. Oxford, 1612.

Sandys, George. *A Relation of a Journey begun ... 1610*. London, 1615.

Settle, Dionyse. *A true reporte of the laste voyage ... by capteine Frobisher*. London, 1577.

Speed, John. *The History of Great Britaine*. London, 1614.

Sledd, Charles. 'A general discourse of the Popes holynes devices'. Miscellanea: Recusant Records, Catholic Record Society 53 (1961), 193–245.

Smith, John (Captain). *Travels and Works of Captain John Smith*, 2 vols. Eds E. Arber and A.G. Bradley. Edinburgh: John Grant, 1910.

*State Papers Foreign, List & Analysis of*. Ed. R.B. Wernham. London: HMSO, 1964–2000.

Sterne, Laurence. *The Life and Opinions of Tristram Shandy*. Ed. Graham Petrie. Harmondsworth: Penguin, 1967.

Stevin, Simon. *Principal Works of Simon Stevin*. Ed. R.J. Forbes. Amsterdam, 1966.

Stow, John. *The abridgement of the English chronicle, first collected by M. John Stow, and continued … unto … 1610 by E.H. Gentleman*. London, 1611.

——. *The annals … of England, begun … by … John Stow, and … continued … unto 1614 by Edmond Howes*. London, 1615.

Stubbes, Philip. *The Anatomie of Abuses*. London, 1595.

Taylor, John. *The Pennyles Pilgrimage*. London, 1619.

——. *The Praise of Hemp-seed*. London, 1620.

——. *The Scourge of Basenesse*. London, 1624.

——. *The Sculler*. London, 1612.

——. *A Verry Merry Wherry-Ferry Voyage*. London, 1622.

Timberlake, Henry. *A True and Strange Discourse of the Travailes of Two English Pilgrimes*. London, 1611.

Walker, Gilbert. *A Manifest detection … of Diceplay*. London, 1552.

Watson, Henry. *The shyppe of fooles*. London, 1509.

Watson, William. A Decacordon of Ten Quodlibeticall Questions. London, 1602.

West, William. *The First Part of Simboleography*. London, 1603.

Wey, William. *The Itineraries of William Wey*. London: Roxburghe Club, 1855.

Wilkins, John. *Mathematicall Magick*. London, 1648.

Wilson, Thomas. *A Discourse upon Usury*. London, 1572.

——. *The Arte of Rhetorique*. London, 1553.

Wood, Anthony à. *Athenae Oxonienses*. Ed. Philip Bliss. London, 1815.

Wotton, Henry. *The Life and Letters of Sir Henry Wotton*. Ed. L.P. Smith. Oxford: Clarendon Press, 1966.

Wright, Edward. *Certain Errors in Navigation*. London, 1610.

## Secondary Sources

Ackerman, E.M. *'Das Schlaraffenland' in German Lit and Folksong*. Chicago, 1944.

Agnew, Jean-Christophe. *Worlds Apart: The Market and the Theater in Anglo-American Thought, 1550–1750*. Cambridge: Cambridge UP, 1986.

Anglo, Sydney. *Spectacle, Pageantry, and Early Tudor Policy*. Oxford: Clarendon Press, 1969.

Ashton, John. *The History of Gambling in England*. London: Duckworth, 1898.

Atkinson, Geoffroy. *The Extraordinary Voyage in French Literature from 1700–1720*. Paris, 1922.

Barbour, Richmond. *Before Orientalism: London's Theatre of the East, 1576–1626*. Cambridge: Cambridge UP, 2003.

——. 'Corporate Praxis and the Legacy of Privateering: The Jacobean East India Company'. *Clio* 41 (2011), 1–29.

Bartlett, K.R. *The English in Italy, 1525–1558: A Study in Culture and Politics*. Geneva: Slatkine, 1991.

Bellhouse, D.R. 'Probability in the Sixteenth and Seventeenth Centuries: An Analysis of Puritan Casuistry'. *International Statistical Review* 56 (1988), 63–74.

Berry, William. *Pedigrees of the Families of the County of Kent*. London: Sherwood, 1830.

Birdwood, G., and W. Foster, eds. *The Register of Letters of the … Company … trading into the East Indies*. London: Quaritch, 1893.

Bland, Mark. 'Ben Jonson and the Legacies of the Past'. *Huntington Library Quarterly* 67 (2004), 371–400.

Boehrer, Bruce. 'The Case of Will Kemp's Shoes', *Ben Jonson Journal* 7 (2000), 271–96.

Bornstein, Diane. *Mirrors of Courtesy*. Hamden, CT: Archon Books, 1975.

Bradley, Katherine, and Richard Bradley, 'William Bush – The Flying Boatman'. *Berkshire Archaeological Journal* 71 (1981–82), 57–70.

Brenner, Reuven. *Gambling and Speculation*. Cambridge: Cambridge UP, 1990.

Brenner, Robert. *Merchants and Revolutions*. Princeton: Princeton UP, 1993.

Briggs, K.M. *A Dictionary of British Folk-Tales in the English Language*. London: Routledge 1970.

Brooks, Christopher W. *Law, Politics and Society in Early Modern England*. Cambridge: Cambridge UP, 2008.

Bruce, John. *Annals of the Honorable East-India Company*. London: Black, 1810.

Brunning, Alison. '"Thou art damned for alt'ring thy religion": The Double Coding of Conversion in City Comedy'. In D. Mehl et al, *Plotting Early Modern London: New Essays on Jacobean City Comedy*. Aldershot: Ashgate, 2004.

Burke, Peter. *Varieties of Cultural History*. Ithaca: Cornell UP, 1997.

Bryson, W.H., ed. *Cases Concerning Equity and the Courts of Equity 1550–1660*. 2 vols. London: Selden Society, 2001.

Campbell, Mary B. *The Witness and the Other World: Exotic European Travel Writing, 400–1600*. Ithaca: Cornell UP, 1988.

Canny, N., ed. *The Origins of Empire*. Vol. 1 of *The Oxford History of the British Empire*. Oxford: Oxford UP, 1998.

Capp, Bernard. *The World of John Taylor the Water-Poet 1578–1653*. Oxford: Oxford UP, 1994.

Caudill, Randall L-W. *Some Literary Evidence of the Development of English Virtuoso Interests in the Seventeenth Century, With Particular Reference to the Literature of Travel*. D.Phil thesis, University of Oxford, unpublished.

Chandler, John. *Travels through Stuart Britain: The Adventures of John Taylor, the Water Poet*. Stroud: Sutton Publishing, 1999.

Chaney, Edward. *The Grand Tour and the Great Rebellion*. Geneva: Slatkine, 1985.

Chapple, Anne S. 'Burton's Geography of Melancholy'. *Studies in English Literature* 33 (1993), 99–130.

Chesney, Elizabeth A. *The Countervoyage of Rabelais and Ariosto*. Durham, NC: Duke UP, 1982.

Chew, Samuel. *The Crescent and the Rose*. Oxford: Oxford UP, 1937.

Clark, Geoffrey. *Betting on Lives: The Culture of Life Insurance in England, 1695–1775* Manchester: Manchester UP, 1999.

Clayton, Roderick. 'John Finet'. *ODNB* 19.596–7.

Craik, Katharine. 'Reading *Coryats Crudities* (1611)'. *Studies in English Literature* 44 (2004), 77–96.

Daston, Lorraine. *Classical Probability in the Enlightenment*. Princeton: Princeton UP, 1988.

——. 'The Domestication of Risk', in L. Kruger et al, *The Probabilistic Revolution*. Cambridge, MA: MIT Press, 1987.

Daston, Lorraine, and Katherine Park. *Wonders and the Order of Nature, 1150–1750*. New York: Zone Books, 1998.

David, F.N. *Games, Gods and Gambling: A History of Probability and Statistical Ideas*. Mineola, NY: Dover, 1998.

Davis, J.C. *Utopia and the Ideal Society: A Study of English Utopian Writing, 1516–1700*. Cambridge: Cambridge UP, 1983.

Davis, Nick. *Stories of Chaos*. Aldershot: Ashgate, 1999.

Deursen, A.T. van. *Plain Lives in a Golden Age: Popular Culture, Religion and Society in Seventeenth-Century Holland*. Cambridge: Cambridge UP, 1991.

Dionne, C., and S. Mentz, eds. *Rogues and Early Modern English Culture*. Ann Arbor: University of Michigan Press, 2004.

Donaldson, Ian. *Ben Jonson: A Life*. Oxford: Oxford UP, 2011.

Duffy, E. 'The Dynamics of Pilgrimage in Late Mediaeval England', in C. Morris and P. Roberts, eds. *Pilgrimage: The English Experience from Becket to Bunyan*. Cambridge: Cambridge UP, 2002.

Dugdale, William. *The Visitation of the County of Yorke, 1665–6*. Vol. 36. London: Surtees Society, 1859.

Duncan, Douglas. *Ben Jonson and the Lucianic Tradition*. Cambridge: Cambridge UP, 1979.

Duncan-Jones, Katherine. 'City Limits: Nashe's "Choise of Valentines" and Jonson's "Famous Voyage"', *Review of English Studies* 56 (2005), 247–62.

Durant, David N. *Bess of Hardwick*. New York: Atheneum, 1978.

Duxfield, Andrew. 'That Horse that Runnes upon the Toppe of Powles'. *Notes & Queries* 252 (2007), 264–5.

Elliott, J.H. *The Old World and the New, 1492–1650*. Cambridge: Cambridge UP, 1992.

Emerson, Ralph W. *English Traits*. Ed. Mumford Jones. Cambridge, MA: Harvard UP, 1966.

Everitt, Alan. 'The Marketing of Agricultural Produce', in Joan Thirsk, *The Agrarian History of England and Wales*, vol. 4, *1500–1640*. Cambridge: Cambridge UP, 1967.

Feil, J.P. *Sir Tobie Matthew and his Collection of Letters*, unpublished dissertation, University of Chicago, 1962.

Ferguson, Arthur. *The Indian Summer of English Chivalry*. Durham: Duke UP, 1960.

Fisher, Raymond H. *The Russian Fur Trade, 1550–1700*. Berkeley: U. of California Press, 1943.

Flynn, Dennis. *John Donne and the Ancient Catholic Nobility*. Bloomington: Indiana UP, 1995.

Footman, John. *History of the Parish Church of Saint Michael and All Angels, Chipping Lambourn*. London: Elliot Stock, 1894.

Forrest, John. *The History of Morris Dancing, 1458–1750*. Toronto: Toronto UP, 1999.

Foucault, Michel. *Madness and Civilisation: A History of Insanity in the Age of Reason*. Trans. Richard Howard. New York: Pantheon Books, 1965.

Franklin, James. *The Science of Conjecture: Evidence and Probability before Pascal*. Baltimore: Johns Hopkins UP, 2001.

Freeman, Arthur. *Elizabethan Eccentrics: Brief Lives of English Misfits, Exploiters, Rogues, and Failures, 1580–1660*. New York: Dorset Press, 1978.

Fuller, Mary. *Voyages in Print: English Travel to America, 1576–1624*. Cambridge: Cambridge UP, 1995.

Galloway, Andrew. 'Latin England', in K. Lavezzo, ed., *Imagining a Medieval English Nation*. Minneapolis: U. of Minnesota Press, 2004.

Gigerenzer, Gerd, et al. *The Empire of Chance: How Probability Changed Science and Everyday Life*. Cambridge: Cambridge UP, 1989.

Glover, Lorri, and Daniel Blake Smith. *The Shipwreck That Saved Jamestown*. New York: Henry Holt, 2008.

Goodman, Jennifer R. *Chivalry and Exploration, 1298–1630*. Rochester, NY: Boydell, 1998.

Gove, Philip B. *The Imaginary Voyage in Prose Fiction*. New York: Columbia UP, 1941.

Gransden, K.W., ed. *Tudor Verse Satire*. London: Athlone Press, 1970.

Grassi, E., and M. Lorch. *Folly and Insanity in Renaissance Literature*. Binghamton, NY: Medieval and Renaissance Texts and Studies, 1986.

Gray, H.D. 'The Roles of William Kemp'. *Modern Language Review* 25 (1930), 261–73.

Green, A.W. *The Inns of Court and Early English Drama*. New Haven: Yale UP, 1931.

Green, R.F. *A Crisis of Truth: Literature and Law in Ricardian England*. Philadelphia: U. of Pennsylvania Press, 1999.

Grosart, A.B., ed. *The Lismore Papers*. London: Chiswick Press, 1886–88.

Hacking, Ian. *The Emergence of Probability*. Cambridge: Cambridge UP, 1975.

_____. *Mad Travelers: Reflections on the Reality of Transient Mental Illness*. Charlottesville: U. of Virginia Press, 1998.

Halasz, Alexandra. *The Marketplace of Print*. Cambridge: Cambridge UP, 1997.

Hale, J.R, ed. *The Travel Journal of Antonio de Beatis*. London: Hakluyt Society, 1979.

Hall, Hubert. *Society in the Elizabethan Age*. London: Sonnenschein, 1892.

Hamilton, Donna B. *Anthony Munday and the Catholics, 1560–1633*. Aldershot: Ashgate, 2005.

Harris, Jonathan Gil. 'Becoming-Indian', in Henry S. Turner, ed., *Early Modern Theatricality*. Oxford: Oxford UP, 2013, 442–59.

Harris, L.E. *The Two Netherlanders*. Cambridge: W. Heffer, 1961.

Helfers, James P. 'The Explorer or the Pilgrim?', *Studies in Philology* 94 (1997), 160–86.

Helgerson, Richard. *Forms of Nationhood: The Elizabethan Writing of England*. Chicago: U. of Chicago Press, 1992.

——. 'The Folly of Maps and Modernity', in A. Gordon and B. Klein, *Literature, Mapping, and the Politics of Space in Early Modern Britain*. Cambridge: Cambridge UP, 2001.

Helms, Mary. *Ulysses' Sail: An Ethnographic Odyssey of Power, Knowledge, and Geographical Distance*. Princeton: Princeton UP, 1988.

Herford, C.H. *Studies in the literary relations of England and Germany in the sixteenth century*. Cambridge: Cambridge UP, 1886.

Herwaarden, Jan van. *Between St James and Erasmus: Studies in Late-Medieval Religious Life*. Leiden: Brill, 2003.

Hutton, Ronald. *Stations of the Sun*. Oxford: Oxford UP, 1996.

Inalcik, H., and D. Quataert, eds. *An Economic and Social History of the Ottoman Empire, 1300–1914*. Cambridge: Cambridge UP, 1994.

Ingram, Jill. 'Economies of Obligation in *E.Ho!*', *Ben Jonson Journal* 11 (2004), 21–40.

Jenkinson, W. *London Churches before the Great Fire*. London: Society for Promoting Christian Knowledge, 1917.

Johnson, Robert C. 'The Lotteries of the Virginia Company, 1612–1621', *Virginia Magazine of History and Biography* 74 (1966), 259–92.

Kaiser, Walter. *Praisers of Folly: Erasmus, Rabelais, Shakespeare*. Cambridge, Mass: Harvard UP, 1963.

Kamps, Ivo. *Historiography and Ideology in Stuart Drama*. Cambridge: CUP, 1996.

Keay, John. *Eccentric Travellers*. London: BBC, 1985.

Kendrick, Christopher. *Utopia, Carnival, and Commonwealth in Renaissance England*. Toronto: Toronto UP, 2004.

Kinney, Arthur. *Humanist Poetics: Thought, Rhetoric, and Fiction in Sixteenth-Century England*. Amhurst: U. of Massachusetts Press, 1986.

Kinsman, Robert S., ed. *The Darker Vision of the Renaissance*. Berkeley: U. of California Press, 1974.

Kirkland-Ives, M. 'The Adornes Family of Bruges and Holy Land Devotion', *Sixteenth Century Journal* 39 (2008), 1041–64.

Knapp, Jeffrey. *An Empire Nowhere*. Berkeley: U. of California Press, 1992.

Kolve, V.A. *Chaucer and the Imagery of Narrative*. Stanford: Stanford UP, 1984.

Langford, Paul. *Englishness Identified*. Oxford: Oxford UP, 2000.

Lerer, Seth. *Chaucer and his Readers*. Princeton: Princeton UP, 1993.

Loxley, James. 'My Gossip's Foot Voyage'. *Times Literary Supplement*, 11 September 2009, 13–15.

Loxley, James, and Julie Sanders. 'My Gossip Joh[n]son his Foot Voyage and Mine into Scotland', in Jonson, *Collected Works*, Electronic Edition.

Lyons, Mathew. 'Dreams of Escape – George Gifford: Courtier, Con-Man, Conspirator', at http://mathewlyons.wordpress.com/2011/10/03/dreams-of-escape.

MacDonald, Michael. *Mystical Bedlam: madness, anxiety and healing in seventeenth-century England*. Cambridge: Cambridge UP, 1981.

Mączak, Antoni. *Travel in Early Modern Europe*. Cambridge: Polity, 1995.

Malcolm, Noel. *The Origins of English Nonsense*. London: HarperCollins, 1997.

Manley, Lawrence. *Literature and Culture in Early Modern London*. Cambridge: Cambridge UP, 1995.

Marcus, Leah. *The Politics of Mirth*. Chicago: U. of Chicago Press, 1986.

Malcolm, Noel. *The Origins of English Nonsense*. London: HarperCollins, 1997.

Manous, Michael L. '"You served God he set you free": Self, Nation and Celebration in the Wager-Voyaging *Adventure* of Richard Ferris'. *Early Modern Literary Studies* 6 (2007). Online.

____. 'An Eagle's Wing and a Vulture's Wing: Poetic Journey and Wager Journey in Jonson's "Famous Voyage"'. *Ben Jonson Journal* 15 (2008), 54–78.

Marshall, Samuel. *A Treatise on the Law of Insurance*. London: J. Butterworth, 1808.

Masson, David. *Drummond of Hawthornden*. London: Macmillan, 1873).

Matar, Nabil. *Islam in Britain 1558–1685*. Cambridge: Cambridge UP, 1998.

Maxwell, Susan M. 'Thomas Cavendish'. *ODNB*, 10.645–9.

McCabe, Richard A. *Joseph Hall: A Study in Satire and Meditation*. Oxford: Clarendon Press, 1982.

McEachern, Claire. *The Poetics of English Nationhood*. Cambridge: Cambridge UP, 1996.

McRae, Andrew. *Literature and Domestic Travel in Early Modern Britain*. Cambridge: Cambridge UP, 2009.

____. '"On the Famous Voyage": Ben Jonson and Civic Space', in A. Gordon and B. Klein, eds. *Literature, Mapping, and the Politics of Space in Early Modern Britain*. Cambridge: Cambridge UP, 2001, 181–203.

____. 'The Peripatetic Muse: Internal Travel and the Cultural Production of Space in Pre-Revolutionary England', in G. Maclean, D. Landry, and J.P. Ward, eds., *The Country and the City Revisited*. Cambridge: Cambridge UP, 1999.

Medine, Peter. 'Object and Intent in Jonson's "Famous Voyage"', *Studies in English Literature* 15 (1975), 100–104.

Midelfort, H.C. Erik. *A History of Madness in Sixteenth-Century Germany*. Stanford: Stanford UP, 1999

Moore, Tim. *Continental Drifter*. London: Abacus, 2002.

Mullaney, Steven. 'Strange Things, Gross Terms, Curious Customs: The Rehearsal of Cultures in the Late Renaissance'. *Representations* 3 (1983), 40–67.

Nelson, Alan H. *Monstrous Adversary: The Life of Edward De Vere*. Liverpool UP, 2003.

Newett, M. Margaret. *Canon Pietro Casola's Pilgrimage to Jerusalem in the Year 1494*. Manchester: Manchester UP, 1907.

Nichols, J.G., ed. *Literary Remains of King Edward the Sixth*. London: J.B. Nichols, 1857.

Niekerk, J.P. van. *The Development of the Principles of Insurance Law in the Netherlands from 1500 to 1800*. Kenwyn: Juta, 1998.

O'Callaghan, Michelle. *The English Wits: Literature and Sociability in Early Modern England*. Cambridge: Cambridge UP, 2007.

——. '"Thomas the Scholer" versus "John the Sculler": Defining Popular Culture in the Early Seventeenth Century', in M. Dimmock and A. Hadfield, eds., *Literature and Popular Culture in Early Modern England*. Farnham: Ashgate, 2009, 45–56.

Ostovich, Helen. 'Hell for Lovers: Shades of Adultery in *The Devil is an Ass*', in *Refashioning Ben Jonson*, ed. J. Sanders et al. Basingstoke: St Martin's Press, 1998.

Page, W.S. *The Russia Company from 1553 to 1660*. London, W. Brown, 1911.

Parks, George. *The English Traveller to Italy*. Roma: Edizione di Storia e Letteratura, 1954.

Parr, Anthony. 'Anarchy and Ordure in Ben Jonson's "On the Famous Voyage"'. *Southern African Journal of Mediaeval and Renaissance Studies* 9 (1999), 45–58.

——. 'Cales and Guiana: John Donne and Elizabethan Foreign Policy'. *Southern African Journal of Mediaeval and Renaissance Studies* 19 (2009), 59–96.

——. '"Going to Constantinople": English Wager-Journeys to the Ottoman world in the Early-Modern Period'. *Studies in Travel Writing* 16 (2012), 1–13.

——. '"Odd Conceits and Crafty Jugglings": The English Nation in Rome in the Late Sixteenth Century'. *Southern African Journal of Mediaeval and Renaissance Studies* 17 (2007), 57–78.

——. 'Thomas Coryat and the Discovery of Europe'. *Huntington Library Quarterly* 55 (1992), 579–602.

——. *Three Renaissance Travel Plays*. Manchester: Manchester UP, 1995.

Peck, Linda Levy. *Court Patronage and Corruption in Early Stuart England*. London: Unwin Hyman, 1990.

Prescott, H.F.M. *Jerusalem Journey: Pilgrimage to the Holy Land in the Fifteenth century*. London: Eyre and Spottiswood, 1954.

Rennie, Neil. *Far-Fetched Facts*. Oxford: Clarendon Press, 1995.

Roberts, Adam. *The History of Science Fiction*. Houndmills: Palgrave Macmillan, 2007.

Robinson, C. *Lucian and his Influence in Europe*. Chapel Hill: U. of North Carolina Press, 1979.

Roover, F.E. de. 'Early Examples of Marine Insurance'. *Journal of Economic History* 5 (1945), 172–200.

Ross, E. Denison. *Anthony Sherley and His Persian Adventure*. London: Routledge, 1933.

Sarton, G. *Simon Stevin of Bruges*. Bruges: Saint Catherine Press, 1934.

Schama, Simon. *The Embarrassment of Riches*. New York: Knopf, 1987.

Schwyzer, Philip. *Literature, Nationalism and Memory*. Cambridge: Cambridge UP, 2004.

Schwyzer, Philip, and Simon Mealor, eds. *Archipelagic Identities: Literature and Identity in the Atlantic Archipelago, 1550–1800*. Aldershot: Ashgate, 2004.

Semenza, G. *Sport, Politics, and Literature in the English Renaissance*. Newark: University of Delaware Press, 2003.

Simpson, A.W.B. *A History of the Common Law of Contract*. Oxford: Clarendon, 1975.

Smith, Bruce. *The Acoustic World of Early Modern England*. Chicago: U. of Chicago Press, 1999.

Smith, R.S. 'Life Insurance in Fifteenth-Century Barcelona', *Journal of Economic History* 1 (1941), 57–9.

Stone, Lawrence. *The Crisis of the Aristocracy, 1558–1641*. Oxford: Clarendon Press, 1965.

Strachan, Michael. *The Life and Adventures of Thomas Coryate*. London: Oxford UP, 1962.

Strong, Roy. *Henry, Prince of Wales, and England's Lost Renaissance*. New York: Thames and Hudson, 1986.

Struik, D.J. *The Land of Stevin and Huygens: A Sketch of Science and Technology in the Dutch Republic*. Dordrecht: D. Reidel, 1981.

Sumption, Jonathan. *Pilgrimage: An Image of Mediaeval Religion*. London: Faber, 1975.

Swain, Barbara. *Fools and Folly During the Middle Ages and the Renaissance*. New York: Columbia UP, 1932.

Timbs. John. *English Eccentrics and Eccentricities*. London: R. Bentley, 1866.

Thomas, Max W. '*Kemps Nine Daies Wonder*: Dancing Carnival into Market'. *PMLA* 107 (1992), 511–23.

Tobler, Titus. *Denkblätter aus Jerusalem*. Konstanz: Scheitlin, 1853.

Trim, D.J.T. 'Henry Cavendish'. *ODNB*, 10.619.

Tyerman, Christopher. *England and the Crusades 1095–1588*. Chicago: U. of Chicago Press, 1988.

Vasvari, Louise O. 'The Geography of Escape and Topsy-Turvy Literary Genres', in Scott D. Westrem, ed. *Discovering New Worlds: Essays on Medieval Exploration and Imagination*. New York: Garland, 1991.

Vicari, Patricia. *The View from Minerva's Tower: Learning and Imagination in 'The Anatomy of Melancholy'*. Toronto: U of Toronto Press, 1989.

Wallace, C.W. 'Gervase Markham, Dramatist'. *Shakespeare Jahrbuch* 46 (1910), 347–50.

Wands, J.M., trans. and ed. *Another World and Yet the Same: Bishop Hall's 'Mundus alter et idem'*. New Haven: Yale UP, 1981.

Webb, Diana. *Pilgrimage in Mediaeval England*. London: Hambledon, 2000.

Welcher, J.K. and G.E. Bush Jr, eds. *Gulliveriana*, vols. 1–5. Gainesville, FL: Scholars' Facsimiles and Reprints, 1970–74.

Wendeborn, G.F.A. *A View of England towards the close of the eighteenth century*. London: G. and J. Robinson, 1791.

Wernham, R.B., ed. *The Expedition of Sir John Norris and Sir Francis Drake to Spain and Portugal, 1589*. Aldershot: Gower, 1988.

Wiles, David. *Shakespeare's Clown: Actor and Text in the Elizabethan Playhouse*. Cambridge: Cambridge UP, 1987.

Willan, T.S. *The Muscovy Merchants of 1555*. Manchester: Manchester UP 1953.

——. *The Early History of the Russia Company, 1553–1603*. Manchester: Manchester UP, 1956

Williamson, James A. *English Colonies in Guiana and on the Amazon, 1604–1668*. Oxford: Clarendon Press, 1923.

Wolfe, Jessica. *Humanism, Machinery, and Renaissance Literature*. Cambridge: Cambridge UP, 2004.

Wood, A.C. *A History of the Levant Company*. Oxford: Oxford UP, 1935.

Wright, Stephen. 'Sir John Pakington (1549–1625)'. *ODNB* 42.429–31.

Wright, Thomas, ed. *Early Travels in Palestine*. London: Henry Bohn, 1848.

Zacher, Christian. *Curiosity and Pilgrimage*. Baltimore: Johns Hopkins UP, 1976.

Zwierlein, Anne-Julia. 'Shipwrecks in the City: Commercial Risk as Romance in Early Modern City Comedy'. In D. Mehl et al. *Plotting Early Modern London: New Essays on Jacobean City Comedy*. Aldershot: Ashgate, 2004.

# Index